Roger Y. Lee

Software Engineering:
A Hands-On Approach

ATLANTIS
PRESS

Roger Y. Lee
Software Engineering and Information
    Technology Institute
Central Michigan University
Mount Pleasant, MI
USA

ISBN 978-94-6239-051-5   ISBN 978-94-6239-006-5 (eBook)
DOI 10.2991/978-94-6239-006-5

Printed on acid-free paper

I dedicate this book to my wife Kay and my children Eric, Joseph, and Ryan

Preface

Theme

Developing efficient software in a timely manner continues to be a struggle for many students and software developers in the real world. As both the size and scope of software systems continues to grow, the complexity of the solutions required to fill the needs of clients, too, increases. Software development has exceeded the mere practice of programming to involve much more planning, analyzing, designing, and delivering; as a result, students must learn how to approach software projects and complete them from start to finish. In light of this trend, a plethora of tools and solutions to any given problem now exists, and developers must know when and how to appropriately use these tools to accomplish the various tasks that come with software engineering projects.

It is not unusual, though, for students to complete many courses only having applied lessons to small problem sets that have limited complexity and freedom. It is also not uncommon for students to learn the science of software engineering without significant hands-on experience. This book aims to ameliorate such gaps in the education of those studying Software Engineering. It recognizes the need to teach key principles, but to also allow the students to gain deeper knowledge that only direct practice can teach. The project-based approach taken by this book reflects the needs observed amongst the students who will one day be a part of teams completing large software projects.

Tools

While many tools for software engineering exist, this book uses some of the most widely used and effective tools available. Most significantly, the object-oriented paradigm and its fundamental principles are used as the primary way to organize and design software. Introduced in phases, the completion of the hands-on project laid out in this book uses various tools for the completion of each phase built on this foundation. UML (Unified Modeling Language), for example, is a choice tool used to model software and is put into practice by the student for their hands-on project. Also extending the object-oriented paradigm are key object-oriented design patterns and analysis tools that will aid the student during requirements specification, system design, and implementation phases of the project. Lastly, standard documentation for each project phase is presented, exposing students to organizational tools often lacking by those new to software engineering.

Principles

In order to better teach software engineering from a practical approach, this book is written with the following principles as a foundation:

Hands-On Learning: Some skills applicable to software engineering are only learned by being fully engrossed in a project with others. Hands-on learning is very important to bridge the gap between academia and the real world as it gives students the chance to learn from mistakes and successes. Professional skills that are both useful and marketable will be learned by students by working with group members, interacting with clients, and applying the tools and techniques taught throughout the book.

Teamwork: The complex software systems of today do not allow any one developer to create solutions on their own; hence, working in teams is a necessary skill all students must learn and experience. Teamwork requires students to work together to define goals and responsibilities, organize tasks, and provide open communication and feedback. These traits of successful teamwork are just as important as the technical knowledge acquired in this book.

Problem Solving: Every software project begins with a problem that must be defined and solved. The solution to such problems will inherently bring about other subsequent problems along the way. A good developer, while knowing the available approaches and methods, must also know how to solve problems that will likely arise as software engineering projects move from phase to phase. The practice of software engineering is always changing solutions to improve to accommodate the endless number of potential problems and ways to solve them.

The Book

This book covers the process, core concepts, and tools of software engineering, from a primarily object-oriented approach, with a hands-on project as the backbone to support the learning and skill development of the student. Divided into parts, the first set of chapters introduce software engineering principles before the subsequent chapters describe the development of a software project from start to finish. A more detailed description of this book's parts and chapters is given below:

Part I: What Is Software Engineering?

In this first part of the text, a brief history and introduction into the science of software engineering and object-oriented principles used in its process are described.

Chapter 1: In this chapter, *Introduction to Software Engineering*, a summary of the definition and need for software engineering is laid out in a historical context; the complexity of software and lack of success rates are detailed as support. The people, tasks, and activities involved in software engineering are also described to provide evidence that software engineering is not merely limited to programming. Lastly, the life cycles of the development process are depicted.

Chapter 2: In *Object-Oriented Concepts*, object-orientation is introduced and underlying concepts such as classes, modularity, inheritance, and abstraction are discussed. This chapter defines key ideas used by more complex tasks described later in this book.

Chapter 3: Entitled *Modeling with UML*, this chapter describes and depicts the variety of diagrams the Unified Modeling Language provides developers. Class, use case, sequence, component diagrams, and others are discussed as well as the basic parts and association types used by many of them.

Part II: The Software Engineering Project

Part II of this book covers the various phases common to software engineering projects. From defining the problem and requirements to implementing designs and models, these chapters describe the tools and methods used by developers to systematically complete a software project.

Chapter 4: *Starting the Project* provides an overview of the project and non-technical activities such as scheduling, communicating, handling problems, and documenting. The skills covered in this section are practical as they help teams to stay on task, work with each other, and quickly adapt to change.

Chapter 5: The topic of this chapter, *Requirements Elicitation*, is the process of defining the different types of requirements that exist for software projects. First, what exactly a requirement is and the difference between functional versus non-functional, and domain requirements versus constraints is described. Next, the methods of requirements elicitation are discussed as well as the issues and problems concerning requirements. Finally, the production of use case models from requirements is outlined.

Chapter 6: This chapter, *Object-Oriented Analysis*, uses object-oriented concepts to cover the analysis phase of the software development process. In this intermediary phase before design, system requirements are evaluated and refined by identifying objects and their relations, identifying use cases, developing scenarios, diagramming, and more. The process and issues in analysis are discussed and demonstrated in this chapter.

Chapter 7: In *System Design*, a chapter covering the transition from analysis to design, different design approaches are detailed for the reader. After learning the categories of system design, approaches detailed include function-oriented, structure-oriented, and finally object-oriented. The key design concepts for each approach are covered and differences between them are analyzed. This phase of the process is important to learn as it allows developers to define how various components will provide functionality to the system.

Chapter 8: The *Object-Oriented Design* chapter is concerned with filling the gaps left by analysis and system design. It describes how object design precisely defines objects, subsystems, and constraints to be used by the software to provide a detailed object model. This stage is the important precursor to implementation in the object-oriented paradigm.

Chapter 9: This chapter, *Implementation*, is about the last phase of the system development life cycle. Described in its contents is the process of planning and executing system design plans using the various tasks of implementation. These tasks are divided amongst the different roles and responsibilities of the stakeholders involved. Furthermore, this chapter uncovers some of the standards for integration, code reuse, language choice, and issues arising from implementation.

Chapter 10: The *Testing* chapter tells students about the ins and outs of software testing. First, the importance of testing is highlighted by describing its important role in the creation of correct software. Then, this chapter details how to plan and manage tests, develop tests, and utilize tests. The appropriate tests to use for certain cases are laid out in this chapter as well. The importance of testing is also highlighted as a means for determining the readiness of a software to be released.

Chapter 11: *Project Wrap-up, Delivery, and Maintenance* is a chapter on the improvement of project management and definition of success criteria. Students will learn about the purpose and importance of project termination and release, wrap-up and presentation to clients, and post-release maintenance as well as how these phases fit into the software development life cycle.

Chapter 12: The chapter *Software Metrics and Measurements* is a description of the theory and practice of establishing and using metrics of many varieties. Metrics are defined and their importance in measuring software quality are detailed in the sections of this chapter. Many broads types of metrics, including design metrics, object-oriented metrics, and project metrics are discussed in relation to the appropriate phases of development they are used in. Similarly, the benefits and drawbacks that inherently exist are detailed.

Chapter 13: Perhaps the most important chapter, *Hands-On Software Engineering Project* provides a complete guideline for completing an academic software project. Presented in order of phase, this chapter clearly introduces the complete software development life cycle and describes important tools to be used to complete the project.

Courses

Geared towards students with a background in an object-oriented language such as Java or C++, this book is intended for courses in introductory software engineering with a semester-long project. This book can be used for other courses, however, with limited or altered use of the book's parts and chapters.

Project-based course: For a project-based course in software engineering, we recommend using the book nearly as-is, following the chapters in the order provided. This provides a smooth transition between concepts and practical use as well as between phases of the development life-cycle. A semester-long project should accompany course instruction and students should practice models, documentation, and other tools detailed by the book, especially those in Chap. 13.

Introductory course: For a course introducing the concepts of object-oriented programming, we suggest primary attention being paid to the first three chapters of this book. Also, various sections of other chapters can be used as necessary to highlight practical uses of material covered in these first three chapters. For example, parts of Chap. 7 cover object-oriented design concepts that rest on principles of the object-oriented paradigm covered in Chap. 2.

Management course: For a course geared towards project management, focus should be placed primarily on Chaps. 4, 5, 9, 10, 11 and 13 as these covers aspects of overall management such as team work, communication, working with clients, project delivery, etc.

Technical course: For students learning object-orientation and software development beyond and introductory level, this books provides a core set of chapters teaching concepts such as modeling with UML, object-oriented design, implementation, and testing. In this case, Chaps. 2, 3, 6–9 and 12 are worth emphasizing.

Support Materials

To better the learning and teaching experience of those using this software engineering textbook, support materials have been provided to enhance courses in the subject. These include:

- PowerPoint presentations for each chapter of the text.
- Multiple choice tests and answers covering the topics discussed in the book.

For more information and support you may contact the author, Dr. Roger Lee, at lee1ry@cmich.edu.

Acknowledgments

There are many individuals and organizations to thank for their dedication and assistance in the creation of this book. Whether it be their influence on my work, support of this endeavor, or review of this text, gratitude and appreciation is due to all of those who helped.

I thank the following colleagues and friends for their help with the completion of this book:

- Chia-Chu Chiang, University of Arkansas–Little Rock
- Dale Karolak, Dart Container Corportation
- Justin Zablocki, Software Engineering and Information Technology Institute
- Lawrence Chung, University of Texas–Dallas

Lastly, I would also like to thank Central Michigan University for its continued support of my research and endeavors. I appreciate this opportunity to contribute to the field of software engineering and, hence, shape its growth. It is my hope that this textbook will be used to better the knowledge and practice of software engineering amongst students and professionals. Thank you again to all.

Contents

Part I   What is Software Engineering?

1   Introduction to Software Engineering 3
- 1.1   Why Do We Need Software Engineering?............... 3
  - 1.1.1   Brief Historical Summary 3
  - 1.1.2   Success Rate of Software.................... 4
  - 1.1.3   The Complexity of Software 4
- 1.2   The Software Engineering Project.................... 5
  - 1.2.1   Defining the Software Engineering Project 5
  - 1.2.2   Who is Involved in a Software Engineering
    Project?................................. 5
- 1.3   Software Engineering Activities 6
  - 1.3.1   Planning 6
  - 1.3.2   Problem Solving........................... 7
  - 1.3.3   Modeling................................ 8
  - 1.3.4   Communication 8
  - 1.3.5   Using and Managing Resources 9
  - 1.3.6   Reaching Milestones and Producing Deliverables ... 9
  - 1.3.7   Maintaining a Product...................... 9
- 1.4   Software Engineering is Not Limited to Programming 10
  - 1.4.1   Computer Science Related.................... 10
  - 1.4.2   Business Related........................... 10
  - 1.4.3   Psychology Related......................... 11
  - 1.4.4   Engineering Related 11
- 1.5   Software Life-Cycles.............................. 11
  - 1.5.1   Understanding the Software Development Process .. 11
  - 1.5.2   Evaluation of the Waterfall Model 12
  - 1.5.3   Evaluation of the Spiral Model................ 14
- 1.6   Chapter Conclusion and Summary 15
- 1.7   Exercises....................................... 16
- References 16

2   Object-Oriented Concepts............................... 17
   2.1   What is an Object?............................... 18
   2.2   Classes 20
        2.2.1   Classes Versus Objects 20
        2.2.2   The Class-Object Hierarchy.................. 21
        2.2.3   Why Use Objects and Classes?............... 21
   2.3   Modularity.. 21
        2.3.1   Reuse 22
        2.3.2   Encapsulation and Information Hiding......... 23
        2.3.3   Access Levels 24
        2.3.4   Delegation 25
   2.4   Inheritance....................................... 25
        2.4.1   Overloading................................. 27
        2.4.2   Overriding.................................. 30
        2.4.3   Polymorphism 30
   2.5   Abstraction 32
        2.5.1   Abstract Classes............................ 32
        2.5.2   Template................................... 34
        2.5.3   Generic Components......................... 35
        2.5.4   Interfaces.................................. 36
   2.6   Chapter Conclusion and Summary 37
   2.7   Exercises.. 37
   References 38

3   Modeling with UML.................................... 39
   3.1   Introduction to the Unified Modeling Language 39
        3.1.1   What is Modeling?......................... 40
        3.1.2   What is the Unified Modeling Language? 40
   3.2   Object, Classes and Actors........................ 41
        3.2.1   Objects 41
        3.2.2   Classes 42
        3.2.3   Actors.................................... 42
   3.3   Associations...................................... 44
        3.3.1   Aggregation............................... 44
        3.3.2   Generalization 45
        3.3.3   Dependency................................ 45
        3.3.4   Uses and Extends 45
        3.3.5   Multiplicity 46
   3.4   Models 47
        3.4.1   Class Diagram 47
        3.4.2   Use Case Diagram 48
        3.4.3   Sequence Diagram 49
        3.4.4   State Diagrams............................. 50
        3.4.5   Activity Diagram 51

	3.4.6	Collaboration Diagram	53
	3.4.7	Component Diagram	54
	3.4.8	Deployment Diagram	54
3.5		Interfaces, Notes, and Packages	54
	3.5.1	Interfaces	54
	3.5.2	Packages	55
	3.5.3	Notes	56
3.6		Chapter Conclusion and Summary	56
3.7		Exercises	57
References			58

Part II   The Software Engineering Project

4	**Starting the Project**		61
4.1		Overview of Project and Planning	61
	4.1.1	Identifying the Purpose of the Project	62
	4.1.2	Identifying the Deliverables of the Project	63
	4.1.3	Cost Estimation	63
4.2		Staying on Task and on Schedule	64
	4.2.1	Deadlines	65
	4.2.2	Work Breakdown Structures	65
	4.2.3	Gantt Chart	67
4.3		Communicating Ideas	67
	4.3.1	Assessing Employee Skill Levels	69
	4.3.2	Team Organization and Role Assignment	70
	4.3.3	Project Communication	71
4.4		Handling Problems and Change	72
4.5		Document Format Specification	73
4.6		Software Project Management Plan	76
4.7		Chapter Summary and Conclusions	78
4.8		Exercises	78
References			80

5	**Requirements Elicitation**		81
5.1		What are Requirements?	81
	5.1.1	Functional Requirements	81
	5.1.2	Non-Functional Requirements or Constraints	82
	5.1.3	Domain Requirements	83
5.2		Requirement Elicitation	83
	5.2.1	Communicating with the Client	83
	5.2.2	Gathering Information	84
	5.2.3	Issues in Requirement Elicitation	85

5.3   Identifying the Requirements   86
        5.3.1   Identifying the Functional Requirements   86
        5.3.2   Identifying the Non-Functional Requirements.   87
        5.3.3   Identifying the Application Domain   89
5.4   Common Problems Concerning Requirements   90
        5.4.1   Problems of Scope   90
        5.4.2   Problems of Understanding   91
        5.4.3   Problems of Volatility. 93
5.5   Validating the Requirements   93
5.6   Producing the Use Case Model.   94
        5.6.1   Structuring Use Cases 95
        5.6.2   Use Case Guidelines 95
5.7   The Software Requirements Specification Document   96
5.8   Chapter Summary and Conclusions.   98
5.9   Exercises   99
References 101

6   Object-Oriented Analysis 103
    6.1   Introduction to Analysis 103
            6.1.1   What is Object-Oriented Analysis?   104
    6.2   Requirements Specification and the Specification
            Document   105
            6.2.1   Evaluating Requirements Specification   106
            6.2.2   Refining Requirements Specification
                    Through Prototyping 107
            6.2.3   Verifying Requirements Specification   108
    6.3   Analysis Modeling Concepts   109
            6.3.1   Analysis Object Models.   110
            6.3.2   Entity, Boundary, and Control Objects   111
    6.4   Scenario-Based Modeling   112
    6.5   Class-Based Modeling. 113
    6.6   Analysis Process. 113
            6.6.1   Identifying Entity, Boundary,
                    and Control Objects 115
            6.6.2   Identifying Use Cases 116
            6.6.3   Scenario Development. 118
            6.6.4   Modeling the System   119
            6.6.5   Class Diagrams.   119
            6.6.6   Use Case Diagrams.   120
    6.7   Issues in Object-Oriented Analysis   121
    6.8   Chapter Summary and Conclusions.   122
    6.9   Exercises 123
    References 124

7   System Design   125
    7.1   Categories of System Design   126
            7.1.1   Global-Based Systems   126
            7.1.2   Group-Based Systems   126
            7.1.3   Local-Based Systems   127
    7.2   Function-Oriented Approach   127
    7.3   Structure-Oriented Approach   128
            7.3.1   Process-Oriented Approach   128
            7.3.2   Data-Oriented Approach   128
            7.3.3   Creating the Data Dictionary   129
    7.4   Object-Oriented Approach   129
            7.4.1   Component-Based Design   131
            7.4.2   Components and Objects   131
            7.4.3   Component Models   131
            7.4.4   The Component Concept   132
    7.5   Structured Versus Object-Oriented System Design   134
            7.5.1   Modularity   134
            7.5.2   Top-Down Versus Bottom-Up Design   135
            7.5.3   Reusability   135
    7.6   Object-Oriented Design Concepts   136
            7.6.1   Abstractions   136
            7.6.2   Architecture   137
            7.6.3   Design Patterns   137
            7.6.4   Modularity   137
            7.6.5   Encapsulation   138
            7.6.6   Refinement   138
            7.6.7   Class Design   139
            7.6.8   Subsystems and Classes   139
            7.6.9   Services and Subsystem Interfaces   140
            7.6.10 Coupling and Cohesion   141
    7.7   Architectural System Design   141
            7.7.1   Data Design   142
            7.7.2   Organization and Refinement   143
    7.8   Issues in Object-Oriented Analysis   143
    7.9   Chapter Summary and Conclusions   144
    7.10 Exercises   145
    References   146

8   Object-Oriented Design   147
    8.1   Overview of Object-Oriented Design   147
            8.1.1   First Steps to OOD   149
            8.1.2   Activities in OOD   150

8.2   Object-Oriented Design Concepts   151
         8.2.1   Functional and Non-Functional Requirements   151
         8.2.2   Types, Signatures and Visibility   151
         8.2.3   Object Contracts: Invariants, Preconditions
                  and Postconditions   152
8.3   Reuse Concepts: Objects and Design Patterns   152
         8.3.1   Objects   152
         8.3.2   Inheritance   153
         8.3.3   The Liskov Substitution Principle   153
8.4   Specifying Interfaces   153
8.5   Interface Specification Concepts   154
         8.5.1   Class Implementer   154
         8.5.2   Object Constraint Language   156
         8.5.3   OCL Collections   160
         8.5.4   OCL Quantifiers   161
8.6   Managing Object Design   161
         8.6.1   Documenting Object Design   161
         8.6.2   Roles in OOD   162
         8.6.3   The Unified Process   163
8.7   Objects as Models   163
         8.7.1   Forward Engineering   164
         8.7.2   Reverse Engineering   164
8.8   Design Tips   164
8.9   Chapter Summary and Conclusions   165
8.10   Exercises   166
References   168

9   Implementation   169
9.1   Introduction to the Implementation Phase   169
         9.1.1   Implementation Standards   170
         9.1.2   Library Utilization and Management   171
         9.1.3   Version Controls   171
9.2   Tasks and Activities   172
         9.2.1   Implementation Updates   172
         9.2.2   New Model Training Plan   173
         9.2.3   Data Entry   174
         9.2.4   Post-Implementation Assessment   174
         9.2.5   Documenting Updates   174
9.3   Roles and Responsibilities   174
9.4   Deliverables   175
         9.4.1   Delivered System   175
         9.4.2   Change Notice   175
         9.4.3   Version Description   175
         9.4.4   Post-Implementation Review   176

9.5		Post-Implementation Considerations	178
9.6		Language Choice	178
9.7		Development Paradigms	179
	9.7.1	Component-Based Development	179
	9.7.2	Extreme Programming	179
9.8		Code Style Standards	180
9.9		Code Reuse	181
9.10		Integration	181
	9.10.1	Top-Down Integration	182
	9.10.2	Bottom-Up Integration	183
	9.10.3	Sandwich Integration	184
	9.10.4	Integration of Object-Oriented Products	185
	9.10.5	Integration Management	185
9.11		Implementation Workflow	185
	9.11.1	Challenges of Implementation Workflow	186
	9.11.2	Metrics of Implementation Workflow	186
9.12		Managing Implementation	187
	9.12.1	Documenting Transformations	187
	9.12.2	Assigning Responsibilities	188
9.13		Chapter Summary and Conclusions	188
9.14		Exercises	189
References			190

10 Testing **191**
10.1		Introduction to Testing	191
	10.1.1	Objective of Testing	192
	10.1.2	Testing Concepts and Theory	192
	10.1.3	Test Planning	194
10.2		Quality and Internal Controls	194
	10.2.1	Assuring Quality Software	194
	10.2.2	Managerial Independence	195
10.3		Testing Management	195
10.4		Non-Execution Based Testing	196
	10.4.1	Walkthrough	196
	10.4.2	Managing Walkthroughs	196
	10.4.3	Inspections	197
10.5		Things to be Tested	198
	10.5.1	Utility	199
	10.5.2	Reliability	199
	10.5.3	Robustness	199
	10.5.4	Performance	200
	10.5.5	Correctness	200
	10.5.6	Usability Testing	200
	10.5.7	System Integration	201

	10.6	Mathematically Proving Correctness	201
	10.7	Execution-Based Testing	202
		10.7.1 Who Should Perform Execution-Based Testing?	203
	10.8	Levels of Testing	203
		10.8.1 Systems Testing	204
		10.8.2 Web Application Testing	204
	10.9	Unit Testing	205
	10.10	Acceptance Testing	206
		10.10.1 Alpha Testing	206
		10.10.2 Beta Testing	208
	10.11	UML Model Testing	209
	10.12	Testing for Object-Oriented Systems	211
	10.13	Testing in a Box	211
		10.13.1 Black-Box Testing	212
		10.13.2 White-Box Testing	212
	10.14	Testing Alternatives	213
	10.15	When to Release the Software	213
	10.16	Chapter Summary and Conclusions	214
	10.17	Exercises	215
	References	. . . .	215
11	**Project Wrap-Up, Delivery, and Maintenance**	217
	11.1	Project Management and Success Criteria	217
		11.1.1 Define Project Success Criteria	217
		11.1.2 Define Business Objectives	218
		11.1.3 Identify Project Constraints	222
		11.1.4 Derive Project Success Criteria	223
	11.2	Project Termination and Release	225
	11.3	Project Wrap-Up and Result Presentation	225
		11.3.1 Postmortem Review	226
		11.3.2 Release Management	227
	11.4	Development and Maintenance	229
	11.5	Why Post-Delivery Maintenance is Necessary	229
	11.6	What is Required of Post-Delivery Maintenance	
		Programmers?	229
	11.7	Managing Post-Delivery Maintenance	230
		11.7.1 Defect Reports	230
		11.7.2 Authorizing Changes to the Product	231
		11.7.3 Ensuring Maintainability	231
		11.7.4 Problem of Repeated Maintenance	231
	11.8	Maintenance of Object-Oriented Software	232
	11.9	Post-Delivery Maintenance Skill Versus	
		Development Skills	232
	11.10	Reverse Engineering	233

11.11   Agile Modeling and Extreme Programming   234
11.12   Testing During Post-Delivery Maintenance   235
11.13   Metrics and Challenges of Post-Delivery Maintenance   235
11.14   Chapter Summary and Conclusions   236
11.15   Exercises   237
References   237

12   **Software Metrics and Measurements**   239
12.1   Theory and Practice   239
        12.1.1   Challenges Using and Understanding Metrics   240
        12.1.2   Properties of a Good Measurement or Metric   241
        12.1.3   Etiquette   241
        12.1.4   Private Versus Public Metrics   242
        12.1.5   Baseline Measurements   242
        12.1.6   Attributes of a Good Metric   243
        12.1.7   Establishing Uniform Measures   244
12.2   Quality Metrics   244
        12.2.1   Garvin's Quality Dimensions   245
        12.2.2   McCall's Quality Factors   246
        12.2.3   ISO 9126 Quality Factors   247
        12.2.4   The Quantitative View   247
12.3   Design Metrics   247
        12.3.1   Interface   248
        12.3.2   Web Design Evaluation   248
        12.3.3   Object-Oriented Design Metrics   249
        12.3.4   Architectural Design Evaluation   250
12.4   Object-Oriented Metrics   250
12.5   Project Metrics   251
        12.5.1   Use-Case Metrics   252
        12.5.2   Size Metrics   252
12.6   Process Metrics   252
12.7   Post Release Metrics   253
12.8   Chapter Summary and Conclusions   253
12.9   Exercises   254
References   254

13   **Hands-On Software Engineering Project**   255
13.1   Phase I: Team Composition and Problem Definition   255
        13.1.1   Team Composition   256
        13.1.2   Writing for Software Engineering   257
        13.1.3   Time and Resource Management   258
13.2   Phase II: Object-Oriented Software Requirements
        Specification   261
        13.2.1   Specification Documentation   264
        13.2.2   Change Management   265

13.3   Phase III: Object Oriented System Design   266
        13.3.1   Stake Holders and Interests List   266
        13.3.2   Use Case   266
        13.3.3   Use Case Diagrams   268
        13.3.4   Class and Object Diagrams   268
13.4   Phase IV: Implementation   271
        13.4.1   Commenting Code   272
13.5   Phase V: System Integration and Testing   273
        13.5.1   Testing   273
        13.5.2   Quality Testing   274
        13.5.3   Performance Testing   275
        13.5.4   Reporting Test Results   275
        13.5.5   When and How to Comprise Time
                  and Functionality   276
13.6   Phase VI: System Demonstration   277
        13.6.1   What to Bring   277
        13.6.2   The Demonstration   278
        13.6.3   Presenting   278
13.7   Phase VII: Product Delivery With Documentation   279
        13.7.1   Peer Reviews   279
13.8   Chapter Summary and Conclusions   280
13.9   Exercises   280
References   281

About the Author   283

Index   285

Part I
What is Software Engineering?

Chapter 1
Introduction to Software Engineering

In the early years of computing, when the new technology was restricted to college campuses and government sponsored labs, software development was often limited to the practice of computer programming, and consisted of writing specific software solutions to unique scientific queries. Today, though, with the use of computers in nearly every imaginable field, simply attempting to program a solution is not enough. Instead, processes borrowed from the field of engineering were applied to the building of software systems to create the field of software engineering.

Software engineering is the process of designing, developing and delivering software systems that meet a client's requirements in an efficient and cost effective manner. To achieve this end, software engineers focus not only on the writing of a program, but on every aspect of the process, from clear initial communication with the client, through effective project management, to economical post-delivery maintenance practices. The IEEE Standard glossary of software engineering terminology defines software engineering as the application of a systematic, disciplined, quantifiable approach to the development, operation and maintenance of software (Ghezzi et al. 1991). As made clear by the above definition, software engineering came about in order to reverse early development practices by establishing a standard development method that could unify and normalize development operations, regardless of the people involved or the goals sought.

1.1 Why Do We Need Software Engineering?

1.1.1 Brief Historical Summary

The term software engineering was first coined in the late 1960s by a NATO study group seeking a solution to a phenomenon that they dubbed the **software crisis**. The software crisis referred to an alarming characteristic that had become definitive of the software development industry: a large volume of software was failing to meet initial budget and timeline specifications, and was either being produced at

R. Y. Lee, *Software Engineering: A Hands-On Approach,*
DOI: 10.2991/978-94-6239-006-5_1, © Atlantis Press and the author 2013

an unacceptably low quality or was being cancelled altogether due to an inability to meet initial requirements. The study group concluded that the application of established practices from the various fields of engineering could result in a more efficient and productive software development process (Schach 2008). In the earliest years of software development, programs were limited in both size and scope. As the technology spread, the need to develop larger, more diverse software systems led to the substandard practices that NATO came to refer to as the software crisis. In turn, the solution that was recommended initiated a new industry that focused not on programming the desired solution, but on the entirety of the development process that would deliver that solution.

1.1.2 Success Rate of Software

The advent of software engineering had an enormous impact on the software development industry, and completely revolutionized the development process. The modern day picture, however, is still far from perfect. A recent study by the Standish Group found that as late as 2004, only 28 % of software projects could be properly termed a success, while an astounding 51 % came in "seriously late, over budget and lacking expected features." The remaining 18 % were cancelled outright (Hayes 2004). All of this points to the need for even greater emphasis on software engineering.

1.1.3 The Complexity of Software

Yet another argument for the software engineering paradigm is the constantly increasing complexity of modern software. The size and scope of software systems has grown steadily since the early days of computer science. Software of the past was typically designed to do one task on a specific computer. Modern software systems, however, can do an abundance of tasks in many different situations, and on many different platforms. This escalation in functionality and portability means these larger systems will be developed by more people across ever diversifying fields of study. The demand for a unified development plan and crystal-clear project management and communication methods has never been greater (Stiller and LeBlanc 2002). No matter how good the tools, a developer must have a sound understanding of the entire software engineering process. A full understanding of the complexity of a software solution is critical in ensuring the delivery of a successful product. Complexity measures can be used to predict critical information about the reliability and maintainability of software systems from an automatic analysis of the source code. They can also provide continuous feedback during a software project to help control the development process. Even during testing and maintenance, complexity measures provide detailed information about software modules to help pinpoint areas of potential instability. Without a full understanding and analysis of the complexity of a project, it is impossible to reach the desired end goals.

1.2 The Software Engineering Project

1.2.1 Defining the Software Engineering Project

The software engineering project is an undertaking that consumes resources in order to produce a software product. The end product described here includes not only the program itself, but all of the documentation, distributions and packaging associated with that program. A software engineering project is driven by the same resources that drive any product development project: time, money and people. Depending on the size of an individual project, the required volume of these three resources can become very large, and at times may seem cumbersome. The potential mismanagement of such myriad resources can be extremely costly, and in some cases may lead to the cancellation of the project. The concept of the software engineering project puts the principals behind software engineering into practice to ensure an efficient and successful development process. To aid in this process, the software engineering project in divided into phases that are optimized to achieve unified project progression; some projects may also be divided into smaller sub-projects. This compartmentalization breaks a large, and seemingly overwhelming, project down into more manageable sections, and it can allow for a more effective utilization of resources. All software engineering undertakings have the potential for mistakes and mismanagement, but proper project organization and management can work to eliminate mishandling and reduce the risk of a failed or cancelled project (Sommerville 2004).

1.2.2 Who is Involved in a Software Engineering Project?

As stated earlier, software engineering is much more than just programming. Similarly, the people involved in a software engineering project are not limited to computer programmers. Rather, the wide range of responsibilities that might be required throughout the project calls for a diversity of skills from any number of fields (Bruegge and Dutoit 2004). The concept of a software engineering project classifies all of the individuals involved in the development process as **stakeholders**. This includes everyone from management, down to the actual clients themselves. There are no limits on the type of software engineering projects that might be requested by a client, and this potential diversity dictates that skills from any conceivable profession could be needed as a part of a software development

Table 1.1 Positions and associated rolls commonly held amongst stakeholders of a software engineering project

Position	Roll
Client	Individual or organization that has commissioned a software project, and for whom the final product is being made. Also referred to as the customer
Project manager	Responsible for overseeing the entire software engineering project. Ensures that the project remains on task, on time and within budget. Manages team leaders
Team leader	Works under project manager and manages teams that are established to handle portions of the software engineering project. Functions as a project manager for smaller 'sub-projects'
System architect	Designs the software system and determines the way in which various parts of the system interact with each other
Programmer/ developer	Responsible for writing the code called for by the system architect. Transforms system model into actual code. Also responsible for creating and maintaining up to date documentation of the code
Tester	Tests software system by using it in the manner prescribed and desired by the client's requirements and specifications
End user	Consumers of the final software product, as intended by the client

team. For this reason, it is not possible to compile an accurate list of all possible stakeholders. However, Table 1.1 details some common positions and associated rolls.

1.3 Software Engineering Activities

Software Engineering is made up of many activities. This section describes some of the general activities that occur throughout all phases of the software engineering project.

1.3.1 Planning

A software engineering project can be a very large and complicated undertaking, composed of many different tasks to accomplish and roles to designate. In order to efficiently and effectively direct this conglomeration of goals and resources, it is crucial to establish comprehensive plans of action.

In the next chapter, we will discuss the phases of the software development process. Planning will not be one of them. It is far too important to be confined to just one phase of the process. Instead, the creation and use of plans is an activity which occurs throughout the entire development process (Schach 2008). In addition, plans are continuously analyzed, evaluated and updated to meet changes encountered, such as updated requirements or specifications from the client or an alteration in the system design from the system architect. This ongoing, flexible planning scheme allows a project to be both well managed and easily adjusted, which makes a timeline oriented process easier to establish. Furthermore, effective planning allows a project to be broken down into separate modules by providing a well understood definition of how the system is supposed to function as a whole, and at what point in the timeline each part is to be completed. Finally, planning is also invaluable in cost estimation and time-requirements computation, as it sets a schedule from which to work.

1.3.2 Problem Solving

Software engineering is, in essence, a form of problem solving. Every existing piece of software and, indeed, every man made tool ever to have existed, can be thought of as a solution to some sort of problem. A client, for example, might request some intuitive application for text entry, storage, reading and editing. The solution: a word processor. In another scenario, a client could be seeking a way to market and sell their merchandise throughout the country without building brick-and-mortar stores in each state. A potential solution could come in the form of an online store that provides a way to view the product, a secure method of payment, and a proper tracking for product orders. In yet a third example, the client might be a videogame firm looking to take their single-player videogame into the realm of multiplayer-gaming. For this client, a software engineering firm might offer two potential solutions; the first could be a peer-to-peer based solution whereby one of the players in a multiplayer session takes on the role of the host, and allows his or her computer to act as a server, collecting, computing and transmitting data to the other players. The second could be a client–server style solution in which all of the players in a session connect to a dedicated server whose sole purpose is to handle the computations and client communications for the game. As these examples above illustrate, the "problem" in problem solving is not necessarily an error to correct or a failure to fix. Rather, it refers to a challenge proposed by the client, for which the software firm implements a software engineering project to create a solution in the form of a software product.

The problem solving methods described here are, of course, not quick and easy jumps from problem to solution. Instead, software engineers use a set of paradigms to work their way through the phases of the software development process. These phases will be discussed in detail in the next two chapters. For now it is sufficient to say that a software engineer must analyze the initial problem, develop a list of possible solutions and evaluate that list to select the best of the group. The software engineer must then design a system to reflect that solution and implement that design into a software product (Blum 1992).

1.3.3 Modeling

As we have stated, in between the identification of the problem and the delivery of
the solution, there lies a series of steps that must be worked through. One
underlying reason for this step-by-step strategy is related to the difficulty of
moving directly from a general concept of the solution to the code that makes up
the software itself. Many deterrents, such as the very large size of some software
engineering projects or the diversity and obscurity of the code needed for the
software, advocate the importance of intermediate steps. The most basic reason,
however, is that, just as it is ill advised to write a paper without first creating an
outline, it is simply bad practice to code from scratch without a well-defined
design to use as a roadmap.

To solve this problem, software engineers use **abstraction** to describe the
intricacies of a software system in an understandable way. They then translate
these concepts into visual representations by engaging in **modeling**. "Simply put,
a model is a simplification of reality" used to provide a conceptually-based picture
of a software system (Booch et al. 1999). This helps to describe the system in an
easy to understand way, and allows software engineers to wrap their heads around
the often very complex ideas and processes involved (Bruegge and Dutoit 2004).

Modeling is not limited to just the software product itself. Rather, software
engineers create models for the initial client problems and the system's operating
environment as well. Presenting engineers with the "bigger picture" helps them to
understand the way in which separate modules of the project fit together, and how
and why a certain design element is to be implemented in a precise way.

Today, most software engineers use a modeling system known as the **Unified
Modeling Language**, or **UML**. UML provides a common framework which is
intuitive to use and can be shared among different engineers. UML will be discussed in further detail in Chap. 9.

1.3.4 Communication

Without a means for communication, it would be nearly impossible for the successful completion of a software development project. The client must communicate to the project manager exactly what he or she wants. The project manager
must communicate with the team leaders to properly explain team rolls. The
developers must communicate with upper management in order to fully understand
what the client wants. Communication never stops in a software engineering
project and it can take many forms, depending on the type of activity it is sup-
porting. To properly monitor progress, participants might communicate and report
their status to team leaders and/or the project leader during regular meetings. It is
also good practice to hold regular client review meetings, in which participants can
communicate project status to the client (Bruegge and Dutoit 2004).

1.3.5 Using and Managing Resources

The materials dedicated to software engineering are nearly boundless. A resource is anything that will be utilized or consumed during a software engineering project. Common resources include time and money; however, resources also include all the people working on the project and the machines on which the project is developed. Improper allocation and management of resources can lead to the failure of a project, while appropriate use can help make the software development process a success.

1.3.6 Reaching Milestones and Producing Deliverables

A software engineering project begins with the elicitation of requirements from the client and ends with the delivery of a software product. As a means of maintaining communication to ensure adequate progress, the client and the software engineers agree on **milestones** to be met along the way. Milestones serve as benchmarks, and allow the client to evaluate the work being done. In addition, a software engineering project is continually producing **deliverables** during the process. A deliverable is any artifact created during the software development process, such as documentation, files, or the code itself, and is classified as either internal or external. An internal deliverable is intended to be seen and used only by those working on the project, whereas an external deliverable is meant for the client. Deliverables are maintained throughout the development process for various reasons, and some, such as documentation, are even delivered to the end users along with the product. These deliverables, along with the meetings of milestones, are a form of communication between the client and a software engineering development team (Sommerville 2004).

1.3.7 Maintaining a Product

It is easy to imagine that the software development process ends with the delivery of the product to the client. This is not the case. At this point, the software engineering project simply moves into its next phase: product maintenance. Even the most successful software engineering firms do not produce perfect software. Bugs will be found. So, if a firm's success is not based on the production of a perfect product, than what is it based on? In part, it is based on effective product maintenance.

The process of maintaining a software product involves three basic steps. First, the existing product is cleaned, meaning that the bugs are fixed. Then, the product is stabilized to ensure that the updated product functions as intended. Finally, any enhancements or additions are added to the product to adjust functionality or improve performance as required by the client. These steps are repeated throughout the life of the software product. They will be discussed further in later chapters, but for now it is important to understand that maintenance is integral to the success of a product.

1.4 Software Engineering is Not Limited to Programming

We have made this point a number of times before, and by now it must seem redundant. Good. It is crucial for anyone interested in the field to understand that software engineering is much more than just programming. This is a very common misconception, when, in fact, programming is just one part of the entire process [only accounting for about 10 % of the overall work (Schach 2008)]. The vast field of software engineering covers a wide range of professions, from business to graphic design, and from public relations to computer science. In this section, we will discuss some of these fields and their relation to the profession of software engineering.

1.4.1 Computer Science Related

The most obvious profession involved in a software engineering project is, of course, computer science. Theories and approaches from the field are used in the software development process, and thus software engineers must have a working knowledge of the concepts of computer science. Theories such as object-oriented design and abstraction are frequently utilized in the development of a software product. These theories, however, cannot always be practically applied. Thus, it is the job of a software engineer to understand the ideas and fundamental concepts behind these theories, rather than simply place them directly into use. The goal is not to understand the inner workings of a computer, but to produce quality software (Sommerville 2004). Software engineering is not a study in the specifics of computer programming or the use of a certain programming language. Rather, it is the practical application of these concepts that leads to the proper development of software.

1.4.2 Business Related

Though computer science may be the first thing that comes to the minds of those unfamiliar with the field, those involved in software engineering understand that it is as much a practice in business theory as anything else. Proper business practices, such as good project management and the efficient organization of workers, can make or break a project. A few of the important business related fields of software engineering are as follows: software product business; distributed product development; digital economy; product data management; information ergonomics; and legal and contractual issues. This business-related side of software engineering focuses on the delivery of software solutions that meet a company's needs, fit within a specified technical environment, and that are delivered on time and on budget. Well established development methods are combined with a suite of development tools to aid in this process.

1.4.3 Psychology Related

Closely related to the business side of software engineering is the management of the people involved in a software engineering project. This often includes a number of teams working on different portions of a project with their own set of goals and deadlines. The efficient and effective management of those individuals is paramount to the development of a successful software product (Schach 2008). Furthermore, every individual involved in the development process must be able to communicate effectively not only with his or her own team, but with all of the other members of the project. To this end, basic psychological concepts of communication and group dynamics are extremely useful in the management of a software project team. Team organization and management will be discussed in detail in later chapters.

1.4.4 Engineering Related

Software engineering is the application of engineering concepts and practices to the field of software development. Engineering can be thought of as a field that relates abstract scientific knowledge to everyday products. This typically means applying science and math in order to design and develop some real world utility, such as a bridge, a toothbrush or the landing gear of a space shuttle. In the field of software engineering, this practitioner uses many of these same engineering-based practices to apply computer science and mathematics to design and implement some sort of software system.

1.5 Software Life-Cycles

1.5.1 Understanding the Software Development Process

There are a number of different approaches for developing high-quality software that satisfies both the needs and expectations of its users. Some of these approaches differ from each other significantly; however they all share a common feature:

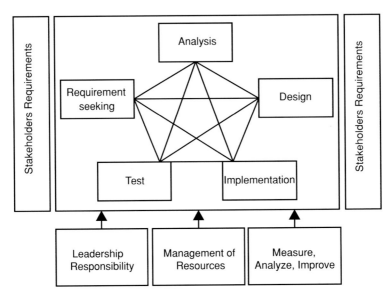

Fig. 1.1 A formal model of the software development process

a quality assurance mechanism that aims to ensure the production of quality software. Figure 1.1 provides an overview of the formal model of the software development process.

1.5.2 Evaluation of the Waterfall Model

The waterfall model, the oldest commonly used software life cycle, is a linear approach to software development that was first suggested by Royce in 1970. This development and maintenance paradigm, also known as the classic life cycle, lays out a set of development phases which are to be completed in order. A new phase begins only when the previous phase has been fully completed, which includes the finalization of all documentation from that phase, as well the approval of completion by the software quality assurance group (Schach 2008). The intent is to create an efficient development process by ensuring that all of the activities involved in a certain stage of development receive the singular attention of the software engineering team, and that as each new stage begins, all of the prerequisite work has been completed. In short, the waterfall model seeks to ensure efficiency by enforcing adherence to a strict development sequence. Figure 1.2 illustrates this sequence.

Today we know that the waterfall model represents an idealized version of the software life cycle. If all clients were able to read and fully understand technical documentation, communicate in a complete and 100 % effective manner, and if everyone involved in the software engineering project performed perfect work

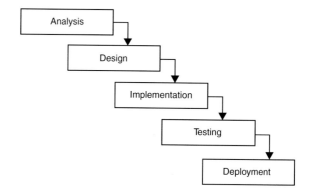

Fig. 1.2 A model of the waterfall life cycle

with no need for modifications or additional functionality beyond the initial product specification, then the classical model would be an easy choice. In practice, however, perfection is often a difficult goal to achieve. Regardless of the energy spent trying to avoid or account for them, miscommunications, misunderstandings, mistakes due to human error, and changes in requirements will occur; and problems will result. When this occurs, the only solution is often to correct the error through a change in the product. The failure to allow proper flexibility for this sort of change is a major weakness of the waterfall model.

The strict sequential structure of the waterfall model attempts to prohibit simultaneous work on different stages. Thus, if a problem that was created in an early development phase is not discovered until a later stage in the development process, the problem must either be ignored or the entire development process must be altered. In the latter case, the earlier development phase, which has been 'signed off' as complete, must now be reopened, and the life cycle must essentially be rewound to this phase. When the problem is corrected, development must continue from that early phase, in order to ensure that all of the proceeding work accommodates for the changes made. For this reason, errors discovered in later phases are extremely time consuming and expensive to fix, as they can require a full overhaul of the project (Sommerville 2004).

In addition to its inflexibility, the waterfall model's reliance on step-by-step development means that no tangible product is available for assessment by the client until late in the development process. This lack of feedback fails to ensure that the product which is being developed is compatible with the desires of the client. The discovery of such a mismatch, like the identification of any other design flaw, at such a late stage in the process can require time-consuming and costly backtracking through the entire development process (Stiller and LeBlanc 2002).

The unpredictability of human error combined with the size and cost of many software engineering projects have made strict use of the waterfall model a risky endeavor. Many of the aspects that originated with this life cycle model, however, have become staples of more secure and flexible development paradigms. The development phases that Royce put forth are still used in nearly every software life

-

cycle, and the dedication paid to continual testing and meticulous quality assurance in order to catch inevitable mistakes have continued to prevent many mistakes from becoming full blown catastrophes (Schach 2008). Today, the waterfall approach is generally only taken when the requirements of a project are well defined and not likely to change.

1.5.3 Evaluation of the Spiral Model

The major downfall of the waterfall model is, in essence, its inherent level of risk. Its use of a rigid development process means that no part of the software product can be tested until far along in the process. Due to this practice, errors and misunderstandings between the client and the developer are often missed until late in development. Fixing these errors is then much more costly to correct than it would have been at earlier stages of development. An alternative software life cycle, the spiral model, seeks to correct this problem by the use of practices designed to minimize risk. Specifically, the spiral model employs prototyping in order to test portions of the software product at various stages of development. This feature is combined with concepts and practices from the waterfall model. The result maintains the use of structure and well specified design phases from the classical model, but allows for greater flexibility and management of change. Figure 1.3 depicts the spiral model, as presented by its creator, Boehm (Schach 2008).

In Fig. 1.3, each cycle represents a phase in the development process. As can be seen, each phase consists of a series of activities, including planning, testing, designing and, most importantly to the model, risk assessment and prototyping. The steps are generalized below.

- System requirements are defined.
- An initial (preliminary) design of the system in created.
- The initial design is translated into a prototype, which is then evaluated based not only on its strength and weaknesses, but its inherent risk.
- The evaluation of the first prototype is used in the creation of a second prototype based on an updated set of plans and requirements. This second prototype is tested and evaluated.
- Consultation with the client is used to evaluate progress. At this point, the decision is reached on whether to abort the project, or to continue on to the development of a new prototype, based on the evaluations of the previous ones.
- At this point, the project enters a loop, iterating over the preceding steps until either the client chooses to abort the project, or the client is satisfied with the most recent prototype.
- The satisfactory prototype is then used to design the final system, which is rigorously tested before final delivery to the client.
- Post-delivery maintenance is carried out for the remaining life of the product.

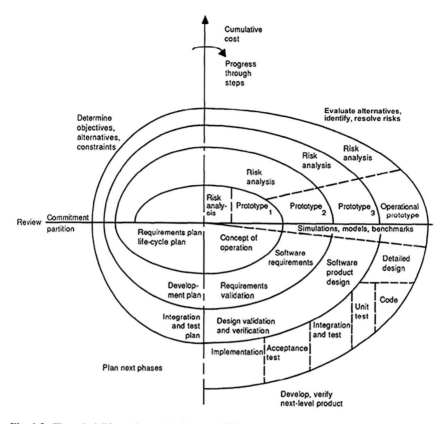

Fig. 1.3 The spiral life cycle model (Boehm 1988)

1.6 Chapter Conclusion and Summary

Software engineering has no simple definition. It can be understood as the application of engineering-based methods to software development for the purpose of delivering a software product on time and within budget. That software product is not just a computer program, but includes all related documentation, distributions and packaging. The product is developed through the collaborative work of stakeholders, which is comprised of all the individuals involved in the software engineering project. The stakeholders engage in a set of software engineering activities to work through the development process in an efficient and effective manner. All of these aspects make up the diverse field of software engineering, which involves not only computer science, but also many aspects from a multitude of other disciplines, such as business and engineering. The upcoming chapters will explore in detail the specific phases and aspects of the software development process.

1.7 Exercises

1. The potential list of professional skills involved in a software engineering project is nearly limitless. List three people involved in a software engineering project who are not computer programmers.
2. The people involved in a software engineering project, the stakeholders, are flexible positions. Describe a situation in which the client, developer and user are the same person.
3. We have said that software engineering is more than just programming and computer science. What do you understand this to mean?
4. We have described software engineering as a practice in problem solving. Pick any software application that you are familiar with, and describe its purpose in terms of an existing challenge, and the solution that it represents.
5. What is modeling and what is its purpose in the software development process?
6. Many video games, like all software systems, are developed using software engineering methodologies and practices. In the production of a video game, what is a potential deliverable aside from the software itself?
7. The word "system" has many meanings and as such many definitions. Look it up in a dictionary and write down all of the definitions that you feel apply to software engineering.
8. What are the risks and benefits of the waterfall model development paradigm?

References

Blum B (1992) Software engineering: a holistic view. Oxford University Press, New York
Boehm B (1988) A spiral model of software development and enhancement. IEEE Computer
Booch G, Ivar, Jacobson, Rumbaugh J (1999) The unified modeling language user guide. Addison Wesley Longman, Inc.
Bruegge B, Dutoit A (2004) Object-oriented software engineering: using UML, patterns, and java, 2nd edn. Pearson Education, Ltd., Upper Saddle River
Ghezz C, Jazayer M, Mandrioli D (1991) Fundamentals of software engineering, 2nd edn. Prentice Hall, New Jersey
Hayes F (2004) Chaos is back. Computerworld. http://www.computerworld.com/printthis/2004/0,4814,97283,00.html. Accessed 8 Nov 2004
Schach S (2008) Object-oriented software engineering. McGraw-Hill Higher Education, Boston
Sommerville I (2004) Software engineering, 7th edn. Peason Education, Ltd., Boston
Stiller E, LeBlanc C (2002) Project-based software engineering. Addison-Wesley, Boston

Chapter 2
Object-Oriented Concepts

Software engineering trends before the mid-1970s followed one basic programming methodology, known as structured programming. The **structured paradigm**, also called the **classical paradigm**, offered a very straight-forward approach to software engineering which seemed sufficient for the time. This model provided a simple view of a software product: the product was either operation oriented or data oriented (Schach 2008). In the first case, primary attention was paid to the functions performed. In the second, the primary focus was on the information being handled. The picture painted by the classical paradigm seemed uncomplicated in the beginning, but as the field of software engineering grew, a fundamental flaw became apparent. Describing a software application based exclusively on either the operations it was to perform or the data it was to manage was just too simplistic.

As solutions to the problem of oversimplification were being investigated, brand new programming concepts began to emerge. The most influential of these, and ultimately the most successful, is known today as the **object-oriented paradigm**. In object-oriented programming, software is not broken down into either operations or data, but rather into abstract software artifacts, called objects. These objects are designed both to manage data and to carry out operations, thus combining the two fundamentally related halves of a software product, which had in the past been kept separate under the classical paradigm.

To better explain this concept, we turn to a real world example: a human being. In the classical model, specific actions and physical characteristics were kept separate from one and other. For example a person's name, eyes, birth date, hands, and taste in music would be separated from the actions he or she is able to perform like, holding a conversation, winking at a friend, having a birthday party, listening to a CD, or shaking an acquaintance's hand. If we apply the object-oriented paradigm however, all of these attributes and actions are combined to make up a single unified object: a human being. This object is able to use its attributes, which are stored internally, to perform actions, and thus can be thought of as a well-defined, independent entity rather than an over encumbering conglomeration of functions and data.

R. Y. Lee, *Software Engineering: A Hands-On Approach*,
DOI: 10.2991/978-94-6239-006-5_2, © Atlantis Press and the author 2013

The advent of the object-oriented paradigm had a profound change on the field of software engineering. The use of objects allows software engineers to create models of the real world in ways that had been previously thought impossible. After all, software seeks to facilitate real-world situations, many of which cannot rightly be broken down into a simple sequence of instructions to be carried out in line-by-line order. Consider a local bank that, like any bank, stores money for some number of clients. The classical model would have led to the creation of a program consisting of many lines of code that dictate the exact order of operations to be performed. Code created in this manner could never be very well organized. This is not due to a fault of the programmer, however, it is the classical paradigm that provided no system for breaking the program down into logical pieces. This created a need for the objected-oriented paradigm, which allows us to model the bank in a way that is logical for our system, capturing and focusing on the important details, while leaving out those that are less important. This concept, known as abstraction, allows us to create various objects that each represent various portions of the bank, such as clients, bank accounts, employees, and money transactions (Jia 2003). In the end, the object-oriented method allows us to design and implement a software system more intuitively, compartmentalized, and manageable than previously possible using the classical method. In this chapter, we will discuss the specifics that make this possible.

2.1 What is an Object?

In the real world, an object can be anything at all from a pencil to a monster truck. If it has a name, certain characteristics, and certain actions that can be done to it or be accomplished with it, then simply put it is an object. Objects characteristics can take on many forms, forms as simple as color to as complex as molecular structure. Likewise, an **object** in the world of computer programming is an entity with attributes that belong to and describe it. These attributes can be actions the object is capable of performing, an interface to access those attributes and actions, and most importantly, a unique identity. An object is a specific instance of a **class**, which can be thought of as a blueprint for that object (classes will be discussed further in the next section). Because a single class can be used to create many objects, an object's unique identity is crucial in distinguishing it from other objects. Think of the monster truck that we mentioned earlier. Just like our software object comes from some defining class, the monster truck object might be an instance of the class truck. We use the identifier "monster truck" to ensure that we can distinguish it from other instances of the truck class, such as fire truck, pickup truck, or dump truck. An object inherits most of its attributes from its class, but these attributes may differ amongst the object instances of that class. An object is described as being in a certain **state** at any given moment, which is defined by the value of its attributes. The state of an object plays a critical role in the functionality of that object. Many of the actions that are performed by or to an object are based on the objects current state.

Programs are written so that a change in the state in an object will in some way affect the program as a whole. For example, the constant monitoring of certain object states is the driving force behind event-driven programming styles, which create programs that react to the occurrence of certain events (specified changes in object states). In this manifestation of object-oriented programming, a program might contain a user interface (UI) that listens for the user to perform a predefined action. For instance, the UI might contain a button that the user can click. When the user clicks said button, the state of some related object changes to reflect that the button has been clicked. This state change then triggers some associated reaction in the program. In this way, the operation of, and progression through, the program is dictated by the states of the objects in it.

We have said that objects are able to both change states and react to state changes. Of course, however, an object cannot simply 'know' how to change states, or how to react to another object's state change. Rather, objects are coded with **methods** that perform tasks when called upon to do so. Think again of the monster truck from before. Monster truck contains a method, which is derived from the truck class (a concept called inheritance, which will be discussed later on the chapter), that turns the engine on. This method might be called start, and it reacts to two specific events: the presence of a key in the ignition, and the turning of that key to the right position. Essentially then, the monster truck object reacts to certain state changes (placing the key in the ignition and turning it) by calling the method start, which turns the vehicle on. This method was implemented in the object by an engineer, much in the way that a software engineer implements methods in a software object.

The methods that are included in an object can vary greatly, as different objects are created for different purposes. There are two methods, however, that are common to most objects: constructors and destructors. Construction is the action of creating an object from its respective class, and initializing its attributes with either assigned values or those that are given to it by default. Object construction physically places that object into the computer's memory. An object's constructor is the actual method that handles the creation and initialization of the object. Likewise, destruction is the action of erasing an object, and thus freeing up the memory in which it resided. The destructor method of an object performs this action. Destruction of an object is used to provide room in the system memory, potentially for the creation of other objects. It also prevents faulty code from creating memory leaks. Constructors and destructors will be discussed in greater detail in Sect. 2.3.4.

Fig. 2.1 Real world objects

```
CAR                      TIM                        LION
Attributes:              Attributes:                Attributes:
Color: Red               Age: 25                    Age: 10
Model: Ford              Address: 300w              Location: Sahara zoo
                         bellows
Methods:                                            Methods:
Drive                    Methods:                   Hunt
Apply brake              Walk                        Eat
Park                     Eat                         Sleep
                         Sleep
```

Fig. 2.2 Real world objects with attributes and methods

In the next section we will discuss classes in further detail; but first, Figs. 2.1 and 2.2 provide examples of real world objects and their associated attributes and methods.

2.2 Classes

The class-object relationship is essential to the object-oriented paradigm. The two are intrinsically linked, and, truly, one cannot be discussed without mention of the other. They are not, however, the same. This section defines classes and describes the relationship and differences between classes and objects. It also explains the distinct roles that the two concepts play in object-oriented programming.

2.2.1 Classes Versus Objects

Objects are instances of classes. It seems natural, then, to say that classes can be thought of as parents to objects. This logic, however, misses a fundamental point in the object-oriented paradigm. To say that classes are related to objects as parents are related to children suggests that classes and objects are the same type of entity, in the way that a parent and his or her child are both human beings. This is not accurate. Rather, using the same example, a class can be thought of as the DNA of an object. DNA is not itself a human being, but the description of a human being's attributes. Both parents and children, on the other hand, can be thought of as objects created according to their DNA. In short, a class is the concept behind an object, or the "essence" of an object, while an object itself is a tangible entity with a place in space and time (or system memory) (Booch 1994).

A second, related definition of a class is similar to the more common definition of the word in everyday speech. In standard use, a class is a "group, set, or kind sharing common attributes" (Merriam-Webster 2009). In object-oriented programming, the usage is the same, but more specifically describes a group of objects with common attributes. This definition is a direct result of the previous definition: objects created using a class will be distinct from each other, but will share the characteristics given to them by that class, and will therefore constitute a group of similar objects. These characteristics include not only the objects' attributes, but also their methods and interfaces, all as defined by the instantiating class.

2.2.2 The Class-Object Hierarchy

We often describe classes and objects in terms of real-world concepts. Fortunately, though, some of the controversies of the real-world do not carry over into the field of software engineering. There is no chicken-egg controversy in object-oriented programming. The class comes first. As we have said, classes are essentially the blueprints or templates behind objects. In our definition from Sect. 2.1, the monster truck object could not exist without the truck class that it is derived from. An object is an **instance** of a certain class, and for that reason a class must be defined before the object can even be conceived. Once a class has been defined, an object of that type can be created from it, using the constructor method specified in that class. This action of creating an object from a class is **instantiation**, and the class used to create the object is referred to as the **instantiating** class. A single class may be used to instantiate any number of objects. All of these objects are then referred to as **members** of the instantiating class.

2.2.3 Why Use Objects and Classes?

We have said a good deal about what objects and classes are, how they related, and what they are capable of doing. However, object-oriented programming only represents one line of thought in the world of computer programming. Why should we use this paradigm? The next sections will describe the key features and advantages of the object-oriented paradigm as afforded by the use of objects and classes.

2.3 Modularity

The move from the classical structured programming model to the modern object-oriented paradigm represented a fundamental shift in the practice of software engineering. One portion of this shift dealt with the conceptualization, organization, and management of a software. If a large software engineering project is attacked as a single program to be written, the resulting code will undoubtedly be cumbersome, arduous to navigate, and extremely difficult to debug. As a solution to this, the use of modularity, borrowed from other engineering fields, worked its way into software engineering. Modular programming focuses on the partitioning of a program into smaller modules in order to reduce its overall complexity. The resulting modules constitute definite and intuitive boundaries within the program, and facilitate the use of multiple software engineering teams, each of which can focus on an individual module. The layout of these modules constitutes the physical architecture of a software system.

Booch describes modularity as "the property of a system that has been decomposed into a set of cohesive and loosely coupled modules" (Booch 1994). This not only covers the advantage of workable units, but also touches on the goal of reducing dependencies among different portions of the program. Such dependencies can make the modification of a program a tremendously large task, as editing a single class will affect all portions of the program which were dependent on that class. Those changes will have to be accounted for throughout the entire system, often at a very high cost. Modularity offers a potential solution to this problem through the isolation of individual program portions from each other. The way in which the objects and classes of a module are accessed can then be easily defined through the implementation of an interface for interaction with other parts of the program.

The theories of encapsulation and information hiding will be discussed in further detail later in this chapter, but it is important to understand that, if implemented properly, they can ensure the integrity and dependability of data across a software system.

The most important benefit of modularization is the efficiency and workability afforded by the separation of different programming concerns into manageably sized, logical modules. The result is a program that is more flexible and much easier to understand, change, and debug. Additionally, because modules are constructed independently, they can be easily reused in other applications or stored for later reference and modification. Modularity also calls for the separate compilation of the modules, which facilitates an incremental development process, and allows for easier unit testing. The following sections will discuss in more detail a few of the specific benefits of modularity.

2.3.1 Reuse

The modularization of a software product results in the creation of any number of independent components, each with a distinct function. One advantage to this approach comes from the potential use of these components in future projects. This practice, known as **reuse**, can save developers from consuming resources in order to remake something that they have developed in the past. For this reason, reuse is a common practice in the field of software engineering, and one which needs not be limited only to software components. Methods of organization, planning procedures and test data may all be reused, as can any other portion of a software engineering project that might serve some function in the development of a different project.

Schach draws the distinction between two types of reuse. The first, opportunistic, or accidental reuse, occurs when a component that was not originally developed with the mindset for future implementation, is discovered to be appropriate for use in a new project. Opportunistic reuse, however, runs an increased risk over the second type, deliberate reuse, which refers to making use of a component that was developed with reusability in mind. In the case of deliberate reuse, attention is paid to ensure that the component in question will have no unintended side effects or disabling dependencies which might have negative consequences for future projects. Opportunistic reuse, on the other hand, has a greater potential for such mistakes, as avoiding them was not a priority during development (Schach 2008). When a software component is developed with reusability in mind, rigorous testing is performed and thorough documentation is compiled to guide software engineers in future implementations of the component in question. This extra attention, however, results in an increased cost for the development of that component.

For the reasons described above, software engineering firms must weigh the potential benefits of reuse against the cost of development when considering the components involved in a software engineering project. A piece of software is developed for a distinct reason, and thus, usually neither the application as a whole nor all of its constituent parts are determined to be viable candidates for reuse. Even pieces of software developed for the most specific purposes will generally make use of very common routines. For this reason, extensive subroutine libraries have been developed for many programming languages. Modules containing common routines, such as math procedures, accounting functions or graphical interface components, are examples of widely used reusable components. Because the development of many such modules took place in the early development of these languages, they are often taken for granted; but in truth, they are the quintessential examples of reusable development, without which software engineers would have to develop each and every portion of a software engineering project from scratch. The myriad benefits of reuse have encouraged many companies to both consider reusability in the development of new software engineering components and to take into account the potential for making use of previously developed components when designing and implementing a new software engineering product.

2.3.2 Encapsulation and Information Hiding

As we have said, a modularized software product is essentially a collection of independent modules which serve distinct purposes and are configured to interact with each other. In addition to lending itself to logical project decomposition and component reuse, this use of the object-oriented paradigm can also provide integrity for a software system. To explain this, let us consider again the `monster truck` and its `start` method that we described in the beginning of the chapter. The `start` method uses the ignition and a key in order to turn the vehicle on. In fact, the insertion and rotation of the key are the only actions needed to start this very complex mechanical system. In software engineering terms, this is referred to as the use of an **interface**. Essentially, an interface provides a defined way for using an object, and for accessing those properties of an object that are intended to be accessed. The processes involved in turning on a vehicle are extremely complex, and involve everything from the use of a proper fuel mixture to the completion of certain electrical circuits to the correctly timed firing of pistons. For the average operator of the vehicle, such in depth knowledge of the vehicle's operation is unnecessary. In fact, were the operator required to manually specify all of the settings and actions required to turn the vehicle on, we can safely assume that our `monster truck` would never leave the sales lot. Luckily for us, these intricacies are hidden from the user, and instead the `monster truck` is engineered to perform these actions on its own, in response to an appropriate interaction with a predetermined interface, in this case the vehicle's ignition.

This practice of hiding a system's inner workings is known as **information hiding**. Information hiding is a key concept in the larger process at work here: **encapsulation**. Booch describes encapsulation as the "process of compartmentalizing the elements of an abstraction that constitute its structure and behavior" (Booch 1994). By this, we mean that objects should be designed to separate their internal composition and function from their external appearance and purpose. As previously stated, this provides integrity in a software system. That integrity results from the closing off of an object's internal workings so that the object in question is only accessed in the desired manner, and unintended changes to the object cannot be made by the program. Furthermore, encapsulation ensures the independence of an object from the rest of a software system. The internalization of an object's attributes and methods means that if a change is made to one part of the system, the object maintains its integrity and functionality, and is still accessed and will still respond in the intended manner. This localization of data facilitates not only changes implemented during the original development process, but also throughout the ongoing maintenance that the software will undergo during its serviceable lifespan.

2.3.3 Access Levels

We have said that the use of modularity and encapsulation can provide integrity within a software system through the use of information hiding. One key practice that leads to this advantage is the designation of access levels within classes, and thus within the objects derived from them. Levels of access are assigned in order to specify how classes, as well as their attributes and methods, can be used by other objects during execution. While cooperation among objects is desirable, these interactions must be controlled in order to ensure stability. The three standard access levels are described below:

Public: the class in question, and instances of it, can be accessed by any other member simply by a call to the class or derived object name.
Protected: can be accessed by the class itself, and by all subclasses that are derived from it.
Private: can only be accessed by the class itself. Thus, only methods that are part of the class are allowed access.

Access levels can be applied to individual attributes or methods within a class, and form the basis of an interface. Those characteristics of a class which we earlier described as the class's "inner workings" are designated as restricted. This might encompass nearly all of a class's attributes and methods. Those characteristics which are left open for access by other parts of the software system constitute the interface, and generally will communicate with the inner workings of the class in a predefined way in order to return information, perform an action, or modify the object in question.

2.3.4 Delegation

In the next section, we will discuss a practice in the object-oriented paradigm called inheritance, which aims to provide a class with the properties of a different class. Here we briefly discuss an alternative method to this practice, known as **delegation**. Delegation provides opportunity for code reuse not by directly inheriting the attributes of some class, but rather by simply using the methods of another class to accomplish the desired result (Bruegge and Dutoit 2004). While inheritance is generally considered a static method of implementing attributes, delegation allows the dynamic use of only those desired attributes at a specified time.

2.4 Inheritance

Object-oriented software engineering aims to efficiently produce reliable software by reducing redundancy and ensuring integrity within a software system. The class-object structure facilitates this end by providing an intuitive system of modularization which easily lends itself to reusability. Central to both of these principles is a feature of object-oriented programming languages known as **inheritance**. Inheritance is a relationship between different classes in which one class shares attributes of one or more different classes. In this way, the class in question, the **subclass**, *inherits* the qualities of other classes that have already been created, the **superclasses**. There are two general cases of inheritance, which are defined by the number of superclasses, or **parent classes**, from which the subclass, or **child class**, directly inherits attributes: **single inheritance** describes a relationship in which a class has only one ancestor from which it directly inherits its attributes. **Multiple inheritance**, on the other hand, occurs when a class calls on more than one superclass for properties. The rest of this section will be devoted to discussing the various principles behind the use of inheritance.

For starters, inheritance offers an obvious solution for the elimination of redundancy through the implementation of reuse. The creation of a new class from some other class with a similar purpose and set of attributes saves the software engineer from rewriting code that is already in use elsewhere. This implementation of inheritance is often used to facilitate the creation of some number of differing classes that share common attributes and a common purpose. Consider, again, the `monster truck` example previously discussed. We described this as being an instance of the `truck` class, along with a few other potential versions of that class: `fire truck` and `dump truck`. In this example, each of our three subclasses of `truck` can be thought of as more specific versions of the superclass. The superclass, `truck`, can then be thought of as a generalization to be used in the formation of those subclasses. This type of class is called an **abstract class** and is not meant to ever be instantiated (that is, no object will be created from it). Rather, it exists only to pass on common characteristics to more specific versions of itself. In our example, these would be characteristics or important information common to all trucks, such as `numberOfWheels`, `allWheelDrive` or `groundClearance`. Each subclass of `truck` might then add more specific characteristics in their separate implementations. `Monster truck`, for instance, might include a `crushCar` method and a `paintJob` attribute. These are examples of single inheritance, which we can now describe as a relationship in which one class inherits a set of characteristics from a more general class. We often refer to this as an "is-a" relationship, a term derived from the situational semantics. That is, a `monster truck` is a `truck`, which is a `vehicle`, and so on from one class to another, more general class.

To understand this further, we can extend our example again to an additional superclass, `vehicle`, of which `truck` is a child. This new class is a step toward greater generalization; an even more abstract class that can be used to create other types of vehicles, such as `car` or `spaceship`. The vehicle class might contain a few very general methods like `move` and `stop`, and some basic attributes like `fuelType` and `manufacturer`, which will most likely be useful to all subclasses. Figure 2.3 illustrates this example.

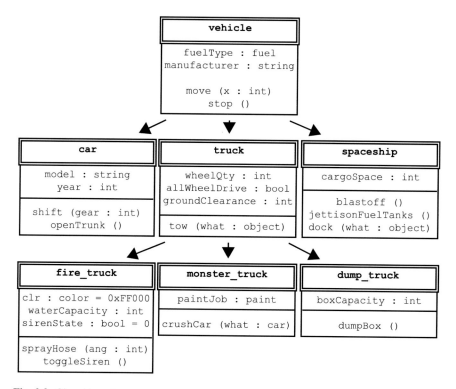

Fig. 2.3 Class hierarchy

2.4.1 Overloading

Overloading is an object-oriented programming practice by which, in certain circumstances, different methods of a class can share the same name. This is known as *overloading* the name with multiple implementations (Jia 2003). One of two criteria must be met in order for two methods to overload the same name:

1. The methods must accept a different number of arguments.
2. The arguments accepted by the methods must be of different data types.

   Due to the potential for overloading, programming languages do not use only the name of a method, but rather the signature, which consists of the name in combination with the arguments passed, in order to determine which implementation of a method to call. The following class description provides an example of overloading.

```
public class ChatterBox {
 protected String fristName;

 public ChatterBox() {
     firstName = "Chatty";
 }

 public ChatterBox(String firstName) {
     this.firstName = firstName;
 }

 public String sayHello() {
     String s = "Hello! My name is " + firstName +
".";

     return s;
 }

 public String sayHello(String userName) {
     String s = "Hello, " + userName + "! My name is
" + firstName + ".";
     return s;
 }

 public String sayHello(int times) {
     String s = "";
     while (times > 0) {
         s += "Hello! ";
         times--;
     }
     s += "My name is " + firstName + ".";
     return s;
 }
}
```

This example, written in Java, uses an overloaded constructor, ChatterBox, to handle the potential need for a default value to be assigned to its only attribute, firstName. This common usage of overloading allows software engineers to apply a minimalist approach to object creation, and avoid writing unnecessary code. In the case of the ChatterBox class, if a string argument is passed with the constructor, that string will be assigned to the firstName attribute. On the other hand, if no string is passed, firstName is given a default value, "Chatty".

The class description above also demonstrates the second usage of overloading: convenience. The three implementations of the sayHello method all serve a slightly different, but related purpose. Overloading is used here to provide logical

Table 2.1 Overloading methods of the `ChatterBox` class

Method	Signature
string sayHello()	sayHello()
string sayHello(String userName)	sayHello(String)
string sayHello(int times)	sayHello(int)

access to the desired actions by differentiating the implementations by the arguments passed. Table 2.1 lists the signatures of each of these implementations.

The following code segment provides examples for possible calls to the `sayHello` method with different arguments.

```
        ChatterBox c = new ChatterBox('Bob');        //invoke
ChatterBox(String)

        c.sayHello();                                //invoke
                                                     sayHello
                                                     ()
                                                     //return
                                                     "Hello!
                                                     My   name
                                                     is Bob."

        c.sayHello('John');                          //invoke
                                                     sayHello
                                                     (String)
                                                     //return
                                                     "Hello,
                                                     John! My
                                                     name   is
                                                     Bob."

        c.sayHello(3)                                //invoke
                                                     sayHello
                                                     (int)
                                                     //return
                                                     "Hello!
                                                     Hello!
                                                     Hello!
                                                     My   name
                                                     is Bob."
```

2.4.2 Overriding

We have said that inheritance permits a class to inherit the characteristics of some
other class. What happens, though if we need to modify some inherited method
within a subclass? **Overriding** is the practice of replacing a method inherited from
a superclass with a newly defined method in the sub class. Unlike overloading,
which differentiates different implementations of methods with the same name by
unique signatures, overriding requires that a method have exactly the same signature and return type as the method it is replacing. The following Java code
segment illustrates the use of overriding on two classes related by inheritance.

```
public class A {
  public String greetings(String userName) {
      String s = "Hello, " + userName;
      return s;
  }
}
public class B extends A {
    public String greetings(String userName) {
        String s = "Hola, " + userName;
        return s;
    }
}
```

In the example above, class B, which uses the Java `extends` keyword to
inherit the structure of class A, requires a different implementation of the
`greetings` method. Thus, the method is overridden by coding a new method
with an identical signature as the inherited method.

Overriding can be extremely useful, but it carries with it significant risks.
Overriding can potentially negate the integrity that is provided by the use of
inheritance. This occurs when the dependencies within a class are disturbed.
Consider the example in Fig. 2.4, which illustrates the subclass `employee` of the
class `person`. Assume that the `setDateOfBirth` method defined in the
`person` class accepts some month-day-year style argument as a date of birth.
Overriding allows us to redefine this method in the `employee` class to accept a
day-month-year style date of birth. However, the `calculateAge` method, which
returns an age based on the current date and the `dateOfBirth` attribute, will
now produce an error unless it too is overridden.

2.4.3 Polymorphism

Imagine for a moment that the only vehicle you had ever driven was a compact
sedan. This is the vehicle that you used when learning to drive, and the only

Fig. 2.4 Overriding

person
dateOfBirth : int
setDateofBirth (mdy_dob : int) calculateAge ()

employee
dateOfBirth : int
setDateofBirth (mdy_dob : int)

vehicle that you have used since. This is the only car that you are familiar with; the only car that you know how to operate. Now, imagine that one day, your compact sedan breaks down. In order to go to work, you are required to borrow a friend's car. This car, though, is not a compact sedan. It is a luxury SUV. How, then, will you be able to drive this vehicle without prior knowledge of its specific operation?

In reality, we know that the problem posed above probably will not be a problem at all. It seems reasonable enough, though, to assume that a compact sedan and a luxury SUV have different enough inner workings to require separate and distinct methods of operation. Why, then, would the knowledge of how to operate one allow us the ability to operate the other? The answer is that both the compact sedan and the luxury SUV share a common interface through which they can be accessed. Simply put, most, if not all, of the control methods for one also work for the other. This common method of access is of course based on some general idea of how an automobile should be used. Put another way, both compact_sedand and luxury_SUV have inherited a common interface from the superclass automobile, which allows them to perform a set of general functions based on the same methods of access.

Polymorphism is an engineering concept concerning the ability of separate classes and their derived instances to be accessed in the same way, assuming they are derived from the same superclass (Booch 1994). This method of access is provided for in a common interface that is defined in the superclass. This provides a level of encapsulation by hiding the inner workings of a class or object from the user, while allowing access in a familiar way. In the example above, the compact sedan and the luxury SUV are both started in the same manner, with the insertion of a key into the ignition, and the turning of that key. The internal actions that fire up the two vehicles, however, may be entirely different from one and other. So, to narrow our definition, polymorphism dictates that a common interface can be used to access the unique inner workings of separate classes that are related by a common superclass. Polymorphism is a powerful tool that permits the use of unique but related objects with only a general understanding of how those types of objects are to be accessed rather than requiring the specific knowledge of the individual objects themselves.

2.5 Abstraction

Abstraction is a fundamental concept in object-oriented software engineering that allows for the efficient management of complexity through the use of generalization. It is the practice of separating those details of a situation that are significant to the current purpose from those that are not, resulting in an abstraction of the situation as a whole. Booch explains that "an abstraction denotes the essential characteristics of an object that distinguish it from all other kinds of objects and thus provides crisply defined conceptual boundaries" of that object (Booch 1994). By this definition, an abstraction is a generalization of an object which includes only those details necessary to define it and to differentiate it from other objects. It describes the "outside view" of an object, and not the objects inner workings, or encapsulated information. An object's abstraction is a simplified form of its original self. It retains only those details required for accurate description and identification of the object, but excludes all other nonessential information (Jia 2003).

The concept of abstraction is closely related to those of encapsulation and information hiding. Essentially, the idea behind the use of an interface is to present a view of an object that includes only the relevant and necessary details; an abstraction of an object. Hiding the inner workings promotes economical use of that object and aids in securing its internal integrity.

2.5.1 Abstract Classes

One of the most fundamental forms of abstraction in object-oriented software engineering is the use of **abstract classes**. Earlier, we briefly described an abstract class as a class which is never meant to be instantiated, but rather exists to pass its characteristics on to more highly specified versions of itself: its subclasses. We can now identify an abstract class as an abstraction comprised of a set of highly generalized, often largely unspecified attributes and methods that are to be passed on to subclasses which are then able to tailor those characteristics to their specific purposes and inner workings. An abstract class is often the root of an inheritance hierarchy and provides the initial interface for the classes that will be derived from it. The abstract class, in this case a base class, expresses the functionality of all subclasses, but does so with such a high level of abstraction that it is impossible to explicitly define all of the implementations behind the interface (McGregor and Sykes 1992).

Though technically identical to other classes in that it consists of methods and attributes which can be used to create instantiations of itself, a class is only considered an abstract class when it is used only as a superclass for other classes,

and is not itself instantiated. An abstract class only specifies properties, that is to
say, it is not used to create objects. Abstract classes provide the structure of all of
the classes in a class hierarchy, while the subclasses are responsible for defining
the specifics of the properties that they inherit. The following code segments
illustrate the use of abstract classes.

```
/*Set of classes for dice with different number of
sides*/

/*This is an abstract class for Dice*/
/*It  is  the  base  class  for  all  other  Dice
Subclasses*/
class Die {
/*Declares   unspecified   protected   variable   for
Number of sides*/
   protected int sides;

/*Declares function to roll Die*/
   public int roll() {
      int   i   =   (int)(Math.ceil(Math.random()   *
this.sides));
      return i;
   }
}

/*Class for six-sided Die*/
class Die_Six extends Die {
   Die_Six() {
      this.sides = 6;
   }
}

/*Class for ten-sided Die*/
class Die_Ten extends Die {
   Die_Ten() {
      this.sides = 10;
   }
}

/*Class for Twenty-sided Die*/
class Die_Twenty extends Die {
   Die_Twenty() {
      this.sides = 20;
   }
}
```

In the code segment above, classes representing dice with different numbers of sides are created using an abstract base class `Die`. In the base class, one attribute and one method are defined. The attribute, `sides`, is an integer that denotes the number of sides on a die. Note that this attribute is only *declared* in our base class, and is not assigned a value. The method defined in the base class is `roll`, which takes advantage of Java's `Math.random` method to select a random integer between 1 and the number denoted by the `sides` attribute. We are able to define this method in our abstract class because its implementation will not change in any of our subclasses: all of our dice will produce a random number based on their number of sides when rolled. It is important to understand, though, that this method cannot be used in our abstract class, because there is no assigned value for the variable `sides`.

The subclasses which we create next are specific version of the abstract class `Die`. That is, they are subclasses of `Die` for which a number of sides is specified (six for `Die_Six`, ten for `Die_Ten`, and twenty for `Die_Twenty`). Each class contains just one method, a constructor which is used to create an instance of the class in the form of an object. In each constructor method, the number of sides for that specific die is assigned to the `sides` attribute, which is inherited from the superclass (or abstraction) `Die`. In addition, each subclass of `Die` also inherits the `roll` method. With this, we now have functioning die objects, which, when this method is called, return a random number between 1 and the value of their individual `sides` attribute.

2.5.2 Template

Closely related to the concept of an abstract class is the concept of **templates**. The use of templates provides for the declaration of the structure and function of subclasses without regard for the data type to be handled by them. In other words, a template is a sort of abstract class definition intended to be used on a data type that is yet to be defined; a *template* for a class. The data type in question is declared only upon the instantiation of an object from the template class, along with the actual class definition. Before this point, in the template itself, a placeholder is used to refer to the data type. Take a look at the following code segment for an example.

```
template class List for X {

    /*Data structure needed to be implemented with
    some sort of list that reacts to the following
    methods*/

    append(X element) { ... };
    X.getFirst() { ... };
    X.getNext() { ... };
}
```

The above template class `List` looks similar to any other class definition, except that the first line denotes it as a template for use with the undefined type X. This identifier, X, is the placeholder that will be replaced when the template class is instantiated by some concrete data type that is to be acted on. The `append` method, for example, will then accept a single argument containing that data type and add it to the list. The data type of the element will be declared upon the creation of a list object, as in the following example.

```
class Apple{

  /*Data structure relating to the qualities of an
apple*/
  Apple() { … };  /*Apple constructor*/

}



  /*Create a List object and specify the data type to
be used*/
  List for Apple appleList;

  /*Make some apples from the Apple class*/
  Apple appleA;
  Apple appleB;

  /*Add them to the list*/
  appleList.append(appleA);
  appleList.append(appleB);
```

In the first bit of code above, we create a class `Apple`. Next, we instantiate the template class `List` into an object named `appleList`, to be used with the data type `Apple`. We go on to create two instances of the `Apple` class, `appleA` and `appleB`, and use the `append` method derived from the template class to add them to `appleList`. The statement `List for Apple appleList` substitutes every occurrence of the placeholder X from our template class with the data type `Apple` for `appleList`. In this way, templates provide for yet another level of abstraction by allowing for dynamic data type declarations with classes.

2.5.3 Generic Components

The principle of abstraction lies at the heart of component based software engineering. Abstraction allows for the creation of generalized components which can be modified and implemented for specific situations. This generalization enhances the reusability of components, assuming that the component in question is generic enough to both be used in different contexts and to capture the common features of those contexts (D'Sourza and Wills 1999). For this reason, software engineers often look to enhance the generic quality of components. This can be performed in several ways, and may result in the modification of a class created for some specific purpose and circumstance, into a more general class which can then be implemented in various other contexts. The use of various forms of inheritance through the creation of templates and abstract classes work toward this end.

2.5.4 Interfaces

We have described the concept behind interfaces at various points throughout this chapter. Simply put, an interface is a system that allows two separate entities to interact with each other. It does this by closing off an object's outward appearance from its inner workings and by providing a set of methods for interaction. As we have said, the interface is not unique to software engineering, but is a common feature that can be found in countless forms: spoken language acts as an interface between people, a keyboard is an interface into a computer, a faucet handle is an interface for controlling water in a sink, and a mouth is an interface between an animal and the food that it consumes.

In software engineering, the use of an interface defines a manner for interacting with a class or an object. In some programming languages an interface is itself a data type, just like any other class. Like a class, an interface defines a set of methods, however, unlike a class the interface never implements those methods. Instead, an interface is used by a class, which implements those methods for its own use. A class can even make use of multiple interfaces to allow for different manners of interaction.

In the example that we have used throughout this chapter, the `monster_truck` class and its class hierarchy define what a `monster_truck` is; what it can and cannot do. A monster truck, however, can be used in other ways. For instance, a monster truck sitting at a car lot must be inventoried, inspected and categorized according to various characteristics, including price. The system responsible for managing the lot's inventory does not care one bit about interacting with a monster truck in the way that a driver would, nor does it care whether or not it is managing a monster truck at all. So, instead of accessing our `monster_truck` class as defined by its normal implementation, the inventory system might set up some other sort of communication protocol to communicate information such as price and model number. The system that it creates, of course, is just another interface through which we are now able to interact with the `monster_truck` class. For this system to work, both the `monster_truck` class and the inventory system must agree to this protocol by implementing their own forms of the interface, and thus all of the methods defined in that interface.

Interfaces are extremely useful tools that are vital to many object-oriented concepts, including information hiding, efficient reuse, abstraction, encapsulation and the proper use of inheritance.

2.6 Chapter Conclusion and Summary

This chapter focused on the object-oriented paradigm and its relationship to software engineering. We defined, first, the base components of object-oriented theory: objects and classes. Classes, as we have said, are not tangible entities, but rather they are blueprints for creating such entities. Objects, on the other hand, are created by classes, which represent the structure of a software system, and are made up of attributes, methods and some unique identifier.

Object-oriented theory is strongly rooted in the concept of modularity. A modular software system is comprised of independent components which are properly implemented in order to function together. The concept of modularity enhances the creation of reusable software components through the proper use of encapsulation and information hiding. Encapsulation allows us to separate an object's inner workings from its outward appearance, and thus lend the object internal integrity.

The creation of a modular software system relies on the use of abstraction to create a general view of the system's components. Through abstraction, a series of generalized components can both provide the boundary to be used in encapsulation and establish a logical class hierarchy for the specification of individual components and classes.

2.7 Exercises

1. Using examples, explain the difference between a class and an object.
2. Explain how the concepts of the object-oriented paradigm are used to reduce the complexity of a software system.
3. We have said that an object consists of attributes and methods. What are these? Describe one attribute and one method of a pencil?
4. Explain how inheritance might jeopardize encapsulation. Can you think of a solution for this?
5. Describe an inheritance hierarchy connecting a button down shit to its root class, clothing.

References

Booch G (1994) Object-oriented analysis and design with applications, 2nd edn. The Benjamin/ Cummings Publishing Companys, Inc., New York

Bruegge B, Dutoit A (2004) Object-oriented software engineering: using UML, patterns, and java, 2nd edn. Pearson Education, Ltd., Upper Saddle River

D'Sourza D F, Wills A C (1999) Objects, components, and frameworks with UML: the catalysis approach. Addison Wesley Longman, Inc., Sydney

Jia X (2003) Object-oriented software development using java: principles, patterns, and frameworks, 2nd edn. Addison-Wesley, Boston

McGregor J D, Sykes D A (1992) Object-oiented software development: engineering software for reuse. Von Nostrand Reinhold Co., New York

Merriam-Webster (2009) Online Dictionary. http://www.merriam-webster.com/dictionary/class. Accessed 30 Jan 2009

Schach S (2008) Object-Oriented Software Engineering. McGraw-Hill Higher Education, Boston

Chapter 3
Modeling with UML

The demand for software has risen tremendously since the early days of software engineering; and, as basic economics teaches us, when the demand for a product rises, so does the value associated with that product. This increase in the value of software has encouraged the software industry to seek out and create ever more efficient methods of software production. Much of the previous two chapters have focused on this never ending pursuit of higher quality software with lower costs and shorter production times. We have outlined many of the concepts central to this goal, including one of the foundations of the object-oriented paradigm, abstraction. Abstraction allows for the useful classification of real world phenomena. The Unified Modeling Language (UML), a graphical system for creating models that has become the "de facto standard for object-oriented modeling", is one of the central tools used to put this concept into practice (Sommerville 2004).

3.1 Introduction to the Unified Modeling Language

As the demand for software has quickly risen, so has the relative complexity of many software products. These increasingly complicated projects require more planning, more engineers, and more code. As this growth continues, clear communication becomes ever more vital to the success of a software project. Standard modeling systems were developed to meet this need. The foremost of these is UML, which has emerged over the last decade as the most popular and is today, in essence, the standard "software blueprint language" (Miller 2003). UML allows everyone involved in software project, from the client to business analysts and from designers to programmers, to have a common understanding of the software being developed. It also allows for the use of a common vocabulary when discussing that software. Furthermore, UML has its foundations in the object oriented paradigm, and thus the central concepts of software engineering are essentially "built in" to the system.

The foundations of UML were laid in the mid-1990s when Booch and Rumbaugh began the unification of two different modeling systems: the Booch

R. Y. Lee, *Software Engineering: A Hands-On Approach*,
DOI: 10.2991/978-94-6239-006-5_3, © Atlantis Press and the author 2013

Method and the Object Modeling Technique (OMT). Jacobson then joined the two, and followed their lead when he merged the Object-Oriented Software Engineering method (OOSE) into their hybrid creation. These efforts resulted in the initial release of the UML. The upkeep of UML was eventually handed over to the Object Management Group (OMG), a software engineering consortium that is still responsible today for setting the standards of the language. OMG's UML specification provides a standard definition for the modeling system: "The Unified Modeling Language visual language for specifying, constructing, and documenting the artifacts of systems. It is a general-purpose modeling language that can be used with all major object and component methods, and that can be applied to all application domains … and implementation platforms" (OMG 2007).

3.1.1 What is Modeling?

Modeling is a critical part of any engineering process. In the field of construction, a model might be a blueprint for a building. Among electrical engineers, a model could be the schematics used to describe an electrical circuit and the components involved. In software engineering, modeling serves the same purpose of allowing those involved in a software engineering project to maintain a common understanding of the product being developed. Models allow all members of a software development team to accurately assess all aspects of a software project, and thus to ensure that a client's requirements are being met. In previous chapters, we have discussed the tremendous costs associated with modifying software late in the development process. Proper modeling practices ensure that the entire project can be accurately visualized at every step of the process to ensure success. For these reasons, modeling is a practice that lies at the heart of analysis and design. It allows us to describe the structure and behavior both of real world phenomena and of the abstractions to be built in a software product. A model can be broken down into three parts. The first of these, the static part, describes an objects state at any given moment. The second part, the dynamic part, represents the state changes that will happen as events occur. The final part, the interactive part, is used to denote the way in which objects interact with one another (D'Sourza and Wills 1999).

3.1.2 What is the Unified Modeling Language?

Booch describes the **Unified Modeling Language** as "a standard language for specifying, visualizing, constructing, and documenting the artifacts of software-intensive systems, as well as for business modeling and other non-software systems" (Booch et al. 1999). UML is a basically a collection of successful software engineering practices that have been compiled into a full-fledged modeling specification. Through the use of this modeling system, object-oriented software engineering projects can be properly visualized and annotated in a standardized way, allowing software engineers to better communicate about the various aspects of the software being designed.

UML was designed to create a standardized modeling language that:

- was expressive and ready-to-use, to provide for the creation of useful, meaningful models;
- was both extensible and able to be specialized to specific projects;
- was programming language independent;
- was development process independent;
- could support higher-level development concepts;
- and integrated various best practices from the field of software engineering.

UML has grown and evolved since its inception. The current version, UML 2.0, includes 13 different diagram types divided into the following three main groups:

- **Structure Diagrams**—class, object, component, composite structure, package, and deployment diagrams
- **Behavior Diagrams**—use case, activity, and state machine diagrams.
- **Interaction Diagrams**—sequence, communication, timing, and interaction overview diagrams.

3.2 Object, Classes and Actors

3.2.1 Objects

In the previous chapter, we defined an object as the core unit of a piece of software, an entity consisting of attributes, methods, an interface, and some unique identifier. With the use of UML, we are able to create visual representations of these objects. Figure 3.1 provides us with a familiar example of a UML object model.

Here we have our `monster_truck` object. Note that the top box shows both the name and type (instantiating class) of the object. In this case, the object is an instance of the `Truck` class. In the bottom box, the object's attributes and related values are displayed.

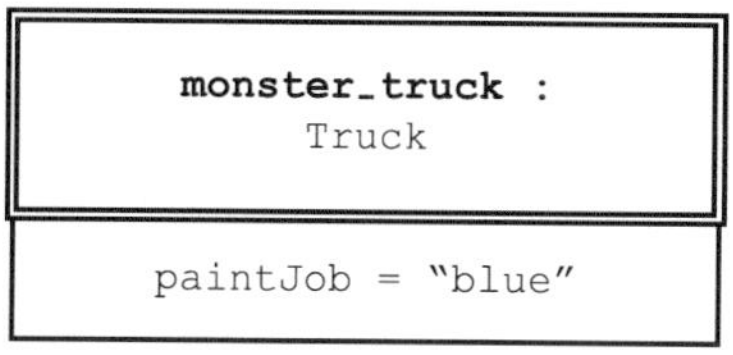

Fig. 3.1 Monster_truck object depicted in UML

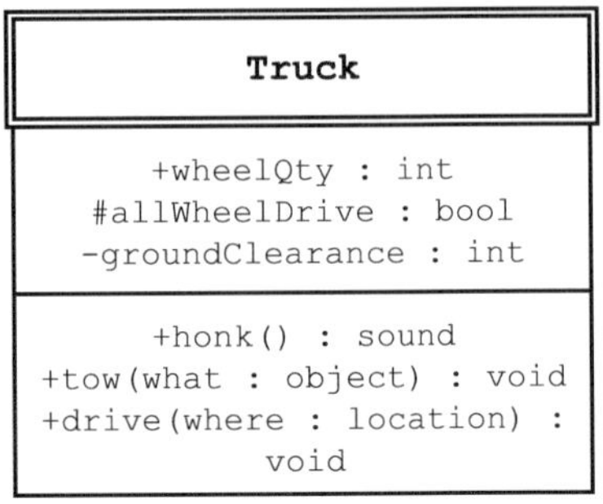

Fig. 3.2 Truck class

Truck
+wheelQty : int #allWheelDrive : bool -groundClearance : int
+honk() : sound +tow(what : object) : void +drive(where : location) : void

3.2.2 Classes

The previous chapter also saw the introduction of the concept of a class, which we described as the blueprint used in the creation of an object. Figure 3.2 shows how this type of abstraction is presented in UML.

Here we see the class that was used to instantiate the monster_truck object in Fig. 3.1, the Truck class. As we can see, a class diagram lists the class' name in the top box, the associated attributes in the middle box, and the operations in the bottom box. Various symbols are used to denote information about the class itself. The symbols preceding the class' attributes and methods are used to express the access levels: a '+' symbol is used for denoting a public attribute, '#' for one that is protected, and a '–' for one that is private. We also see that each attribute declaration is made up of two parts separated by a ':' symbol: the first is the attribute's name; the second is the attribute's type. So, the wheelQty attribute, for instance, has the type integer, or int. The method representations follow this same schema, but appear slightly more complicated. Directly following a method's name, we find a set of parentheses, '(' and ')', sometimes with information enclosed. The enclosed information describes the arguments that a particular method is to accept, in the familiar attribute form. If there is no information here, the method accepts no arguments. The final portion of a method definition, following the ':', describes the method's return type. A method defined for return type void does not return anything. To put this all together, let's look at the tow method defined in +tow (what : object) : void. This is a public method which accepts one argument, what, which is an object, and produces no return.

3.2.3 Actors

Unlike objects and classes, which are software entities within a software system, an actor is an external entity, such as a person or an organization, that interacts with a software system. More specifically, an actor is the role played by such entities when interacting with the system. An actor is who or what is responsible

Fig. 3.3 Example of an actor

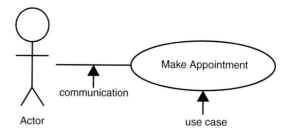

for initiating user events within a software system. Actors, like objects, have unique names so that they can be identified as entities within the system. Figures 3.3 and 3.4 illustrate the relationship that an actor has with a system. The oval labeled Make Appointment represents a use case that describes the systems response to an externally initiated event (use cases will be discussed in greater detail later in the chapter). The event in question is denoted by the line linking the use case to the actor itself, represented by a stick figure. In this example, the actor, a patient, is using the system to make an appointment. In the next example, Fig. 3.4, we are shown a situation in which multiple actors interact with the system. This diagram describes a point-of-sale checkout system in a convenience store. The Sales_Clerk interacts with the system to begin the interaction. In this case, imagine the Customer has elected to pay by debit card. The Customer must now interact with the system on its own to enter in a personal identification number. The actor-use case standard allows both members of a software engineering team and the client to visualize and discuss the external interactions that a software system intends to handle.

Fig. 3.4 Example of multiple user situation

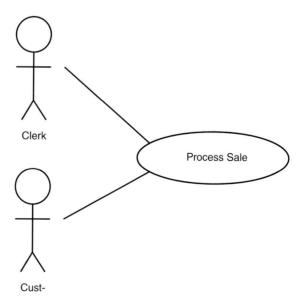

Fig. 3.5 Association
between classes

3.3 Associations

Computer programming has long been considered a related field to that of lin-
guistics. After all, programming languages are simply a combination of grammar
and vocabulary created for a specific purpose. In a related sense, we can think of
classes as nouns in our modeling language. They represent things; entities that
exist within the system. In order to form proper and complete sentences, though,
we need verbs to describe what it is that our nouns do. In this case, our verbs are
associations. Associations express the relationships between classes, and thus
describe the actions that define their interactions. In the same way that objects are
instances of classes, associations too have instances, called links in UML. Associations describe the relationships between classes. Links describe the relationships between objects. As we described in the previous section, associations are
depicted by a line connecting two classes. In Fig. 3.5, an association called
Consults defines the relationship between classes A and B.

3.3.1 Aggregation

Aggregation is a relationship in which one class completely contains another
class. Real world examples could include a hotel class that contains a
hotel_room or a soccer_team class which contains a soccer_player.
The UML diagram below denotes aggregation between a Country class and a
State class.
    Figure 3.6 the Country is the owner class. The diamond ended line connecting
the two classes denotes the aggregation relationship, with the diamond end always
pointing to the owner class. The State class in this example is called the owned,
part, or component class. In most cases, the owner is responsible for construction
and destruction of the owned class.

Fig. 3.6 Example of
aggregation

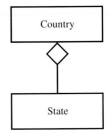

Fig. 3.7 Generalization

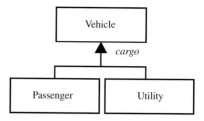

3.3.2 Generalization

Generalization is another type of relationship that can be described using UML. Generalization describes inheritance, which we previously described as a relationship in which a class is derived from a more generalized version of itself. The figure below denotes a superclass, `Vehicle`, that has two child classes, `Passenger` and `Utility`. The relationship is denoted by a solid line with an arrowhead that points to the superclass (Fig. 3.7).

Earlier in the book, we explained that an inheritance hierarchy was a path of related classes. The starting point on this path has the greatest amount of generalization, and the derived classes become more specific as they move along it. In UML diagrams of generalization, the arrow will always point toward the more general end of the hierarchy.

3.3.3 Dependency

A dependency relationship occurs when one entity depends upon or requires the resources of another. Real life examples of this include a bank account, which requires a bank, or a flashlight, which is dependent upon a battery to work. In UML, dependency is indicated by a dashed line, with an arrow at one or both ends. The arrow originates from the independent entity, and points toward the entity that is dependent. In other words, the entity at the tail end of the arrow is dependent upon the entity that is being pointed to. An entity indicator with an arrow at both ends depicts a relationship in which both objects are dependent upon each other, signifying co-dependency. In a dependency relationship, changes to the independent entity will have an effect on the dependent entity. Figure 3.8 illustrates such a relationship.

3.3.4 Uses and Extends

Uses and **Extends** are two types of relationships utilized in use case diagrams. The first, uses, specifies that the semantics of the source element are dependent upon the semantics of the public portion of the target element. The second, extends,

Fig. 3.8 Dependency

dictates that the target use case adopts the behavior of the source. Both relationships involve selecting common behavior from several use cases for use in a single
use case, which is then used or extended by other use cases. The extends relationship is used when the intent is to adopt a certain set of behaviors and then build
on those behaviors to create an entity with increased capability. The uses relationship, on the other hand, allows for the straight forward adoption of some
common behavior, providing for reuse so that the behavior need not be copied
again and again.

3.3.5 Multiplicity

Relationships within the object-oriented paradigm come in a few different flavors,
defined by the number of possible associations that a class can have. This is known
as **multiplicity**, which defines the number of instances of an individual class that
may be associated with a single instance of another class. For a real world
example, imagine the fingers on a human hand. One hand may contain up to five
fingers. The hand has what is called a **one-to-many** relationship with its fingers.
Each finger, however, may be associated with only one hand, known as a **one-to-
one** relationship. Multiplicity in a UML diagram is denoted either by a single digit,
signifying the exact number of relationships that an entity will have, or using the
form "x..y". In the second instance, "x" and "y" are numbers, or symbols representing numbers, and the entity will have a number of relationships that falls
somewhere within the range "x" to "y". Table 3.1 lists the most common types of
multiplicities, and the Fig. 3.9 illustrates a UML diagram indicating multiplicity.

Table 3.1 Types and definitions of various multiplicities

Multiplicity	Meaning
0..1	0 or 1 instance
0..*	0 to infinite instance (There is no limit of the number of instances)
1	Exactly 1 instance
1..*	At least 1 instance (There must be a minimum of 1 instance)

Fig. 3.9 Multiplicity

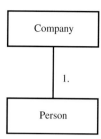

3.4 Models

3.4.1 Class Diagram

A **class diagram** is a way of visualizing a software system based on the abstractions, or classes, that it is comprised of and the relationships between them. Class diagrams are generated throughout the software development process. During the analysis phase of development, class diagrams are used to indicate the common roles and responsibilities associated with all of the entities that define the system's behavior. Class diagrams are used in the design phase to describe the system's architecture, based on the structure of the classes, which it is composed of. A given class diagram may not represent a system's entire class structure, but rather can be specified and tailored for the situation at hand.

The major component of the class diagram is, of course, the class. As we said earlier, a model of a class consists of the class' name, attributes and methods. We can now add constraints enforced upon the class to this list, such as the class's multiplicity. The Booch abstract image of a class and the important information that will be shown in the model is given below in Fig. 3.10.

A class diagram consists of many classes, and is used to depict their structure and relationships in a logical and meaningful way. Class diagrams are considered static. That is, they are used to illustrate which classes interact, but they do not go so far as to describe what occurs when said interaction occurs. In the figure below, a class diagram is used to model a customer order system. The diagram is centered around the Order class, which interacts with both a Customer class, and a Payment class. Contained within the Order class is an OrderDetail class,

Fig. 3.10 Booch class image
(Booch 1994)

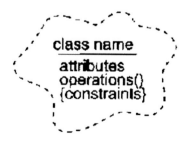

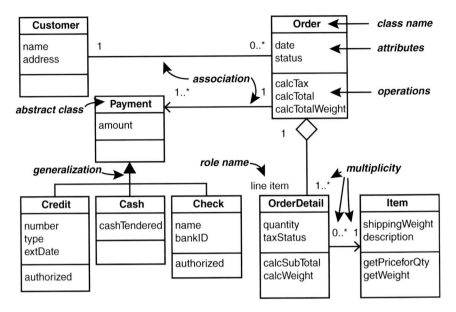

Fig. 3.11 Class diagram (Miller 2003)

which is associated with an `Item` class that describes the actual item being ordered, and contains information regarding specific individual orders. From the `Payment` class, we find three derived classes, `Credit`, `Cash`, and `Check`, all of which are, quite literally, different types of `Payment` (Fig. 3.11).

3.4.2 Use Case Diagram

As we briefly explained earlier, a use case represents an interaction between a software system and an external entity. A **use case diagram** then, similarly, models the system from the view of an external observer. Like class diagrams, use case diagrams are considered static views of a system. They are also a type of abstraction in that they limit the information presented to that which is necessary and useful for an external understanding of a system. In essence, while many aspects of software development focus on the intricacies of how a software system works, a use case diagrams describes a system based on what it does. A **scenario** describes what takes place when some external entity interacts with the system. The entity that interacts with the system in a scenario is an actor. A use case, then, is a compilation and summary of all of the scenarios involved in an individual task. The figure below illustrates a use case diagram for a patient's interactions with a medical clinic.

Figure 3.12 includes 4 use cases and 4 actors. Remember, each use case is denoted by an oval, and each actor by a stick figure. Note that in this use case diagram, each use case involves 2 separate actors. When all of the information is

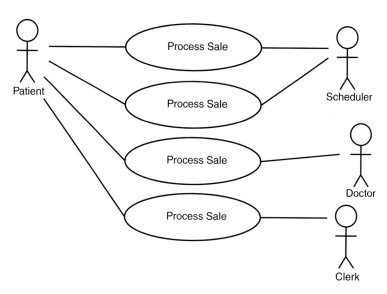

Fig. 3.12 Use case diagram (Miller 2003)

presented together, as it is here, the result is a use case diagram which describes not how this medical clinic functions, but, rather, what it does.

Use case diagrams are helpful in determining the features of a system, as each scenario can reveal some new information; in communicating with clients by providing a non-technical visualization of what a system will do; and in testing, by providing scenarios which can be used to develop test cases.

3.4.3 Sequence Diagram

As we have said, class and use case diagrams are considered static models of a system. They describe the structure and function of a system. **Sequence diagrams**, on the other hand, are a type of interaction diagram, which describe what takes place when the various entities associated with a system interact. A sequence diagram details not what operations are meant to do, but how they are performed, which includes the following: what information is changed, what communication takes place, and when those actions occur. Sequence diagrams, as the name suggests, are sequential based and derive their structure from a timeline. The top of a diagram represents the earliest time in the sequence, which then progresses downward. The actions performed are known as **communications** and can be thought of as the sending of messages. The objects involved in a message sequence are listed from left to right according to the order in which they participate in that communication. The diagram below is used to represent making a hotel reservation (Fig. 3.13).

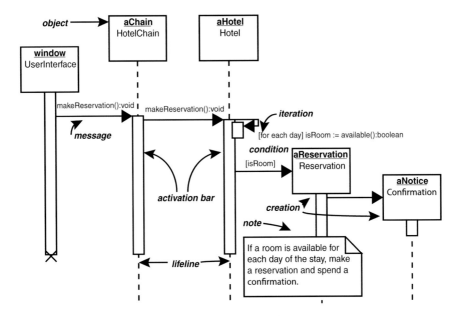

Fig. 3.13 Sequence diagram (Miller 2003)

In the figure above, the sequence is initiated by the UserInterface instance of the window class, which sends a message to the HotelChain object via the makeReservation method. At this point, HotelChain then sends a makeReservation message to Hotel. Here we can see an iteration through which Hotel moves in order to test whether or not a room is available for each day requested. If this condition is met, Hotel creates the Reservation object, which in turns creates a Confirmation notice to complete the sequence. In this image, each box represents an object and each straight arrow depicts a message call. The vertical dotted lines represent lifelines, which define how long an object exists before destruction. The activation bars shown denote the time for the executing of the message. The topmost message call made by the Hotel object is a call back to itself, and is an iteration, which is denoted by the asterisk. Expressions shown in square brackets are conditions that are tested. The note contained in the rectangle is simply for clarification, and can be used in any UML diagram.

3.4.4 State Diagrams

An object's state describes that object based on all of its properties and their values at a given instant in time. An object's behavior is a response to its state, and thus changes based on its current state. Similarly, a **state diagram** describes a software system based on its behavior, and thus in relation to the states of the objects that

make it up. For the creation of a state diagram to be possible, the system must have
a finite number of states, or an abstraction must be used to this end. State transition
diagrams, similarly, depict all of the information involved in a state change,
including the events that trigger the change and the actions that occur as a result of
it. Harel provided the following common notations for use in state diagrams
(Figs. 3.14, 3.15, 3.16).

The first image is used to depict a state, which is given a unique name and, if
necessary, some actions that are associated with it. The second shows a history
icon, which can be attached to a state to indicate its' lastly assumed state, which it
will go into upon entry. The last image depicts state nesting, in which a superstate
consists of some number of substates.

Actions are often associated with states in the sense that they occur when a state
changes (i.e.: when a state is entered or exited). State transitions connect one state
to another or one state back to itself, and denote the specific changes in state. Each
state transition is unique, that is, given a certain set of circumstances (the overall
state of the system) a certain trigger even must result in exactly one new state.

3.4.5 Activity Diagram

Similar to a state diagrams, **activity diagrams** provide a way of understanding a
system based on the processes that occur within it. While a state diagram's main

Fig. 3.14 State icon (Harel
1987)

Fig. 3.15 History icon
(Harel 1987)

Fig. 3.16 Nesting (Harel
1987)

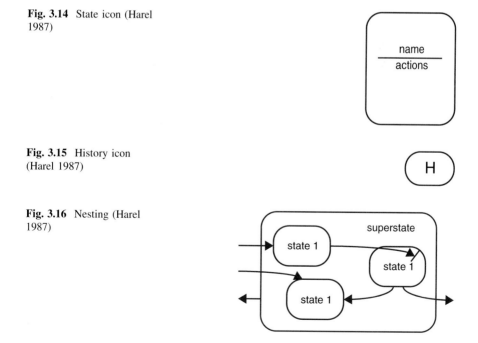

focus is on an object and its response to changes in state, an activity diagram
depicts all of the activities associated with a single process and the dependencies
that relate those activities. The diagram below shows the processes involved in
withdrawing money from an ATM. The black circle labeled start indicates the
beginning of the process, and the similar circle labeled end denotes where the
process stops.

As depicted in Fig. 3.17, activity diagrams are divided into sections called
swimlanes. The names at the top of each swimlane represent the three objects
involved in our example: Customer, ATM Machine, and Bank. Each object is

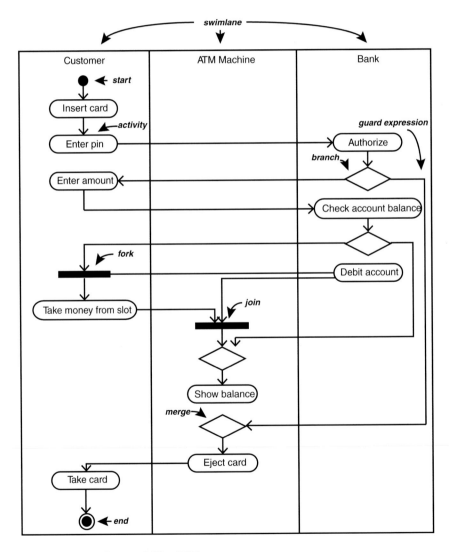

Fig. 3.17 Activity diagram (Miller 2003)

responsible for all of the activities contained within its swimlane. The arrows depict transitions. Each activity results in a single outgoing transition, which can then branch into separate transitions, as denoted by the diamond symbol. For example, the outgoing transition from the `Authorize` activity branches into two possible transitions, one to the `Enter Amount` activity and the other to the merge diamond before the `Eject Card` activity. At runtime, the transition used will be determined by the existence of either the `Valid PIN` or `InvalidPIN` state. As evidenced by the branches-merge combination in this example, transitions branch apart due to some varied data and will eventually merge together again when the set of activities dependent on that data is complete. The solid black rectangles in the diagram depict forks, at which one transition forks into two or more parallel activities. Similar to a branch, the transitions created in a form will later join back together when the activities being carried out in parallel have been completed. The same solid black rectangle is used to indicate a join.

3.4.6 Collaboration Diagram

Like activity, state, and sequence diagrams, **collaboration diagrams** are inter-action diagrams that describe what a system does. They are very similar to sequence diagrams in that they show the same information, but collaboration diagrams focus on object-roles rather than a timeline. As the name suggests, object-roles describe the role that an object is to play; what it is to do as relative to the software system. The following diagram gives an example of a collaboration diagram (Fig. 3.18).

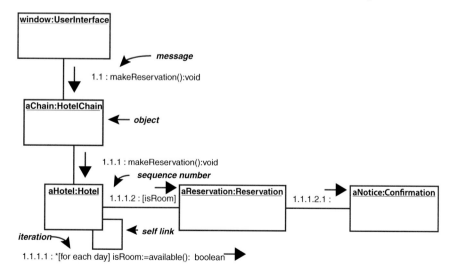

Fig. 3.18 Collaboration diagram (Miller 2003)

Fig. 3.19 Component

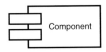

The rectangles in the diagram represent object-roles, labeled by the object name, class name or both (class names are always preceded by a colon (:). The arrows represent the messages being sent, and each is labeled with a number, with the top level message labeled 1. For each level below the top, a new number is appended, preceded by a decimal point. Messages on the same level share the same prefix number, different suffixes determined by the order in which they occur. For example two messages, one labeled 1.1.1 and 1.1.2, both originated at the second level down from the top, but the second occurred before the first.

3.4.7 Component Diagram

A **component diagram** is a code model used to indicate how various components are linked together in order to form either larger components or an entire software system. These provide an easy to understand visual for a system's architecture. A component diagram is a very high level view of a software system, and is made possible by the generous use of abstraction. In a sense, a component diagram can be used as a map for the software system, made up of logical units of decomposition (Fig. 3.19).

3.4.8 Deployment Diagram

A **deployment diagram** depicts the physical configuration of a software system upon hardware. This is a useful way of presenting a software project because it allows both the client and the developers to gain an understanding of the system's distribution across physical resources from a unique overview. Figure 3.20 depicts such a system.

3.5 Interfaces, Notes, and Packages

3.5.1 Interfaces

Many of the fundamental principles of the object-oriented paradigm are centered on the creation of independent, self-contained entities that exhibit characteristics such as encapsulation and data hiding to ensure the integrity of the software

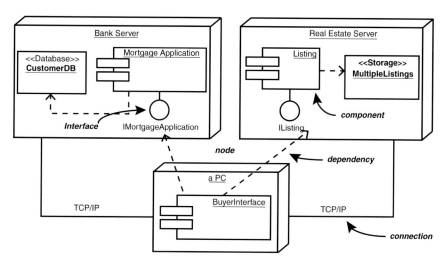

Fig. 3.20 Deployment diagram (Miller 2003)

system. This practice leads to the use of interfaces to allow controlled communication with an entity while concealing that entity's inner working from the user.
An interface is, of course, an integral part of the software system, and must be
designed, implemented, and documented like any other portion of a software
engineering project. Figure 3.21 shows an interface in a component diagram,
represented by a circle containing the interface's name.

It is important to note that a component may implement any number of interfaces (including none at all), and that multiple components may implement the
same interface.

3.5.2 Packages

A **package** is a "UML grouping concept denoting that a set of objects or classes
are related" (Bruegge and Dutoit 2004). Essentially, a package is a collection of
related models. Figure 3.22 illustrates this concept.

As evidenced in this diagram, a package is denoted in UML by a single tab
containing the package name. In Fig. 3.22, "Sched" is the package name. A
package is a development concept used for grouping, as distinct from a component, which exists at runtime.

Fig. 3.21 Component
interface

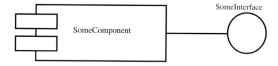

Fig. 3.22 Simple package
diagram

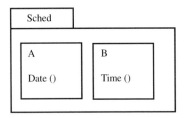

3.5.3 Notes

A note is an extremely useful UML concept. Exactly the same as its real world
counterpart, a note is simply a bit of useful information to be tacked onto a
diagram. Notes do not represent a piece of the software system. Rather, they are
used to relay contextual information along with a model. In UML, a note is
represented by a rectangle with a folded, or dog-eared, upper corner. Textual
information is written within the rectangle (Fig. 3.23).

3.6 Chapter Conclusion and Summary

The use of modeling is intrinsic to both the object-oriented paradigm and to the
successful completion of any software engineering project. Without this practice,
effective communication between members of the software development team, not
to mention between the team and the client, would be nearly impossible.

In this chapter, we covered all of the vital elements of the Unified Modeling
Language, as well as the diagrams that those models comprise. To review, the
UML diagrams we have discussed are as follows: class, object, use case, sequence,
state, activity, collaboration, component and deployment. A class diagram states
the relationships among the abstractions of a system. Use case diagrams describe
what a system does from the standpoint of an external observer. Sequence diagram
are a type of interaction diagram that details how operations are carried out. A
state diagram is used to illustrate the cumulative results of a software system's
behavior.

Fig. 3.23 Example of a
package with a note attached

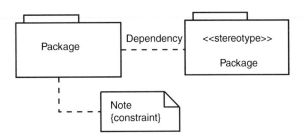

An activity diagram focuses on the flow of activities involved in a single process. Collaboration diagrams are another form of interaction diagram, which focuses on object roles to describe a process. Component diagrams are physical analogs of class diagrams, that is, they convey the actual distribution of a software system across physical computer systems. Deployment diagrams show the configuration of run-time processing nodes. An interface is a collection of operations that define the way in which an external entity is to interact with a class or package. A package is a collection of model elements. A note is simply a symbol for relaying useful information about a UML model.

3.7 Exercises

1. Last chapter, we asked you to explain the difference between a class and an object using examples. Now, present the same difference, this time using models.
2. Think yet again about the `truck` class and its `vehicle` superclass that we have used throughout this book. Create a different subclass of `vehicle` with at least two unique attributes and two unique methods. Finally, create an instantiation (object) of this new class. Diagram your new class, depicting its relationship with the `vehicle` superclass and the object you chose to create.
3. Consider the following sequence involved in starting the `monster_truck` object:

   Step 1: Insert `key` into `ignition` and turn. Sends message to ...
   Step 2: `ignition_controller` performs calculations and sends message to ...

   Step 2.1: `fuel_injector` injects fuel [if there is `fuel`] and sends message to ...
   Step 2.2: `spark_plug` ignites [if there is `power`] and sends message to...

   Step 3: `piston`, at which point the monster truck is started and the `ignition` reverts back to its initial state.

At each step in this sequence, an object performs an action, and then sends some message to the next object in the sequence. In the second step, a fork is initiated and two separate transitions appear next, which then join again in the third step. Each parallel process initiated after step two checks for some condition (contained in brackets ([])), which must be true for the sequence to continue on. If these conditions are met, the `piston` reacts. If not, it remains static. In either case, the sequence ends after this step, when the `ignition` reverts to its inactive state. Illustrate this sequence using a sequence diagram.

4. Illustrate the sequence from the last question again, this time using an activity diagram. Don't forget to include swimlanes! (HINT: the sequence will both begin and end in the swimlane of the ignition object)

5. Create a UML diagram for the following two entities: Band and Album. In the Band entity, include the attributes band_name, band_members, and music_style. The Album entity, which will be dependent on the Band entity, inherits all attributes from Band, and adds the new attributes album_name and release_date. Be sure to indicate the multiplicities for each object, as well as the direction of dependency.

References

Booch G (1994) Object-oriented analysis and design with applications. The Benjamin/Cummings Publishing Company, Inc., New York

Booch G, Ivar, Jacobson, Rumbaugh J (1999) The unified modeling language User guide. Addison Wesley Longman, Inc

Bruegge B, Dutoit A (2004) Object-oriented software engineering: using UML, patterns, and java, 2nd edn. Pearson Education, Ltd., Upper Saddle River

D'Sourza D F, Wills AC (1999) Objects, components, and frameworks with UML: the catalysis approach. Addison Wesley Longman, Inc., Sydney

Miller R (2003) Practical UML: A hands-on introduction for developers. Available via Embarcadero. http://edn.embaracardero.com/article/31863. Accessed 1 Dec 2003

OMG (2007) Unified modeling language (OMG UML). Infrastructure v2.1.2. Available via OMG. http://www.omg.org/docs/formal/07-11-04.pdf. Accessed 4 Nov 2007

Sommerville I (2004) Software engineering, 7th edn. Peason Education, Ltd., Boston

Part II
The Software Engineering Project

Chapter 4
Starting the Project

4.1 Overview of Project and Planning

All of the technical and managerial activities required to deliver a software product to a client are collectively referred to as a **software project**. A software project has a specific duration, consumes resources, and produces deliverables. From the perspective of a developer, a software project consists of project functions, activities and tasks. Figure 4.1 depicts a project model, as described by Bernd Bruegge (Bruegge 2004). A project function is an activity, or set of activities, that spans the entire duration of the project. Examples of project functions include configuration management, documentation, quality control, training, and testing. Each of these activities begins in the early stages of the development process, and continues through the development life of the software product. An activity is described as a smaller unit of work. Activities are often small enough for adequate planning and tracking but also large enough to quickly complicate micro management. Finally, a task is the smallest unit of management accountability. Tasks are the building blocks of the development process, and larger units of work are composed of multiple, complimentary tasks. Tasks, by nature, have a predetermined, finite duration, require specific resources, and produce tangible results, such as code, documentation, etc.

The decomposition of a software engineering project into units of work allows for a development team to both focus effort on specific jobs, and to easily classify and organize the entire project in a useful and understandable way. Such practices have led developers to define tasks in such a way that all of their characteristics may be specified in a meaningful way. Bruegge lists the following attributes of a task that should be specified during planning and development:

- Name and description of work to be done.
- Preconditions for starting, required resources, and task duration.
- Task completion criteria: tangibles to be produced and acceptance criteria for those tangibles.
- Risk involved.

R. Y. Lee, *Software Engineering: A Hands-On Approach*,
DOI: 10.2991/978-94-6239-006-5_4, © Atlantis Press and the author 2013

Fig. 4.1 Model of a software project and the constituent activities (Bruegge 2004)

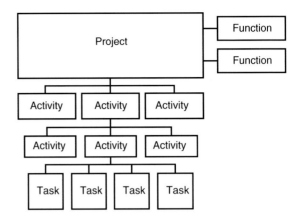

(Bruegge 2004)

Proper project planning deals with the identification of activities, milestones, and deliverables that are to be produced as the result of a project. A plan is drawn up in order to guide the development process toward the established project goals. Cost estimation is a closely related activity, concerned with estimating the resources needed for the successful completion of a project (Sommerville 2004). This activity will be explained in detail later in this chapter.

4.1.1 Identifying the Purpose of the Project

Project planning begins with a simple goal: determination of software scope and purpose. This may seem like an obvious first step, but for that very reason it is often overlooked. If an effective and well-defined purpose is not laid out at the onset, developers and clients will not be able to understand the connection between the development process and the final product. This will result in the project quickly getting off track due to a loss of focus. For this reason, the basic objectives of the project should be considered and determined at the project's onset. The required function and performance of the software being developed should be assessed in order to establish a project scope that is unambiguous and under-standable at both the managerial and technical levels. Of course, many aspects of a project are somewhat hazy at the beginning of the development process. Often, a final product will get defined and the basic goals and objectives will be enunciated. However, the information necessary to define the scope (a prerequisite for esti-mation) is commonly not yet generated from the relationship between real the world phenomena to be represented and the abstractions that will make up the final software product. For this reason, it is of paramount importance to permit the use of adequate time and resources in order to develop an effective project plan.

The scope of a software project is used to describe the function, performance, constraints, interfaces, and reliability of, as well as the data to be processed by, the software system. Functions are initially described in the statement of a system's scope, are later evaluated and, if needed, refined in order to provide the proper level of detail required for accurate and successful estimation phases. Because both cost and schedule estimates are function oriented, a degree of decomposition is often useful in providing a meaningful picture of the development process. A scope's statement of performance encompasses both processing and response time requirements for the software system. The statement of a system's constraints is used to identify the limits within which the software system will exist, as imposed by factors such as external hardware, available memory, or other preexisting systems.

4.1.2 Identifying the Deliverables of the Project

Following the identification of a project's purpose and scope, the software engineering team must now create a set of goals to be met throughout the process. This is accomplished through the establishment of a series of **milestones**, or recognizable endpoints for specific development activities. This practice allows a project to be broken down into distinct, logical sections. Closely related to this concept is that of producing **deliverables**. Deliverables make up the tangible results of the development process such as code, documentation, cost estimates, or reports from engineers. As a milestone is reached, the deliverables produced by the included development activities are completed. The relationship between a milestone and the related deliverables allows both, for the sequential production of the various portions of the software project, as well as the assessment of the development team's progress.

4.1.3 Cost Estimation

Finally, the third activity involved in project planning is **cost estimation**. Cost estimation is the practice of calculating the amount of resources required to successfully complete the software project. These resources come in two basic categories: money and time. Certainly, there are other types of resources, such as personnel or work space, however, resources of this type can usually be reduced back to money; in this case salary and rent. Both estimate types are of critical importance to the relationship between the client and developer. They are also at the core of establishing the cost the client will pay.

Schach defines two types of money cost estimates, as characterized by the party for which they are intended. The **internal cost** is the cost for the development team, while the **external cost** is the price tag that will be given to the client (Schach 2008). The internal cost is the composition of the various costs the development team must pay out. These include employee salaries, hardware and software costs, and overhead costs such as rent and utilities. In other words, the internal cost is the actual cost required to develop the software. The external cost, then, includes both the internal cost, as well as any additional profit that the development team intends to generate from the client. The difference between the internal and external costs varies from project to project and from organization to organization. The amount of profit added by a development firm in order to calculate the external cost is based on many factors. This is a key component in a client's decision to accept one firm's bid over that of another. For this reason, cost estimation and the determination of an appropriate profit margin are the determining factors of whether or not the project in question will even exist.

The proper estimation of a project's timeline is equally as important as financial projections. The development team is responsible for establishing a development schedule, which provides the client with both a final delivery date, as well as a timeline by which it can judge the development team's progress. Failure to stick to this schedule on the part of the developer can lead to a number of negative consequences. These can include the loss of future business or in some cases, may even lead to the application of financial or legal penalties.

Before a specific software engineering firm is selected and a project is begun, the organizations bidding for the project develop initial time, or duration, and financial estimates, and then submit these to the client. From these estimates, the client can determine the feasibility and potential profit of the product in question. If the client chooses to undertake the project, they will then select an organization based on the list of projections. From this point on, it is the responsibility of the chosen development firm to uphold the contract constituted by those estimates. Right away, the selected firm begins to develop more detailed estimates, which will be used to plan the upcoming development process. Throughout the development cycle, additional estimates are created to continually guide the project. As we can clearly see, software engineering cost estimates are not just a tool for initial conjecture, but rather, they are also a continually updated progress report, and an adaptable, multipurpose planning tool.

4.2 Staying on Task and on Schedule

In the Sect. 4.1.3, we explained the importance of effective planning and accurate cost estimation. These two development aspects are vital to the software engineering project, and set the development team on track to realizing the final goal. They are, however, only the beginning of the process. After plans are laid out and estimates are generated, either at the start of the project or periodically throughout, the development team must constantly work to ensure that the plan is being followed, and that the costs are not being exceeded. The Sect. 4.2.1 discusses the critical concepts related to ensuring a software project is completed on time and within budget.

4.2.1 Deadlines

Effective project planning revolves around the establishment of efficient, yet attainable **deadlines**. These deadlines, like the milestones discussed earlier, allow a project to be broken down into a series of related activities. These activities can then be managed individually, as modular components of the larger software project. In addition, deadlines also allow project managers and clients to evaluate the efficiency of the development team. If activities are being completed after their intended deadline, a project's feasibility and release date can be reevaluated by the client. On the other hand, if activities are being completed ahead of time, the project's overall timeline can be adjusted for more efficient time management.

Successfully setting and meeting deadlines requires effective project management by the software engineering firm. To this end, project managers must be familiar with the requirements of the project, the abilities of the development team, and the expectations of the client. They must then be able to combine this information into well understood and properly organized sets of activities and deadlines. Finally, effective project managers must be able to properly manage the development team in an efficient manner in order to reach the predefined.

4.2.2 Work Breakdown Structures

As we have stated, effective project and time management are based on the decomposition of a software project into smaller, more manageable activities, each with individual goals and deadlines. Of course, these activities can, if needed, be broken down further into smaller and more manageable work units. At its top level, it can be difficult to understand how a specific function benefits the final goal of a piece of software. For this reason, the decomposition process can be repeated if necessary, to create a modular software project consisting of useful, manageable units of work with well understood goals. The units can then be planned out individually, and resources can be dedicated in a manner that makes sense to everyone involved (Ghezzi et al. 1991).

A common engineering practice, known as a **Work Breakdown Structure** (**WBS**), can achieve this decomposition by organizing the development process in a tree-like, activity-based format. In a fashion related to the concepts of abstraction and generalization, a WBS provides a view of the development activities in which some activity is described at a certain level of specificity. It is then decomposed into constituent activities that branch off to the next highest level of specificity. These activities can again be broken down, as described in the previous paragraph, into even more specific activities. The result is a tree model in which the most general activity being described, or the **root node**, sits at the base of the diagram, and is expanded upon by more specific nodes on various higher levels. In the case

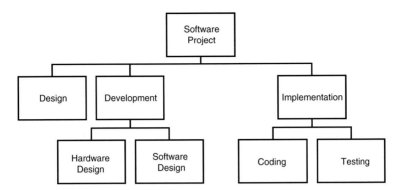

Fig. 4.2 Generic work breakdown structure

of a WBS that describes an entire software project, the root node will be the final piece of software itself. Figure 4.2 provides a basic illustration of this concept.

If created properly, a WBS will describe an entire project by all of the activities that will comprise it. That is, an ideal WBS will identify all of the activities that must be accomplished in order to complete the project as a whole. When considered alongside a timeline, this will describe exactly what must be performed when, and if the project is to be realized. Tools such as this can be invaluable during the planning and estimating phases of a software engineering project. Given sufficient specificity, the development team is able to accurately predict the resources required for the entire project by calculating those needed for each individual activity (a much more reasonable task, which produces a higher degree of accuracy) and compiling that information into a final estimate. In addition, once the activities involved in the project have been identified and ordered, they can be assigned to developers. Because the WBS is centered around manageable units of work, the activities it generates are designed with assignment and implementation in mind. To further aid in this process, a WBS can be extended to the desired level of specificity through the addition of important information, such as tasks and resources needed to the nodes. This will create a model of the project based on not only the activities to be performed, but all of the information required for a basic understanding of those activities. In this way, a WBS is a multipurpose diagram which helps with the organization of the activities of a project, and also with resource allocation, cost estimation, task assignment, and timeline creation. Finally, a properly formatted WBS can be a useful tool in communicating with the client by describing what activities must be performed when, and for what reason, in order to complete the project successfully and on time.

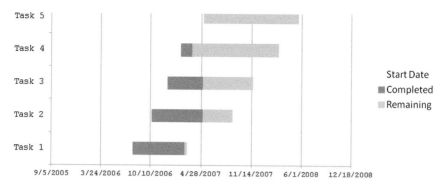

Fig. 4.3 Gantt chart

4.2.3 Gantt Chart

Another useful project planning strategy, closely related to the WBS, is the use of **Gantt Charts**. A Gantt Chart is essentially a specific type of bar graph, tailored to illustrate the progression of a project. It does this by mapping out the activities involved in a software engineering project over the project's timeline. That is, a period of time is displayed along one axis of the graph, while the activities to be completed during that period of time are displayed in the order that they occur along the other axis. Figure 4.3 provides an example of a Gantt Chart.

As you can see, the various activities (Task 1, Task 2, etc.) are mapped along the vertical axis of the chart, and are graphed over the dates of the project, which are laid out along the horizontal axis. Each task spans from its start date to its projected end date, and is shaded to illustrate current progress. Since their creation, Gantt Charts have been enhanced in various ways, and other common management tools have been incorporated into them. For instance, relationships are often depicted between the various activities on the chart in order to show task dependencies. Like the other planning tools that we have discussed, Gantt Charts show a selected level of project decomposition, which can be modified to suit the needs of the developer. As with a WBS, the various elements of a Gantt Chart can again be decomposed into other Gantt Charts of their own, to show the constituent tasks of the activity in question. In fact, quite often, the elements of a Gantt Chart are actually decomposed into a WBS, thus incorporating the various methods of project abstraction.

4.3 Communicating Ideas

In addition to planning the development process, project managers are also charged with organizing, managing, and motivating the people who work on the project. These people are, after all, the greatest assets that any software engineering firm maintains. Regardless of the amount of capital, or the sophistication of the technology used, no software engineering project can be successfully completed without a competent, motivated development team. To this end, both proper staff selection skills and effective people management abilities are critical characteristics for the ideal project manager.

A project is composed of the individuals that work on it. Thus, a project can only be successful if the development team is also successful. To achieve this end, a project manager must know the strengths and weaknesses of his or her team, as well as the technical requirements of the project. Proper use of this information will allow the employees of a software engineering firm to be efficiently allocated according to their abilities. Furthermore, the work produced will be maximized when a project manager is able to assign effective, and realistic workloads that do not overburden the team.

On the other hand, if a project manager is unfamiliar with either the assets of the development team, or the requirements of the project, the development process is all but guaranteed to be inefficient and off schedule. This will result in the development team to be most likely either under-challenged or overworked. These results occur when a manger imposes unrealistic deadlines for activities, improperly allocates resources, or misunderstands the skills of his or her team.

To avoid the problems mentioned above, an effective project manager must take the time to get to know the development team and the project in question. The key to reaching this goal is effective communication. Communication with the development team will help a project manager to understand what the team is capable of, and the time within which they can complete certain activities. It will also help to identify any problems encountered during the development process. Once such a problem has been brought to the forefront, continued consultation with the employees involved can help to find the cause of the problem, and to present possible solutions. As we have stated, a software engineering firm's most valuable assets are its employee's, and they should be given the respect and deference due to them. They are the ones involved with the intricacies of an activity, and thus have the best view of the problem, which results in them being best equipped to find a solution. Consulting the members of the development team and acting on the information that they provide encourages a team mentality in which all members feel they are an integral part of the project. In addition, project managers should reward employees for effective work. These rewards can take on many forms, such as financial bonuses or increased responsibility. The combination of respect, through communication consultation, recognition, and reward, will foster an ideal work environment, in which every member of the development team understands what is expected of him or her, and understands the importance of his or her job.

In addition to communicating with the members of the development team, the project manager is also responsible for communication with the client. It is crucial that an effective means of exchanging ideas with the customer be established at the onset of any software engineering project. Without this foundation, it is unlikely that the work completed by the development team will match the ideas envisioned by the client, even if a functioning piece of software is built. Later in this section, we will discuss common practices used by software engineers and project managers to ensure that the product produced and the product requested are the same piece of software.

4.3.1 Assessing Employee Skill Levels

We explained in the Sect. 4.3 that the proper assignment of development activities and the establishment of efficient yet realistic production goals depend on a project manager's understanding of the skills of his or her employees. Because people's abilities and attitudes can be difficult to quantify, this can present a challenge. However, we are software engineers and creating meaningful abstractions of real world information is our job.

Employee assessment begins with information. Said information comes in three forms: that which is provided by the employee up front; that which is attained from those who have worked with the employee in the past; and that which is gathered directly by management at the software engineering firm. The first type of information is usually provided as a résumé, or curriculum vitae (CV). These resources contain material regarding an individual's education, motivation, goals, and relevant work experience. They also provide a deeper insight into a person's communication and organization skills. The way in which they are written (level of formality, proper spelling, correct use of grammar, etc.) describes both the written communication skills, and attention to detail that can be expected from the candidate. The way in which they are formatted, on the other hand, can be used to assess the organizational skills of the candidate. That is, a résumé that lacks flow and a meaningful system of organization might be a warning sign that an individual is unable to effectively order his or her thoughts. On the other hand, a well composed document can indicate that a candidate can easily and usefully arrange his or her thoughts, and can use those skills to effectively communicate ideas.

The second resource in assessing a potential team member is the information gained from those who have worked with the candidate before; this provides a real world understanding of the individual's skills. Recommendations from previous supervisors or coworkers compliment the information provided in a résumé or CV by establishing that a candidate is actually capable of putting their education and experience to use in a practical way. Furthermore, the use of references can provide an understanding of a candidate's strengths and weaknesses in a real world context. Finally, communication with those who have worked with a candidate in the past can help a project manager be aware of the candidate's ability to work with others in a team scenario.

The last way of assessing a candidate's ability is to actually interview him or her. Many consider this to be the most useful method, and it is often the deciding factor in whether or not a candidate will be assigned to a development team. First off, an interview gives a candidate the chance to restate the information already provided via a résumé or CV. Allowing them to explain the context of their education or work experience, and to emphasize those points they feel are particularly important or relevant. This can be particularly useful to a project manager, who might have a difficult time understanding why the candidate felt certain experiences warranted mentioning. An in-person assessment also allows a candidate to comment on or account for the information gathered during the reference/ recommendation phase. In addition, an interview also gives a project manager the chance to ask the candidate about things that he or she feels were missing or ill-described in the earlier phases of assessment. During an interview, a project manager should be mindful of the characteristics exhibited by the candidate. For instance, this time can be used to further assess communication skills, level of respect, or work ethic.

The three methods described above are common ways of gauging a potential team member. More important than the method used though, is the end result. In order to be effective, a project manager must be able to organize the information gathered through both these methods and any others that are deemed useful. They must then synthesize that information into a meaningful evaluation of the candidate, and finally determine whether or not that candidate meets the firm's standards and will thus be an asset to the project. If the candidate in question is chosen to join the development team, the information gathered during the assessment period will also play a crucial part in determining the role the new team member will play in the project.

4.3.2 Team Organization and Role Assignment

In this chapter, we have described how a software engineering project can be efficiently organized based on decomposition of the entire project into development activities. These resulting activities intuitively lend themselves to team-based development. That is, various portions of the project can be developed semi-independently from one another by separate teams. The benefits provided by this practice include the ability to complete different activities in parallel, the ability to assign a specific activity to the developers that are best suited for it, and the ability to adjust some development activity without changing the entire project plan.

In a team-based software engineering project, each development team functions as a smaller version of the whole. That is, each team is led by a team leader, who acts similar to a project manager on reduced scale, and is composed of engineers. The team leader is responsible for managing and supervising the progress of the team, as well as for communicating with the project manager. Within the team, the leader assigns specific roles and tasks in order to accomplish the activity with which the team has been charged. The team works to complete a development activity, and thus to produce any deliverables related with that activity, such as software or documentation. A team completes a specific activity when they have met the criteria put forth in the planning phase.

As we have explained with other project management strategies, a team can be further decomposed into smaller teams, each charged with completing tasks involved in the original activity. In this case, each sub-team will have its own team leader, who will report to the team leader above him or her.

Many factors can complicate effective teamwork. Conflicting personalities, differences in working habits, or ineffective communication can lead to misunderstandings or disagreements within a team. For this reason, deliberate and careful team assignment on the part of the project manager and team leaders is important in the successful completion of a project. In addition, managers and leaders must be prepared to handle conflicts between team members, and to resolve them effectively and efficiently.

4.3.3 Project Communication

We have said many times that effective communication is crucial to the success of a software engineering project. This statement however, is extremely open ended, as there are many forms of communication which will take place during a projects development life. The term **project communication** is used to describe the interactions that occur between the client and the development team. It can include anything from the elicitation of requirements, to the exchange of design models, to conflict resolution.

The most important communication that takes place during a software engineering project, without question, is that between the development team and client. Without effective communication at this level, there is no project. The best way to achieve successful communication with the client is to get the communication process started early. Interviews and preliminary meetings are of course necessary in dictating the requirements and expectations of the software to be developed; but this is not their only role. In addition, they serve as the foundation for all further communication between the software engineers and the client. If these initial meetings are handled poorly, a shadow may be cast over the rest of the project. Simply said, the initial communications set both the standard and the mood for the rest of the project. A common approach to ensuring effective early communication is to minimize the potential for confusion and misunderstanding between the software engineers and the client. That is, the software engineer should open with abstract questions, not specific, technical ones. These questions should help both parties to articulate what the software is to accomplish in a very general sense, and not *how* it is to function. From here, when both parties are comfortable with the problem and the solution is presented, discussions can move into greater specifics.

The use of the initial, context-free questions is crucial to making both the client and engineer comfortable with what is being discussed. The first set of questions should be general enough to only cover the people and economic benefits involved with the solution being presented, and not the details of the solution itself. They should allow the customer to articulate the goal of the project and the return they will gain from it. In addition, alternative solutions should also be considered.

The second set of questions should focus on the problem being addressed, and should help the engineer to understand just what the client hopes to accomplish in his or her own words. The client should be asked to explain how they understand the problem, and what result they expect the solution to generate. Questions relating to the environment in which the solution will be used, including obstacles and constraints, and the qualities required for a solution to be considered successful, should also be posed.

The last set of questions should focus on the meeting itself. The engineer should assess the quality and reliability of the answers by asking if the responses are "official responses," as well as whether or not anyone else should be consulted about the questions that have been posed. The engineer should then double check his or her own work by inquiring about the effectiveness of the questions being asked. He or she will ask the client if they feel satisfied that all relevant information has been discussed, or if any additional information is necessary.

These sorts of questions can help to establish the level of comfort required for effective client-engineer communication, as well as to actually establish the goals and scope of the project.

4.4 Handling Problems and Change

Project planning is used to create a model of what a project's development process is supposed to look like. We have discussed the ways in which it can be used as a roadmap to lead a development team through a project's development life, and to monitor a project's progress over time. What we have not yet discussed, however, is the way in which project plans can be used as safeguards against, and warning of, deviation within a project. As development moves forward, progress is noted and recorded, and is then compared to the projected schedule according to plans that were developed earlier. This practice provides a clear-cut, intuitive method for viewing any deviations from the intended course that project encounters over its lifetime. Detecting such changes from the plan, though, is only the first step, and is certainly not a solution. When such deviations are found, it becomes the job of the project manager to correct these issues and to get the project back on track.

Delays and setbacks are encountered in any schedule-based job. In many fields, the solution involves increasing the work on a particular activity to make up for lost time. This can often be accomplished by augmenting the number of workers involved or by increasing the amount of time spent on the activity per day (overtime). Software engineering, however, is not generally driven by manpower, but by intellectual capital. The best solution, of course, is to avoid the problem all together. Careful analysis and planning can sometimes allow a project manager to foresee potential problems, and adjust resource allocation to prevent them. The most important aspect of this resource allocation is the assignment of engineers with appropriate talents to specific activities. Similarly, when a problem is encountered, a project manager may choose to reassign an engineer, or engineers, with skills appropriate for correcting the issue. If this does not appear to be a viable solution, a software engineering firm may also choose to hire new engineers to pick up the extra workload, with careful attention paid to the relevance of those engineers' skill sets to the problem in question.

If the development team is unable to find an answer that seems reasonable, it may be necessary to resort to modifying the original project specifications. This can result in the elimination of certain system requirements that are not deemed absolutely necessary. This practice, known as **requirements scrubbing**, is a risky endeavor, though. The project manager must be able to identify those extra requirements which can be removed without significantly reducing the functionality of the system, or altering the final product from that envisioned by the client. To aid in this, it is important to maintain constant communication with the client, so that changes in requirements do not come as a surprise when the final product is delivered. The use of an incremental development process provides for the potential of such alterations. This concept dictates that the most important activities and requirements of a software system are finished first, and that further development progresses incrementally iterates through less critical portions of the project. This way, if the decision is made to scrub a component, that component will most likely not have been completed at the time the decision is made, which would negate the whole purpose.

If neither reassigning of engineers, nor the scrubbing of certain components will adequately correct for deviation within a project, a more serious course of action must be taken. At such a point, it is crucial to admit the mistake, rather than attempt to make up for it with a solution that will never succeed. Instead, it is important to recognize that the initial plan was infeasible, and to review and analyze the requirements and resources in an attempt to create a new, more effective plan. This, of course, will most likely result in the loss of work, an adjustment to the final schedule, and possibly an alteration of the end product. It is therefore absolutely critical to spend the time and resources required to develop an effective plan *before* a project gets underway. If a change must be made any later in the development cycle, it will be costly.

4.5 Document Format Specification

1. **Introduction**

   1.1 **Purpose of this document**
   Describes the purpose of the document, and the intended audience.
   1.2 **Scope of this document**
   Describes the scope of this requirements definition effort. Introduces the

requirements elicitation team, including users, customers, system engineers, and developers.

1.3 **Overview**

Provides a brief overview of the product defined as a result of the requirements elicitation process.

1.4 **Business context**

Provides an overview of the business organization sponsoring the development of this product. This overview should include the business's mission statement and its organizational objectives or goals.

2. **General Description**

2.1 **Product Functions**

Describes the general functionality of the product, which will be discussed in more detail below.

2.2 **Similar System Information**

Describes the relationship of this product with any other products. Specifies if this product is intended to be stand-alone, or else used as a component of a larger product.

2.3 **User Characteristics**

Describes the features of the user community, including their expected expertise with software systems and the application domain.

2.4 **User Problem Statement**

This section describes the essential problem(s) currently confronted by the user community.

2.5 **User Objectives**

This section describes the set of objectives and requirements for the system from the user's perspective.

2.6 **General Constraints**

Lists general constraints placed upon the design team, including speed requirements, industry protocols, hardware platforms, and so forth.

3. **Functional Requirements**

This section lists the functional requirements in ranked order. Functional requirements describe the possible effects of a software system, in other words, *what* the system must accomplish. Each functional requirement should be specified in a format similar to the following:

4. **Interface Requirements**

This section describes how the software interfaces with other software products or users for input or output. Examples of such interfaces include library routines, token streams, shared memory, data streams, and so forth.

4.1 **User Interfaces**

Describes how this product interfaces with the user.

4.1.1 GUI

Describes the graphical user interface if present. This section should include a set of screen dumps or mockups to illustrate user interface features. If the system is menu-driven, a description of all menus and their components should be provided.

4.1.2 CLI

Describes the command-line interface if present. For each command, a description of all arguments and example values and invocations should be provided.

4.1.3 API

Describes the application programming interface, if present. For each public interface function, the name, arguments, return values, examples of invocation, and interactions with other functions should be provided.

4.1.4 Diagnostics of ROM

Describes how to obtain debugging information or other diagnostic data.

4.2 Hardware Interfaces

Describes interfaces to hardware devices.

4.3 Communication Interfaces

Describes network interfaces.

4.4 Software Interfaces

Describes any remaining software interfaces not included above.

5. Performance Requirements

Specifies speed and memory requirements.

6. Design Constraints

Specifies any constraints for the design team using this document.

6.1 Standards Compliance
6.2 Hardware Limitations
6.3 Others as Appropriate

7. Other Non-Functional Attributes

Specifies any other particular non-functional attributes required by the system. Examples are provided below:

7.1 Security
7.2 Binary Compatibility
7.3 Reliability
7.4 Maintainability
7.5 Portability
7.6 Extensibility
7.7 Reusability
7.8 Application Affinity/Compatibility
7.9 Resource Utilization

7.10 **Serviceability**
7.11 **Others as Appropriate**

8. Preliminary Object-Oriented Domain Analysis

This section presents a list of the fundamental objects that must be modeled within
the system to satisfy its requirements. The purpose is to provide an alternative,
"structural" view on the requirements stated above and how they might be satisfied in the system.

9. Operational Scenarios

This section should describe a set of scenarios that illustrate, from the user's
perspective, what will be experienced when utilizing the system under various
situations.

10. Preliminary Schedule

This section provides an initial version of the project plan, including the major
tasks to be accomplished, their interdependencies, and their tentative start/stop
dates. The plan also includes information on hardware, software, and wetware
resource requirements. The project plan should be accompanied by one or more
PERT or GANTT charts.

11. Preliminary Budget

This section provides an initial budget for the project, itemized by cost factor.

12. Appendices

Specifies other useful information for understanding the requirements. All SRS
documents should include at least the following two appendices:

12.1 **Definitions, Acronyms, Abbreviations**
    Provides definitions of unfamiliar definitions, terms, and acronyms.
12.2 **References**
    Provides complete citations to all documents and meetings referenced or
    used in the preparation of this document.

4.6 Software Project Management Plan

Effective project management is, simply, the effective use of human capital. It is
"the creation and maintenance of an internal environment … where individuals,
working together in groups, can perform efficiently and effectively toward the
attainment of group goals" (Koontz et al. 1980). Project management is resource
allocation, communication, and organization. A project manager is given a set of
resources, including engineers, and a goal to achieve. The course he or she

establishes in order to realize success is the development process. Unfortunately, there is no exact science that dictates how to get from one end of this route to the other. Instead, a project manager is responsible for synthesizing a number of different concepts and schemes, in order to produce an environment that enables the individual members of the development team to work together to reach a common goal. Ghezzi describes the following five goals that can guide a project manager is this endeavor (Ghezzi et al. 1991):

- **Planning**—The project manager is charged with identifying the goals, and establishing the plans needed to meet those goals. This includes the assignment of workers, the allocation of other resources, and the creation of a schedule. A project's plan describes the course it will take, and the pattern it will follow on its way to the creation of the final project.
- **Organizing**—A project manager must lay out clear lines of authority and must make sure that development teams and engineers understand their duties and responsibilities. Organizing must take place at all the various levels of the development team hierarchy, from a small team of programmers, up to the group of team leaders. Organizational structure must be tailored to ensure efficiency and effectiveness, and must be based on the goals of both the project in question, and the software engineering firm as a whole.
- **Staffing**—A project manager must select and assign the workers involved in a project in an effective and efficient manner. This includes the assessing of, and hiring of candidates as discussed earlier in the chapter. In addition, a manger must see that employees are appropriately trained and compensated.
- **Directing**—A project manager is responsible for leading the workers of the project, and for coordinating the activities in which they are involved. Employees should understand not only what it is that they are doing, buy why they are doing it and what part it plays in the project as a whole. They should also be given specific goals to achieve.
- **Controlling**—A project manager must constantly assess the progress of the software engineering project. This includes monitoring for deviations from the project's plans and schedules as well as ensuring that the initial goals are being reached. In addition, a project manager must be able to take action to correct for errors encountered in the process.

The management aspects described above are general responsibilities required of a project manager. The personal style of one manager may differ significantly from another, but may be just as effective. What is important is to ensure that these goals are realized. In addition, it is important to keep in mind that management is not performed only by the project manager, but at various levels throughout a project hierarchy. Team leaders, for instance, must effectively manage their team using the same concepts. To achieve these management objectives, a tool known as a **software project management plan (SPMP)** is often used. A SPMP is essentially a document that specifies practices that will be used during the development process, both technical and managerial. A SPMP is accompanied by a **software requirement analysis document (SRAD)**, which, as its name suggests, helps to further describe the project being undertaken.

4.7 Chapter Summary and Conclusions

In this chapter we have discussed the critical concepts to planning and managing a software engineering project. A project must begin with communication. The initial communication with the client is used to identify the software solution envisioned by the client, and the functionality that they require from it. The information gathered from the client is then utilized to create a plan for the project. Project planning seeks to identify the activities, milestones, and deliverables that are to be achieved throughout the project. Planning begins with the determination of a software systems purpose and scope. Next, the project manager identifies the activities to be undertaken during the project, the milestones that will define them, and the deliverables that they will produce. Finally, the project plan must include estimations of resources to be consumed, including manpower, time, and money. From this estimation, a schedule is created for the development process. The project manager is responsible for managing this schedule for the entirety of the project. One tool a project manager might use in this endeavor is called a Work Breakdown Structure, WBS, which lays out a project according to the activities that make it up. In addition, project managers can use Gantt Charts to map out the project's schedule, and to monitor progress.

In addition to planning the project, a project manager is responsible for communicating with, and supervising all of the individuals involved in the project. This includes everyone from the client to the individual engineers. When a project begins, the project manager must select staff based on ability, and assign that staff to activities at which they can perform effectively.

Finally, a project manager is responsible for monitoring a software engineering project to ensure that it follows the intended course and achieves the specified goal. If deviation from the plan or schedule is encountered, the project manager must take appropriate action to see that it is corrected. This can include the reassignment of engineers, the hiring of new engineers, or the scrubbing of certain requirements.

4.8 Exercises

1. Last chapter, we asked you to explain the difference between a class and an object using examples. Now, present the same difference, this time using models.

2. Explain why the process of project planning is iterative and why a plan must be continually reviewed during a software project.
3. What is the critical distinction between a milestone and a deliverable?
4. Explain the difference between task and activity?
5. Can a role be shared between two or more participants? Why or why not?
6. To which role would you assign the following tasks?

    a. Change a subsystem interface to accommodate a new requirement.
    b. Communicate the subsystem interface change to other teams.
    c. Change the documentation as a result of interface change.
    d. Design a test suite to find defects introduced by the change.
    e. Ensure that the change is completed on schedule.

7. Select at a random a working day in your work week. Log all the activities that qualify as communication activities (e.g., talking to a friend over phone, providing information and obtaining information to a fellow) which fraction of your working day does communication represent?
8. Why do software development projects generate so much documentation?
9. As a programmer, you are offered a promotion to project management but you feel that you can make a more effective contribution in a technical rather than a managerial role. Discuss whether you should accept the promotion.
10. Explain why the best programmers do not always make the best software managers. You may find helpful to base your answer on the list of project activities described in Sect. 4.1.
11. You work for a large mobile phone manufacturer. You have been nominated project manager for the design project of a new mobile phone model. The project scope has already been determined. You have chosen a very simple work breakdown structure, and the included activities have been named. You must now plan the project schedule and calculate project duration, as well as estimate the resources needed and calculate project costs. Your boss wants the schedule and resource plan on his table in a few weeks' time.

    a. You have already made the following table (Table 1) that includes all the activities required in the project, the duration of each activity (in weeks), and resources (in men). Also, dependencies between activities have been identified. Dependency refers to the activity number of the preceding activity. The preceding activity must be fully completed before work on the following activity can be started (all dependencies are Finish to Start dependencies).
    b. Draw a Gantt-chart corresponding to the shortest duration for the project, and mark the floats of the activities in the chart. Mark the two most important milestones in the Gantt.

References

Bruegge B, Dutoit A (2004) Object-oriented software engineering: using UML, patterns, and java, 2nd edn. Pearson Education, Ltd., Upper Saddle River

Ghezzi C, Jazayer M, Mandrioli D (1991) Fundamentals of software engineering, 2nd edn. Prentice Hall, New Jersey

Koontz H (1980) The management theory jungle revisited. Acad Manag Rev, pp 175–187

Schach S (2008) Object-oriented software engineering. McGraw-Hill Higher Education, Boston

Sommerville I (2004) Software engineering, 7th edn. Peason Education, Ltd., Boston

Chapter 5
Requirements Elicitation

5.1 What are Requirements?

Requirements define expected services of the system and constraints that the system must obey. These services can be grouped into those that describe the scope of the system and those that comprise the business functions, which are called functional requirements. Statements can be classified into different categories of restrictions imposed on a system; these are called constraints (Maciaszek 2001). Requirements derived from the application domain of the system rather than from the specific needs of users are called domain requirements. A **requirement** can be a description of *what* a system must do. This type of requirement specifies something that the delivered system must be able to do. Another type of requirement is one that specifies something about the system itself, and how well it performs its functions. Such requirements are often called 'non-functional requirements', 'performance requirements' or 'quality of service requirements.'

5.1.1 Functional Requirements

Functional requirements are associated with specific functions, tasks, or behaviors the system must fully support. The functional requirements address the quality characteristic of functionality while the other quality characteristics are concerned with various kinds of non-functional requirements. Use cases have quickly become a widespread practice for capturing functional requirements. This is especially true in the object-oriented community where they originated, however, their applicability is not limited to object-oriented systems.

R. Y. Lee, *Software Engineering: A Hands-On Approach,*
DOI: 10.2991/978-94-6239-006-5_5, © Atlantis Press and the author 2013

5.1.2 Non-Functional Requirements or Constraints

Non-functional requirements are essentially constraints placed on various attributes of these functions or tasks. Because of this, non-functional requirements tend to be stated in terms of **constraints** that are placed on the results of tasks considered functional requirements (e.g., constraints on the speed or efficiency of a given task). A task-based functional requirements statement is commonly a useful "skeleton" upon which to construct a complete requirements statement. It can be helpful to think of non-functional requirements as adverbially related to tasks or functional requirements: how fast, how efficiently, how safely, etc. Non-functional requirements in software engineering presents a systematic and pragmatic approach to 'building quality into' software systems. Systems must exhibit software quality attributes such as accuracy, performance, security and modifiability. However, such non-functional requirements (NFRs) are difficult to address in many projects, even though there are many techniques to meet functional requirements in order to provide desired functionality. Non-functional requirements in software engineering demonstrates the applicability of the NFR framework to a variety of NFRs, domains, system characteristics and application areas. This will help readers apply the Framework to NFRs and domains of particular interest to them. Detailed treatments of particular NFRs—accuracy, security and performance requirements—along with treatments of NFRs for information systems are presented as specializations of the NFR framework. The use of the framework for particular application areas is illustrated for software architecture, as well as enterprise modeling. Feedback from domain experts in industry and government provides an initial evaluation of the framework and some case studies (Chung et al. 1999).

5.1.2.1 Sources of Non-Functional Requirements

Non-functional requirements arise from the operating environment, the user(s), and competitive products such as:

- System Constraints.
- User Objectives, Values and Concerns.
- Competitive Analysis of Features.
- Development Organization Constraints.
- Development Organization Objectives, Values and Concerns.
- Product requirements: Requirements that specify a products behavior.
- Organizational requirements: Policies and procedures of customer and developer's organization.
- External requirements: All requirements that are derived from factors external to the system.

5.1.3 Domain Requirements

Domain requirements include specialized domain terminology or reference to domain concepts. Since these are specialized, software engineers often find it difficult to understand how they are related to other system requirements. Domain experts may leave information out of requirement simply because it is so obvious to them. However, it may not be obvious to the developers of the system, and they may, therefore, implement the requirement in the wrong way. There could be a request for a user interface specification or a copyright constraint on a particular software released. The developers in the first case must find out how to design the specified user interface and in the second case the developers must design copyright information available to all the users, popping up when a user attempts to use the software. These are two extra requirements that will be added according to the operation performed by the software (Sommerville 2004).

5.2 Requirement Elicitation

Requirements definition conversations often center on what to do, techniques to use, or methods to follow. But requirement definition either succeeds or fails based on how well people can work together. Success of the requirement elicitation process depends on dealing with interpersonal, cultural and organizational aspects of adopting these methods. A business analyst discovers the system requirements through customers and experts in the problem domain. Requirements elicited from the customers are expressed in use case scenarios. The task of a business analyst is to combine the two sets of requirements into a business model. Requirement elicitation is distinguished into two categories as traditional and modern methods. Traditional methods involve interviewing customers, questionnaires, observation and studying documents. However, the modern method involves prototyping, Joint Application development (JAD), Rapid Application Development (RAD) (Maciaszek 2001).

5.2.1 Communicating with the Client

First the developers and customers must develop a shared understanding of problems and technical solutions. Then the team leaders and members who did not talk to customer need to understand what was learned through proper team conversations. Finally, organizational functions-design, engineering, marketing, documentation, testing and customers must also understand the problem and agree to the technical solution. Customer-centered techniques necessitate face-to-face communication, continuous, synchronous team work in design meetings, shared decision-making, and consensus (Holtzblatt and Beyer 1995).

(a) **Involvement and Control**: Effective requirements definition requires mutual control of process by all players. No one likes to feel out of control of their time, their work activities, or their goals. Team members don't want their activities dictated to them. Team members really own their processes and have the desired skills to solve a particular problem. A successful requirements process includes effective ways to foster a healthy partnership between the customer, designer, and team members. It must reveal the ownership of the activities of the design by customers and team members (Holtzblatt and Beyer 1995).

(b) **Client-Developer links**: In the software arena these links are defined as techniques or channels that allow customers and developers to exchange information. Today, there is a wide variety of links available to software developers. The tremendous variety of links that are available today represents both opportunity and a challenge for software development managers. Opportunity is easier to obtain input from clients and the challenge is deciding on the type of links. By focusing on links we are able to draw insights on degree of participation that should be used to engage customers in development process. According to Keil and Carmel three results can be drawn regarding the links:

1. The more links the better
2. Reduce indirect links
3. Consider links not traditionally used in environment (Keil and Carmel 1995)

5.2.2 Gathering Information

One concern is how to gain access to information we may need that is hidden in the minds of users or in the environment. Another concern is how to broaden the users' perspective in efforts to accomplish the goals (Thayer and Dorfman 1990). In traditional methods of requirement elicitation, interviews and questionnaires were the primary technique of fact finding and information gathering. Interviews would be either formal or informal interviews. The information collected through such interviews can address organizational and contextual factors, provided that the right questions are asked. Likewise, if the right people are interviewed, the information will represent multiple stakeholders' opinions across a large number of different communities affected by the development of the proposed system being elicited. The organization and expression of the information collected through interviews is a commonly neglected issue. There is a lack of standardized procedures for structuring information received via interviews: other limitations with eliciting requirements primarily or exclusively through interviews result from the tremendous responsibility placed on the requirements analyst. Assuming that the interview data was collected from the different communities affected by the system being elicited, the analyst must integrate these different interpretations, goals, objectives, communication styles, and use of terminology into a single set of requirements. This integration is a difficult task unless the interviews are structured in some way. For example, the use of a glossary of system-specific terms may reduce the number of inconsistencies in interviews that subsequently have to be resolved by the analyst. Even with well-structured interview data, the analyst still must perform complex tasks such as deciding whether a particular piece of information is premature design information or a requirement. These tasks require that the analyst is experienced in both the system domain and with development techniques; making qualifications for such a position often difficult to satisfy. With so much decision-making resting with the analyst, the elicitation stakeholders may not understand how the resulting requirements were derived and may refuse to share ownership in and approve these requirements. The requirements themselves may not be easily understood, e.g., if written with a behavioral tone in very domain specific terms, the users may comprehend everything, however, the developers could have many issues with fully grasping the terminology. The integration and decision-making performed by the analyst takes time and given that requirements are volatile, the longer this process takes the more likely it is that the subsequent requirements no longer match the stakeholder communities' needs and expectations. Other techniques can be used in conjunction with interviews to help structure them and facilitate optimal integration.

5.2.3 Issues in Requirement Elicitation

There are many problems associated with requirements engineering, including problems in defining the system scope, problems in fostering understanding among the different communities affected by the development of a given system, and problems in dealing with the volatile nature of requirements. These problems will often lead to poor requirements and the cancellation of system development, or the development of a system that is later judged unsatisfactory or unacceptable, has high maintenance costs, or undergoes frequent changes. By improving the requirement elicitation process, the requirements engineering process can also be greatly improved, resulting in enhanced system requirements and potentially a much better system.

Requirements engineering can be decomposed into the activities of requirement elicitation, specification, and validation. Most of the requirements techniques and tools today focus on specification, i.e., the representation of the requirements.

A list of ten elicitation problems given in one source could be classified according to the following framework:

- problems of scope
- the boundary of the system is ill-defined
- unnecessary design information is given
- problems of understanding
- users have incomplete understanding of their needs
- users have poor understanding of computer capabilities and limitations
- analysts have poor knowledge of problem domain

- user and analyst speak different languages
- ease of omitting "obvious" information
- conflicting views of different users
- requirements are often overly vague and untestable, e.g., "user friendly" and "robust"
- problems of volatility
- requirements evolve over time

   The remainder of this section will discuss these problem areas in further detail. (Christel and Kang 1992)

5.3 Identifying the Requirements

A system will often times consist of hundreds or thousands of requirement statements. To properly manage such a large number of requirements, they have to be numbered with some type of identification scheme. There are several techniques, a few of which are listed as follows: (Maciaszek 2001)

- Unique identifier—usually a sequence number is assigned
- Sequential number within document hierarchy—assigned with consideration to the requirement's position within the requirements document.
- Sequential number within requirement's category—assigned a mnemonic name that identifies the category of requirement.

5.3.1 Identifying the Functional Requirements

Functional requirements capture the intended behavior of the system. This behavior may be expressed as services, tasks or functions that the system is required to perform. In product development, it is useful to distinguish between the baseline functionality necessary for any system to compete in that product domain and the *features* that differentiate the system from competitors' products, and from variants in your company's own product line/family. Features may be additional functionality or differ from the basic functionality along some quality attribute (such as performance or memory utilization). One strategy for quickly penetrating a market, is to produce the core or a stripped down, basic product, and adding features to variants of the product to be released shortly thereafter. This release strategy is obviously also beneficial in information systems development, staging core functionality for early releases and adding important features over the course of several subsequent releases. In many industries, companies produce product lines with different cost/feature variations per product in the line. Many product families include a number of product lines targeted at somewhat different markets or usage situations. What makes these product lines part of a family are some common elements of functionality and identity. A platform-based development approach leverages this commonality, utilizing a set of reusable assets across the family. These strategies have important implications for software architecture. In particular, it is not just the functional requirements of the first product or release that must be supported by the architecture. The functional requirements of early (nearly con-current) releases need to be explicitly taken into account. Later releases are accommodated through architectural qualities such as extensibility, flexibility, etc. The latter are expressed as non-functional requirements. As such, use cases have quickly become a widespread practice for capturing functional requirements. This is especially true in the object-oriented community where they originated, but their applicability is not limited to object-oriented systems.

5.3.2 Identifying the Non-Functional Requirements

Non-functional requirements are requirements that are not directly concerned with specific functions delivered by the system. They may relate to emergent system properties such as reliability, response time, etc. Therefore, they may specify system performance, security, availability and other emergent properties. How-ever, failing to meet non-functional requirements can mean that the whole system is unusable. Identifying non-functional requirements means identifying the origin. Nonfunctional requirements arise through user needs, because of budget con-straints, organizational policies and the need for interoperability with software or hardware systems. A problem with non-functional requirements is that they are difficult to verify since users often state these requirements in terms that are overly vague. (Sommerville 2004). Here are some questions for identifying non-func-tional requirements (Malan and Bredemeyer 2001).

User interface and human factors:

- What type of user will be using the system?
- Will more than one type of user be using the system?
- What sort of training will be required for each type of user?
- Is it particularly important that the system be easy to learn?
- Is it particularly important that users be protected from making errors?
- What sort of input/output devices for the human interface are available, and what are their characteristics?

Documentation

- What kind of documentation is required?
- What audience is to be addressed by each document?

Hardware considerations

- What hardware is the proposed system to be used on?

- What are the characteristics of the target hardware, including memory size and auxiliary storage space?

Performance characteristics

- Are there any speed, throughput, or response time constraints on the system?
- Are there size or capacity constraints on the data to be processed by the system?

Error handling and extreme conditions

- How should the system respond to input errors?
- How should the system respond to extreme conditions?

System interfacing

- Is input coming from systems outside the proposed system?
- Is output going to systems outside the proposed system?
- Are there restrictions on the format or medium that must be used for input or output?

Quality issues

- What are the requirements for reliability?
- Must the system trap faults?
- What is the maximum time for restarting the system after a failure?
- What is the acceptable system downtime per 24-hour period?
- Is it important that the system be portable (able to move to different hardware or operating system environments)?

System Modifications

- What parts of the system are likely candidates for later modification?
- What sorts of modifications are expected (levels of adaptation)?
- Are the users willing to tailor an application?
- What kind of interface is required?
- Might unwary adaptations lead to unsafe system states?

Security Issues

- Must access to any data or the system itself be controlled?
- Is physical security an issue?

Resources and Management Issues

- How often will the system be backed up?
- Who will be responsible for the back up?
- Who is responsible for system installation?
- Who will be responsible for system maintenance?

NFRs are commonly perceived as difficult to express. Reasons for this include:

- Certain constraints are related to the design solution that are unknown at the requirements stage.
- Certain constraints are highly subjective and can only be determined through complex, empirical evaluations.
- Non-functional requirements tend to be related to one or more functional requirements.
- Non-functional requirements tend to conflict and contradict.
- There is no 'universal' set of rules and guidelines for determining when non-functional requirements are optimally met.

5.3.3 Identifying the Application Domain

Domain analysis is a term used to describe the systematic activity of identifying, formalizing and classifying the knowledge in a problem domain. Our view of domain analysis encompasses those domains which enable or provide supportive function to the application domain. Therefore, we are interested in acquiring quantifiable characteristics of the application, related execution, architectural design, and algorithmic domains. We use these characteristics to further constrain non-functional requirement goals, thereby producing realistic and achievable non-functional requirements. During domain analysis, we seek answers to questions such as 'What are the essential performance criteria for this type of application?', 'Where will the application be utilized, and what are the performance features of this environment, i.e., throughput, delay, loss?' and 'What are the performance characteristics of specific algorithms?' Answers to such questions would vary based on the domain. For example, domain analysis within the execution domain may produce information regarding processor speed, radio range for wireless devices, battery life for mobile devices, average throughput, delay and loss characteristics of the network, etc. In addition, domain analysis within the application domain will hopefully produce quantifiable characteristics that are inherent to all applications of that type. An example of such an application characteristic is the 150 ms one way path propagation delay requirement for IP telephony applications. Studies show that humans tolerate delays in speech of approximately 150 ms. After 150 ms of delay, we begin to talk over or interrupt the speech of the other person. Furthermore, regarding the algorithmic domain, we are interested in the performance of algorithms that may be used to satisfy a specific non-functional requirement. For example, performance specifications of an encryption algorithm may be used to assess the feasibility of employing the encryption algorithm to provide confidentiality and protect the data's integrity (Hill 2004).

5.4 Common Problems Concerning Requirements

Problems of requirement elicitation can be grouped into three categories (Christel and Kang 1992):

1. Problems of scope in which the requirements may address too little or too much information
2. Problems of understanding within groups as well as between groups such as users and developers
3. Problems of volatility, i.e., the changing nature of requirements.

5.4.1 Problems of Scope

Elicitation techniques need to be broad enough to establish boundary conditions for the specified target system, yet they still should focus on the creation of requirements as opposed to design activities. Avoiding contextual issues can lead to requirements which are incomplete, not verifiable, unnecessary and unusable. Focusing on broader design activities improperly emphasizes developers' issues over the users' needs, and may result in poorly defined requirements as well. Requirement elicitation must begin with an organizational and contextual analysis to determine the boundary of the target system, as well as the objectives of the system. Less ambitious elicitation techniques not addressing this concern run the risk of producing requirements which are incomplete and potentially unusable, because they do not adhere to the user's or organization's true goals for the system. Performing an organizational and contextual analysis allows these goals to be properly captured, and then put to use in verifying that the requirements are indeed usable and correct. Elicitation techniques can be overly ambitious as well. Elicitation must focus on the creation of requirements, not design activities, in order to adequately address users' concerns and not just developers' needs. Elicitation strategies which produce requirements in the form of high level designs run the risk of creating requirements which are overly ambiguous to the user community. These requirements may not be verifiable by the users because they cannot adequately understand the intricate design language. Also, requirements expressed as a design are much more likely to incorporate additional decisions not reflecting user or sponsor needs, i.e., the requirements will not be precise and necessary. There are at least three broad categories which affect the requirements and the requirements engineering process for a proposed system:

- Organization
- Environment
- Project

A number of a restricting assumptions and misunderstandings such as "the boundary of the system is ill-defined or the customers/users specify unnecessary

technical detail that may confuse rather than clarify..." and, similarly, "the cus-
tomers/users ... have a poor understanding of the capabilities and limitations of
their computing environment,..." (Pressman 2005) can set up a team for difficulty
down the road. Environmental factors include:

- Hardware and software constraints imposed on a target system (the target sys-
  tem will typically be a component of some larger system with an existing or
  required architecture already in place)
- The maturity of the target system's domain
- The certainty of the target system's interfaces to the larger system
- The target system's role within a larger system

However, the initial requirements are typically underspecified, unnecessary,
and incomplete; or at times they are over-specified but burdened with needless
design constraints. Thus, elicitation activities which are either too narrow or too
broad in scope may result in requirements which are ambiguous, incomplete, not
verifiable, unnecessary, and unusable. The requirements may be unusable because
they do not reflect true user needs, or else because they are not implementable
under given environmental or project constraints.

5.4.2 Problems of Understanding

Problems of understanding during elicitation can lead to requirements which are
ambiguous, incomplete, inconsistent, and even incorrect because they do not
address the requirement elicitation stakeholders' true needs.
   Problems of understanding can be separated into three issues:

1. The communities involved in the elicitation process, possess a variety of
   backgrounds and experience levels, creating a situation where common
   knowledge to one group may be completely foreign to another. This makes it
   difficult for a requirements analyst to interpret and integrate information
   gathered from these diverse communities.
2. The language used to express the requirements back to these stakeholder
   communities may be too formal or too informal to meet the needs of each of the
   groups, again because of the diversity of the communities.
3. The large amount of information gathered during elicitation necessitates that it
   be structured in some way. The understanding of this structure is dependent on
   the characteristics of the stakeholder communities.

The stakeholders involved in requirements elicitation come from at least five
communities: customers/sponsors, users, developers, quality assurance teams, and
requirements analysts. The requirements should be expressed in a form which:

- Promotes communication and understanding between customers and users;
- Allows the developer to determine whether the expressed requirements are implementable; and
- Lets quality assurance teams verify that an implementation meets these requirements.

The stakeholder communities may be multilevel. More specifically, the involved parties may be in managerial positions within a contributing organization; gathering information of this variety can be a difficult task. System developers and requirements analysts may have limited knowledge of the application domain, while the system users may not know design methods for the development of systems with a significant software component. The customer may not understand what can be done to solve a given problem, nor have a full appreciation for the difficulty involved with getting the analyst and developer to understand the problem in the customer's domain. The analyst is often ignorant of the customer's problems, goals, and wishes. Requirements elicitation starts with inherently informal knowledge and typically involves people not literate in software-intensive systems. To avoid misunderstandings due to terminology differences, requirements have traditionally been expressed back to the elicitation communities using natural language text. Requirements, therefore, may be difficult to understand by the elicitation communities because of the sophisticated form used to express the requirements. Requirements are typically not the product of a single person's work, but, rather, they are the result of many peoples' expressed needs across a multitude of different communities. These multiple and often varying inputs present problems in regards to redundancy of data, inconsistency, and point-of-view. Each particular different group involved in requirements elicitation have different interpretations of what the requirements say and different expectations of what a system built to these requirements will deliver.

Requirements may also be misunderstood because of their large size. Often times this is because requirements are so complex that the client and practitioner may have difficulty focusing attention on one single aspect at a time. This can lead to issues with perceiving interactions between requirements, or problems with the specified system being impossible to visualize from the resulting specification. Problems in understanding results from the necessary involvement of requirements analysts, sponsors, developers, and end users in requirements elicitation are common and can lead to many issues if not properly handled. The requirements are produced and interpreted by people with vastly different experience levels and backgrounds. The form in which the requirements are expressed and the size of the system described by the requirements also affect understanding. If the participants in elicitation do not adequately understand the output of the process, then the resulting requirements may be ambiguous, inconsistent, and incomplete. The requirements may also be incorrect not fully addressing the true needs of the elicitation communities. In summary, good communication among users, customers, and developers is very important in solving pragmatic system problems, an issue too often overlooked when system analysis is approached only from a pure computer science standpoint.

5.4.3 *Problems of Volatility*

Requirements will change over time. During the time it takes to develop a system, the users' needs may mature because of increased knowledge brought on by the development activities, or they may shift to a new set of needs because of unforeseen organizational or environmental pressures. If such changes are not accommodated, the original requirements set will become incomplete and inconsistent with the new situation, potentially creating an unusable system because the captured information has since become obsolete. One primary cause of requirements volatility is that "user needs evolve over time". The requirements engineering process of elicit, specify, and validate should not be executed only once during system development, but rather should be returned to so that the requirements can reflect the new knowledge gained during specification, validation, and subsequent activities. A requirements engineering methodology should be iterative in nature, "so that solutions can be reworked in the light of increased knowledge". Due to political climate and other factors, the needs of a particular group may be overemphasized in the elicitation of requirements. Later prioritization of the elicitation communities' needs may correct this oversight and result in requirements changes. Both the traceability of requirements and their consistency may be affected if these changes are frequent and not anticipated. Organizational complexity is another common cause of requirements volatility. Organizational goals, policies, structures, and work roles of intended end users all may change during the course of a system's development, especially as the number of users affected by a system's development increases. Due to the problems of understanding and scope discussed earlier, user needs may not be clearly expressed initially in the requirements, and the developer or requirements analyst may make some incorrect assumptions based on this ambiguity. With an iterative process, those mistaken assumptions can be detected faster and corrected sooner.

5.5 Validating the Requirements

Validating requirements is the process of showing that the requirements define the system in a fashion that accurately represents what the customer wants. Requirement validation often results in reworking the elicitation process because of errors discovered during development of the system. Recent techniques used for validation are:

- Prototyping
- Quality Function Deployment
- Requirements Reviews
- Test case generation

1. Prototyping can be used to develop early executable versions of the requirements model. Prototyping may be costly which is not the ultimate solution when working with a fixed budget.
2. Quality Function Deployment (QFD) is another useful technique for validation. QFD helps to identify user requirements that have not been addressed by the developer, as well as developer-proposed features that do not support any requirements. In addition to highlighting such omissions, QFD also documents requirements that are highly rated by the user and receive little attention by the developer-proposed features.
3. Requirement Reviews: The Requirements are analyzed by a team of reviewers. Requirement reviews could be either formal or informal.
4. Test case generation: Requirements should be testable. If the tests for the requirements are devised as part of validation process, this reveals requirement problems.

5.6 Producing the Use Case Model

A *use case* defines a goal-oriented set of interactions between external actors and the system under consideration. *Actors* are parties outside the system that interact with the system. An actor may be a class of users, roles users can play, or other systems. Cockburn (1997) distinguishes between primary and secondary actors. A *primary* actor is one having a goal requiring the assistance of the system. A *secondary* actor is one from which the system needs assistance. A use case is initiated by a user with a particular goal in mind, and is considered successful when that goal is satisfied. It describes the sequence of interactions between actors and the system necessary to deliver the service that satisfies the goal. It also includes possible variants of this sequence, e.g., alternative sequences that may also satisfy the goal, as well as sequences that may lead to failure to complete the service because of exceptional behavior, error handling, etc. The system is treated as a "black box", and the interactions with the system, including system responses, are as perceived from outside the system. Thus, use cases capture *who* (actor) does *what* (interaction) with the system, for what *purpose* (goal), without dealing with system internals. A complete set of use cases specifies all the different ways to use the system, and therefore defines all behavior required of the system, defining the scope of the system. Generally, use case steps are written in an easy-to-understand structured narrative, using the vocabulary of the domain. This is engaging for users who can easily follow and validate the use cases. Also the increased accessibility encourages users to be actively involved in defining the requirements.

Scenarios

A scenario is an instance of a use case, and represents a single path through the use case. Thus, one may construct a scenario for the main flow through the use case, and other scenarios for each possible variation of flow through the use case (e.g., triggered by options, error conditions, security breaches, etc.). Scenarios may be depicted using sequence diagrams.

5.6.1 Structuring Use Cases

UML provides three relationships that can be used to structure use cases. These are generalization, include and extends. An *include* relationship between two use cases means that the sequence of behavior described in the included (or *sub*) use case is included in the sequence of the base (including) use case. Including a use case is thus analogous to the notion of calling a subroutine (Coleman 1992). The *extends* relationship provides a way of capturing a variant to a use case. Extensions are not true use cases, but they are changes to steps in an existing use case. Typically, extensions are used to specify the changes in steps that occur in order to accommodate an assumption that is false (Coleman 1992). The extends relationship includes the condition that must be satisfied if the extension is to take place, and references to the extension points which define the locations in the base (extended) use case where the additions are to be made. A *generalization* relationship between use cases "implies that the child use case contains all the attributes, sequences of behavior, and extension points defined in the parent use case, and participates in all relationships of the parent use case." The child use case may define new behavior sequences, as well as add behavior into and specialize the existing behavior of the parent.

5.6.2 Use Case Guidelines

Creation
  The following provides an outline of a process for creating use cases:

1. Identify all the different users of the system
2. Create a user profile for each category of user, including all the roles the users play that are relevant to the system. For each role, identify all the significant goals the users have that the system will support. A statement of the system's value proposition is useful in identifying significant goals.
3. Create a use case for each goal following the use case template. Maintain the same level of abstraction throughout the use case. Steps in higher-level use cases may be treated as goals for lower level (i.e., more detailed), sub-use cases.
4. Structure the use cases. Avoid over-structuring, as this can make the use cases harder to follow.
5. Review and validate with users

Use case writing process:

1. Name the system scope.
2. Brainstorm and list the primary actors.

   Find every human and non-human primary actor, over the life of the system.

3. Brainstorm and exhaustively list user goals for the system.
4. Select one use case to expand.

   Consider writing a narrative to learn the material.

5. Write the main success scenario (MSS).

   Use steps 3 to 9 to meet all interests and guarantees.

6. Brainstorm and exhaustively list the extension conditions.

   Include all that the system can detect and must handle.

7. Write the extension-handling steps.

   Each will end back in the MSS, at a separate success exit, or in failure.

8. Extract complex flows to sub use cases; merge trivial sub use cases.

   Extracting a sub use case is easy, but it adds cost to the project.

9. Readjust the set: add, subtract, merge, as needed.

5.7 The Software Requirements Specification Document

Software Requirements Specification (SRS) consists of a complete description of the external behavior of the software system. SRS could be written by a potential user of a system or a developer of a system. The two scenarios create different situations.

The following is a SRS template:

1. **Introduction**

   This section provides an overview of the entire requirement document. This document describes all data, functional and behavioral requirements for software.

   1.1 **Goals and Objectives**
   1.2 **Statements of Scope**
   1.3 **Software Context**
   1.4 **Major Constraints**

2. Usage Scenario

This section provides a usage scenario for the software. It organized information collected during requirements elicitation into use-cases.

2.1 User Profiles
2.2 Use Cases
2.3 Special Usage Considerations

3. Data Model and Description

3.1 Data Description
3.2 Data Objects
3.3 Relationships
3.4 Complete Data Model
3.5 Data Dictionary

4. Functional Model and Description

4.1 Description for Function n

A description of each major software function, along with data flow or class hierarchy (OO) is presented.

4.1.1 Processing Narrative (PSPEC) for Function n
4.1.2 Function n Flow Diagram
4.1.3 Function n Interface Description
4.1.4 Function n Transforms

4.1.4.1 Transform k Description (processing narrative, PSPEC)
4.1.4.2 Transform k Interface Description
4.1.4.3 Transform k Lower Level Flow Diagrams
4.1.4.4 Transform k Interface Description

4.1.5 Performance Issues
4.1.6 Design Constraints

4.2 Software Interface Description

4.2.1 External Machine Interfaces
4.2.2 External System Interfaces
4.2.3 Human Interface

4.3 Control Flow Description

5. Behavioral Model and Description

A description of the behavior of the software is presented.

5.1 **Description for Software Behavior**

   5.1.1 **Events**
   5.1.2 **States**

5.2 **State Transition Diagrams**
5.3 **Control Specification (CSPEC)**
6. **Restrictions, Limitations, and Constraints**

Special issues which impact the specification, design, or implementation of the software are noted here.

7. **Validation Criteria**

The approach to software validation is described.

7.1 **Classes of Tests**
7.2 **Expected Software Response**
7.3 **Performance Bounds**

8. **Appendices**

Presents information that supplements the Requirements Specification.

8.1 **System Traceability Matrix**
8.2 **Product Strategies**
8.3 **Analysis Metrics to be Used**
8.4 **Supplementary Information (as required)**

5.8 Chapter Summary and Conclusions

Requirements for a system are the descriptions of the services provided by the system and its operational constraints. Functional requirements are associated with specific functions, tasks or behaviors the system must support. Non-functional requirements are constraints on various attributes of these functions or tasks. Domain requirements include specialized domain terminology or references to domain concepts. Since these are specialized, software engineers often find it difficult to understand how they are related to other system requirements. Requirement elicitation is distinguished into two categories as traditional and modern methods.

Communicating with the client involves the developers and customers developing a shared understanding of problems and of technical solutions. Effective requirements definition requires mutual control of process by all players. In traditional methods of requirement elicitation, interviews and questionnaires were the primary technique of fact finding and information gathering. This chapter explains the way to identify the functional and non-functional requirements, as well as domain requirements. Domain analysis is a term used to describe the systematic activity of identifying, formalizing and classifying the knowledge in a problem domain. Problems of requirements elicitation can be grouped into three categories: problems of scope, problems of understanding, and problems of volatility. Validating requirements is showing that the requirements properly define the system that the customer wants. Then this chapter describes how to derive use cases from the requirements. Creating use cases involves:

- Identifying all the different users of the system
- Creating a user profile for each category of user

Software Requirements Specification (SRS) consists of a complete description of the external behavior of the software system. Finally, this chapter displays the complete template of SRS.

5.9 Exercises

1. Specify which of these are functional and non-functional requirements:
   - The ticket distributor must enable a traveler to buy weekly passes
   - The ticket distributor must be written in java
   - The ticket distributor must be easy to use
   - The ticket distributor must always be available
   - The ticket distributor must provide a phone number to call when it fails

2. Identify and briefly describe three types of requirements that may be defined for a computer based system.
3. Describe types of non-functional requirements that may be placed on a system. Give examples of each of these types of requirement.
4. Write a set of non-functional requirements for the ticket-issuing system. Suggest how the engineer is responsible for drawing up a system requirements specification and how they might keep track of the relationships between functional and non-functional requirement.
5. Using your knowledge of how an ATM is used, develop a set of use-cases that could serve as a basis for understanding the requirements for an ATM system.
6. Give a non-functional requirement that can be handled without having detailed knowledge about the target software product.
7. Distinguish between a use case and a use case diagram.
8. During requirement elicitation we try to reconcile domain knowledge requirements and use case requirements. Explain the difference between these two kinds of requirement. Should one of them take precedence over the other in the requirement determination process? Give reasons why.
9. Describe the typical structure of a requirement specification document.

10. Requirements specification of a patient monitoring system is given below. Answer the remaining questions based on this:

a. Patients are taken to the hospital and discharged from a hospital. The patients can be in the regular ward, in the intensive care unit (ICU) or in the monitored aftercare unit (MACU).

b. A patient can be in several wards during his or hers stay in a hospital and within the same ward, different beds can be allocated to him or her.

c. When staying in a ward, it may happen that the patient is outside the bed from time to time (e.g. when an operation is performed). In that case, the monitoring function has to be interrupted. It has to be resumed as soon as the patient returns into the bed.

d. For each patient the system monitors a set of parameters. Depending on the patient, some patient-specific parameters have to be taken into account as well.

e. New parameters have to be added to the monitoring function when the equipment of the medical practice is changed.

f. The system has to analyze images recorded by the video camera system in order to check the patient's emotional condition.

g. All ICU- and MACU-patients are to be monitored. In the case of MACU-patients, usually the parameters are monitored less when compared to ICU-patients. In all other aspects they are treated the same way.

h. Patients in normal wards are not monitored.

i. ICU-patients are more important than MACU-patients.

j. Patient parameters are monitored by means of analog or digital devices being controlled by software. All devices are equipped with a standard hardware interface providing a digital data output. The data format used in the messages passed at the device's output depends on the function of the device.

k. The devices are connected to the computer by means of data cables. They are provided by the connector panel that every bed is equipped with. The devices are able to identify themselves; this is way the software can determine which device is connected to which data cable by a simple query.

l. Two limits are assigned to every parameter and every device: standard limits, device limits and patient limits.

m. An "Excel" database application on a PC stores both the parameters of all patients, as well as the messages that came up (alarms and display journal look-up requests).

n. In the nurses room a master display panel is installed. In the ICU room other display panels are used. The MACU rooms are equipped with portable display panels.

o. Three different kinds of messages can be displayed: alarms, status messages and journal look-ups.

p. When requested, the status message of a specific patient can be shown on every display panel.

q. A journal look-up returns all journal entries available for a specific patient and can be requested from any display panel.
    They system has to be made easy to use and reliable

11. Assign each requirement section to one or more of the following categories:

Functional Requirement
Quality Requirement
Implementation Requirement
Hardware Requirement
No Requirement

12. Check if it is possible to meet the requirement in question.
13. Check if the information given by each requirement section is consistent. In the solution table either "Yes" has to be entered, or the number of the requirement section being in contradiction to the current one.
14. Check if the information given by each requirement section is unambiguous.
15. Check if the implementation of the requirement in question can be verified in the system, when the development has been finished.

References

Chung L, Nixon A, Yu E, Mylopoulos J (1999) Non-functional requirements in software engineering. Kluwer Academic Publishers

Christel M G, Kang K C (1992) Issues in requirements elicitation. Technical Report CMU/SEI-92-TR-12

Coleman D (1992) A use case template: draft for discussion. Fusion Newsletter, April 1998

Hill R, Wang J, Nahrstedt K (2004) Quantifying non-functional requirements: a process-oriented approach. In: Proceedings of the 12th IEEE International Requirements Engineering Conference

Holtzblatt K, Beyer H R (1995) Requirement gathering: the human factor. In: Communication of the ACM, vol 38

Keil M, Carmel E (1995) Requirement gathering: the human factor. In: Communication of the ACM, vol 38

Maciaszek L A (2001) Requirements analysis and system design. Addison Wesley

Malan R, Bredemeyer D (2001) Architecture resources for enterprise advantage. Bredemeyer Consulting, Bloomfield, Indiana

Pressman R (2005) Software engineering: a practitioner's approach, 6th edn. McGraw-Hill

Sommerville I (2004) Software engineering, 7th edn. Peason Education, Ltd., Boston.

Thayer R H, Dorfman M (1990) System and software requirement engineering. IEEE Computer Society: Press Tutorial

Further Reading:

'Software Requirements Revision, Objects, Functions and States', This book discusses the latest, highly practical research results from requirements arena (Alan M Davis, 1993, Prentice Hall).

'Requirements Engineering: Processes and techniques' This book covers all aspects of the requirement engineering process and discusses specific requirements specification techniques (G. Kotonya and Ian Sommerville, 1999, john wiley and sons)

'System and software requirement Engineering' This is a collection of papers on requirement engineering that includes several relevant articles such as 'verifying and validating Software requirements', a discussion of the IEEE standard for requirements documents. (R.H Thayer and M. Dorfman, 1990, IEEE computer Society Press).

Chapter 6
Object-Oriented Analysis

6.1 Introduction to Analysis

During the requirements elicitation phase of the software life cycle, information that will be used to define the software system is gathered from numerous sources and organized for this purpose. This information comes in the form of requirements, which are categorized into functional and non-functional requirements. Functional requirements lay out what a system must do, while non-functional requirements dictate the environment and constraints within which a system must operate. At the end of the requirements phase, this information is composed into an initial system specification that provides both a general outline for the system and a detailed view of the qualities that the system will have. So, with our requirements understood and our system defined, are we ready to move onto design?

No, we are not. It is crucial to never forget the vast difference between "understood" and "well understood", and between "defined" and "well defined". The requirements specification produced during the elicitation phase does provide some level of definition for our system, but this is a rough draft at best. To ensure the success of a software engineering project, this initial specification must be scrutinized, appended, and refined as many times as needed to produce a requirements specification that satisfies the client's demands, meets the user's needs, does not exceed the system constraints, and is fully understood by the software development team. All of this must be fully accomplished before system design begins, and encompasses the second phase of the software engineering life cycle: Analysis.

Analysis is the systematic evaluation, modification, and refinement of a system's requirements, gathered during the requirements elicitation phase, into a final, functional requirements specification. During analysis, systems analysts review requirements with a goal of identifying and correcting missing or erroneous information. As a part of this, they ensure that no requirements were left out during the elicitation phase, neither due to incomplete interviews and information gathering nor due to the decision made by an engineer that some piece of information was too obvious to include. They also review the questions asked during client and user interviews, to ensure that both the interviewer and the interviewee were

R. Y. Lee, *Software Engineering: A Hands-On Approach,*
DOI: 10.2991/978-94-6239-006-5_6, © Atlantis Press and the author 2013

talking about the same thing. If not controlled, such miscommunications and misunderstandings can lead to inaccurate responses and thus incorrect requirements. Similarly, the analysts must ensure that requirements are written using terminology and concepts that are well understood by everyone involved in the project. Failure to do so can lead to a misunderstanding between those who conducted the interviews and the engineers who will be responsible for designing and building the system. This will result in a system that does not meet the client's intended requirements, even though the system is representative of their understanding of what was thought to be a complete requirements specification.

When the analysts discover errors or omissions during this evaluation period, new information is gathered to fill in the gaps, using improved techniques or new interview questions. If requirements are determined to be poorly worded, ambiguous, or incomplete, they are corrected and rewritten. This new information is then composed into a more well-refined, updated requirements specification. Various methods will be used to verify this new system definition. Then, when the results are in, the analysts will start the whole process over again. This sequence will be repeated as needed, as the requirements specification evolves from the initial rough draft to a final, workable characterization of the intended system. The resulting requirements specification must be composed of requirements that are well understood, concise, able to be measured and tested, realistic, and sufficiently detailed for system design.

6.1.1 What is Object-Oriented Analysis?

Requirements analysis is a traditional practice in the field of engineering. As we have discussed with other concepts throughout this book, the concepts behind the object-oriented paradigm have been applied to this field to produce a new practice: **object-oriented requirements analysis**. During requirements analysis, the problem statement is studied to identify objects or classes of objects and the relationship between objects. A set of scenarios or use cases are developed that help identify objects and describe the behavior of the system. The objects and their relationships are expressed graphically on an object diagram. A State Transition Diagram (STD) depicts the permitted states of an object and the events that cause a change of state. This captures the dynamic behavior of the system. Finally, functional relationships and data requirements are shown on a Data Flow Diagram (DFD) We shall extract software requirements from all three diagrams to build our software requirements specifications (SRS). A common problem in requirements analysis is determining the difference between a software requirement and a design implementation. Since the object-oriented models created during the requirements analysis phase are adorned with design information in later phases, there is a tendency to over specify, which adds design constraints to requirements. The Institute of Electrical and Electronics Engineers (IEEE) recommended practice for SRSs (IEEE 1998) provides guidance for differentiating requirements from design.

A requirement specifies an externally visible function or attribute of a system. A design describes a particular subcomponent of a system or its interfaces with other subcomponents or both. This criterion should be applied throughout the creation of the requirements analysis diagrams; the addition of any design details to the requirements models should be delayed until the design phase. Once the use case is complete, we can analyze the use case for object interactions, state changes contained within the use case, and the functional or data requirements of the use case. These requirements are discovered and documented in the corresponding object, state transition, and DFDs. Again, only externally visible objects and object interactions should be captured. Not all associations, attributes, and methods are shown in the diagrams. In addition, most of the classes represented in our object diagram will each yield a single object in the finished system. We have blurred the distinction between classes and objects. When writing specifications, it is important to state whether the requirement applies only to an object of the class or to the entire class being specified.

Once all externally visible objects and behavior have been captured graphically, it is a simple matter to translate the pictures into words. The translation is accomplished by walking through the diagrams and stating the associations depicted in plain language. It is sometimes helpful to select aggregate constructs from the object diagram and describe their requirements first. This helps establish the context for the rest of the system. We recommend conducting an informal peer review prior to translation to make sure all requirements are contained in the diagrams and that no design information has been included. Each requirement should be numbered or otherwise marked for inclusion in a requirements-tracking database. Requirements tracking is needed to complete the trace tables in the testing documentation and to verify requirements flow down from higher level specifications. In our example, requirement numbers are contained in parenthesis following the requirement. The external interface requirements are readily visible from the DFD. When capturing interface requirements, care must be taken to avoid specifying design detail when adding the DID-required data characteristics. By the same token, design constraints that form externally visible restrictions on interfaces must be specified. A detailed example of an SRS section is given in the sidebar at the end of the article titled "Sample SRS Section".

6.2 Requirements Specification and the Specification Document

A software system is characterized based on its behavior, which must be engineered to suit the needs of the client and end user. As we discussed in the previous chapter, these needs are known as requirements, and are initially gathered during the requirements elicitation phase of the software life cycle. In the last section, we introduced the concept of requirements analysis, whereby those requirements gathered during the elicitation phase are evaluated, modified, and refined in order to extend the work done during requirements elicitation into a complete, accurate, and unambiguous description of the software system. At the end of the analysis phase, a final **requirements specification** or **requirements specification statement** is formed into the **specification document**, a document that formally expresses all of the requirements that make up the system (Stiller and LeBlanc 2002).

After the system's requirements specification has been thoroughly generated, the specification document serves as the basis for the next phase in the software life cycle: system design. In order to serve this purpose, the document must be of sufficient detail to enable engineers to draw up the design (Schach 2008). Analysts must use great care when working toward this level of detail as any errors, ambiguities or omissions that are not corrected during analysis, before the finalization of the document, will be written into the design. Mistakes that are not caught will have to be corrected later in the development process, and at a much higher cost.

In addition to providing the primary resource for system design, the specification document also serves as a contract between the client and the developer. Analysts must therefore balance the engineers' need for detail with the client's need for a sufficiently understandable (non-technical) description of the product being developed. After all, the specification document provides a picture of the system that *will* be developed, and the client is not likely to elect to continue development if they are unable to comprehend, and thus agree to, the proposed system itself. To this end, the document will contain a set of acceptance criteria. These criteria constitute tests that have been agreed upon by both the client and developer which will be carried out during development and upon product completion in order to verify that the final product meets the stated needs of the client (Schach 2008). These tests will cover both the capabilities of the system (functional requirements) as well as the system's ability to operate within the necessary constraints (non-functional requirements). When the acceptance criteria are successfully met, the development team has successfully finished its job.

The analysis phase presents an important challenge for a software development team. Analysts must constantly consider the different, and often contradictory, goals of their task. Producing a final specification document that meets the needs of both the engineers and the client is critical to the successful completion of a software engineering project. The rest of this chapter discusses practices and techniques designed to meet this end.

6.2.1 Evaluating Requirements Specification

The requirements specification produced during the requirements elicitation phase will not be sufficiently accurate, complete, and unambiguous to correctly describe the software system being developed. To assume otherwise would be a costly mistake that could entirely derail a project and ruin the reputation of a software engineering firm. Instead, analysts must continue to engage the client and the end user in order to highlight incomplete or incorrect information, and then must use this information to evaluate the requirements specification. During this evaluation, analysts must keep in mind that analysis serves two distinct purposes based on two distinct groups, the client and the engineers, and that each group will view the specification from a different point of view. The vocabulary and technical information included in the specification document must thus meet the needs of both without exceeding the comprehension of either. In addition, assumptions about information made by one group cannot be assumed to be understood by the other.

To ensure that such mistakes do not occur, in depth discussions concerning the specification should be conducted amongst all of the parties involved in development (Stiller and LeBlanc 2002). Keeping in mind the issues of accuracy, completeness and ambiguity, analysts must read over the requirements in order to formulate questions about the system, which will provide the basis for these discussions. These questions often come in two major forms. The first expressly covers the information provided in the existing requirements. Is it accurate? Is it complete? Is it unambiguous? The second questions, which are much harder to compose, seek to uncover information that was left out of the original specification entirely. Often times, experts may consider some piece of information to be too obvious to include at all, or too simple to require specifying. Unfortunately, such omissions may represent critical gaps in the system's specification and may result in the reduced functionality of the final system, which may no longer meet the client's requirements. To ensure that all necessary information is included in the final requirements specification, the evaluation must be exhaustive and in depth. It is far better to provide too much information, which can be refined before the finalization of the specification document, than to provide too little.

6.2.2 Refining Requirements Specification through Prototyping

True to its object-oriented roots, the requirements analysis is an iterative process, creating a more complete, accurate, and unambiguous specification document with each cycle. At the beginning of the phase, analysts evaluate the requirements specification for errors. This information is then added to the specification to create an updated set of requirements. This updated set is then evaluated again, and the information gained from that second evaluation is used to create an even more refined version of the set. This sequence is repeated and improved upon until the requirements specification meets the needs of the project. With each iteration, the questions produced during the evaluation should better target the needs of the analysts, and, as such, the discussions that are held should be more efficient and more focused. The process should refine not only the requirements themselves, but the communication that takes place.

A popular method for producing this desired refinement is to create a mock up of the system based on the existing requirements, which will be used to evaluate its effectiveness and to identify its weaknesses. This mock up, known as a **prototype**, is essentially a scaled down version of the software system, produced with limited functionality. When working to create the prototype, certain problems, such as ambiguities and outright errors will become apparent as they hinder the creation process. Evaluating the prototype is achieved by allowing users to interact with the system and recording the experience. This method allows users to provide actual feedback about the system's functionality, and is easier to gauge than a vague discussion about intangible system characteristics (Stiller and LeBlanc 2002).

6.2.3 Verifying Requirements Specification

All requirements should be verifiable. The most common method is by test. If this is not the case, another verification method should be used instead (e.g. analysis, demonstration, inspection, or review of design). Certain requirements, by their very structure, are not verifiable. These include requirements that say the system shall never or always exhibit a particular property. Proper testing of these requirements would require an infinite testing cycle. Such requirements must be rewritten to be verifiable. As stated above all requirements must be verifiable.

Non-functional requirements, which are unverifiable at the software level, must still be kept as a documentation of customer intent; however, they may be traced to process requirements that are determined to be a practical way of meeting them. For example, a non-functional requirement to be free from backdoors may be satisfied by replacing it with a process requirement to use pair programming. Other non-functional requirements will trace to other system components and be verified at that level. For example, system reliability is often verified by analysis at the system level. Avionics software, with its complicated safety requirements, must follow the DO-178B development process.

Verifiability is necessary for a requirement, but there are other important issues as well. A requirement can be verifiable yet incorrect; and assessing verifiability alone will not detect incorrect requirements. Moreover, verification is totally irrelevant with regard to a requirement which has been overlooked. Mere analysis, inspection, or review alone will find some of these issues but, generally, is far weaker than usually is realized.

Only through effective communication between the client and the developers can a system be accurately defined, and only with this clear definition can a project hope to be successful. This process begins with the understanding of problems and of technical solutions. Then the team leaders and members who did not talk to the developer need to understand what was learned through team conversations. Finally, organizational functions such as design, engineering, marketing, docu-mentation, testing, and customers must also understand the problem, and agree/correlate to the technical solution. Customer-centered techniques necessitate face-to-face communication, continuous, synchronous team work in design meetings, shared decision-making, and consensus (Holtzblatt and Beyer 1995).

- **Involvement and Control**: Requirements can only be effectively defined when all members of the development process are involved. No one likes to feel out of control of their time, their work activities or their goals. Team members don't want their activities dictated to them. Team members really owns their process and have skills to solve particular problem. A successful requirements process includes effective ways to foster partnership between customer and designer and team members. It must reveal the ownership of the activities of the design by customers and team members (Holtzblatt and Beyer 1995).
- **Client-Developer Links**: A software project is built of techniques or channels that allow customers and developers to exchange information. We refer to these as **links**. A wide variety of links are available to software developers. The tremendous variety of links that are available today represents both opportunity and a challenge for software development managers. Opportunity is easier to obtain inputs from clients and challenge is deciding on the type of links. By focusing on links we are able to draw insights on degree of participation that should be used to engage customers in development process. Keil and Carmel lay out three basic guidelines regarding these links: the more links the better; avoid indirect links; and always be sure to consider links that may be considered non-traditional for the environment (Keil and Carmel 1995).

6.3 Analysis Modeling Concepts

In the case of Object-Oriented Analysis Design (OOAD) with UML, your models consist primarily of diagrams: static diagrams that depict the structure of the system, and dynamic diagrams that depict the behavior of the system. The dynamic diagrams allow you to trace through the behavior and analyze how various scenarios play out. With the static diagrams, you can ensure that each component or class has access to the interfaces and information that it needs to fully carry out its responsibilities. The best part is that it's very easy to make changes to these models, such as: adding, moving, or deleting a line. It is also great for reviewing the change in a diagram which takes only minutes. Contrast that with actually building the code, which can take hours to simply implement the change and hours more to test and review it.

Your core artifact of the OOAD process is the model. In fact, you will likely have multiple models:

- **Analysis Model**. This is a model of the existing system, the end user's requirements, and a high-level understanding of a *possible* solution to those requirements.

- **Architecture Model**. This is an evolving model of the structure of the solution to the requirements defined in the Analysis Model. Its primary focus is on the architecture which includes: the components, interfaces, and structure of the solution; the deployment of that structure across nodes; and the trade-offs and decisions that led up to said structure.
- **Component (Design) Models**. This is a number of models (roughly, one per component) that depict the internal structure of the pieces of the Architecture Model. Each Component Model focuses on the detailed class structure of its component, and allows the design team to precisely specify the attributes, operations, dependencies, and behaviors of its classes.

Depending on your development process, you may have even more models: a business model, a domain model, and possibly even others. The major benefit of models is that you can make *model* changes far earlier in the development cycle than you can make *code* changes, and this is also far easier. Due to the fact that you can make changes early, you can also make corrections early. And that's a good thing, because early detection and correction is cheap detection and correction. Modeling will let you catch your most costly bugs sooner which can save you a factor of 50–200 on the cost and schedule of a bug fix.

6.3.1 Analysis Object Models

Analysis modeling provides a representation of the software system from the point of view of the user. To achieve this, a model is created based on the interactions between the user and the system, and the responses that the system generates. This model, known as the **analysis object model**, describes the individual classes, attributes, and operations that are manipulated by the system through the use of UML class diagrams. These diagrams create a visual representation of the system that is made up of the various portions of the system that are seen and interacted with by the user (Bruegge and Dutoit 2004).

A complementary portion of the analysis model focuses on what takes place within the system in response to user interaction and changes in the system's state. This model, called the **dynamic model**, depicts the behavior of the software system through the use of sequence diagrams and statecharts. The sequence diagrams are used to describe a single use case based on the interactions that occur among a set of objects. The resulting image details object relationships. The statecharts, on the other hand, are used to represent the behavior of a single object, or the ways in which it responds to stimuli (Bruegge and Dutoit 2004). The dynamic model pinpoints classes, attributes, and relationships in the software system, and can also be used to indicate where, when and for what purpose new ones should be created and instituted.

6.3.2 Entity, Boundary, and Control Objects

Entity objects are classes that encapsulate the business model, including rules, data, relationships, and persistence behavior, for items that are used in your business application. For example, entity objects can represent the logical structure of the business, such as product lines, departments, sales, and regions. They could also be used to represent business documents, such as invoices, change orders, and service requests. In another scenario, entity objects could be used to depict physical items, such as warehouses, employees, and equipment. From an object-oriented perspective, an entity object represents an object in the real-world problem domain. From a relational database perspective, an entity object provides a Java representation of data from a database table. Advanced programmers can map entity objects to other types of data sources, such as spreadsheets, flat files, and XML files. Depending on how you want to work, you can automatically create entity objects from existing database tables or define entity objects and use them to automatically create database tables.

Business logic should be written into entity objects, because they consistently enforce information for all viewing of any data, accessed via any type of client interface. Business logic can include the following items:

- **Business Rules and Policy**: When adding or modifying data, you should ensure that the data complies with your organizations' procedures before adding it to the database. For example, you could increase the salary when an employee is promoted, give an employee 3 weeks of vacation after they have been at a company 3 years or change the status of an order to shipped after all items in an order have been mailed to a customer.
- **Validation Logic**: When adding new data, you should ensure that the data is valid before storing it in the database. For example, you could ensure that a job code is an existing valid job code.
- **Deletion Logic**: You should make sure that data is deleted only when appropriate and that any dependencies are handled. For example, you could prevent an on-leave employee from being wrongly removed.
- **Calculations**: You should efficiently perform data calculations in the business logic tier. For example, you could calculate an employee's monthly pay based on a given hourly rate.
- **Default Value Logic**: When creating new data, you should add appropriate default values. For example, you could provide a default benefit plan based on an employee's job code.
- **Security**: You should make sure that data is read and modified only by users with the appropriate authority. For example, you could ensure that only the direct manager of a given employee can change said employee's salary.

Boundary Objects represent the interactions between the user and the system. These often represent input/output systems which the user utilizes (Schach 2008). For example, if a user needs to extract information from the system, boundary objects will be used to define the ways in which the user communicates with the system in order to make his or her request, and the ways in which the system responds directly back to the user.

Control Objects are used to model the internal workings of the software system itself. That is, they represent the complex algorithms and computations used to process information and perform actions (Schach 2008). Control objects are the means by which use cases are fully realized from start to finish. They handle all of the activity that the system is responsible for carrying out.

6.4 Scenario-Based Modeling

In computing, a scenario is a narrative describing foreseeable interactions by various types of users (characters) and the system. Scenarios include information about goals, expectations, motivations, actions and reactions. Scenarios are neither predictions nor forecasts, but rather attempts to reflect on or portray the way in which a system is used in the context of daily activity. Scenarios are frequently used as a part of the system's development process. They are typically produced by usability or marketing specialists, often working in harmony with end users and developers. Scenarios are written in plain language, with minimal technical details, so that stakeholders (designers, usability specialists, programmers, engineers, managers, marketing specialists, etc.) have a common example for which they can focus their discussions. Increasingly, scenarios are used directly to define the wanted behavior of software; replacing or supplementing traditional Functional requirements. In the agile style of software development, scenarios are written as brief user stories. In the more deliberate style of software development, scenarios are written as structured use cases.

Scenarios can be used in various ways. First, they can be used as vision pieces. Vision pieces provide a high level picture of an envisioned system or product. They can also be used to focus on the value offered by a system, showing how it offers an advantage over the way things are. This type of scenario may be used to 'sell' an idea within the organization that is considering developing the system.

Use-oriented techniques are widely used in software requirement analysis and design. Use cases and usage scenarios facilitate better system understanding and provide a common language for communication. In this model, scenarios are organized hierarchically and they capture the system functionality at various abstraction levels including scenario groups, scenarios, and sub-scenarios. Combining scenarios or sub-scenarios can form complex scenarios. Data are also separately identified, organized, and attached to scenarios. This scenario model can be used to cross-check the UML model. It can also direct systematic scenario-based testing including test case generation, test coverage analysis with respect to requirements, and functional regression testing.

Fig. 6.1 Booch class image
(Booch 1994)

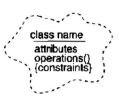

6.5 Class-Based Modeling

This section is a review of the class diagrams which were discussed earlier in the book. Class-based modeling offers a view of the system under development based on the classes that make it up. A **class diagram** is a way of visualizing a software system based on the abstractions, or classes, that make it up, and the relationships between them. Class diagrams are useful throughout the entire software development process. During the analysis phase of development, class diagrams are used to indicate the common roles and responsibilities associated with all of the entities that define the system's behavior. Class diagrams are used in the design phase to describe a system's architecture based on the structure of the classes of which it is composed. A given class diagram may not represent a system's entire class structure, but rather can be specified and tailored for the situation at hand.

The major component of the class diagram is, of course, the class. As we said earlier, a model of a class consists of the class's name, attributes, and methods. We can now add constraints upon the class to this list, such as the class's multiplicity. The Booch abstract image of a class and the important information that should be contained in the model is displayed below in Fig. 6.1.

A class diagram consists of many classes, and is used to depict their structure and relationships in a logical and meaningful way. Class diagrams are static. That is, they are used to illustrate which classes interact, but they do not go so far as to describe what occurs when they interact. In the figure below, a class diagram is used to model a customer order system. The diagram is centered around the Order class, which interacts both with a Customer class and a Payment class. Contained within the Order class is an OrderDetail class which is associated with an Item class, describing the actual item being ordered, and contains information about a specific order. From the Payment class, we find three derived classes, Credit, Cash, and Check, all of which are, quite literally, different types of Payment (Fig. 6.2).

6.6 Analysis Process

The first step of an analysis process demands that we obtain requirements and complete them as necessary. In our case, we want to describe the OOA process, so we can refer to the previous section describing default steps and activities as the

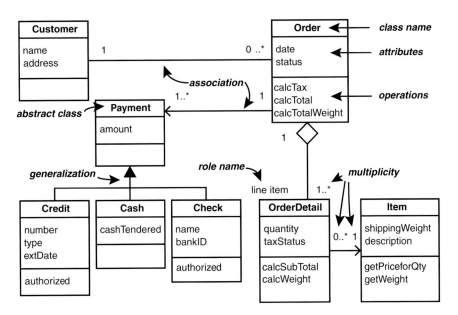

Fig. 6.2 Class diagram (Miller 2003)

requirements document for this enterprise. Subsequently, we ought to provide for system-context interaction, subsystem delineation and vocabulary development. We will, however, bypass these steps. Our abstraction level eliminates the analyst. We cannot effectively discuss system-context interaction or model construction. Additionally, the OOA process is too abstract to allow subsystems to be properly distinguished. The vocabulary consists of concepts such as: class, relationship, instance, attribute, constraint, transition network, state, transition, etc. Such a vocabulary allows us to go straight into class elaboration.

In the analysis phase, a model of the real-world application is developed showing its important properties. It abstract concepts from the application domain aid in the describing of what the intended system must do, rather than how it will be done. Most proponents of object-oriented analysis (OOA) claim that the use of object-oriented concepts in the analysis phase (i.e., OOA) increases the understanding of problem domains, that OOA promotes a smooth transition from the analysis phase to the design phase, and that OOA provides a more natural way of organizing specifications (Coad and Yourdon 1990). Extant object-oriented approaches can be classified into three categories (Monarchi and Puhr 1992): combinative approaches use different modeling techniques in different stages of the system development process; adaptive approaches apply existing techniques (e.g., data-flow diagram and entity-relationship approach) in object-oriented ways to analyze the problem domain; and pure approaches adopt an object-oriented perspective in systems analysis and design.

6.6.1 *Identifying Entity, Boundary, and Control Objects*

Transforming use cases and scenarios into an effective analysis model begins with the identification and classification of the concepts enunciated in the requirements specification. These models must be broken down and torn apart in order to pinpoint the entity, boundary, and control objects that make them up. Great care must be taken to ensure that no objects are missed, or, conversely, that an excessive number of objects are not created. It is also vital to ensure that the objects identified are correctly interpreted and classified.

This process begins with the identification and determination of **participating objects**, which are candidate objects assigned to use cases. These participating objects are used to determine which concepts are to be used and manipulated in each use case, and should be standardized across all use cases. Because these objects are defined based on the requirements elicited during the various elicitation and analysis interviews, natural language analysis can be used for identification. The system of natural language analysis, put forth by Abbott (1983), is is "an intuitive set of heuristics for identifying objects, attributes, and associations" from within the requirements specification (Bruegge and Dutoit 2004). This system is used to map various language constructs, such as nouns, verbs, and adjectives, to component models. The following list illustrates related examples:

- **Proper Noun**: Instance of a class (an object). For example, *Whiskers* the cat.
- **Common Noun**: Class. For example, a *cat*.
- **Doing Verb**: Operation. For example, Whiskers *eats*.
- **Being Verb**: Inheritance. For example, a cat *is a* kind of animal.
- **Having Verb**: Aggregation. For example, a cat *has* the fur of a mammal.
- **Modal Verb**: Constraints. For example, a cat *must be* a mammal.
- **Adjective**: Attribute. For example, a cat is *cute*.

When a use case is analyzed, these concepts can be used for object identification. Unfortunately, natural language analysis is an imprecise method. The outcome hinges on the writing style and ability of the analyst, as well as his or her consistency and level of language competence. We said earlier that inconsistency and ambiguity are highly detrimental to a requirements specification. This is never more true than when analyzing those requirements for object identification. Developers must be sure to refine and clarify the requirements specification during the identification process in order to establish a standard set of objects and ensure the use of a standard set of terms. However, even after such clarification, natural language analysis still faces another issue: "there are many more nouns than relevant classes" (Bruegge and Dutoit 2004). Beyond this, the use of nouns in normal speech does not always correspond with the concepts laid out in Abbott's heuristics. Many nouns are used not to identify objects or concepts, but to convey attributes or likenesses. In addition, multiple nouns can be used to describe the same concept, further complicating the identification process. Tearing apart the various meanings and uses of such nouns can be a very lengthy and repetitive process. For this reason, Abbott's heuristics are well suited to the initial stage of the identification process, when candidate objects are determined.

Bruegge and Dutoit have created an additional set of heuristics to be used together with Abbott's heuristics in determining each of the three analysis objects: entity, boundary, and control objects. They suggest the following list be used in identifying entity objects:

- Terms that must be clarified by developers or users to get a better understanding of the use case.
- Nouns that show up multiple times.
- Real world entities that are to be tracked by the system.
- Real world activities that are to be tracked by the system.
- Data sources.

The following list they recommend for the identification of boundary objects:

- User interface controls that must be initiated by the user.
- Forms utilized by the user to pass data to the system.
- Responses the system presents to the user, such as notices, messages, and warnings.
- NOT visual aspects of the interface.

Finally, they suggest the following list be used to in conjunction with Abbott's heuristics to identify control objects:

- One control object per use case.
- One control object per actor in the use case.
- The lifespan of a control object should correspond with the lifespan of the use case or user session being considered (Bruegge and Dutoit 2004).

6.6.2 Identifying Use Cases

The best way to find use cases is to consider what each actor requires of the system. For each actor, human or not, ask:

- What are the goals that the actor will attempt to accomplish with the system?
- What are the primary tasks that the actor wants the system to perform?
- Will the actor create, store, change, remove, or read data in the system?
- Will the actor need to inform the system about sudden external changes?
- Does the actor need to be informed about certain occurrences, such as unavailability of a network resource, in the system?
- Will the actor perform a system startup or shutdown?

Understanding how the target organization works and how this information system might be incorporated into existing operations gives an idea of a system's surroundings. That information may reveal other use case candidates. Give a unique name and brief description that clearly describes the goals for each use case. If the candidate use case does not have goals, ask yourself why it exists, and then either identify a goal or eliminate the use case. The following process describes a technique that can be used to identify use cases:

First, prioritize the candidate list based on user input and importance to the release being built and begin describing the use cases. Define the use case, considering the system as a black box, and focus on the interaction of the actors with the system. Remember that use cases can be represented both textually and graphically.

Next, describe the main interactions with the system. Focus on the priority use cases and on the basic course. These priority use cases are sequences of events and interactions that contain fundamental information about the system functions. Consider each primary function of the system in order to properly document decisions made about the actions and sequence, provide an effective communication vehicle for requirements, and serve as a set of instructions for the final implementation. Focus on the main interactions in the system. Start with an external user's interactions with the system (e.g., for a bank, start with deposit cash, withdraw cash). Create a narrative that describes what happens as the system responds to the event. Use a checklist of questions to help build a complete description. Assess your descriptions using the guidelines for use case descriptions and the use case quality checklist. Use a sequence diagram to show the messages and responses of the objects with each other to complete the sequence. In analysis, describe the message with descriptive text. As the model is refined, use message names and parameter lists. Remember that use cases do not define the object model. Return to the object model to review inheritance, examine state transitions, or document flow of control.

The next step is to structure the use case. Use cases most often deal with varying degrees of complexity. Each use case considers only those objects relevant to the use case itself. An individual object may participate in many use cases. All responsibilities of an object are easily identified by considering all of the use cases in which it participates. Even the most complex systems can usually be described with a modest number of high-level use cases. These high-level use-cases, of course, can be used for organization as many more detailed use cases as are required by the given project. As the object model gets larger and more complex, use cases may be identified for subsets of the entire model, in an effort to refine the interactions and responsibilities of objects at a more detailed level.

Finally, the use case should be extended to subordinate use cases. A subordinate use case is a sequence of events and interactions that contains supplemental information about the system functions. The subordinate use case is used to document the following:

- Alternate paths through the sequence.
- Exceptions.
- Variations in the main functionality.

Define the subordinate as a complete stand-alone use case documenting the applicable sequence. Use it to support the main use case, however, do not repeat the information. For each main use case, consider the alternatives. For example, an application received by mail may have slightly different processing, than an application received in person. Identify the main exception processes. For example, applicants for driver's license renewals may have their renewals automatically issued, unless they have outstanding summonses. Review the interactions by developing sequence diagrams for the subordinate use cases.

6.6.3 Scenario Development

The use of scenarios is a development technique by which the developer maps the possible user interactions with the system. An individual scenario represents the experience of a single actor during an interaction with the system. In order to identify the scenarios that will be used, developers observe users and create a set of scenarios to represent the functionality that the system will have. These scenarios represent hard evidence for the way in which the system will be used. They also provide another chance to gain user feedback on the system. Scenarios are distinct from use cases in that they provide information about "specific instances and concrete events" (Bruegge and Dutoit 2004). For this reason, they cannot replace use cases, but they are extremely useful tools for communication with the user and client, and for classifying that information in a way that is meaningful to the development team. The following list provides a number a scenario types (Carroll 1995):

- **As-is Scenario**: Describes a current situation. Provides a picture of the system based on scenarios derived from observing users and classifying their actions. User input can be used to ensure that the scenarios are correct and accurate.
- **Visionary Scenario**: Describes a future system. Used in refining the developer's understanding of the system being developed by serving as a point in the modeling space. Also used as a way to communicate with users in order to elicit new requirements. Commonly considered a cheap, idea-based prototype.
- **Evaluation Scenario**: Evaluates the system by describing user tasks which have been selected for use as testing criteria for the system. Used to refine and improve the functionality definitions that they test.
- **Training Scenario**: Tutorials designed to introduce a new user to, and allow that user to get acquainted with, the system. The user is walked through common tasks via a step-by-step tutorial of the system.

A scenario represents a single actor's interactions with the system, and is thus a sequence of events that the system will manage and handle. In this way, a specific scenario describes one possible process and outcome for a single use case. Because a use case may be worked through in various ways, multiple scenarios may be needed to describe it completely (Stiller and LeBlanc 2002).

6.6.4 Modeling the System

Analysis modeling uses a combination of text and diagrammatic forms to depict requirements for data, functions, and behaviors in a way that is relatively easy to understand, and, more importantly, straightforward to review for correctness, completeness and consistency. This section presents resources for conventional and object-oriented analysis (OOA) methods as well as resources for UML.

Data modeling is a method used to define and analyze data requirements needed to support the business processes of an organization. The data requirements are recorded as a conceptual data model with associated data definitions. Actual implementation of the conceptual model is called a logical data model. To implement one conceptual data model successfully, may require the implementation of multiple logical data models. Data modeling defines the relationships between data elements and structures. Data modeling techniques are often used to model data in a standard, consistent, predictable manner in order to properly manage it as a resource. The use of this standard is strongly recommended for all projects requiring a standard means of defining and analyzing the data resources within an organization. Such projects include:

- Incorporating a data modeling technique into a methodology;
- Using a data modeling technique to manage data as a resource;
- Using a data modeling technique for the integration of information systems;
- Using a data modeling technique for designing computer databases.

Data modeling may be performed during various types of projects and in multiple phases of the projects. Data models are progressive; there is no such thing as the final data model for a business or application. Instead a data model should be considered a living document that will change in response to a changing business. The data models should ideally be stored in a repository so that they can be retrieved, expanded and edited over time. Bentley (2004) determined two types of data modeling:

- Strategic data modeling: This is part of the creation of an information systems strategy, in which an overall vision and architecture for information systems is defined. Information engineering is a methodology that embraces this approach.
- Data modeling during systems analysis: In systems analysis, logical data models are created as part of the development of new databases.

6.6.5 Class Diagrams

We have described class diagrams in previous chapters. In this section, we will review that information in a way that is relevant to the analysis phase. Class diagrams are used to describe a class based on the elements that make it up, as well as its relationships to other classes. In a previous chapter, we said that class diagrams are made up of classes, interfaces, relationships and collaborations. More than one diagram may be necessary to describe a specific class, as varying levels of specificity are needed to describe the class in a specific context.

6.6.6 Use Case Diagrams

This walkthrough will set out one example of how to go about a use case analysis. There are many variations of how to develop a use case analysis, and finding the right method can take time. First, a use-case realization describes how a particular use case is realized within the design model, in terms of collaborating objects. The Realization step sets up the framework within which an emerging system is analyzed. This is where the first, most general, outline of what is required by the system is documented. This entails a rough breakdown of the processes, actors, and data required for the system. These are what comprise the classes of the analysis.

Once the general outline is completed, the next step is to describe the behavior of the system that will be visible to the potential user of the system. While internal behaviors can be described as well, this is more related to designing a system rather than gathering requirements for it. The benefit of briefly describing internal behaviors would be to clarify with potential users that the system is not missing a vital component externally due to it not being completed internally. The overall goal of this step is to provide just enough detail to understand what classes are required for the system. Too much detail can make it difficult to change the system later on.

The next step narrows down the class list into those classes that are capable of performing the behavior needed to make the system function successfully. If no classes yet exist for a system, they must be created before this step can be completed. Classes can be created in many ways from many sources. A few examples are: previous—but similar—systems, enterprise models, and data mining. Once classes are created and narrowed down, relationships must be developed between classes, now called analysis classes, which model the tasks of the system.

For each analysis class identified in the previous step, the responsibilities of the class must be detailed clearly. This will ensure that an individual class has a task to complete for which no other class in the system will also perform. The responsibilities of the different classes should not overlap.

After detailing the responsibilities of each analysis class, the relationships between the classes must be clarified next. There are four parts to this step. First, identify the classes to be used. Then, identify possible relationships between the classes. Next, for those with relationships, describe the nature of the relationship. Finally, if applicable, identify the multiplicity of the relationship, meaning determine how many of the first class correspond to one object in the second class of the relationship.

Once the relationships between classes is understood, the next process is to detail the behavior the classes will exhibit and how they will interact in order to complete the system. This entails determining how the classes communicate and send messages along the timeline of the system process being developed. This is derived from the responsibilities of the classes previously identified. Determining what class the message goes to is a simple matter of following the associations set up in the previous step.

Throughout the use case analysis so far, attributes of the classes and objects may have been discovered that are necessary for the classes to complete their tasks. These could be in the form of data variables or functions. Some of these attributes can be derived from the previous steps, while others are general assumptions from common knowledge (e.g. all operational modern-day computers have an operating system, a processor, and input/output devices).

The final step is to identify components that provide a solution to the problem domain. This would include databases to hold the data, security, exception handling, and communication between processes or programs.

6.7 Issues in Object-Oriented Analysis

Even with careful identification of sources of information and careful characterization of requirements information, there will still be many problems. It is difficult to provide a clean set of requirements. Software engineers must make sure that they are addressing the problem and not adding useless enhancements to it. Software Engineers must continuously think whether the solution to the problem is important and necessary, or else it's an enhancement. Common problems with requirement information are (Berard 1993):

- **Omissions**: We refer to the process of focusing on the essential (or important) details of an item or situation while ignoring the inessential. Very often, the initial set of user-supplied information is incomplete. This means that, during the course of analysis, the software engineer will be expected to locate and/or generate new requirements information. This new information is, of course, subject to the approval of the client.
- **Contradictions**: Contradictions may be the result of incomplete information, imprecise specification methods, a misunderstanding or a lack of a consistency check on the requirements. If the user alone cannot resolve the contradictions, the software engineer will be required to propose a resolution to each problem.
- **Ambiguities**: Ambiguities are often due to lack of precision in the specification method and incompletely defined ideas.
- **Duplications**: Replication of information in the same format. Software engineer must be careful in removing these.
- **Inaccuracies**: Most commonly inaccuracies are due assumptions. These inaccuracies must be brought to the client's attention and resolved.

- **Too much design**: One of the greatest problems in requirement analysis is finding the solution to the defined problem in the same stage. A meta-requirement is a design decision that is presented in the form of a system (product) requirement. Meta-requirements describe situations and items that are *not* externally-discernible characteristics of the system to be delivered. True meta-requirements are not suggestions. They are items that the customer absolutely requires in the solution.
- **Failure to identify properties**: Sometimes, software engineers make the mistake of assuming that any solution to the customer's problem can *only* contain items that were explicitly mentioned in the problem description and/or the problem-space module. Some of the requirements properties could be implicit and hidden in other requirements.
- **Irrelevant information**: One straightforward way to describe a solution to a problem is to focus on what is essential, while ignoring what is inessential.

6.8 Chapter Summary and Conclusions

A requirement is a quality that a software system must have. This could be an activity that it must perform, an interface that it must contain or an environment within which it must operate. Requirements are criteria that a system must meet if it to work as intended, and thus must be considered mission critical if a software engineering project is to be successfully completed. In the last chapter, we discussed the process of eliciting these requirements from the client and from the end user. Those requirements first elicited, however, are often times far from perfect.

In this chapter we discussed the analysis phase of the software life cycle. This phase is focused on refining, improving and finalizing the requirements specification, a formalized understanding of the system that will be the primary resource for the rest of the development process. At the beginning of the analysis phase, requirements usually suffer from one or more of the following problems:

- omitted information
- contradictory information
- ambiguous information
- inaccurate information
- irrelevant information

The analysis phase seeks to correct these problems through the systematic evaluation, modification and refinement of a system's requirements. The system requirements gathered during the requirements elicitation phase are then complied into a final, functional requirements specification. During analysis, systems analysts review requirements with a goal of identifying and correcting, missing or erroneous information. Interviews used in the requirements elicitation phase are reviewed. When the analysts discover errors or omissions during this evaluation period, new information is gathered to fill in the gaps by carrying out new, improved interviews. At the end of the analysis phase, a final requirements specification or requirements specification statement is formed into the specification document, a document that formally expresses all of the requirements that make up the system.

6.9 Exercises

1. Does Object-oriented Analysis preclude any kind of software implementation?
2. Describe how, in the face of changing problems, practices and people, analysis has evolved, or should have evolved. Include a consideration of the appropriateness of the terms that have been used for the job.
3. Consider a file system with GUI. The following objects were identified from a use case describing how to copy a file from a floppy disk to a hard disk: FILE, ICON, Trashcan, Folder, Disk, Pointer. Start the analysis process on this.
4. Assuming the same file system before, consider a scenario consisting of selecting a File on a floppy, dragging it to Folder and releasing the mouse. Identify attributes and look for irrelevant objects.
5. Depict the above scenario through UML diagrams (any model described in the chapter can be used).
6. Consider a traffic light system at a four-way crossroads. Assume the simplest algorithm for cycling through the lights. Identify objects, states, attributes and draw a statechart diagram describing them.
7. You are asked to design a group scheduler. The software allows you to arrange meetings among individuals or groups and to reserve a limited number of conference rooms. Implement the object-oriented analysis phase on this.
8. Perform OOA on the following requirements for a checkers game:

   - Checkers is played by two people, one with light and one with dark pieces.
   - Pieces move diagonally and opponents are captured by jumping over them.
   - A Piece can only move and capture forward.
   - When a piece makes it to the other side of the board, it becomes a king and can move diagonally in any direction as far as it wants.
   - Capturing is mandatory. A piece (or king) that is captured is removed from the board.
   - The player who has no pieces left or cannot move anymore has lost the game.

9. Complete the OOA phase for a Tic-Tac-Toe Computer Game using the following description. Tic-Tac-Toe is a 2 player game played on a 3 × 3 board. Players alternate placing a marker in one of the squares on the board. If a player gets 3 of their markers in a row, they win. If all squares are full, and neither player has 3 in a row, the game is a draw. Statistics should be kept for each player on total games won, lost and drawn. Traditional Markers are X and O.

10. Design using UML any of the OOA models for worm game application. In this game, a worm, controlled by the user, navigates the 2 dimensional screen and eats pieces of "candy". When a piece is eaten, the worm grows by one segment. If the worm runs into the wall, or runs into itself, the worm dies and the game is over. As time increases, the speed of the worm increases. You should focus on the states of the application, but not the worm. Start from the initial state (application is not initialized) and final state (application is destroyed). Define the states between these two. Then connect states with events and transitions (events can come to the game from "outside" also).

Consider, for example, the following events:

- Start game
- Stop game
- Restart game
- Worm died
- Candy eaten
- Timer tick

Are there any other events or transitions, such as time events, signals, or self-transitions?

References

Abbott RJ (1983) Program design by informal English descriptions. Commun ACM 26(11):882–894
Bentley LD, Dittman KC, Whitten JL (2004) Systems analysis and design methods
Berard EV (1993) Essays on object-oriented software engineering, vol. 1. Prentice-Hall, Inc..
Booch G (1994) Object-oriented analysis and design with applications. The Benjamin/Cummings Publishing Company, Inc., New York
Bruegge B, Dutoit A (2004) Object-oriented software engineering: using UML, patterns, and java, 2nd edn. Pearson Education, Ltd., Upper Saddle River
Carroll JM (1995) Scenario-based design: envisioning work and technology in system development
Coad P, Yourdon E (1990) Object-oriented analysis. PrenticeHall, Englewood Clis, New Jersey
Holtzblatt K, Beyer HR (1995) Requirement gathering: the human factor. Commun ACM, vol 38
IEEE Computer Society (1998) Software Engineering Standards Committee, and IEEE-SA Standards Board. IEEE Recommended Practice for Software Requirements Specifications, Institute of Electrical and Electronics Engineers
Keil M, Carmel E (1995) Customer-developer links in software development. Commun ACM, vol 38
Miller R (2003) Practical UML: a hands-on introduction for developers. Available via Embarcadero. http://edn.embaracardero.com/article/31863. Accessed 1 Dec 2003
Monarchi DE, Puhr GI (1992) A research typology for object-oriented analysis and design. Commun ACM 35(9):35–47
Schach S (2008) Object-oriented software engineering. McGraw-Hill Higher Education, Boston
Stiller E, LeBlanc C (2002) Project-based software engineering. Addison-Wesley, Boston

Chapter 7
System Design

System design involves a process to fulfill user requirements. Constraints imposed on the project and on the user requirements may interact in complex ways to produce several designs rather than a single design. The result of the design phase is several system design deliverables as a design report which is ready for evaluation. System design as described by Sommerville is concerned with how the system functionality is to be provided by different components of the system. The activities in the process are (Sommerville 1996):

- Partition requirements: During this phase requirements are analyzed and formed into groups.
- Identify sub-systems: This activity is concerned with identifying different sub-systems which meet the requirements.
- Assign requirements to subsystems: In this phase, the requirements are assigned to subsystems. In principle there is never a clean match between requirements partitions and identified sub-systems.
- Specify sub-system functionality: this may be seen as a system design phase or software system design phase.
- Define sub-system interfaces: This critical activity involves defining the interfaces that are provided and expected by each sub-system (Fig. 7.1).

The system analysis and design phase depend on each other. This Phase of the SDLC continues from the Detailed System Analysis and describes how the proposed system will be built. The design is specific to the technical environment that the system will operate in and the tools used in building the system. The results of this phase significantly impact the build and implementation phases of the system. The project manager is responsible for producing the deliverables associated with the detailed system design. A good system design process should therefore result in a system which can be implemented in either hardware or software. However, the project manager usually delegates responsibility for some or all of these deliverables to the development team. If some or all of the phase's deliverables have been delegated, the project manager maintains overall responsibility for producing quality deliverables submitted.

R. Y. Lee, *Software Engineering: A Hands-On Approach*,
DOI: 10.2991/978-94-6239-006-5_7, © Atlantis Press and the author 2013

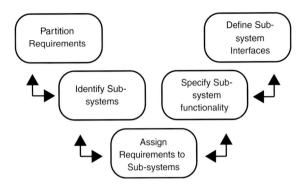

Fig. 7.1 System Design
Process

7.1 Categories of System Design

There are two broad approaches called structure-oriented design and object-oriented design. Detailed categories include:

- Global-based systems
- Group-based systems
- Local-based systems

7.1.1 Global-Based Systems

Global-based design refers to complete overhaul or replacement of all the systems design components. The following changes are common in this design (Burch 1992):

- Old output formats are changed to new output display devices
- New processes are developed
- Input to systems is through improved techniques rather than erroneous ones.
- Old hierarchical database is converted to relational database
- Various control are installed
- New platforms are used

To develop a global-based systems design, several alternatives are presented. Once they are thoroughly reviewed by systems professionals, it is moved to the evaluation phase.

7.1.2 Group-Based Systems

The group based system, though connected to global-based system, services a branch, department or a special group of users in the enterprise. These groups will have special purpose to work and make proper decisions. System designers who are working on a group-based system should have a workable global based system already in place. The design focus is generally on output, input, process, and control which pertain to a specific group (Burch 1992).

7.1.3 Local-Based Systems

A local-based system is typically designed for few people, or for an ad hoc application. A systems professional is generally called into work with the user in analyzing and designing requirements, evaluating different systems, acquiring one, and implementing it, along with network and support. Another example is an executive information system developed for decision makers (Burch 1992).

7.2 Function-Oriented Approach

A function-oriented design strategy relies on decomposing the system into a set of interacting functions with a centralized system state shared by these functions. Functions may also maintain local state information, but only for the duration of their execution. Function-oriented design has been practiced informally since programming began. Programs were decomposed into subroutines which were functional in nature. In the late 1960s and early 1970s several books were published which described 'top-down' functional design. Function-oriented design conceals the details of an algorithm in a function, but system state information is not hidden. This can cause problems because a function can change the state in a way which other functions do not expect. Changes to a function and the way in which it uses the system state may cause unanticipated changes in the behavior of other functions. A functional approach to design is therefore most likely to be successful when the amount of system state information is minimized and information sharing is explicit.

Systems whose responses depend on a single stimulus or input and which are not affected by input histories are naturally functionally-oriented. Many transaction-processing systems and business data-processing systems fall into this class. In essence, they are concerned with record processing where the processing of one record is not dependent on any previous processing. An example of such a transaction processing system is the software which controls automatic teller machines (ATMs) which are now installed outside many banks. The service provided to a user is independent of previous services provided so it can be thought of as a single transaction (Sommerville 1996). Figure 7.2 shows the design view of the function-oriented approach.

Fig. 7.2 Function–oriented
design view

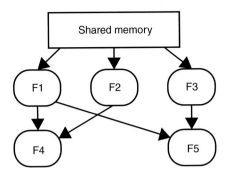

7.3 Structure-Oriented Approach

The structure-oriented approach to system design is a set of methodologies, techniques, and modeling practices based on the structured approach to software engineering. This approach can be broken down into two subcategories: the process-oriented approach and the data-oriented approach. Both of these focus on identifying all of the data attributes that will constitute the system being developed. In this section, we will explain these approaches and their associated practices, as well as the ways in which they come together to form the larger structure-oriented approach to system design.

7.3.1 Process-Oriented Approach

Process-oriented approach is used to examine input, output and processing of a given application to determine the data needs of the system. Applying the process-oriented approach, system professionals look at all reports, display screens, calculations and decisions needed for a process. Data flow Diagrams are used for a process-oriented approach. The process-oriented approach works well if the systems professionals know input, process and output from a system in advance. This approach is effective for transaction-based applications such as accounts, payroll etc. Each of these applications usually has a very stable set of input.

7.3.2 Data-Oriented Approach

The system professionals working with future users use a data-based approach. This approach is used when processes of a system, inputs, and outputs are undefined. The focus of the data requirements for the decisions is based on the data. The first step of a data-oriented approach is to discuss potential decisions that will be made from the system with the users of the system. The second step in data-oriented approach is to model the decision support system through the use of flexible modeling tools such as an entity relationship diagram (ERD). The third step in data-oriented approach is to divide each criterion into its attributes. The fourth step is to break down the attributes identified above into their most fundamental data components.

7.3.3   Creating the Data Dictionary

Once the data is identified for a system using either process-oriented or data-oriented approach, systems professionals use the information to create a data dictionary. The data dictionary includes the following attributes:

- Size
- Type
- Description
- Limits and exceptions
- Ranges
- Security level
- Access privileges

   Three aspects of data dictionaries are:

- Changes: The data dictionary is not a static document that is never changed
- Description: Attributes names must describe data defined fully
- Order: Attributes should be arranged in some form of standard order

7.4   Object-Oriented Approach

The design process is concerned with describing how a requirement is to be met by the design product. In other words, design is a creative process of transforming the problem into a solution. Good design is the key to effective engineering. However, it is not possible to formalize the design process in any engineering discipline. It must be practiced and learnt by experience and study of existing system (Turner et al. 2003). Software design can be viewed in the same way. We use the requirements specification to define the problem. Then, we declare something to be a solution to the problem if it satisfies all the requirements in the specification. The nature of the solution may change as the solution is described or implemented (Pfleeger 2001).

   Object-oriented design is a design strategy based on information hiding. It differs from the functional approach to design in that it views a software system as a set of interactive objects with its own private state, rather than as a set of functions that share a global state. Outside the business systems domain it is the predominant design strategy for new software systems. In an object-oriented design, the system state is decentralized and each object manages its own state information. Objects have a set of attributes defining their own state and operations which act on these attributes. Objects are usually members of an object class whose definition defines attributes and operations of class members. These may be inherited from one or more super-classes so that a class definition need only set out the differences between that class and its super-classes. Conceptually, objects communicate by exchanging messages; in practice, most object communication is achieved by an object calling a procedure associated with another object.

The stages in object-oriented approach according to Sommerville (2004) are:

1. Understand and define the context and the modes of use of system
2. Design the system architecture
3. Identify the principal objects in the system
4. Develop design models
5. Specify object interface

All the activities here are interleaved and influence each other. Here, objects are identified and the interfaces fully or partially specified as the architecture of the system is defined. As the object models are produced, these individual object definitions may be refined, which leads to changes to system architecture. The aim of the object-orientation is to employ reusable components rather than writing the modules from scratch. This approach would result in increased systems development productivity and higher systems quality (Burch 1992).

In the preceding section, it was remarked that in identifying the benefits that could be obtained through using the principle of information hiding, (Parnas 2001) also recognized that it was difficult to produce such structures by following any well-formed set of procedures. By the time the object-oriented philosophy began to coalesce in the late 1970s, it was obvious that this difficulty with providing any form of design process that incorporated encapsulation still remained a significant problem, and, indeed, that the problems were increased further by the nature of the object-oriented model being so very different from the forms previously experienced. A further spur to finding a design process that could encompass object-oriented principles came from the development of the Ada programming language, which became an ANSI standard in 1983. While the 1983 form of Ada is not strictly an object-oriented programming language, it can be considered to be object-based in its form, since its structures support the use of:

- **Abstraction**, both in terms of data typing and through the generic mechanism with the latter allowing for some abstraction in the description of the algorithmic part;
- **Encapsulation**, since the scope of data instances can be controlled via the private/public mechanism;
- **Modularity**, through the use of the package construct (and arguably by using the 3 task and the procedure mechanisms).

7.4.1 Component-Based Design

Component-based software engineering (CBSE) is commonly considered the next step after object-oriented programming. It is not surprising that components are often related to objects and sometimes the term component is simply used as a synonym for object. However, the concepts of components and objects are independent, although most component models are based on object-oriented concepts. To avoid further confusion we will briefly characterize objects and components and outline their differences.

7.4.2 Components and Objects

Objects are entities that encapsulate state and behavior, and have a unique identity. The behavior and structure of objects are defined by classes. A class serves multiple purposes: First, it implements the concept of an abstract data type (ADT) and provides an abstract description of the behavior of its objects. Class names are often used as type names in strongly typed systems. Second, a class provides the implementation of object behavior. Third, a class is used for creating objects, that is, instances of the class.

Nearly all modern component models are based on the object-oriented programming paradigm. The basic premise of object-orientation is to construct programs from sets of interacting and collaborating objects. This does not change with component based approaches. Components are similar to classes. Like classes, components define object behavior and create objects. Objects created by means of components are called component instances. Both components and classes make their implemented functionality available through abstract behavior descriptions called interfaces.

Unlike classes, the implementation of a component is generally completely hidden and sometimes only available in binary form. Internally, a component may be implemented by a single class, by multiple classes, or even by traditional procedures in a non-object-oriented programming language. Unlike classes, component names may not be used as type names. Instead, the concept of type (interface) and the concept of implementation are completely separated. Finally, the most important distinction is that software components conform to the standards defined by a component model.

7.4.3 Component Models

A component model defines a set of standards for component implementation, naming, interoperability, customization, composition, evolution, and deployment. A component model also defines standards for associated component model implementations, i.e., the dedicated set of executed software entities that are required to support the execution of any component that conforms to said component model.

There are numerous component models currently available. The main competing component models today are OMG's CORBA Component Model (CCM), Microsoft's (D)COM/COM family, and SUN Microsystems JavaBeans and Enterprise JavaBeans. We need generally accepted component models to create a global component market-place. It is not necessary to agree on one standard, but at the same time there should not be too many standards. The market share of a particular standard has to be large enough to make the development of compliant components worthwhile. In this chapter we comment on important elements constituting a component model (Weber et al. 2000).

In the global software component marketplace, components are independently deployed and subject to third-party composition. This marketplace requires standards. Standards for communication and data exchange among components from different component producers are obvious. Such an interoperability standard, sometimes called a wiring or connection standard, is a central element in a component model. Other basic elements of a component model are standards for interfaces, naming, meta data, customization, composition, evolution, and deployment.

A component model can also have specialized standards for describing domain specific features required for certain applications. For example, the composition of components in domains with concurrent activities requires appropriate standardized threading models and synchronization mechanisms. An open distributed processing system requires standards for remote method invocation and security.

7.4.4 The Component Concept

Although the goal of reusing elements of one system in other systems has long been associated with the object-oriented paradigm, it really has a much longer history. Actual reuse through object-orientation would appear to be quite difficult to achieve. At the 'system facilities' level there are some successful examples such as Java's Abstract Windowing Toolkit (AWT). For this type of example, reuse is motivated both by the need to avoid rewriting major low-level elements of software, and also by the influence of human factors, since users generally like to see a consistent presentational style for the images on a screen, regardless of the application producing them.

For other domains in which design is an important process, the idea of component reuse is fairly well established, although systematic practices to support such reuse are relatively informal. One motivation for reuse of components is that it reduces the manufacturing costs of the final product, something that of course does not have any parallel for software development and distribution. Indeed, although the concept of 'product lines' appears to have become established by the early 1900s, the adoption of manufacturing (and hence design) reuse on an incredibly large scale would appear to have been highly motivated by the need to increase manufacturing volume drastically during the Second World War.

Perhaps one of the most visible examples of designing around reusable components that can be encountered in the current era is that of the motor car. While a given manufacturer's models may differ substantially in appearance, many elements such as switches, instruments, starter motors etc. will be common across manufacturers. Design reuse is also (if less visibly) used very successfully in such domains as electronics, as well as in the building industry (for example, through the standardization of dimensions for windows, doors, pipes), and in many other domains. The motivation may well be ease of both manufacturing and maintenance. While the former is more relevant to software, the latter may also be a significant factor when viewed across the often-long lifetimes of software products, even if maintenance of these is interpreted in a rather different way.

While such reuse may often be centered upon quite small elements, larger, possibly composite, ones are reused too (car engines provide a good example). However, there are two important characteristics of such reuse that we need to note here.

- The first is that it is commonly based upon well-defined functionality. Most physical components have very well defined roles (starter motor, pump, switch, etc.), making it easy for the designer to identify the appropriate manufacturer's catalogues, and then search them in order to view what is available to them.
- The second is that the elements themselves have well-defined interfaces. Indeed, an important corollary of this is that there may also be several manufacturers who are able to provide a given component ('second sourcing'). Substitution may be an exact functional and non-functional match (as it tends to occur for integrated circuits), or may differ slightly in terms of non-functional characteristics, while still conforming to the specified interface.

These are not accidental properties, but rather ones that are driven by several economic factors. These include the need to minimize the cost of manufacturing an item, pressure to maintain a marketplace position, and the user's need to protect their supply chain (here the 'user' is another manufacturer who makes use of a given component for integration into their own product). Sometimes the standards necessary to enable this emerge from marketplace factors, leading to the acceptance of one manufacturer's format as a standard for all; at other times an industry may set up a standards body to undertake the role of agreeing standards. Whatever the route leading to the standards, there is significant pressure on manufacturers to conform to them. For the engineering designer, as mentioned above, catalogues of components are now readily available in many domains, with examples ranging across electronic and electrical, to mechanical and civil engineering. However, the *ways* in which these catalogues are used during the design process appear to be a rather more elusive concept. A good example of this is given in Pugh, which provides the following quotation from Cooke:

> The designer of electronic-based products has available an enormous range of basic building blocks of high or still increasing complexity. What he often does not have is

either training or well-established conceptual tools for working out levels of sophistication.

A situation which still seems largely unchanged similarly in Pahl et al. (1996), widely cited as a repository of engineering design knowledge, the discussion of 'design catalogues' is almost entirely confined to consideration of how such a catalogue should be constructed. The authors suggest that component classification should be based upon function, since the assumption is that the catalogue will be searched for components that will meet specific sub functions of the conceptual design. Indeed, their view of component reuse is very much that this is a subsidiary element of the design process.

Turning to software, the above characteristics take very different forms. Functionality is apt to be blurred and can be extended or modified with relative ease, whereas no-one would even think of modifying the design of a car's starter motor so that it can also be used to power the engine's cooling fan. It is easy to generate variants of a software unit, and hence there are few catalogues of software components only of the end products. Interfaces are rarely standardized to any great degree and producers are much less motivated to conform to such standards that may exist. Likewise, although standards bodies may exist, they are likely to be less effective than their manufacturing counterparts. Second, sourcing of components from more than one supplier in order to protect a supply chain exists only in a limited form, —although the motivations for adopting this practice may not be so different. All of this is important when we come to examine the ways in which the component concept has been mapped on to the software domain. In the rest of this section we examine how the concept has been interpreted, identify the characteristics of a software component, and consider how business models may have to be modified to cope with these characteristics. The following sections then examine more design-centered ideas about how to design with components and how to design components for reuse, as well as considering the effects of the 'proprietary factor'.

7.5 Structured Versus Object-Oriented System Design

With structured thinking you would start by forming a skeleton framework of an overall plan, and from that plan work downwards to sort out all the structural elements at an ever increasing level of detail. With object-oriented thinking, you do not need to have a fixed or definite plan of the final structure, but you might start anywhere, building up a structure from small self contained subsections which are fitted together as you go along.

7.5.1 Modularity

In structure-oriented design, a module is a unit of software code that performs a well defined function. In object-oriented design, a module is an object that encapsulates attributes and program code to behave in a certain manner. Modularity is a degree to which modules are standardized and independent, and show variety in use. If any systems design is composed of n modules, the connections between modules should be maximum n (n − 1) because too many connections lead to error. Controlling the amount and form of communication between modules is the essence of modularity, and the key objective of modularity is autonomous, stand-alone modules. But object-oriented proponents argue that a structure-oriented approach cannot build designs that are highly independent, or very loosely tied to other modules.

7.5.2 Top-Down Versus Bottom-Up Design

In the **top-down** model an overview of the system is formulated without going into detail for any part of it. Each part of the system is then refined by designing it in further detail. Each new part may then be refined again, defining it in yet more detail until the entire specification is detailed enough to validate the model from the highest-level specification describing the project as a whole, or the application logic, downwards to individual operations. By contrast in **bottom-up** design, individual parts of the system are specified in detail. The parts are then linked together to form larger components, which are in turn linked until a complete system is formed. Working up from the specific operations in the problem domain that you know you will need to perform is a main concept in the bottom-up design. A designer working from the top down will start by thinking about the program's main event loop, and plug in specific events later. A designer working from the bottom up will start by thinking about encapsulating specific tasks and glue them together into some kind of coherent order later on. The end of the stack you start with matters a lot because the layer at the other end is quite likely to be constrained by your initial choices. In particular, if you program purely from the top down, you may find yourself in the uncomfortable position where the domain primitives your application logic and your wants don't match the ones you can actually implement. On the other hand, if you program purely from the bottom up, you may find yourself doing a lot of work that is irrelevant to the application logic—or merely designing a pile of bricks when you were trying to build a house. Figure 7.3 shows an example of the top down approach.

7.5.3 Reusability

The big promise of the object-oriented design approach is reusability. Designers aim at creating libraries so that systems professionals can look through object class catalogs to select the appropriate object class and reuse it. In structured design, SCLC goes through all the phases from user requirements to systems design, to

Fig. 7.3 Top down design

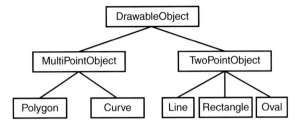

detailed system design. Object-oriented design has led to object-oriented approach in the software world.

7.6 Object-Oriented Design Concepts

Object-oriented design intuitively revolves around the specification and elicitation of objects. The purpose of OOD is not only to determine what objects are needed, but the methods and attributes of these objects. Relationships between the objects also must be determined, and in some manner documented. This documentation, even though it is not intended to be executed by a computer, must be capable of human understanding.

7.6.1 Abstractions

A model is essentially an **abstraction** of the real world. It captures only the essential and relevant characteristics of the real world (Jia 2003). Abstraction should lead to the development of models. These models should be able to mimic the behavior and form of the physical world when implemented. Just like the real world understanding of an entity, an abstraction can only maintain a portion of the actual information concerning the entity. For example, if you were to abstract a chair (the common ordinary dining room table type) into a class you very easily could come up with attributes such as height, weight, color, if it can swivel, the material it is made out of etc. This may sound like a perfectly complete, including any other items you may realized were missing from my list. Yet, there are many more items that could be added to both our lists; where the raw materials originated, density, age, manufacturer and how much dust resides on it. The list could go on forever and that is why only the important aspects of the chair (or anything else) should be included in the abstraction.

7.6.2 Architecture

Large systems can be decomposed into sub-systems that provide some related set of services. The initial design process of identifying these sub-systems and establishing a framework for sub-system control and communication is called **architectural design** (Sommerville 2004). Object-oriented Architecture is very close in comparison to that of the more commonly known architecture, that of homes and buildings.

This parallel is very useful for constructing mental images of software architecture. Software architecture suffers from the same caveats of traditional architecture. Some of the major parallels are that:

- Different models exist for both software architecture and a building architect.
- Bad design cannot be made right through implementation.
- Elegant design does not guarantee proper implementation.

Using the above listed correlations between designing object-oriented software and designing a home, it is easier to see the most important aspect is a well designed architecture. Software though may not be tangible in the same sense that a building is, but it still has very real implications. Poorly architected software can cause fiscal harm possibly easier than poorly architected buildings.

7.6.3 Design Patterns

A **design pattern** represents a generic and reusable solution to a recurring problem. Design Patterns were first published en masse by Gamma et al. in 1995. Gamma et al. were able to separate design patterns into three distinct groups (Jia 2003):

1. Creational patterns: concern the creation of objects.
2. Structural patterns: these patterns deal with the composition of objects.
3. Behavioral patterns: these patterns reflect the interactions of objects within a system.

7.6.4 Modularity

Modules, or classes, are the most important derivation of object-oriented design. This being said, **modularity** is the use of divide and conquer to create a set of cohesive and loosely coupled modules (Jia 2003). This means that each module is an entity on its own connected to the other modules in the system by simple and loose connections. To do this, each module performs a specific function or serves a unique purpose. Any module in this system can be replaced by any other module that maintains the same interfaces for interconnecting modules.

7.6.5 Encapsulation

Modularity is achieved mainly by the separation of interface from implementation. This separation is known as **encapsulation**. With a correctly encapsulated object the developer does not need to know how the internals of the class work, they need to merely know the input parameters and the corresponding return type. Each of these independent modules allows for greater simplicity of the system due to property that you can remove any module and replace this module with another that offers the same interfaces. This replacement and interface agreement does not, however, result in guaranteed simplicity. This is due to the fact that the functionality of the object can be obscured by poor naming conventions and insufficient documentation. As the internals of the object are unknown it may be difficult to determine its correct use when documentation is unavailable.

Encapsulation is a method of hiding implementation details from the consumers of the object. Just because the internal implementation may not be available to anyone using the object, this does not mean that you can write poor code internally and not worry since the interface is the only portion that is observed. The effects of your programming will be noticed and all interfaces rely on proper internal composition of the class to create satisfactory results.

7.6.6 Refinement

As a project, the progress from concept to delivery can make many details change or become clearer. This extends to not only the project understanding and implementation as a whole, but to each component, class, object and subsystem. A well designed and implemented architecture will permit refinement. **Refinement** is a modification to the system resulting from any attitude, desire, or requirement (functional or non-functional), as well as any intrinsic or extrinsic event that concerns the project. Although it is impossible to prevent alterations to specifications after a project has begun, it is the part of good design practice to have the understanding how these concepts will be handled.

Business models are necessary to convey business ideas from the client to the design and implementation teams. These models should not be static, but dynamic in nature to provide for the most fluid and natural process of implementing of changes. Keeping track of requirements using use case diagrams and a list of requirements is a simple and inexpensive way of maintaining system functionality with the client's expectations (Schach 2008). Since Object-Oriented Design is iterative, these changes can be implemented in varying stages and they are not always necessarily required to be rushed to the production floor.

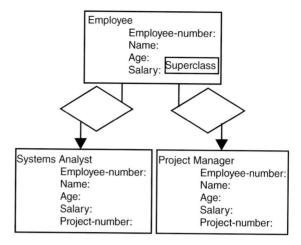

Fig. 7.4 Example of a class diagram

7.6.7 Class Design

There are various design principles that allow for classes and their objects to gain the most from object-oriented design. Classes describe the attributes and methods of objects. Collectively classes can be enumerated with those that they are related to. Collective class enumeration details the interactions of the classes and their relationships with one another (Fig. 7.4).

How to get from a design concept to the model shown above can be a cumbersome process. Schach points to an iterative and incremental three step approach (Schach 2008). This method is described in the Architectural Design portion of this chapter. However, at this point it is useful to know that successful design methodologies allow for the maximum amount of reuse and growth with the least complexity.

7.6.8 Subsystems and Classes

A correct modular design revolves around a sliding scale of granularity. This granularity can be as coarse as the entire project or as fine as a single class, or even smaller with the attribute of a class. Subsystems are one of the most useful levels of abstraction when a developer wishes to gain an overview of how to componentize a system. **Subsystems** are merely a collection of modules where some are visible to other subsystems and some modules are not externally visible (Booch 1994). These subsystems and the classes that compose them provide many benefits for developers that include:

1. The ability to logically break a system into segments more easily understood by people.

Fig. 7.5 Top-Level Module
Diagram (Booch 1994)

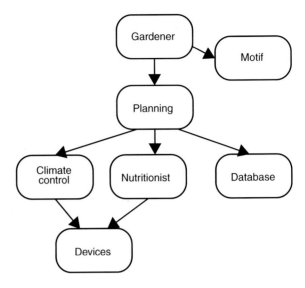

2. The ability to isolate errors based on the component failure.
3. The ability to loosely couple subsystems in the same way classes are loosely coupled providing the ability to replace one subsystem with another offering the same interfaces (Fig. 7.5).

Like anything else poorly designed or implemented, subsystems that are of bad quality provide little to no benefit to anyone. There are a few considerations to make the optimal subsystem organization. First, think of the system as interactive parts, such as what parts can function without the others (normally the ones seen outside of the system). You must also consider if there is logic carried out that can be implemented via inputs and outputs. This can be seen in the "Planning" module of Fig. 7.5. The gardener in this scenario would provide the planning information, such as the number of plants and their variety, and the planning module would provide the pertinent information to each of the modules below it using the appropriate interfaces. There may also be accessible controls. In this scenario they are grouped in the "Devices" module.

7.6.9 Services and Subsystem Interfaces

Each module must provide some service or functionality otherwise they would not need to be included in the system. To do this, each service needs an interface to the service requestor(s). This interface is a subsystem interface, and subsystem interfaces should function similarly to those of class level interfaces. They should provide the smallest pieces of data necessary as well as retain only one functionality.

7.6.10 Coupling and Cohesion

Coupling measures the degree of independence and interaction between modules. A module's independence results from its freedom from the modification of its variables by other objects (Burch 1992). Thus, if two modules have very little interaction they are said to be **loosely coupled.** The opposite being **tightly coupled**, or when two modules have a great level of interaction. When two modules are tightly coupled they are said to be dependent on the other. Dependency causes one module to be modified when the other is modified.

If two modules have no interaction then they would have no relationship. This, however, is not relevant as it is only pertinent to realize coupling when it extends to coexisting entities. The coupling to be concerned with is that of two modules that interact. Good coupling is that of when two modules share data. Better coupling results from smaller pieces of data. In general, the smaller and less complex the data is, the looser the coupling.

The measure of how closely components are related is known as **cohesion**. Cohesion, unlike coupling, is better the more of it that there is. There are several forms of cohesion: coincidental, logical, temporal, procedural, communicational, sequential and functional (Sommerville 2004). Modules should be loosely coupled, meaning they communicate by passing the most basic data available. Highly cohesive means that they should maintain as many forms of cohesion with the modules in the system.

7.7 Architectural System Design

Architecture, when concerning software concerns the implementation or design. This is how you can name UNIX applications and client–server or embedded systems as an architectural style. Similarly, these concepts when applied to design can form multiple genres of design styles which can include Model Driven Architecture, Service-Oriented Architecture, Object-oriented Architecture and the like. All these methodologies have some things in common such as iteration and implementation in small increments.

The architectural system design is used to reflect the system as planned and to help flush out problems before implementation. A common model is typically used for the platform on which a model is designed, though it is not necessarily consistent due to the complexity of large system design. A system design model consists of diagrams and text in some uniform notation. The model should contain classes, interactions, and how these classes and interactions build a working system. Schach describes a three step iterative and incremental system for class design (Schach 2008):

Step 1: The first step is functional model. This is where the scenarios are designed using use case models.

Step 2:   The next step is to design a class diagram. Determine the attributes and the
          methods of each class.
Step 3:   Dynamic modeling is the final step. In this step the actions of all classes
          and subclasses should be described in a state chart.

You may be wondering what is meant by "iterative and incremental". What
iterative means is that this will continue over and over again in the same basic
form, but with slight modifications to the inputs each time. Incremental in this case
means that the whole project may not need tackled at the same time. It may be
necessary to get a general overview of the system and then break the architecture
down into smaller units or subsystems. Putting these terms together shows that this
process is not a big bang approach, where you go from nothing to something with
little in between. In fact with this approach it is the sheer opposite.

This architecture is very much akin to city planning and development. When a
city is being planned the planners begin by zoning the land they have to work with
to determine what function it will serve, such as residential, industrial, commercial, etc. This is the same as creating a functional model where actors are used to
showing the interaction with the system. City planners use maps and zoning code
to show how people will interact in that part of the city. Second, city planners
would need to attract business, or display some reason for people and their money
to come to where ever it is this new city will be. The layout of each business and
the resulting development (for example the homes to house employees of a large
factory) can be seen as the classes and their relations to one another. Finally,
highways, utilities and services must be in place. In order to do this it needs to be
understood what, when and how each entity needs to function. This is closely akin
to a state chart where the systems function is laid out for closer examination. This
example is very reliant on the fact that the method is incremental and iterative. If
the planners had to fill every inch of the city instantly at its conception they would
never succeed, but since details can be created and modified over time it becomes
much easier to manage the development process.

7.7.1 Data Design

Data hiding or encapsulation has been the concern of object-oriented design since
its inception. Code reuse creates an abundance of easily accessible code entities for
easy and tested use. The next step in code reuse is a common data representation
format. Abstract Data Types (ADTs) are the answer to this problem. The modules
resulting from the procedural programming proceeding OOD give no hint on how
to implement them as meaningful components (Elienes 1995).

For instance, without ADT's a programmer may produce several separate
pieces of code, individually and invariably differently from each other or they
could create the least common denominator of the data type and allow for specific
types to be applied dynamically. Assume this programmer is creating a queue, a

queue enqueues and dequeues, and holds some sort of entity after it is enqueued and before it is dequeued. This behavior remains no matter if the queue contains strings, integers, or people objects. Making this queue flexible enough to hold all these types is proper data design.

7.7.2 Organization and Refinement

The iterative nature of the software development model allows the greatest ease of refinement. The refinement can consist of a more loosely coupled organization to greater cohesion. It is generally a given that software (or any work for that matter) will not be perfect in the first installment or the last. Allowing for refinement, reorientation, and testing provides software engineers a means to understand and resolve some of the problems in their work.

7.8 Issues in Object-Oriented Analysis

Even with careful identification of sources of information and careful character-ization of requirements information, there will still be many problems. It is dif-ficult to provide a clean set of requirements. Software Engineers must make sure that they are addressing the problem and not adding useless enhancements to it. Software Engineers must continuously determine if their solution to the problem is important and necessary, or if it's an enhancement. Problems with requirement information are (Berard 1993):

- **Omissions**: We refer to the process of focusing on the essential (or important) details of an item or situation while ignoring the inessential. Very often, the initial set of user-supplied information is incomplete. This means that during the course of analysis, the software engineer will be expected to locate and/or generate new requirements information. This new information is, of course, subject to the approval of the client.
- **Contradictions**: Contradictions may be the result of incomplete information, imprecise Specification methods, a misunderstanding, or lack of a consistency check on the requirements. If the user alone cannot resolve the contradictions, the software engineer will be required to propose a resolution to each problem.
- **Ambiguities**: Ambiguities are due to a lack of precision in specification method and incompletely defined ideas.
- **Duplications**: Replication of the information in the same format or replication of information in different places of same format. Software engineer must be careful in removing these.
- **Inaccuracies**: Most of the inaccuracies would be due assumptions. These inaccuracies must be brought to the client's attention and resolved.

- **Too much design**: one of the greatest problems in requirement analysis is finding the solution to the defined problem in the same stage. A metarequirement is a design decision that is presented in the form of a system (product) requirement. Metarequirements describe situations and items that are *not* externally-discernible characteristics of the system to be delivered. True metarequirements are not suggestions. They are items that the customer absolutely requires in the solution.
- **Failure to identify properties**: Sometimes, software engineers make the mistake of assuming that any solution to the customer's problem can *only* contain items that were explicitly mentioned in the problem description and/or the problem-space module. Some of the requirements properties could be implicit and hidden in other requirements.
- **Irrelevant information**: One straightforward way to describe a solution to a problem is to focus on what is essential, while ignoring what is inessential.

7.9 Chapter Summary and Conclusions

A requirement is a quality that a software system must have. This could be an activity that it must perform, an interface that it must contain, or an environment within which it must operate. Requirements are criteria that a system must meet if it is to work as intended, and thus if a software engineering project is to be successfully completed. In the last chapter, we discussed the process of eliciting these requirements from the client and from the end user. Those requirements first elicited, however, are far from perfect.

In this chapter we discussed the analysis phase of the software life cycle. This phase is focused on refining, improving, and finalizing the requirements specification, and a formalized understanding of the system that will be the primary resource for the rest of the development process. At the beginning of the analysis phase, requirements usually suffer from one or more of the following problems:

- omitted information
- contradictory information
- ambiguous information
- inaccurate information
- irrelevant information

The analysis phase seeks to correct these problems through the systematic evaluation, modification, and refinement of a system's requirements gathered during the requirements elicitation phase, into a final, functional requirements specification. During analysis, systems analysts review requirements with a goal of identifying and correcting missing or erroneous information. Interviews used in the requirements elicitation phase are reviewed. When the analysts discover errors or omissions during this evaluation period, new information is gathered to fill in the gaps by carrying out new, improved interviews. At the end of the analysis phase, a final requirements specification or requirements specification statement is formed into the specification document, which is a document that formally expresses all of the requirements that make up the system.

7.10 Exercises

1. Does object-oriented analysis preclude any kind of software implementation?
2. Describe how, in the face of changing problems, practices, people, and analysis has evolved, or should have evolved. Include a consideration of the appropriateness of the terms that have been used for the job.
3. Consider a file system with GUI. The following objects were identified from a use case describing how to copy a file from a floppy disk to a hard disk: FILE, ICON, Trashcan, Folder, Disk, Pointer. Start the analysis process on this.
4. Assuming the same file system before, consider a scenario consisting of selecting a File on a floppy, dragging it to a Folder and releasing the mouse. Identify attributes and look for irrelevant objects.
5. Depict the scenario from exercise 7.4 through UML diagrams (any model described in the chapter can be used).
6. Consider a traffic light system at a four-way crossroads. Assume the simplest algorithm for cycling through the lights. Identify objects, states, attributes and draw a state chart diagram describing them.
7. You are asked to design a group scheduler. The software allows you to arrange meetings among individuals or groups, and to reserve a limited number of conference rooms. Implement the object-oriented analysis phase on this.
8. Perform OOA on the following requirements for a checkers game:

   - Checkers is played by two people, one with light and one with dark pieces.
   - Pieces move diagonally and opponents are captured by jumping over them.
   - A piece can only move and capture forward.
   - When a piece makes it to the other side of the board, it becomes a king and can move diagonally in any direction as far as it wants.
   - Capturing is mandatory. A piece (or king) that is captured is removed from the board.
   - The player who has no pieces left or cannot move anymore has lost the game.
   - Complete the OOA phase for a Tic-Tac-Toe Computer Game using the following description: Tic-Tac-Toe is a 2 player game played on a 3 × 3 board. Players alternate placing a marker in one of the squares on the board. If a player gets 3 of their markers in a row, they win. If all squares are full, and neither player has 3 in a row, the game is a draw. Statistics should be kept for each player on total games won, lost and drawn. Traditional Markers are X and O.
   - Design using UML and any of the OOA models for a worm game application. In this game, a worm, controlled by the user, navigates the 2 dimensional

screen and eats pieces of "candy". When a piece is eaten, the worm grows by one segment. If the worm runs into the wall, or runs into itself, the worm dies and the game is over. As time increases, the speed of the worm increases. You should focus on the states of the application, but not the worm. Start from the initial state (application is not initialized) and the final state (application is destroyed). Define the states between these two. Then connect states with events and transitions (events can come to the game from the "outside" also).

Consider, for example, the following events:

- Start game
- Stop game
- Restart game
- Worm died
- Candy eaten
- Timer tick

Are there any other events or transitions, such as time events, signals, or self-transitions?

References

Berard EV (1993) Essays on object-oriented software engineering, vol 1. Prentice-Hall, Inc..

Booch G (1994) Object-oriented analysis and design with applications. The Benjamin/Cummings Publishing Company, Inc., New York

Burch J G (1992) Systems analysis, design, and implementation. Boyd and Fraser Publishing Company, Boston, MA

Elienes A (1995) Principles of object-oriented software development. United Kingdom University Press, Cambridge, United Kingdom

Jia X (2003) Object-oriented software development using java, 2nd edn. Pearson Education Inc., Boston

Pahl, G., & Beitz, W. Engineering Design: A Systematic Approach. ed. K. Wallace. 1996

Parnas DL (2001) On a 'buzzword': hierarchical structure. In Pioneers and their contributions to software engineering, pp. 499–513. Springer, Berlin, Heidelberg

Pfleeger SL (2001) Software engineering: theory and practice, 2nd edn. Prentice Hall, Upper Saddle River, NJ

Schach S (2008) Object-oriented software engineering. McGraw-Hill Higher Education, Boston

Sommerville I (2004) Software engineering, 7th edn. Peason Education, Ltd., Boston

Sommerville I (1996) Software engineering, 5th edn. Peason Education, Ltd., Boston

Turner M, Budgen D, Brereton P (2003) Turning software into a service. Computer 36(10):38–44

Weber CA, Current J, Desai A (2000) An optimization approach to determining the number of vendors to employ. Supply Chain Manage: Int J 5(2):90–98

Chapter 8
Object-Oriented Design

8.1 Overview of Object-Oriented Design

Object design is primarily adding details to the requirements analysis and making implementation decisions. Object design serves as the basis for implementation in an object-oriented paradigm. During object design, developers define solution domain objects to bridge the gap between the analysis model and the hardware/software platform defined during system design. This includes precisely describing object and subsystem interfaces, selecting off-the-shelf components, restructuring the object model to attain design goals such as extensibility and understandability, and optimizing the object model for performance. An object model describes how a component or system works, down to programming language classes or some other level that can be coded. The result of the object design activity is a detailed object model annotated with constraints and precise description for each element (Bruegge and Dutiot 2004). The following figure shows object design in the software lifecycle (Bruegge and Dutoit 1999). "Object design should consist solely of expanding the requirements model to account for the complexities introduced in selecting a particular implementation—e.g. multiple computational resources, added objects to manage other objects, added objects to manage external interfaces, continue from analysis to design" (Coad and Yourdon 1990) (Fig 8.1).

Eliens describes the distinction between object-oriented analysis and design primarily as emphasis—emphasis on modeling the reality of the problem domain versus emphasis on providing an architectural model of a system that lends itself to implementation (Eliens 1995).During object design we close the gap between the application objects and the off-the-shelf components by identifying additional solution objects and refining existing objects. This is shown in Fig. 8.2. Object design includes Reuse, Service Specification, Object Model Restructuring, and Object Model Optimization. Object design like system design is not algorithmic. It's the developers who restructure and optimize the object model to address design goals such as maintainability, extensibility, efficiency, response time or timely delivery. Analysis reduces the gap between the problem and the machine by identifying objects representing problem-specific concepts. System design reduces

R. Y. Lee, *Software Engineering: A Hands-On Approach*,   147
DOI: 10.2991/978-94-6239-006-5_8, © Atlantis Press and the author 2013

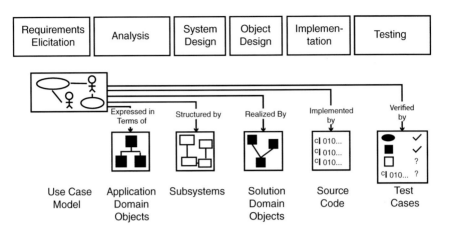

Fig. 8.1 Software life cycle activities

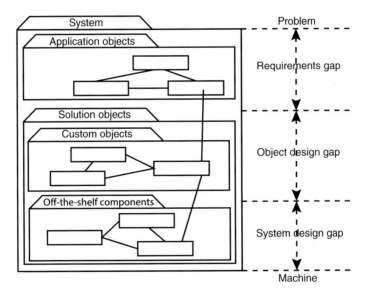

Fig. 8.2 Object design closes the gap between the application objects and the off-the-shelf components

the gap between the problem and machine through a virtual machine, using reusable class and libraries. After several iterations of analysis and system design, the developers are usually left with a few pieces missing. These pieces are found during object design. Some of these pieces are new solution objects, adjusting off-the-shelf components, and specifying each subsystem interface and class (Bruegge and Dutiot 2004).

8.1.1 First Steps to OOD

Edward Berard presents the following steps as if they were sequential, some of them may be re-ordered, and some may even be accomplished in parallel.

The first part of the OOD process requires that the software engineer accomplish two different goals: identify the objects of interest, and specify how these objects will affect a solution to the problem. A software engineer must construct an object-oriented model of the proposed solution. The object-oriented model can be accomplished using any one of a number of strategies:

(a) Writing a paragraph: Identifying the objects from the nouns, pronouns, noun phrases, adjectives etc.
(b) Constructing a graphical model using such things as semantic networks, state transition diagrams, Petri net graphs, or any other variety of diagrams.
(c) Using an automated tool to sketch a solution, e.g. Smalltalk, Trellis.

Once the strategy is agreed upon, the objects of interest can be identified. The designer should also gather information about each object and localize it with the appropriate object.

The next major step requires the designer to identify suffered and required operations for each object. A "suffered" operation is something which happens to a given object, e.g. adding an element to a list, directing an elevator to go up, and querying a temperature sensor as to its current value. A "required" operation is an operation for an object other than the encapsulating object, and is necessary to ensure the correct and desired behavior of the object. For example, if we wish a list object to be ordered, it will require that the items contained in the list furnish a "<" (less than) operation (Berard 2002).

Object design includes four groups of activities:

Reuse Class libraries and components are selected for basic data structures and services. Design patterns are selected for solving problem and for protecting specific classes from future change. Often, components and design patterns need to be adapted before they can be used. This is done by wrapping custom objects around them or refining them by using inheritance.

Interface Specification During this activity, the subsystem services identified during system design are specified in terms of class interfaces, including operations, and exceptions. The result of service specification is a complete interface specification for each subsystem. The subsystem specification is called subsystem Application Programmer Interface (API).

Restructuring activities manipulate the system model to increase code reuse or meet other design goals. Restructuring activities include transforming n-ary associations into binary associations, implementing binary associations as references, merging two classes into a single class or collapsing classes, and rearranging to increase inheritance and packing.

Optimization activities address performance requirements of the system model. This includes changing algorithms to respond to speed, memory requirements, reducing multiplicities in associations to speed up queries, rearranging execution order, and adding derived attributes to improve the access time to objects.

Object design is not sequential. The activities described occur concurrently. Interface specifications and reuse activities occur first, yielding an object design model that is then checked against the use cases. Restructuring and optimization activities occur next, once the object design model for subsystem is relatively stable. Focusing on interfaces, components and design patterns result in an object design model that is easier to modify.

8.1.2 Activities in OOD

During object design our understanding of each object deepens. As the focus of system design was on identifying large chunks of work that could be assigned to individual teams or developers, the focus of object design is to specify the boundary between objects. At this stage a large number of developers refine and change many objects and their interfaces. Interface specification activities of object design include (Bruegge and Dutiot 2004):

- Identifying missing attributes and operations
- Specifying type signatures and visibility
- Specifying invariants
- Specifying preconditions and postconditions

During system development we would have made decisions about the system and produced several models:

- The analysis object model describing the entity, boundary and control objects that are visible to user. The analysis object model includes attributes and operations for each object.
- Subsystem decomposition describes how these objects are partitioned into cohesive pieces that are realized by different teams of developers. Each subsystem includes high-level service descriptions that indicate which functionality it provides to others.
- Hardware/Software mapping identifies the components that make up the virtual machine on which we build solution objects. This may include classes and APIs defined by existing components.
- Boundary use cases describe, from the user's point of view, administrative and exceptional cases that the system handles.
- Design patterns selected during object design reuse describe partial object design models addressing specific design issues.

All these models however reflect partial view of the system. The goal of the object design is to produce the object design model that integrates all of the above information into a coherent and precise whole. The interface specification includes the following activities:

- Identify missing attributes and operations: During this activity, we examine each subsystem service and each analysis object.
- Specify visibility and signatures: During this activity, we decide which operations are available to other objects and subsystems and which are used only within a subsystem.
- Specify contracts: During this activity, we describe in terms of constraints the behavior of the operations provided by each object.

8.2 Object-Oriented Design Concepts

8.2.1 Functional and Non-Functional Requirements

Requirements come in two main types: functional and nonfunctional. Nonfunctional requirements are the requirements that are not related to how the system functions. These include, but are not limited to: performance, reliability, and aesthetics. Functional requirements on the other hand provide information on how the system operates. From the interfaces of classes to the user interface requirements are all examples of functional requirements.

8.2.2 Types, Signatures and Visibility

During analysis we identified attributes and operations without specifying their types or their parameters. During object design we redefine the analysis and system design models by adding type and visibility information. The type attribute specifies the range of values the attribute can take and the operations that can be applied to the attribute. For example attributes could be integer, float etc. The type of the attribute also denotes the operations we could apply, like addition or subtraction. Given an operation, the tuple made out of the types of its parameters and the type of return value is called a signature of the operation. Visibility of an attribute or an operation specifies whether it can be used by other classes or not. UML defines four levels of visibility:

- Private: A private attribute can be accessed only by the class in which it is defined.
- Protected: A protected attribute or operation can be accessed by the class in which it is defined and any descendent class.
- Public: A public attribute or operation can be accessed by any class.
- Package: Accessible to only other classes in the package.

Visibility is denoted in UML by prefixing the symbol—for private, # for protected, + for public and ~ for package to the name of the attribute or operation.

8.2.3 Object Contracts: Invariants, Preconditions and Postconditions

Contracts are constraints on a class that enable the caller and callee to share the
same assumptions about the class. Contracts include three types of constraints:

Invariant is a predicate that is always true for all instances of a class. Simply
speaking, this is to say the class is/has/will [*any word here*] is a predicate. This
simply allows for a description of contracts between classes.

Precondition is a predicate that must be true before an operation is invoked.
Preconditions are used to specify constraints that a caller must meet before calling
operation. An example of this would be check to make sure a number that will be
used to divide by is not zero, as in most instances this results in undesirable
behavior.

Postcondition is a predicate that must be true after an operation is invoked.
Postconditions are used to specify constraints that the object must ensure are
fulfilled after the invocation of operation (Bruegge and Dutiot 2000).

8.3 Reuse Concepts: Objects and Design Patterns

8.3.1 Objects

Class diagrams are used to model application domain and solution domain.
Application objects also called "domain objects", as they represent concepts of
domain that are relevant to the system. They are identified by the application
domain specialist and domain specialists and end users. Solution objects represent
components that do not have a counterpart in the application domain, such as
persistent data stores, user interface objects or middleware. They are identified by
developers. An example of each is shown below (Bruegge and Dutoit 1999). Most
of the entity objects identified in analysis process are application objects. They are
independent and specific to the system. During analysis the solution objects
identified are visible to the user such as forms, windows etc. During system design
we identify solution objects, and during object design we refine both application,
as well as solution objects needed to bridge the object design gap (Bruegge and
Dutiot 2004) (Figs. 8.3 and 8.4).

Fig. 8.3 Requirement
Analysis (Language of
application Domain)

Fig. 8.4 Object Design
(Language of solution
Domain)

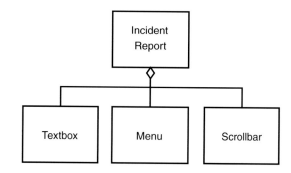

8.3.2 Inheritance

Inheritance is the ability of a class to take on the attributes and methods of a
superclass (Schach 2008). The ability to transfer details from a higher level class to
a lower level permits code reuse. Classes can be seen as children and parents.
Children have all the same properties as their parents, but may implement their
own new methods and attributes. Their children, in turn, by definition have all the
attributes of their parent class and what could be termed their grandparent class.
Though all object-oriented languages support inheritance, not all languages support multiple inheritance. True to its name, multiple inheritance is the ability for a
child class to be derived from multiple parent classes.

8.3.3 The Liskov Substitution Principle

The Liskov Substitution principle provides a formal definition for specification
inheritance. It essentially states that if a client code uses the methods provided by a
superclass, then developers should be able to add new subclasses without having to
change the client code (Bruegge and Dutiot 2004).

8.4 Specifying Interfaces

During the object design our understanding of each object deepens. As the focus of
system design was on identifying large chunks of work that could be assigned to
individual teams or developers, the focus of object design is to specify the
boundary between objects. At this stage a large number of developers refine and

change many objects and their interfaces. Interface specification activities of object design include (Bruegge and Dutiot 2004):

- Identifying missing attributes and operations
- Specifying type signatures and visibility
- Specifying invariants
- Specifying preconditions and postconditions

During system development we would have made decisions about the system and produced several models:

- The analysis object model describing the entity, boundary, and control objects that are visible to user. The analysis object model includes attributes and operations for each object.
- Subsystem decomposition describes how these objects are partitioned into cohesive pieces that are realized by different teams of developers. Each subsystem includes high-level service descriptions that indicate which functionality it provides to others.
- Hardware/Software mapping identifies the components that make up the virtual machine on which we build solution objects. This may include classes and APIs defined by existing components.
- Boundary use cases describe, from the user's point of view, administrative and exceptional cases that the system handles.
- Design patterns selected during object design reuse describe partial object design models addressing specific design issues.

All of these models, however, reflect partial view of the system. The goal of the object design is to produce an object design model that integrates all of the above information into a coherent and precise whole. The interface specification includes the following activities:

- Identify missing attributes and operations: During this activity, we examine each subsystem service and each analysis object.
- Specify visibility and signatures: During this activity, we decide which operations are available to other objects and subsystems, and which are used only within a subsystem.
- Specify contracts: During this activity, we describe in terms of constraints the behavior of the operations provided by each object.

8.5 Interface Specification Concepts

8.5.1 Class Implementer

A good class definition and implementation must have many desirable properties. Because a class captures an abstraction, the class must have all of the properties of a good abstraction. But as an executable representation, a class must also have other properties beyond those of an abstraction. The three major properties that a class must possess are that it be (Implementing a class 2006):

- **Correct**: An object of the class must maintain its state properly and respond to invocations of its methods with the expected results. The most stringent level of correctness is a formal proof, though such proofs are usually reserved for safety–critical components due to the high cost of proving correctness of software. More common are less stringent levels achieved through testing. No amount of testing establishes the formal correctness of a class. However, useful and measurable degrees of reliability and dependability can be achieved.

- **Safe**: Classes should provide reliable and correct results when implemented in a manner consistent with the documentation. That is, they should not cause harm to the system or provide harmful parameters when assigned to another object type.

- **Efficient**: The object should make efficient use of the processor and memory resources. While the most important means for ensuring efficiency reside in the overall system design and the choice of critical data structures and algorithms, the class implementer has several ways of improving the efficiency of the implementation. Given the desired properties of abstractions and those of a class, it is clear that good object-oriented design is a creative and challenging activity.

The class implementer is responsible for realizing the class under consideration. Class implementers design the internal data structures and implement the code for each publication operation. The implementer of classes must be a proficient user of basic tools. In addition to the obvious need for a compiler, is the need for proficiency in using a symbolic debugger during development and testing. Any system beyond the most trivial ones also require the use of tools to (re)build the executable system from its source code when some part of that code has changed. For trivial systems, all of the code can be recompiled every time any part of it is changed. With modest and large systems, this brute force approach is impractical because the time to recompile and relink the system is excessive. However, it is not practical for the implementer to remember all of the ways in which parts of the system must be rebuilt when some parts have changed. Thus, tools must be used to make the (re)building process efficient and accurate.

The class user invokes the operations provided by the class under consideration during the realization of another class, called the client class. For class users, the interface specification discloses the boundary of the class in terms of the services it provides and the assumptions it makes about the client class.

The class extender develops specializations of the class under consideration. Like class implementers, class extenders may invoke operations provided by the class of interest, and focus on specialized versions of the same services. For them, the interface specification both specifies the current behavior of the class, and any

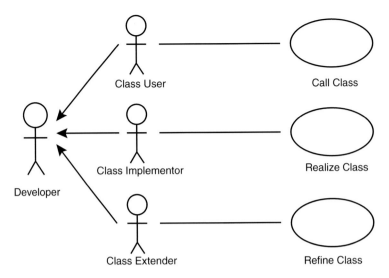

Fig. 8.5 Class Implementor, Class extender, Class user role

constraints on the services provided by the specialized class. Figure 8.5 shows the role of each of the above described developers in class implementation.

8.5.2 Object Constraint Language

The Object Constraint Language (OCL) is a notational language for the analysis and design of software systems. It is a subset of the industry standard Unified Modeling Language (UML) that allows software developers to write constraints and queries over object models. These constraints are particularly useful, as they allow a developer to create a highly specific set of rules that govern the aspects of an individual object. As many software projects today require unique and complex rules that are written specifically for business models, OCL is becoming an integral facet of object development. The Object Constraint Language (OCL) is a language that enables one to describe expressions and constraints on object-oriented models and other object modeling artifacts. An *expression* is an indication or specification of a value. A *constraint* is a restriction on one or more values of (or part of) an object-oriented model or system. Various constraint languages have been used in object-oriented modeling methods (Syntropy, Catalysis, and BON), and programming languages (Eiffel). The OCL is a standard query language, which is part of the Unified Modeling Language (UML) set by the Object Management Group (OMG) as a standard for object-oriented analysis and design.

8.5.2.1 Types of Expressions

Expressions can be used in a number of places in a UML model such as:

- To specify the initial value of an attribute or association end.
- To specify the derivation rule for an attribute or association end.
- To specify the body of an operation.
- To indicate an instance in a dynamic diagram.
- To indicate a condition in a dynamic diagram.
- To indicate actual parameter values in a dynamic diagram.

8.5.2.2 Types of Constraints

There are four types of constraints:

- An *invariant* is a constraint that states a condition that must always be met by all instances of the class, type, or interface. An invariant is described using an expression that evaluates to true if the invariant is met. Invariants must be true all the time.
- A *precondition* to an operation is a restriction that must be true at the moment that the operation is going to be executed. The obligations are specified by postconditions.
- A *postcondition* to an operation is a restriction that must be true at the moment that the operation has just ended its execution.
- A *guard* is a constraint that must be true before a state transition fires.

8.5.2.3 The Context of an OCL Expression

The *context definition* of an OCL expression specifies the model entity for which the OCL expression is defined. Usually this is a class, interface, data type, or component. In terms of the UML standard, this is called a *classifier*. Sometimes the model entity is an operation or attribute, and rarely it's an instance. It is always a specific element of the model, usually defined in a UML diagram. This element is called the *context* of the expression (Introduction to OCL 2005).

Next to the context, it is important to know the *contextual type* of an expression. The contextual type is the type of the context, or of its container. It is important because OCL expressions are evaluated for a single object, which is always an instance of the contextual type. To distinguish between the context and the instance for which the expression is evaluated, the latter is called the *contextual instance*. Sometimes it is necessary to refer explicitly to the contextual instance. The keyword *self* is used for this purpose.

For example, the contextual type for all expressions in Fig. 8.6 is the class *LoyaltyAccount*. The precondition (*pre: i > 0*) has context as the operation *earn*.

Fig. 8.6 UML class diagram as an example for context definition (Introduction to OCL 2005)

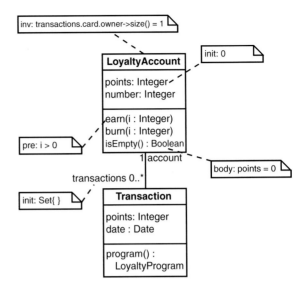

When it is evaluated, the contextual instance is the instance of *LoyaltyAccount* for which the operation has been called. The initial value (*init: 0*) has context as the attribute *points*. The contextual instance will be the instance of *LoyaltyAccount* that is newly created.

8.5.2.4 Invariants on Attributes

The simplest constraint is an invariant on an attribute. Suppose our model contains a class *Customer* with an attribute *age*, then the following constraint restricts the value of the attribute:

context Customer **inv**:
age $> = 18$

8.5.2.5 Invariants on Associations

One may also put constraints on associated objects. Suppose our model contains the class *Customer* that has an association to class *Salesperson*, with the role name *salesrep* and multiplicity 1, then the following constraint restricts the value of the attribute *knowledgelevel* of the associated instance of Salesperson:

Context Customer inv:
salesrep.knowledgelevel $> = 5$

8.5.2.6 Collections of Objects

In most of the cases, the multiplicity of an association is not 1, but more than 1. Evaluating a constraint in these cases will result in a collection of instances of the associated class. Constraints can be put on either the collection itself, e.g. limiting the size, or on the elements of the collection. Suppose in our model the association between Salesperson and Customer has the role name *clients* and multiplicity 1..* on the side of the Customer class, then we might restrict this relationship by the following constraint:

context Salesperson **inv**:
clients- > size() <= 100 and clients- > forAll(c: Customer I c.age > = 40)

8.5.2.7 Pre- and Postconditions

In pre- and postconditions, the parameters of the operation may be used. Furthermore, there is a special keyword called *result* which denotes the return value of the operation. It can be used in the postconditions only. As an example we have added an operation *sell* to the Salesperson class:

context Salesperson::sell(item: Thing): Real
pre: self.sellableItems- > includes(item)
post: not self.sellableItems- > includes(item) and result = item.price

8.5.2.8 Derivation Rules

Models often define derived attributes and associations. A derived element does not stand alone. The value of a derived element must always be determined from other (base) values in the model. Omitting the way to derive the element value will result in an incomplete model. Using OCL, the derivation can be expressed in a derivation rule. In the following example, the value of a derived element *usedServices* is defined to be all services that have generated transactions on the account:

context LoyaltyAccount::usedServices : Set(Services)
derive: transactions.service- > asSet()

8.5.2.9 Initial Values

In the model information, the initial value of an attribute or association role can be specified by an OCL expression. In the following examples, the initial value for the attribute *points* is *0*, and for the association end *transactions,* it is an empty set:

context LoyaltyAccount::points : Integer
init: 0

context LoyaltyAccount::transactions : Set(Transaction)
init: Set{ }

Note the difference between an initial value and a derivation rule. A derivation rule states an invariant: The derived element should always have the same value that the rule expresses. An initial value, however, must hold only at the moment when the contextual instance is created. After that moment, the attribute may have a different value at any point in time.

8.5.2.10 Body of Query Operations

The class diagram can introduce a number of query operations. Query operations are operations that have no side effects, i.e., do not change the state of any instance in the system. Execution of a query operation results in a value or set of values, without any alterations in the state of the system. Query operations can be introduced in the class diagram, but can only be fully defined by specifying the result of the operation. Using OCL, the result can be given in a single expression, called a *body expression*. In fact, OCL is a full query language, comparable to SQL. The use of body expressions is an illustration thereof.

The next example states that the operation *getCustomerName* will always result in the name of the card owner associated with the loyalty account:

context LoyaltyAccount::getCustomerName() : String
body: Membership.card.owner.name

8.5.2.11 Broken constraints

Note that evaluating a constraint does not change any values in the system. A constraint states "this should be so". If for a certain object the constraint is not true, in other words, it is broken, the only thing we can conclude is that the object is not correct, and it does not conform to our specification. Whether this is a fatal error or a minor mistake, what should be done to correct the situation is not expressed in the OCL (Introduction to OCL 2005).

8.5.3 OCL Collections

Local attribute: The constraint involves an attribute that is local to the class of interest.

Directly related class: The expression involves the navigation of a single association to a directly related class.

Indirectly related class: The constraint involves the navigation of a series of associations to an indirectly related class.

All of the constraints can be built using a combination of these three basic cases of navigation that are listed below. Once we know how to deal with these cases of navigation, we can build any constraint.

- OCL sets are used when navigating a single association.
- OCL sequences are used when navigating a single ordered association.
- OCL bags are multisets: they can contain he same object multiple times. Bags are used to accumulate the objects when accessing indirectly related objects (Bruegge and Dutiot 2004).

8.5.4 OCL Quantifiers

There are two operations on collections which enable us to iterate over collections and test expressions on each element:

1. Forall (variablel expression) is true if expression is true for all elements in the collection.
2. Exists (variablel expression) is true if there exists at least one element in the collection for which expression is true (Bruegge and Dutiot 2004).

8.6   Managing Object Design

There are two primary management challenges during object design. The first challenge is an increased communication complexity: The number of participants involved during this phase of development increases dramatically. The object design models and code are the result of the collaboration of many people. Management needs to ensure that decisions among these developers are made consistently with project goals. The second challenge is the consistency with prior decisions and documents: Developers often do not appreciate completely the consequences of analysis and system design decisions before object design. When detailing and refining the object design model, developers may question some of these decisions and reevaluate. The management challenge is to make sure all documents reflect the current state of development (Bruegge and Dutiot 2004).

8.6.1   Documenting Object Design

The first section of the ODD is an introduction to the document. It describes the general trade-offs made by developers, guidelines and conventions, and an overview of the document. Interface documentation guidelines and coding conventions are the single most important factor that can improve communication between developers during object design. A few examples of conventions include (ee.hawii.edu):

- Classes are named with singular nouns.
- Methods are named with verb phrases, fields, and parameters with noun phrases
- Error status is returned via exception, not a return value.

The second section of the ODD, package(s), describes the decomposition of subsystems into packages and the file organization of the code. This portion details exactly where to find the files and how the subsystems are divided logically. This is important before moving to section three where the details of the classes themselves are covered.

The third section, class interfaces, describes the classes and their public interfaces. This includes an overview of each class, its dependencies with other classes and packages, its public attributes, and, finally, operations or exceptions they can raise.

The initial version of the ODD can be written soon after the subsystem decomposition is stable. The ODD is updated every time new interfaces become available or existing ones are revised. In Java, the javadoc tool generates webpages from the source code comments. Developers annotate interfaces and class declarations with tagged comments.

For a system of useful size, the ODD represents a large amount of information that can translate to several hundreds or thousands of pages of documentation. Moreover, the ODD evolves rapidly during object design and integration, as developers understand better other subsystem's needs and find faults with their specifications (Bruegge and Dutiot 2004).

8.6.2 Roles in OOD

Object design is characterized by a large number of participants accessing and modifying a large amount of information. To ensure that changes to interfaces are documented and communicated in an orderly manner, several roles collaborate to control, communicate, and implement changes. These include the members of the architecture team who are responsible for inter-team communication and configuration managers who are responsible for tracking change. The following are the roles assigned during object design:

- The core architect develops coding guidelines and conventions before object design starts. The core architect is also responsible for ensuring consistency with prior decisions documented in the System Design Document (SDD) and Requirements Analysis Document (RAD).

- The architecture liaisons document the public subsystem interfaces for which they are responsible. This leads to a first draft of the ODD, which is used by developers. The architecture liaisons and the core architect form the architect team.
- The object designers refine and detail the interface specification of the class or subsystem they implement.
- The configuration manager of a subsystem releases changes to the interfaces and the ODD once they become available. The configuration manager also keeps track of the relationship between source code and ODD revisions.
- Technical writers from the documentation team clean up the final version of ODD. They ensure that the document is consistent from a structural and content point of view. They also check for compliance with guidelines.

The architecture team is the integrating force of object design. The architecture team ensures that changes are consistent with project goals. The documentation team, including the technical writers, ensures that the changes are consistent with the guidelines and conventions.

8.6.3 The Unified Process

The Unified Process is a life cycle for software engineering proposed by Booch, Jacobson and Rumbaugh (Bruegge and Dutiot 2000). Different from the spiral model (the most common model used in OOD), it offers no names for the stages. Instead it makes evident the parallel nature of the development progression by referring to activities as workflows. A **workflow** is any activity in the development process.

These parallel tasks allow for the stages of traditional development to run in parallel. For instance, design and implementation may occur at the same time. In this scenario the design process may provide feedback to the live and functioning design team before their disbandment. This live interaction between teams provides more efficient and accurate changes to the project.

8.7 Objects as Models

UML notation provides a standard and widely accepted method for the description of program constructs as a diagram. This diagram is easier to understand than code entities, as it provides a visually appealing and intuitive interface to the workings of what can be a complex and obfuscated source code. While new projects can be modeled by engineers trained in UML and these diagrams can be translated to code by hand, there exists the ability to forward and reverse engineer UML models as objects.

Source code may be generated from UML using templates and translation tools. These tools can automate a large share of the source code generation, but fall short of 100 % automation (Eriksson et al. n.d.). However, many case studies show that costs and turnaround times are shortened using UML to source code tools. In turn, maintenance of software systems can be eased using reverse engineering. As software products make it to the market with little or no proper documentation, even internally documentation may be lacking. Reverse engineering provides a mechanism to turn compiled code into models. These models allow developers to more easily understand the system. Reverse engineering objects provides insight more quickly and accurately than black-box investigation techniques.

8.7.1 Forward Engineering

Forward engineering most simply stated takes a higher level of abstraction to that of a lower level (Schach 2008). This engineering process provides source code from models. Software engineers find that this sort of engineering is very beneficial for the accuracy and speed of which objects may be constructed from models.

8.7.2 Reverse Engineering

Reverse engineering is exactly the opposite of forward engineering; reverse engineering can turn the objects and low level executable code to high level pictorial representations. Collectively, reverse and forward engineering is termed **restructuring** (Schach 2008). As reverse engineering produces models and forward engineering can create executable code, software maintainers can rely on improved code generation algorithms to generate better code than the original developers produced. This improvement of implementation without modification of a function is the essence of restructuring.

8.8 Design Tips

This section contains a brief overview of object-oriented design methods that allow for the most reliable and productive development. The following is a brief list of the most important concepts and ideas required for object-oriented design.

1. Keep close to the problem domain. Do not stray too far or the scope of the project will grow to an uncontrollable size.

2. Discover objects, do not invent them. Objects should be obvious and necessary. If you are forcing them, then they are most likely not correct.
3. Using a standard naming convention. These vary from project to project, but some common practices consist of using nouns as class names and attributes. Using verbs for method names is also common.
4. Modern languages and toolkits provide almost every data structure and low level component you can imagine. Use them. These classes built into the language are widely understood, documented, and implemented. There is no need to rebuild something that is already proven and readily available.

8.9 Chapter Summary and Conclusions

This chapter focuses on object design. Object design is adding details to the requirements analysis and making implementation decisions. The process of object design serves as the stepping stone to implementation. This phase closes the gap between the application objects and the off-the-shelf components by identifying additional solution objects and refining existing objects. At the end of this step there should be a complete design that is ready to be implemented.

Objects are categorized in a few different groups. Application objects, also called "domain objects", represent concepts of domain that are relevant to the system. Solution objects represent components that do not have a counterpart in the application domain, such as persistent data stores, user interface objects, or middleware.

Inheritance is embodied by all object-oriented languages. It provides a crucial and necessary mechanism to promote reusability. The focus of inheritance during object design is to reduce redundancy and enhance extensibility.

A clear and concise design revolves around well enumerated and documented interfaces to the outside world. Whereas internal components are not seen or directly manipulated (this does not mean that they should not be thought out) by the end user interfaces. This can make or break a project in terms of usability. Interface specification activities of object design include:

- Identifying missing attributes and operations
- Specifying type signatures and visibility
- Specifying invariants
- Specifying preconditions and postconditions

The class implementer is responsible for realizing the class under consideration. Class implementers design the internal data structures and implement the code for each class. Class extenders may invoke operations provided by the class of interest, and they focus on specialized versions of the same services.

A constraint is a restriction on one or more values of (part of) an object-oriented model or system. The context definition of an OCL expression specifies the model entity for which the OCL expression is defined.

Managing object design adds a couple of new layers of complication. The two main considerations added during object design in relation to communication are as follows:

- Increased communication complexity: Object design revolves around UML, OCL and many other methodologies. These techniques are normally out of the scope of many stake holders understanding. Using simple and concise documentation is the key to demonstrating ideas and concepts.
- Consistency with prior decisions and documents is increasingly problematic as the complexity of the system increases, and flaws may be found in the work of previous stages. Also, stake holders may change their requirements. Object design teams should work closely with the other teams to create the most accurate rendition of the requirements. However, do not forget to document these changes before moving to the next phase.

The Object Design Document (ODD) provides insight into the Object design phase. The following information is essential for maintaining a complete and useful document:

- Communication among stakeholders. This should be documented and time stamped. A complete and coherent dialogue will help in the resolution of conflicts and assure that all features desired are implemented.
- Level of detail and rate of change are essential for tracking progress of a project.
- Level of detail and elicitation effort. Detailing the effort allows for a comparison between the rate of change and the effort (or the man hours). Using this information, managers can determine if the project is on schedule.
- Testing requirements will provide a metric by which the delivery system should perform.

8.10 Exercises

1. Give an outline of steps required in object-oriented design.
2. For each of the following objects, indicate if it is an application object or a solution object:

   - League
   - League store
   - Match
   - Match view
   - Move

3. Indicate which occurrences of the following inheritance relationship is specification inheritance and which implementation inheritance is:

   - A Rectangle class inherits from a Polygon class

- A Set class inherits from a BinaryTree class
- A Set class inherits from a Bag class
- A Player class inherits from a User class
- A Window class inherits from a Polygon class

4. Consider Polyline, Polygon, and Point classes Write the following constraints in OCL:

   - A polygon is composed of a sequence of at least three points
   - A polygon is composed of a sequence of points starting and ending at the same point
   - The points returned by the getpoints (bbox) method of a polygon are within the bbox rectangle

5. Why is maintaining consistency between the analysis model and the object model difficult? Illustrate your point with a change to the object design model.

6. **Group Diary**

   A group diary and time management system is intended to support the timetabling of meetings and appointments across a group of co-workers. When an appointment is to be made that involves a number of people, the system finds a common slot in each of their diaries and arranges the appointment for that time. If no common slots are available, it interacts with the user to rearrange his or her personal diary to make room for the appointment.

   - *For the bored*: Announce successful meetings per email. Permit people to block out personal time. Set up provisional meetings that must be confirmed by all participants before they are finalized.
   - Identify possible objects in your system and develop an object-oriented design for it. You may make any reasonable assumptions about the systems when deriving the design.
   - Draw a sequence diagram showing the interactions of objects in your system.
   - Draw a state chart showing the possible state changes in one or more of the objects defined.
   - Write a precise interface in Java of the objects you have defined.

7. Define: (a) precondition; (b) postcondition; (c) assertion; (d) invariance condition; (e) Types; (f) signature

8. How do you decide whether something is to be modeled as an attribute or a class?

9. Define the terms: pattern, design pattern, analysis pattern, and organizational pattern architectural pattern. Give examples of each.

10. Produce a framework template for school timetable preparation: allocating suitable classrooms, qualified teachers, ten subjects, and five one-hour timeslots per weekday. Include all invariants; e.g. Chemistry needs a classroom with sinks and there must be at least five hours of Math and English per week.

Are there any rules that are hard to express in OCL? Why is this? Apply the same framework to factory production scheduling.

11. Write patterns to deal with the following situations:

   a. The needs to inform all users of e-mail of a change to their e-mail addresses, when some may be on holiday;
   b. Users in a workshop continually disagree with each other;
   c. Management resists object technology because they consider it too risky.

Compare two architectural styles from the following list: layers, pipes and filters, peer-to-peer, and client–server.

References

Berard E V (2002) Object-oriented design. The Object Agency, Prolouge

Bruegge B, Dutoit A (1999) Object-oriented software engineering: conquering complex and changing systems. Pearson Education, Ltd., Upper Saddle River

Bruegge B, Dutoit A (2000) Object-oriented software engineering: conquering complex and changing systems. Pearson Education, Ltd., Upper Saddle River

Bruegge B, Dutoit A (2004) Object-oriented software engineering: using UML, patterns, and java, 2nd edn. Pearson Education, Ltd., Upper Saddle River

Coad P, Yourdon E (1990) Object-oriented analysis. PrenticeHall, Englewood Clis, New Jersey

Eliens A (1995) Principles of object-oriented software development. Addison-Wesley

Schach S (2008) Object-oriented software engineering. McGraw-Hill Higher Education, Boston

Implementing a class. In: Object-oriented software design and construction. Virginia Tech. http://peopl.cs.vt.edu/~kafura/cs2704/implementing.html. Accessed 15 July 2006

Introduction to OCL. The professional website of Jos Warmer and Anneke Kleppe. http://www.klasse.nl/ocl/ocl-introduction.html. Accessed 15 July 2006

http://www.objenv.com/cetus/oo_ooa_ood_tools.html. Accessed 28 Sept 2006

http://www.toa.com/pub/ood_article.txt. Accessed 28 Sept 2006

http://ee.hawaii.edu/~tep/EE467/BDLecs/html/odd.html. Accessed 1 July 2009

Chapter 9
Implementation

9.1 Introduction to the Implementation Phase

Implementation is the act of translating a design into a working system. This phase revolves around coding, but maintains several theoretical aspects as well. Effective implementation standards include requirements that programmers and other project participants discuss in effort to form design specifications before programming begins. The procedures help to ensure that the programmers clearly understand program designs and functional requirements.

Programmers use various techniques to develop computer programs. The large transaction-oriented programs associated with financial institutions have traditionally been developed using procedural programming techniques. Procedural programming involves the line-by-line scripting of logical instructions that are combined to form a program.

Procedural programming activities primarily include the creation and testing of source code and, the refinement and finalization of test plans. Typically, individual programmers write and review (desk test) program modules or components, which are small routines that perform a particular task within an application. Completed components are integrated with other components and reviewed, often by a group of programmers, to ensure the components properly interact. This process continues as component groups are progressively integrated and as interfaces between component groups and other systems are tested.

Advancements in programming techniques include the concept of "object-oriented programming." Object-oriented programming centers on the implementation of reusable program routines (modules) and the classification of data types (numbers, letters, dollars, etc.) and data structures (records, files, tables, etc.). Linking pre-scripted module objects to predefined data-class objects reduces implementation times and makes programs easier to modify. Refer to the "Software Implementation Techniques" section for additional information on object-oriented programming.

Organizations should complete testing plans during the implementation phase. Additionally, they should update conversion, implementation, and training plans as well as user, operator, and maintenance manuals.

R. Y. Lee, *Software Engineering: A Hands-On Approach,*
DOI: 10.2991/978-94-6239-006-5_9, © Atlantis Press and the author 2013

Fig. 9.1 Software life cycle
model (Raymond 2003)

9.1.1 Implementation Standards

Implementation is the process of translating the detailed design into code. When
this is done by a single individual, the process is relatively well understood. But,
most real-life products today are too large to be implemented by one programmer
within the given time constraints (Schach 2007). Code is produced from the deliverables of the design phase during implementation, and this is the longest phase
of the software development life cycle. For a developer, this is the main focus of
the life cycle because this is where the code is produced. Implementation may
overlap with both the design and testing phases. Many tools exists (CASE tools) to
actually automate the production of code using information gathered and produced
during the design phase. Figure 9.1 shows the general life cycle model including
the implementation phase.

In the implementation phase, the system or system modifications are installed
and made operational in a production environment. Activities in this phase include
notification of implementation to end users, execution of the previously defined
training plan, data entry or conversion and post implementation review. This phase
continues until the system is operating in production, and is in accordance with the
defined user requirements. The new system can fall into three categories,
replacement of a manual process, replacement of a legacy system, or upgrade to an
existing system. Regardless of the type of system, all aspects of the implementation phase should be followed. This will ensure the smoothest possible transition
to the organization's desired goal.

Implementation standards should be in place to address the responsibilities of
application and system programmers. Application programmers are responsible for
developing and maintaining end-user applications. System programmers are
responsible for developing and maintaining internal and open-source operating
system programs that link application programs to system software and subsequently to hardware. Managers should thoroughly understand development and
production environments to ensure they appropriately assign programmer
responsibilities.

Implementation standards should prohibit a programmer's access to data,
programs, utilities and systems outside their individual responsibilities. Library
controls can be used to manage access to, and the movement of programs between,
implementation, testing and production environments. Management should also
establish standards requiring programmers to document completed programs and
test results thoroughly. Appropriate documentation enhances a programmer's
ability to correct programming errors and modify production programs.

Coding standards, which address issues such as the selection of programming
languages and tools, the layout or format of scripted code and the naming conventions of code routines and program libraries, are outside the scope of this

document. However, standardized, yet flexible, coding standards will enhance an organization's ability to decrease coding defects while simultaneously increasing security, reliability and maintainability of application programs. Examiners should evaluate an organization's coding standards and related code review procedures (IRM 2003).

9.1.2 Library Utilization and Management

Libraries are collections of stored documentation, programs and data. Program libraries include reusable program routines or modules stored in source or object code formats. Program libraries allow programmers to access frequently used routines and add them to programs without having to rewrite the code. Dynamic link libraries include executable code programs + can automatically run as part of larger applications. Library controls should include:

Automated Password Controls: Management should establish logical access controls for all libraries or objects within libraries. Establishing controls on individual objects within libraries can create security administration burdens. However, if similar objects (executable and non-executable routines, test and production data, etc.) are grouped into separate libraries, access can be granted at library levels.

Automated Library Applications: When feasible, management should implement automated library programs, which are available from equipment manufacturers and software vendors. The programs can restrict access at library or object levels and produce reports that identify who accessed a library and what, if any, changes were made.

9.1.3 Version Controls

Library controls facilitate software version controls. Version controls provide a means to systematically retain chronological copies of revised programs and program documentation. Implementation version control systems are sometimes referred to as concurrent version systems. Such systems assist organizations in tracking different versions of source code during implementation. The systems do not simply identify and store multiple versions of source code files. They maintain one file and identify and store only changed code. When a user requests a particular version, the system recreates that version. Concurrent version systems facilitate the quick identification of programming errors. For example, if programmers install a revised program on a test server and discover programming errors, they only have to review the changed code to identify the error.

9.2 Tasks and Activities

Tasks and activities in the implementation phase are associated with certain deliverables. The tasks and activities actually performed depend on the nature of the project. A few sample tasks taken from a project of applabs (A large software testing corporation) is provided below (Applabs 2006):

- Follow the naming and coding standards for developing the source code
- Follow the implementation plans/programming specifications
- Conduct peer reviews of software source code of each unit
- Place the software source code under software configuration management
- Execute all unit test cases mentioned in the Unit Test plan
- Document and track problems identified during unit testing to closure
- Review and close reported defects
- Perform software regression testing at unit test level when software source code is changed
- Change software source code when software designs are changed
- Update the Project Data Collection Sheet.

9.2.1 Implementation Updates

The implementation notice should be sent to all users and organizations affected by the implementation. Additionally, it is good policy to make internal organizations not directly affected by the implementation aware of the schedule so that allowances can be made for a disruption in the normal activities of that section. Some notification methods are email, internal memo to heads of departments, and voice tree messages. The notice should include:

- The schedule of the implementation;
- A brief synopsis of the benefits of the new system;
- The difference between the old and new system;
- Responsibilities of end user affected by the implementation during this phase; and
- The process to obtain system support, including contact names and phone numbers.

The Implementation Plan describes how the information system will be deployed, installed and transitioned into an operational system. The plan contains an overview of the system, a brief description of the major tasks involved in the implementation, the overall resources needed to support the implementation effort (such as hardware, software, facilities, materials, and personnel) and any site-specific implementation requirements. The plan is developed during the Design Phase and is updated during the Development phase; the final version is provided

```
┌─────────────────────────────────────────────────────────────────────────┐
│  Cover Page                                                               │
│  Table of Contents                                                        │
│                                                                           │
│  1.0      INTRODUCTION                                                    │
│           1.1        Purpose                                              │
│           1.2        System Overview                                      │
│                      1.2.1      System Design                             │
│                      1.2.2      System Organization                       │
│           1.3        Project References                                   │
│           1.4        Glossary                                             │
│                                                                           │
│  2.0      MANAGEMENT OVERVIEW                                             │
│           2.1        Description of Implementation                        │
│           2.2        Points of Contact                                    │
│           2.3        Major Tasks                                          │
│           2.4        Implementation Schedule                              │
│                      2.4.1      System Security Features                  │
│                      2.4.2      Security during Implementation            │
│                                                                           │
│  3.0      IMPLEMENTATION SUPPORT                                          │
│           3.1        Hardware, Software, Facilities, and Materials        │
│                      3.1.1      Hardware                                  │
│                      3.1.2      Software                                  │
│                      3.1.3      Facilities                                │
│                      3.1.4      Material                                  │
│           3.2        Personnel                                            │
│                      3.2.1      Personnel Requirements and Staffing       │
│                      3.2.2      Training and Implementation               │
│           3.3        Performance Monitoring                               │
│                                                                           │
└─────────────────────────────────────────────────────────────────────────┘
```

Fig. 9.2 Outline of implementation plan

in the Integration and Test Phase, and is used for guidance during the Implementation Phase. The outline below, Fig. 9.2, shows the structure of the Implementation Plan (IRM 2003).

9.2.2 New Model Training Plan

It is always a good business practice to provide training before the end user uses the new system. Because there has been a previously designed training plan established, complete with the system user manual, the execution of the plan should be relatively simple. Typically what prevents a plan from being implemented is a simple lack of funding. Good budgeting practices should prevent this from happening.

9.2.3 Data Entry

With the implementation of any system, typically there is old data which is to be included in the new system. This data can be in a manual or an automated form. Regardless of the format of the data, the tasks in this section are twofold, data input and data verification. When replacing a manual system, hard copy data will need to be entered into the automated system. Some sort of verification that the data is being entered correctly should be conducted throughout this process. This is also the case in data transfer, where data fields in the old system may have been entered inconsistently and therefore, will affect the integrity of the new database. Verification of the old data becomes imperative to a useful computer system. One of the ways verification of both system operation and data integrity can be accomplished is through parallel operations. Parallel operations consist of running the old process or system and the new system simultaneously until the new system is certified and considered stable. In this way if the new system fails in any way, the operation can proceed on the old system while the bugs are worked out (IRM 2003).

9.2.4 Post-Implementation Assessment

After the system has been fielded, a post-implementation review is conducted to determine the success of the project through its implementation phase. The purpose of this review is to document implementation experiences in order to recommend system enhancements and provide guidance for future projects. In addition, change implementation notices will be utilized to document user requests for fixes to problems that may have been recognized during this phase. It is important to document any user request for a change to a system in order to limit misunderstandings between the end user and the system programmers.

9.2.5 Documenting Updates

During this phase, the Requirements Analysis Phase is revised. The System Security Plan, Security Risk Assessment, Software Development Document, System Software and the Integration Document are also revised and finalized during the Implementation Phase (IRM 2003).

9.3 Roles and Responsibilities

- Project Manager: The project manager is responsible and accountable for the successful execution of the Implementation Phase. The project manager is responsible for leading the team that accomplishes the tasks discussed above. The project manager is also responsible for reviewing deliverables for accuracy, approving deliverables and providing status reports to management.

- Project Team: The project team members (regardless of the organization of permanent assignment) are responsible for accomplishing assigned tasks as directed by the project manager.
- Contracting Officer: The contracting officer is responsible and accountable for the procurement activities and signs contract awards.
- Oversight Activities: Agency oversight activities, includes providing advice and counsel for the project manager on the conduct and requirements of the Implementation Phase. Additionally, oversight activities provide information, judgments and recommendations to the agency decision makers during project reviews and in support of project decision milestones.

9.4 Deliverables

The following deliverables are initiated during the Implementation Phase:

9.4.1 Delivered System

After the Implementation Phase Review and Approval Certification is signed by the Project Manager and the System Proponent representative, the system—including the production version of the data repository—is delivered to the customer for the Operations and Maintenance Phase.

9.4.2 Change Notice

The change notice is a document of a formal nature. This document should detail the changes that have been made, any changes that were planned and not implemented, as well as who is in charge of the changes being made. This document is essential for properly communicating the features and caveats of each release.

9.4.3 Version Description

The version description should be thorough and yet not loaded down with technical jargon. It should be detailed enough to allow anyone to point out the differences

```
┌─────────────────────────────────────────────────────────────────────┐
│                    VERSION DESCRIPTION DOCUMENT                       │
│                                                                       │
│  Cover Page                                                           │
│  Table of Contents                                                    │
│                                                                       │
│  1.0      INTRODUCTION                                                │
│           1.1        Roles and Responsibilities                       │
│           1.2        Process                                          │
│                                                                       │
│  2.0      SCOPE                                                       │
│           2.1        Identification                                   │
│           2.2        Applicability                                    │
│           2.3        System Overview                                  │
│           2.4        Documentation Overview                           │
│           2.5        Points of Contact                                │
│                                                                       │
│  3.0      REFERENCE DOCUMENTS                                         │
│                                                                       │
│  4.0      VERSION DESCRIPTION                                         │
│           4.1        Inventory of Materials Released                  │
│           4.2        Inventories of Software Contents                 │
│           4.3        Changes Installed                                │
│           4.4        Interface Compatibility                          │
│           4.5        Adaptation Data                                  │
│           4.6        Bibliography of References Documents              │
│           4.7        Installation Instructions                        │
│           4.8        Possible Problems and Known Error                 │
│           4.9        Glossary                                         │
│                                                                       │
└─────────────────────────────────────────────────────────────────────┘
```

Fig. 9.3 Version description document

between features with terms they are familiar with using. It is inevitable that some jargon may need to be incorporated. In these instances it is best practice to fully explain the term and then if prudent or possible, by in house standards allow for indexing the terminology at the end of the document (Fig. 9.3).

9.4.4 Post-Implementation Review

The review is conducted at the end of the Implementation Phase. A post-implementation review shall be conducted to ensure that the system functions as planned and expected; to verify that the system cost is within the estimated amount; and to verify that the intended benefits are derived as projected. Normally, this shall be a one-time review that occurs after a major implementation; it may also occur after a major enhancement to the system. The results of an unacceptable review are submitted to the System Proponent for its review and follow-up actions. The System Proponent may decide to return the deficient system to the responsible system development Project Manager for correction of deficiencies (IRM 2003) (Fig. 9.4).

POST-IMPLEMENTATION REVIEW DOCUMENT

Cover Page
Table of Contents

1.0   INTRODUCTION
      1.1   Project Identification
      1.2   Requesting Organization
      1.3   History of the System
      1.4   Functional System Description and Data Usage

2.0   EVALUATION SUMMARY
      2.1   General Satisfaction with the System
      2.2   Current Cost-Benefit Justification
      2.3   Needed Changes or Enhancements

3.0   ANALYSIS AND IMPLEMENTATION
      3.1   Purpose and Objectives
      3.2   Scope
      3.3   Benefits
      3.4   Development Cost
      3.5   Operating Cost
      3.6   Training

4.0   OUTPUTS
      4.1   Usefulness
      4.2   Timeliness
      4.3   Data Quality

5.0   SECURITY
      5.1   Data Protection
      5.2   Distaster Recovery
      5.3   Controls
      5.4   Audit Trails
      5.5   Allowed Access

6.0   COMPUTER OPERATIONS
      6.1   Control of Work Flow
      6.2   Scheduling
      6.3   User Interface
      6.4   Computer Processing
      6.5   Peak Loads

7.0   MAINTENANCE ACTIVITIES
      7.1   Activity Summary
      7.2   Maintenance Review
      7.3   System Maintenance

Fig. 9.4 Post-implementation review outline

9.5 Post-Implementation Considerations

Once a system has been developed, tested, and deployed it will enter the Operations and Maintenance Phase. All development resources and documentation should be transferred to a library or the operations and maintenance staff (IRM 2003).

9.6 Language Choice

In most cases, programming language for implementation is not an issue. Unless the client wants a particular language to be used, allowing for the possibility of unforeseen limitations, and issues. Such details are most commonly irrelevant to the client. However, if the product has to be implemented on a specific computer and only a specific language is available on that computer then there is no choice. In these types of cases the choice of programming language is clearly predetermined and unchangeable due to factors that cannot be controlled. The most interesting situation is choosing the most suitable programming language when it is not specified (Schach 2007). Object-oriented programming languages (OOPLs) are the natural choice for implementation of an Object-Oriented Design because they directly support the object notions of classes, inheritance, information hiding, and dynamic binding. Because they support these object notions, OOPLs make an object-oriented design easier to implement. An object-oriented system programmed with an OOPL results in less complexity in the system design and implementation, which can lead to an increase in *maintainability*. Current OOPLs include C++, Objective C, Smalltalk, Eiffel, Common LISP Object System (CLOS), Object Pascal and Java. The use of OOPL technology requires a corporate commitment to formal training in the proper use of the OOPL features and the purchase of the language compiler. Object-oriented (OO) applications can be written in either conventional languages or OOPLs, but they are much easier to write in languages especially designed for OO programming. OO language experts divide OOPLs into two categories, hybrid languages and pure OO languages. Hybrid languages are based on some non-OO model that has been enhanced with OO concepts. C++ (a superset of C), Ada 95, and CLOS (an object-enhanced version of LISP) are hybrid languages. Pure OO languages are based entirely on OO principles; Smalltalk, Eiffel, Java, and Simula are pure OO languages. In terms of numbers of applications, the most popular OO language in use is C++. One advantage of C++ for commercial use is its syntactical familiarity to C, which many programmers already know and use; this lowers training costs. Additionally, C++ implements all the concepts of object-orientation, which include classes, inheritance, information hiding, polymorphism and dynamic binding. One disadvantage of C++ is that it lacks the level of polymorphism and dynamics most OO programmers expect. The major alternative to C++ or Ada 95 is Smalltalk. Its advantages are its consistency and flexibility. Its disadvantages are its unfamiliarity (causing an added training cost for developers) and its inability to work with existing systems (a major benefit of C++) (Bray 2005).

9.7 Development Paradigms

9.7.1 Component-Based Development

Described as a reuse-oriented approach to software development, component-based development of software relies on the reuse and integration of software components. This approach aims to improve efficiency and reduce risk in development by reducing the amount of software to be developed. Between requirements specification and system validation in usual stages of the software process, this approach requires the following stages (Sommerville 2004):

1. **Component Analysis:** This stage requires the team to find components that at least partially fit the functionality needs of the software as laid out during requirements specification.
2. **Requirements Modification:** Requirements are altered to match the available functionality of the found software components to be used. If requirements are unable to be altered to fit the components, better solutions may be searched for.
3. **System Design with Reuse:** A framework for the software is designed or re-implemented to fit the components that are being reused.
4. **Development and Integration:** Components that were not found for reuse may be developed and integrated with reused components in the system.

9.7.2 Extreme Programming

Extreme programming (XP) represents a process for the agile development of software (Pressman 2005). Agile development, aiming to produce incremental software delivery, can be done via the methods and activities laid out in the XP approach. This approach, in general, will break software into releasable increments and aim to quickly and simply develop those increments. XP can be broken into four major activities of development; these activities include the following:

1. **Planning.** To begin development using the extreme programming paradigm, planning will occur in which the customer will begin by customer writes a set of *stories* describing features of the desired software. These stories, which break up features into small enough parts so that each story will only take a few weeks of development, are ranked by both the customer and team for priority and cost respectively (cost refers to the length of time needed to develop it).

The team will work with the customer to decide which stories and in what order they will be grouped and produced for various releases of the software.

2. **Design.** The design phase of XP encourages simple design, CRC cards, and spike solution prototypes. CRC cards, or class-responsibility cards, designate classes to be used in the development of the current software increment; the team produces only these are their method for organizing design. A spike solution is a working prototype of a specific portion of the design that is potentially difficult; these are made in order to reduce problems and risk related to the portions future implementation.

3. **Coding.** Often recommending two programmers coding at once, XP will have team members develop tests for the various stories in the current increment. Code created by the pairs will be implemented as a part of the whole increment with other pairs' code, often integrating these parts on a continuous basis.

4. **Testing.** While testing and small problem correction is done by the team on a continuous basis, rather than fixing major problems near the end, the customer will specify and review tests as well before the release of the increment.

Once completed, the increment is released and the next is began. It is worth noting that the XP paradigm often times prefers to make use of the object-oriented approach.

9.8 Code Style Standards

Coding standards can be both a blessing and a curse. A useful rule of thumb is that if statements should not be nested to a depth that is greater than three. If programmers are shown examples of unreadable code resulting from nesting if statements too deeply, then it is likely that they will conform to such regulation. Below are the few rules Schach describes

- Nesting of if-statements should not exceed a depth of three
- Modules should consist of between 35 and 50 statements
- The use of goto statements should be avoided

The aim of coding standards is to make maintenance easier. However, if the effect of a standard is to make the life of software developers difficult, then such a standard should be modified, even if such a modification must occur in the middle of a project. Overly restrictive coding standards such as those just listed regarding nesting of if statements, module size, and goto statements, coupled with a mechanism for deviating from those standards, can lead to improved software quality, which, after all, is a major goal of software engineering (Schach 1999).

Many recommendations on good coding style are language specific. Here are a few programming practices that are generally considered to be acceptable. (Schach 1999).

Use consistent and meaningful variable Names: This implies that the programmer developing a module is merely the first of many other programmers who will work on module. It is counterproductive for a programmer to give names to variables that are meaningful to only that programmer; within the context of software engineering, meaningful means "meaningful from the viewpoint of future maintenance programmers".

Self-document the code: The important point is whether the module can be understood easily and unambiguously by all the other programmers who will read the code. Prologue comments are mandatory in every single module. The minimum information that must be provided for every module is: module name; brief description of what the module does; programmer's name; date when the module was coded; list of module arguments; list of variables names; known faults if any.

Use parameters: There are very few genuine constants, that is variables whose values never change. All such apparent constants should be treated as parameters. If a value should change for any reason, this change can be implemented quickly and effectively.

Readable code layout: Indentation is perhaps the most important technique for increasing readability. It also helps to clarify which statements belong with which block. Another useful aid is the proper use of blank lines.

9.9   Code Reuse

Reuse refers to using components of one product to facilitate the development of a different product, with a different functionality. A reusable component need not necessarily be a module or a code fragment—it could be a design, a part of a manual, a set of test data, or a duration and cost estimate. There are two types of reuse, opportunistic reuse and deliberate reuse. If the developers of a new product realize that a component of a previously developed product can be reused in the new product, then this is opportunistic reuse, sometimes referred to as accidental reuse. On the other hand, utilization of software components constructed specifically for possible future reuse is considered to be systematic reuse or deliberate reuse. A potential advantage of systematic reuse in comparison to opportunistic reuse is that components specially constructed for use in future products are more likely to be easy and safe to reuse; such components generally are robust, well documented, and thoroughly tested. Maintaining is made to be a much easier task with systematic reuse but, it can be expensive (Schach 2007).

9.10   Integration

One approach towards integration of the product is to code and test each individual code artifact separately, followed by linking together all the code artifacts and then testing test the product as a whole. There are two common difficulties with this

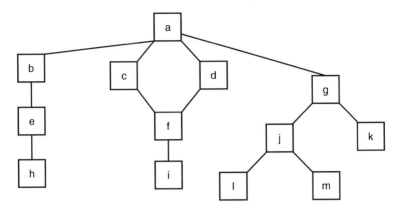

Fig. 9.5 Interconnection diagram

approach. Consider artifact a. It cannot be tested on its own, because it calls artifacts b, c, and d. Therefore in order to unit test a, artifacts b, c and d must be coded as stubs. A stub is empty artifact, and it should return values corresponding to preplanned test cases (Damian 2007).

9.10.1 Top-Down Integration

In top-down integration, if module **mAbove** calls module **mBelow**, then **mAbove** is implemented/integrated before **mBelow**. Suppose that the same product (Fig. 9.5) is to be implemented/integrated in a top-down manner. One possible top-down ordering is **a, b, c, d, e, f, g, h, i, j, k, l, m**. First, module **a** is coded and tested with **b**, **c** and **d** implemented as stubs. Next, stub **b** is expanded into module **b**, linked to module **a**, and tested with module **c e** implemented as a stub. Implementation/integration proceeds this way until all of the modules have been integrated into the product. Another possible top-down ordering is **a, b, e, h, c, d, f, i, g, j, k, l, m**. With this latter ordering, portions of the implementation/integration can proceed in parallel in the following way. After **a** has been coded and tested, one programmer can use module **a** to implement/integrate module **b**, **e**, and **h**, while another programmer can use **a** to work in parallel on **c**, **d**, **f**, and **i**. Once **d** and **f** are completed, a third programmer can start to work on **g**, **j**, **k**, **l**, and **m**.

9.10.1.1 Advantages

Suppose that module **a** executes correctly by itself on a specific test case. However, when the same data sets are submitted after **b** has been coded and integrated into the product (now consisting of modules **a** and **b** linked together), the test fails. The fault can be in one of two places; namely, in module **b** or in the interface between modules **a** and **b**. This holds true in general whenever a new module is added to the product.

A major strength of top-down integration is that *major design flaws show up early*. The modules of a product can be divided into two groups: *logic modules* and *operational modules*. Logic modules incorporate the high-level decision making flow of the product, and are generally situated close to the root of the module interconnection diagram. From Fig. 9.5, it is reasonable to expect that modules **a, b, c, d**, and perhaps **g** and **j** are logic modules. The operational modules perform the actual operations of the product, such as **getLineFromTerminal** or **measureReactorTemperature**. These modules are generally found at the lower levels, close to the leaves of the module interconnection diagram. In Fig. 9.5, modules **e, f, h, i, k, l**, and **m** may be operational modules. By coding and testing the logic modules before the operational modules, top-down integration will exploit any major design faults early in the development process.

9.10.1.2 Disadvantages

The main disadvantage of top-down integration is that potentially reusable modules may not be adequately tested. These are the operational modules, which implement fundamental functions and therefore, are likely candidates for use in future projects. Unfortunately, these modules are generally the lower-level modules and as such, are often not tested as thoroughly as the upper-level modules. For example, if there are 184 modules, the root module will be tested 184 times, but the last module integrated will be tested only once. This makes the reuse of operational modules a much more risky proposition.

9.10.2 Bottom-Up Integration

In bottom-up integration, if module **mAbove** calls module **mBelow**, then **mBelow** is implemented/integrated before **mAbove**. Returning to Fig. 9.5 one possible ordering is **l, m, h, i, j, k, e, f, g, b, c, d**, and **a**. In order to have the product coded and tested by a team, a better bottom-up ordering would be as follows: **h, e** and **b** are given to one programmer and **i, f** and **c** to another. The third programmer starts with **l, m, j, k** and **g**, and then implements **d** and integrates his/her work with that of the second programmer. Finally, when **b, c**, and **d** have been successfully integrated, **a** can be implemented/integrated.

9.10.2.1 Advantages

The operational modules are more thoroughly tested when using a bottom-up strategy. Bottom-up integration also provides fault-isolation, as does top-down integration.

9.10.2.2 Disadvantages

Major design faults will be left undetected until late in the development cycle, since the logic modules are integrated last. This may result in large costs being necessary for redesigning and recoding.

9.10.3 Sandwich Integration

Since top-down and bottom-up strategies have their own unique strengths and weaknesses, the solution is to combine the two so as to capitalize upon their strengths and minimize their weaknesses. This leads to the idea of sandwich integration. Consider the module interconnection diagram shown in Fig. 9.6. Six of the modules, namely, **a, b, c, d, g** and **j** are logic modules, and therefore should be implemented/integrated in a top-down manner. Seven are operational modules, namely, **e, f, h, i, k, l** and **m**, and should be implemented/integrated in a bottom-up manner. Therefore, because neither top-down nor bottom-up implementation/integration is suitable for all the modules, the solution is to partition them. The six logic modules are implemented/integrated top-down and any major design faults can be detected early.

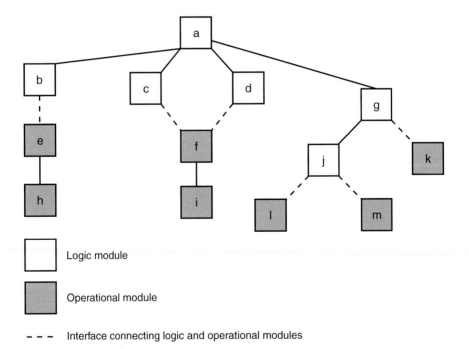

Fig. 9.6 Sandwich integration

The seven operational modules are implemented/integrated bottom-up, receiving a thorough testing, and therefore can be used with confidence in other products.

9.10.4 Integration of Object-Oriented Products

Objects can be integrated either bottom up or top down. If top-down integration is chosen, then stubs are used for each method in the same way as with classical modules. If bottom up integration is used, the objects that do not send messages to other objects are implemented and integrated first. Then, the objects that send messages to those previous objects are implemented and integrated and so on, until all the objects in the product have been properly implemented and integrated. Because top-down and bottom-up integration are supported, sandwich integration can be used. If the product is implemented in a hybrid object-oriented language like C++, the classes generally are operational artifacts and, therefore, integrated through the means of bottom up (Schach 2007).

9.10.5 Integration Management

A problem for management is discovering, at integration time, that the code artifacts simply do not fit together. A problem like this can arise when a change is made to only one copy of the design document, without informing all the members of the development group. Both the programmers know that they are right; neither is prepared to compromise, because the programmer who gives in must recode large portions of the product. To solve these and similar problems all the code artifacts have to be tested and combined into single product (Schach 2007).

9.11 Implementation Workflow

The aim of the implementation workflow is to implement the target software product in the selected implementation language. A large software product is commonly partitioned into smaller subsystems, which are then implemented in parallel by coding teams. The subsystems, in turn, consist of components or code artifacts. As soon as the code artifact has been coded, the programmer is satisfied that the code artifact is correct. It is then passed onto the quality assurance group for further testing. A number of different types of testing have to be performed during implementation workflow including unit testing, integration testing, product testing and acceptance testing.

9.11.1 Challenges of Implementation Workflow

It is hard to properly achieve code reuse if it is attempted as late as the implementation workflow. For example, suppose the decision is made to implement a product in language L. Now after half the code artifacts have been implemented and tested, management decides to utilize package P for the graphical user interfaces of the software product. No matter how powerful the routines of P may be, if they are written in a language that is hard to interfere with L, then they cannot be reused in the software product.

Even if language interoperability is not an issue, there is little point in trying to rescue an existing code artifact unless the item to be reused fits the design exactly. More work may be needed to modify the existing code artifact than to create a new code artifact from scratch. Code reuse therefore, has to be built into a software product from the very beginning. Reuse has to be a user requirement as well as a constraint of specification document. Also, the design document must state which code artifacts are to be implemented and which are to be reused. From a purely technical viewpoint, the implementation workflow is relatively straight forward. If requirements, analysis and design workflows were carried out satisfactorily, the task of implementation should pose few problems to competent programmers. However, management of integration is of critical importance (Schach 2007).

9.11.2 Metrics of Implementation Workflow

The usual fault statistics must be maintained for code inspections. The total number of faults is important, because if the number of faults detected in a code artifact exceeds a predetermined maximum, then that code artifact must be redesigned and recoded. In addition, detailed statistics need to be kept regarding the types of faults detected. Typical fault types include misunderstanding the design, lack of initialization, and inconsistent use of variables. The fault data can be incorporated into checklists to be used during the code inspections of future products. A number of metrics specific to the object-oriented paradigm have been put forward. Object-oriented metrics can relatively accurately predict the number of lines of code added, changed, and deleted in agile processes, however, they are of little use in predicting the same measures in a framework-based process. There is a need, specifically for object-oriented metrics, as opposed to classical metrics that can be applied equally to object-oriented software (Schach 2007).

9.12 Managing Implementation

9.12.1 Documenting Transformations

Implementation and transformations enable us to improve specific aspects of the object design model and to convert it into source code. By providing systematic recipes for recurring situations, transformations enable us to reduce the amount of effort and the overall numbers of errors in the source code. However, to retain this benefit throughout the lifetime of the system, we need to document the application of the changes to the object design model or source code. Reverse engineering attempts to alleviate this problem by allowing us to reconstruct the object design model from source code. If we could maintain a one-to-one mapping between the source code and the object design model, we would not need any documentation. Most useful transformations are not one-to-one mappings. As a result, information is lost in the process of applying transformations (Bruegge and Dutoit 2000).

Association multiplicity and collections. Unidirectional one-to-many associations and many-to-many associations map to the same source code. In general, information about association multiplicity is distributed in several places in the source code, including checking code in the boundary objects.

Association multiplicity and buried association. One-to-many associations and one-to-one associations implemented as a buried association in a database schema suffer from the same problem. Most of the time associations are realized as separate tables and all information about association multiplicity are lost.

When mapping contracts to exception handling code, we generate checking code only for preconditions. Postconditions and invariants are not mapped to source code. Changes in postconditions or invariants make the system inconsistent.

The following principles reduce consistency problems when applied systematically:

- For a given transformation, use the same tool. If you are using a modeling tool to map associations to code, use the same tool when you change association multiplicities. Modern modeling tools generate markers as source code comments to enable the repetitive generation of code from the same tool. However, this mapping can break when developers use different text editors or different association tools.
- Keep the contracts in the source code, not in the object design model. Contracts describe the behavior of methods and restrictions on parameters and attributes. Developers change the behavior of an object by modifying the body of a method, not by modifying the object design model.
- Use the same names for the same objects. When mapping an association to source code or a class to a database schema, use the same names on both sides of the transformation. If the name is changed in the model, change it in the source code. By doing this you make it easier for developers to identify transformations.

- Make transformations explicit. When transformations are applied by hand, it is critical that the transformation is made explicit in some form so that developers can apply the transformation the same way. For example implementation should be documented in coding conventions so that two developers produce the same code when applying the same transformation. The developers should use standard conventions, rather than actual conventions.

9.12.2 Assigning Responsibilities

Several roles collaborate to select, apply and document transformations and the conversion of the object design model into source code (Bruegge and Dutoit 2000):

- The core architect selects the transformations to be systematically applied. For example, if it is critical that the database schema is modifiable, then the core architect decides that all associations should be implemented as separate tables.
- The architecture liaison is responsible for documenting the contracts associated with subsystem interfaces. When such contracts change, the architecture liaison is responsible for notifying all classes of users.
- The developer is responsible for following the conventions set by the core architect and actually applying the transformations and converting the object design model into source code. Developers are responsible for maintaining the up-to-date source code comments with the rest of the models.
- Identifying and applying transformations for the first time is trivial. The challenge is reapplying the transformations after change occurs.

9.13 Chapter Summary and Conclusions

This chapter presents details about the implementation phase in the software development life cycle. Implementation is the process of translating the detailed design into code. In most cases, choosing a programming language for implementation is not an issue. Object-oriented programming languages (OOPLs) are the natural choice for implementation of an object-oriented design.

Section 9.1 describes how to document transformations and the principles to reduce inconsistencies with that. Several roles collaborate to select, apply, and document transformations:

- The core architect.
- The architecture liaison.
- The developer.

Section 9.9 describes many coding standards and good programming practices that the developers should follow. Reuse refers to using components of one product to facilitate the development of a different product with a different functionality. This is followed with discussions on integration. Integration of the product is the process of coding and testing each code artifact separately, followed by linking together all of the code artifacts and testing the product as a whole.

Later, Sect. 9.10 describes different types of integration and their advantages and disadvantages. The aim of the implementation workflow is to implement the target software product in the selected implementation language.

The next section presents the challenges in implementation workflow. Code reuse, therefore, has to be built into a software product from the very beginning. If requirements, analysis, and design workflows were carried out satisfactorily, the task of implementation should pose few problems.

9.14 Exercises

1. How do coding standards for a one-person software production company differ from those in organizations with 300 software professionals?
2. A user has a word-processor and a drawing package open. The word processor's window is upper most. The user then clicks on the drawing window. The drawing window then pops to the front. Describe in detail the things that the window manager and applications perform during the processing of the mouse click in the above scenario. Explain any assumptions you make about the kind of window manager or application toolkits that are being used.
3. A designer described the following interface for a save operation. The users initially see a screen with a box where they can type the file name. The screen also has 'list' button that they can use to obtain a listing of all the files in the current directory (folder). This list appears in a different window. When the user clicks the 'save' button the system presents a dialogue box to ask the user to confirm the save.
4. Two programmers independently coded the interface using two different window managers. Programmer A used an event-lop style of program where as programmer B used notifier (callback) style.
5. Sketch out the general structure of each program.
6. Highlight any potential interface problems you expect from each programmer and how they could attempt to correct them.
7. Your instructor has asked you to implement the Elevator problem. Which language would you choose? and why? Of various languages available to you list their benefits and costs. Do not attach dollar values to the cost.
8. Repeat the problem 9.5 for automated library circulation system.
9. Repeat problem 9.5 for the product that determines whether a bank statement is correct.

10. How do coding standards for a software company that develops and maintains software for intensive-care units differ from those in an organization that develops and maintains accounting products?
11. What is the role of the SQA group during implementation?

References

Applabs (2006) Software development process. http://www.applabs.com/pdf/Development_ Process.pdf# search=%22implementation%20constraints%20in%20software%20 development %20life%20cycle%22. Accessed 29 Sept 2006

Bray M (2005) Object-oriented programming languages. http://www.sei.cmu.edu/str/descriptions/ oopl.html. Accessed 19 July 2006

Bruegge B, Dutoit A (2000) Object-oriented software engineering: conquering complex and changing systems. Pearson Education, Ltd., Upper Saddle River

Damian D (2007) Practical software engineering. http://sern.ucalgary.ca/courses/CPSC/451/W00/ Testing.html. Accessed 19 July 2009

Information Resource Management (2003) Systems development life cycle guidance document. http://www.usdoj.gov/jmd/irm/lifecycle/table.htm. Accessed 29 Sept 2006

Pressman R (2005) Software engineering: a practitioner's approach, 6th edn. McGraw-Hill

Raymond (2003) Software development life cycle model: the general model. http://codebetter.com/ blogs/raymond.lewallen/archive/2005/07/13/129114.aspx. Accessed 29 Sept 2006

Schach S R (1999) Classical and object-oriented software engineering with UML and C ++, 4th edn. McGraw-Hill

Schach S R (2007) Object-oriented and classical software engineering, 7th edn. McGraw-Hill

Sommerville I (2004) Software engineering, 7th edn. Peason Education, Ltd., Boston

Further Reading:

'Object-Oriented Implementation of Numerical Methods: An Introduction with Java & Smalltalk'. This book offers a wide-ranging set of objects for common numerical algorithms. Written for the math-literate Java and Smalltalk programmer, this volume demonstrates that both languages can be used to tackle common numerical calculations with ease. (Didier H. Besset, 2000, The Morgan Kaufmann Series)

'A Functional Pattern System for Object-Oriented Design'. This book integrates the vital areas of object-orientation, functional programming, design patterns, and language design. (Thomas Kühne, Verlag Dr. Kovac, Hamburg, Germany, 1999)

Chapter 10
Testing

10.1 Introduction to Testing

Testing is an integral component of the software process and an activity that must be carried out throughout the life cycle: During the requirements workflow, the requirements must be checked; during the analysis workflow, the specifications must be checked; and the software production management plan must undergo similar scrutiny. The design workflow requires meticulous checking at every stage. During the implementation workflow, each code artifact certainly must be tested; and the product as a whole needs testing when it has been fully integrated. After passing the acceptance test, the product is installed and post-delivery maintenance begins. There are two types of testing: execution-based and non-execution-based testing. For example, it is impossible to execute a written specification document; that only alternatives are to review it as carefully as possible or subject it to some form of analysis. However, once there is executable code, it becomes possible to run test cases, that is, to perform execution-based testing (Schach 2007).

A robust model for testing starts with early **test planning** to assure that the environments are available when needed, the system is itself testable in an optimal manner, and all resources are present at the time that they are required. Some organizations start with a Master Test Plan that identifies how many levels of test will be required, as well as the attributes that distinguish them. After the planning, there is usually some kind of test **design** (documented or undocumented) where there is refinement of the approaches and establishment of the coverage goals. Specific **test cases** (the input and corresponding expected output) are selected and then executed. Actual results are recorded. Some organizations record all results, while on the other hand others record only the defects that are found. After each test level is executed, some assessment is made as to the success or failure of it. Retesting occurs as fixes are made.

R. Y. Lee, *Software Engineering: A Hands-On Approach*,
DOI: 10.2991/978-94-6239-006-5_10, © Atlantis Press and the author 2013

10.1.1 Objective of Testing

Testing has a distinct and definitive role in the software development process. Testing closes the gap between inception and delivery, verifying systematically and reproducibly that the design and implementation are not flawed. Only in the most trivial systems is it possible to eradicate 100 % chance of failure, but testing aims to minimize the amount of down time a client experiences.

Testing should occur at all levels internally. As systems are designed and implemented they should be checked and validated. Once again, as systems are assembled they should be testing for computability. The testing phase, however, revolves solely around diagnosis and isolation of bugs.

The testing process can be divided into three phases (Hetzel and Hetzel 1991): planning, acquisition and execution & evaluation. The planning phase provides description for the tester to determine what to test and how to test it. Acquisition phase is during which the required testing software is manufactured, data sets are defined and collected, and detailed test scripts are written. During the execution and evaluation phase the test scripts are executed and the results of that execution are evaluated to determine whether the product passed the test.

10.1.2 Testing Concepts and Theory

The major output of the planning phase is a set of detailed test plans. In a project that has functional requirements specified by use cases, a test plan should be written for each use case. Advantages to this include: Since many managers schedule development activity in terms of use cases, the functionality that becomes available for testing will be in terms of use cases. This facilitates determining which test plans should be utilized for a specific build of the system. Second, this approach improves the tractability from the test cases back into the requirements model (McGregor 1994).

10.1.2.1 Testing the Requirements Model

Writing the detailed test plans provides a thorough investigation of the requirements model. A test plan for a use case requires the identification of the underlying domain objects for each use case. Since an object will typically apply to more than one use case, inconsistencies in the requirements model can be located. Typical errors include conflicting defaults, inconsistent naming, incomplete domain definitions and unanticipated interactions and are identified.

The individual test cases are constructed for a use case by identifying the domain objects that cooperate to provide the use and by identifying the equivalence classes for each object. The equivalence classes for a domain object can be thought of as subsets of the states identified in the dynamic model of the object. Each test case represents one combination of values for each domain object in the use scenario.

As the use case test plan is written, an input data specification table captures the information required to construct the test cases. That information includes the class from which the domain object is instantiated, the state space of the class and significant states (boundary values) for the objects. As the tester writes additional test plans and encounters additional objects from the same class, the information from one test plan can be used to facilitate the completion of the current test plan (McGregor 1994).

10.1.2.2 Testing Interactions

Creating use case-level test plans also facilitates the identification and investigation of interactions,: situations in which one object affects another one or one attribute of an object affects other attributes of the same object. Certainly many interactions are useful and necessary. That is how objects achieve their responsibilities. However, there are also undesirable or unintended interactions where an objects state is affected by another object in unanticipated ways. For example, two objects might share a component object because a pointer to the one object was inadvertently passed to the two encapsulating objects. This phenomenon may happen instead of a second new object being created and passed to one of them. A change made in one of the encapsulating objects is seen by the other encapsulating object.

Even an intended interaction gone badly can cause trouble. For example, if an error prevents the editing of a field, then it is more probable that the same, or a related, error will prevent us from clearing that same field. This is due to the intentional use of a single component object to handle both responsibilities.

The brute force technique for searching for unanticipated interactions is to test all possible permutations of the equivalence classes entered in the input data specification table. If this proves to be too much information or require too many resources for the information gained, the tester can use all possible permutations of successful execution but only include a single instance of error conditions and exceptional situations. These selection criteria represent successively less thorough coverage but also require fewer resources.

Since the tester often does not have access to the code, the identification of interactions is partially a matter of intuition and inference. The resources required for the permutation approach can be reduced further by making assumptions about where interactions do not exist. That is, there is no need to consider different combinations of object values if the value of one object does not influence the value of another. Test cases are constructed to exercise permutations within a set of interacting objects, but not to include other objects that we assume are independent of the first group. Obviously this opens the door to faults not being detected, but that is true of any strategy other than an all permutations strategy (McGregor 1994).

10.1.3 Test Planning

Testing can be a resource intensive activity. This means that tests should be planned in a very specific manner as to provide testers with the resources that they need, including adequate time. Test planning should be planned and scheduled before the conception of the project to facilitate tractability throughout the entire process (Sommerville 2004). By planning far ahead, resources that must be ordered or specialists that must be hired will have time to arrive and there will be adequate time for the testers to complete their tasks before their results are due.

The tester may need to reserve special hardware or he may have to construct large, complex data sets. They will have to spend large amounts of time verifying that the expected results section of each test case accurately corresponds to the correct behavior. In this next section, I want to present two techniques for determining which parts of the product should be tested more intensely than other parts. This information will be used to reduce the amount of effort expended while only marginally affecting the quality of the resulting product (McGregor 1994).

10.2 Quality and Internal Controls

A fault is injected into the software when a human makes a mistake. One mistake on software may cause several faults; conversely, various mistakes may cause the identical fault. A failure is observed as incorrect behavior of the software product as a consequence of a fault, and the error is the amount by which a result is incorrect. The word defect is a generic term for a fault, failure, or error. The term quality implies excellence of some sort, but this unfortunately is infrequently the meaning intended by software engineers. The quality of software is the extent to which the product satisfies its specifications. The task of every software professional is to ensure high-quality software at all times. That is, each developer and maintainer is personally responsible for checking that his or her work is correct. Quality is not something added afterward by the software quality assurance group, but rather must be built in by the developers from the very beginning. One role of SQA group is to ensure that developers are indeed doing high quality work (Schach 2007).

10.2.1 Assuring Quality Software

One aspect of the role of the SQA group is to test that the developers' product is correct. More precisely, once the developers have completed a workflow and carefully checked their work, members of the SQA group have to ensure that the workflow has indeed been carried out correctly. Software quality assurance goes further than just testing at the end of workflow or the end of the development process. For example, the responsibilities of the SQA group include the development of various standards to which the software must conform as well as the establishment of the monitoring procedures for ensuring compliance with those standards. In brief, the role of the SQA group is to ensure the quality of the software process and thereby ensure the quality of the product (Schach 2007).

10.2.2 Managerial Independence

It is important to have managerial independence between the development team and the SQA group. If serious defects are found in the product as the delivery deadline approaches, the software organization must now choose between two unsatisfactory options. These options include the product being released on time with faults, or the developers fixing it and delivering it late. Both problems should be reported to the manager and he should decide which choice would be in the best interests of both the software development organization and the client. Without an SQA group, every member of the software development organization would have been involved to some extent with quality assurance activities. In case small software company, it may simply not be economically viable to have a separate SQA group. The best that can be done is to ensure that the analysis artifacts are checked by someone other than the person responsible for producing those artifacts (Schach 2007).

10.3 Testing Management

Managing tests is at the least as critical as developing, planning and executing them. Tests must be managed in a manner that provides isolation of the tester from recourse of every issue they may encounter. If this isolation is not present, the tester may not report the actually entity as incorrect and instead chose not to report it. Worse yet, it may seem a good idea to deviate the implementation from the design to gain the correct results.

Schach proposes that test managers need to have a level of mathematics ability more substantial than most professionals in the field. This is due to the statistical analysis required to determine when it is time for testers to test more, move on, or continue their present plan. Only with the correct techniques correctly carried out can the tests provide the best results possible. This knowledge of what, when and how is the main purpose of a testing manager.

10.4 Non-Execution Based Testing

Testing software without running test cases is termed non-execution-based testing. The principle underlying non-execution-based testing techniques, such as walk-throughs and inspections, is that a review by a team of experts with a broad range of expertise increases the chance of finding a fault. It is not a good idea for a person responsible for drawing up a document to be the only one responsible for reviewing it. Almost everyone has blind spots that allow faults to creep in the document. Therefore, a review task must be assigned to someone other than the original author of the document. In addition, having one reviewer may not be adequate. The strength of a review by a team of experts is that the different skills of the participants increase the chances of finding fault. Walkthroughs and inspections are two types of reviews. The fundamental difference between them is that walkthroughs have fewer steps and are less formal than inspections (Schach 2007). Non-execution-based testing was remarkably effective at the Jet Propulsion Laboratory (JPL). JPL study showed that on average each two-hour inspection exposed four major and fourteen minor faults, resulting in a saving of approximately $25,000 per inspection. Another JPL study shows that the number of faults detected decreases exponentially by phase. In other words, inspections result in faults being detected early in the software process, thereby saving both time and money. An alternative non-execution-based technique is *correctness proving*. This consists of using a mathematical proof to show that a product is correct, that is, satisfies its specifications. However, even if a product is proved correct, it must nevertheless be subjected to thorough execution-based testing (Schach 1996).

10.4.1 Walkthrough

A walkthrough team should consist of four to six individuals. An analysis walk-through team should include at least one representative from the team drawing up the specifications, the manager responsible for the analysis workflow, a client representative, a representative of the team that will perform the next overflow of the development and a representative of the software quality assurance group. The members of the walkthrough team should be experienced senior technical staff members because they tend to find the important faults (Schach 2007).

10.4.2 Managing Walkthroughs

The walkthrough should be chaired by an SQA representative because the SQA representative has the most to lose if the walkthrough is performed poorly and faults slip through. In contrast, the representative responsible for analysis workflow may be eager to have specification document approved as soon as possible to start some other task. The quality of the product is a direct reflection of the professional competence of the SQA group. The person leading the walk-through guides the other members of the walkthrough team through the document to uncover any faults. It is not the task of the team to correct faults, but merely to record them for later correction. There are four reasons for this:

1. A correction produced by a committee within the time constraints of the walkthrough is likely to be lower in quality than a correction produced by an individual trained in the necessary techniques.
2. A correction produced by a walkthrough team of five individuals takes at least as much time as a correction produced by one person.
3. Not all the items flagged as faults actually are incorrect.
4. There simply is not enough time in the walkthrough to both detect and correct faults. No walkthrough should be longer than 2 h.

There are two ways of conducting a walkthrough. The first is participant driven. Participants present their lists of unclear items. The second way of conducting a review is document driven. A person responsible for the document walks through with the reviewers interrupting either with their prepared comments or comments triggered by the presentation. This approach is likely to be more thorough. The primary role of the walkthrough leader is to elicit questions and facilitate dis-cussion. A walkthrough is an interactive process; it is not supposed to be one-sided instruction by the presenter. It also is essential that the walkthrough is not used as a means of evaluating the participants. To prevent this conflict of interests, the person responsible for a given workflow should not also be directly responsible for evaluating any member of the walkthrough team for that workflow (Schach 2007).

10.4.3 Inspections

Inspection goes far beyond a walkthrough and has five formal steps:

1. An overview of the document to be inspected is given by one of the individuals responsible for producing that document.
2. In the preparation, the participants try to understand the document in detail.
3. To begin the inspection, one participant walks through the document with the inspection team, ensuring that every item is covered and that every branch is taken at least once.
4. In the rework, the individual responsible for the document resolves all the faults and problems noted in the written report.
5. In the follow-up, the moderator must ensure that every issue raised has been resolved satisfactorily.

The first step ensures that everyone is informed of the tests. This allows all team members to bring up any valid and significant points they may have concerning the system. Also, by informing all members of the development team of the inspection they will be aware and not feel as if they are personally being targeted. A strong understanding of the document is crucial to the following steps. If it is not comprehensible it must go back to the design team to rework it until it is understandable. If the document is intelligible the next step provides the testers with a group execution, as the testers move through all possibilities and analyzes the outcomes. This walkthrough should be thorough and ideas should be shared among all members, but precautions should be made to avoid group think. Some suggestions are as follows:

- Have all team members write down (and not cross out ideas) before they bring them up with the group.
- Create a friendly and conductive environment, by not prohibiting some off topic ideas as long as it is not the main activity at the meeting.
- Make sure that team meetings are not directly proceeding holidays or inconvenient times. If the members do not wish to be there, their mind will be elsewhere.

The person that knows the document or section of the document under review will be the one the one that wrote it. Allowing that person to address the issues in the final report will be the most efficient as they are the most familiar with the issues. It is important however that they should not feel as if they are being blamed, but that they are just making corrections to the document as are the rest of the team. This promotes corrections are implemented correctly and efficiently. Finally, once the group moderator has deemed that all issues have been addressed and resolved then the group may dissolve.

10.5 Things to be Tested

Execution based testing is a process of inferring certain behavioral properties of a product based, in part, on the results of executing the product in a known environment with selected inputs. This has three implications:

1. First, the definition states that testing is an inferential process. The tester takes the product, runs it with known input data, and examines the output. The tester has to infer what, if anything is wrong with the product.
2. A problem with definition is the phrase "known environment". We never really can know our environment, either the hardware or the software.
3. Another worrisome phrase is "with selected inputs". In the case of real-time system, frequently no control is possible over the inputs to the system.

10.5.1 Utility

Utility is the extent to which a user's needs are met and a correct product is used under conditions permitted by its specifications. In other words, a product that is functioning correctly is now subjected to inputs that are valid in terms of the specifications. Irrespective of the issues such as performance, ease and cost effectiveness have to be tested. If the product is not cost effective then there is no point in buying it. Therefore, when considering the buying of an existing product, the utility of the product should be tested first, and if the product fails, testing should be stopped.

10.5.2 Reliability

Another aspect that must be tested is reliability. Reliability is a measure of the frequency and criticality of product failure. Reliability has to do with the quality of measurement. Failure is a consequence of fault. In other words, it is necessary to know how often the product fails and how bad the effects of that failure can be. When a product fails, an important issue is how long it takes to repair the results of the failure. This point is frequently overlooked in instances such as if the software fails and completely erases the information needed. The information can be retrieved using backups, but the system will be inoperable for a few days, resulting in the low reliability of the system. There are four *general classes of reliability estimates*, each of which estimates reliability in a different way. They are:

- **Inter-Rater or Inter-Observer Reliability** Used to assess the degree to which different raters/observers give consistent estimates of the same phenomenon.
- **Test–Retest Reliability** Used to assess the consistency of a measure from one time to another.
- **Parallel-Forms Reliability** Used to assess the consistency of the results of two tests constructed in the same way from the same content domain.
- **Internal Consistency Reliability** Used to assess the consistency of results across items within a test.

10.5.3 Robustness

Another aspect of every product that requires testing is its robustness. Robustness essentially is a function of a number of factors, such as the range of operating conditions, the possibility of unacceptable results with valid input, and the acceptability of effects when the product is given invalid input. A product with a wide range of permissible operating conditions is more robust than a more restrictive product. A robust product should not crash when the product is not used under permissible operating conditions. A system which informs the user as to why the data failed is more robust than a product that crashes whenever the data is slightly deviated.

10.5.4 Performance

Performance is another aspect of the product that must be tested. It is essential to know the extent to which the product meets its constraints with regard to response time or space requirements. Real-time software is characterized by hard time constraints, that is, time constraints of such a nature that is a constraint is not met, information is lost. With all real-time systems, the performance must meet every time constraint listed in the specification.

10.5.5 Correctness

Correctness is satisfied if the output specifications of a product are satisfied. In other words, if input that satisfies the input specifications provided and the product is given all the resources it needs, then the product is correct if the output satisfies the output specifications. This also has worrisome implications. Suppose the product is tested against a broad variety of test data. Does this mean that the product is acceptable?

Unfortunately, it does not. If a product is correct, all that means is that it satisfies the specifications. What if specifications themselves are incorrect? After all, the correctness of a product is meaningless if its specifications are incorrect. The fact that a product is correct is not sufficient because the specifications in terms of which it was shown to be correct may be wrong. With all the difficulties associated with execution-based testing, computer scientists have tried to come up with other ways of ensuring that a product does what it is supposed to do.

10.5.6 Usability Testing

Especially useful for web application testing, usability testing is important for determining how easy the interface of a system makes it on the user, i.e. how well does the interface guide the user in a timely and consistent manner (Pressman 2005). In order to test usability, Pressman discusses a sequence of steps:

1. Define testing categories and goals
2. Design tests to evaluate each goal
3. Select participants

4. Measure participant interaction during testing
5. Devise means for assessing usability

The categories Pressman provides for testing usability include: interactivity, layout, readability, aesthetics, display characteristics, time sensitivity, personalization, and accessibility. Some of these apply more directly to Web apps than others.

10.5.7 System Integration

Systems may be designed from the top-down or bottom-up, however, regardless of the approach chosen, components are created and may provide difficulty when attempting to identify the source of errors as components are integrated into the system. In order to reduce the difficulty that comes from integration of system components, Sommerville points out that an incremental approach to system integration and testing is beneficial (Sommerville 2004). In this approach, you integrate as few components as possible into the system and run sets of tests. Then, components and test sets can be added to the minimal system and tested repeatedly throughout this incremental process. Rather than testing the system will many or all components, this approach will simplify testing and error location.

10.6 Mathematically Proving Correctness

A correctness proof is a mathematical technique for showing that a product is correct, in other words, that it satisfies its specifications. The technique is sometimes termed verification. In addition, verification is also often used to denote all non-execution based-techniques, not only correctness proving. For clarity, this mathematical procedure will be termed correctness proving. A number of software practitioners have put forward reasons why correctness proving should not be viewed as a standard software engineering technique. First, it is claimed that software engineers lack adequate mathematical training. Second, it is suggested that proving is too expensive to be practical; third proving hard (Schach 2007).

1. Nontrivial proofs require that input specifications, output specifications, and loop invariance be expressed in first-or second-order predicate calculus or its equivalent. Not only does this make the proof process simpler for a mathematician, it allows correctness proving to be done by a computer. Fortunately, most computer science majors today either take courses in the requisite material or have the background to learn correctness-proving techniques on the job. Therefore, colleges now are producing computer science graduates with sufficient mathematical skills for correctness proving.

2. The claim that proving is too expensive for use in software development also is false. On the contrary, the economic viability of correctness proving can be determined on a project-by-project basis using cost-benefit analysis.
3. Despite the claim that correctness proving is too hard, many nontrivial products successfully have been proven correct, including operating system kernels, compilers and communication systems. Many tools such as theorem provers assist in correctness proving. The theorem prover then attempts to prove mathematically that the product, when given input data satisfying the inputs specifications, produces output data satisfying the output specifications.

There are some difficulties with correctness proving:

1. How can we be sure that a theorem prover is correct? What reliability can be placed on the output of a theorem prover? One suggestion is to submit a theorem prover to it and see whether it is correct.
2. A further difficulty is finding the input and output specifications, and especially the loop invariance or their equivalents in other logics such as modal logic. Suppose a product is correct. Unless a suitable invariant for each loop can be found, there is no way of proving the product correct
3. What if the specifications themselves are incorrect?

Proving product correct is an important, and sometimes vital, software engineering tool. Proofs are appropriate where human lives are at stake or where otherwise indicated by cost-benefit analysis. Because the aim of software engineering is the production of quality software, correctness proving is indeed an important software engineering technique. A fundamental issue in execution-based testing is which members of the software development team should be responsible for carrying it out.

10.7 Execution-Based Testing

It has been claimed that testing is a demonstration where faults are not present. Program testing can be a very effective way to show the presence of faults, but it is hopelessly inadequate for showing their absence. With test data if output is wrong, then the product definitely contains fault. But if the output is correct, then there still may be a fault in the product; only information that can deduced from that particular test is that the product runs correctly on that particular set of test data. The goal of execution-based testing is therefore to highlight as many faults as possible while accepting that there is no way to guarantee that all faults have been detected. A reasonable way to proceed is first to use black-box test cases (testing to specifications) and then to develop additional test cases using glass-box techniques (testing to code). The art of black-box testing is to use the specifications to devise a small, manageable set of test cases to maximize the chances of detecting a previously undetected fault while minimizing the chances of wasting a test case by having the same fault detected by more than one test case. There are a number of different forms of glass-box testing, including statement, branch, and path coverage. The most powerful form of structural testing is path coverage that is, testing all possible paths (Schach 1996).

10.7.1 Who Should Perform Execution-Based Testing?

Testing is a destructive process. On the other hand, the programmer doing the testing ordinarily does not wish to destroy his or her work. A successful test finds faults. It means that, if the code artifact passes the test, then the test has failed. Conversely, if the code artifact does not perform according to specifications, then the test succeeds. An inescapable conclusion is that programmers should not test their own code artifacts. A second reason why execution-based testing should be done by someone else is that the programmer may have misunderstood some aspect of the design or specifications. If testing is done by someone else, such faults may be discovered. The programmer must try out the flowchart or pseudocode with various test cases, tracing through the detailed design to check that each test case is executed correctly. When the programmer is satisfied that the code artifact operates correctly, systematic testing commences. This Systematic testing should not be performed by the programmer. If programmers are allowed to test their own code, then there always is the danger that the programmer will see what he or she wants to see. The same danger can occur even when the testing is done by someone else. While the product is being maintained, regression testing must be performed (Schach 2007).

10.8 Levels of Testing

The fact that the last module has been successfully integrated into the product does not mean that the task of the developers is complete. The SQA group must still perform a number of testing tasks in order to be certain that the product will be successful. There are two main types of software: COTS and custom software. The aim of developing COTS is to ensure that the product is sold to as many buyers as possible. The aim of COTS product testing is to ensure that the product as a whole is free of faults. When product testing is complete, the product then undergoes alpha and beta testing, as described in the next section. Custom software, on the other hand, undergoes a somewhat different type of product testing. The SQA performs a number of testing tasks in order to be certain that the product will not fail its acceptance test, the final hurdle that the custom software development team must overcome. To ensure a successful acceptance test, the SQA group must perform product testing. First, black-box test cases for the product as a whole must be run. The test cases which are set as module-by-module or object-by-object must satisfy specifications. Second, robustness of the product as a whole must be tested. In addition, the product must be tested to stress testing and volume testing. Third, the SQA Group must check that the product satisfies all its constraints (Schach 1999).

10.8.1 Systems Testing

System testing is the process of testing the integrated software in the context of the total system that it supports. System testing ensures that the complete system complies with the functional and nonfunctional requirements. Tests conducted at this level include the following:

- Functional Testing: Functional testing, also called requirement testing, finds difference between the functional requirements and the system.
- Performance testing: Performance testing finds difference between the design goals selected during system design and the system (Bruegge and Dutoit 2004).
- Recovery Testing: A system test forces the software to fail in various ways and verifies that complete recovery is properly performed.
- Security Testing: Test cases are conducted to verify that proper controls have been designed and installed in the system to protect it from a number of risks.
- Stress Testing: This type of testing, similar in concept to security testing, executes a system in a manner that demands resources in abnormal quantity, frequency or volume (Burch 1992).

10.8.2 Web Application Testing

The distributed and decentralized nature of web technologies imposes some unique testing issues for developers. Web applications are executed in one of the most brutal environments an application can be placed, the internet. Web applications are susceptible to a continuous barrage of attacks, irregular usage patterns, high load and a desired high availability. This gives us the outline of what we must test for in order to provide the most efficient and thorough testing of our web platform.

- Security: web applications must be secure. This includes correct security certificates, file permissions and hardware configurations of wide area network interface components when doing in house hosting.
- Functionality: all links, animations, images and downloads should be available and responsive. There are many suites and toolsets to accomplish this, but it is hard to beat the manual site walk through.
- Compatibility is a large portion of what makes web interfaces complex to design. The W3C provides standards and guidelines for web design. However, not all web browser developers are capable of following the rendering recommendations to the letter so you will need to verify your page at least does not appear deformed or dysfunctional on a wide variety of web engines.

- Searchability is a very difficult thing to test for, but it is a great asset to your web site. If you would like to allow web crawlers to index your page there are a couple tips to make this more efficient.
- If using Ajax, use comment tags to hold content that may be dynamically inserted. This provides proper indexing.
- Do not use images for text. Image text is harder to index and most web crawlers will not index the internal text of images. If you do use images for text use the alt attribute to insert a brief and proper description.
- Do not try to get higher page ranks by placing what you believe to be highly searched terms in the head tags.

10.9 Unit Testing

Unit testing is testing of the systems components, as components rather than a system as a whole. First, unit testing reduces the complexity of overall test activities, allowing us to focus on smaller units of the system. Second, unit testing makes it easier to pinpoint and correct faults, given that few components are involved in the test. Third, unit testing allows parallelism in the testing activities; that is, each component can be tested independently of the others. The specific candidates for unit testing are chosen from the object model and the system decomposition. The minimal set of objects to be tested should be the participating objects in use cases. Subsystems should be tested after each of the objects and classes within that subsystem have been tested individually. Existing subsystems, which were reused or purchased, should be treated as components with unknown internal structure. That does not mean they should not be tested, on the other hand it means that they should be tested rigorously, as it is impossible to examine and walkthrough the internals.

Unit testing may be called component testing. Components that will require testing include the following:

1. Individual functions or methods within the object.
2. Object classes that have attributes and methods (most all do).
3. Composite components, packages or binary files that will be linked to the project.

When testing object classes, tests which cover all the features of the object should be tested (Sommerville 2004).The tests should be thorough, meaning that they should cover all possible points of failure as well as input ranges. It is crucial to include tests out of the scope of the specification to check error handling and not only check the values for which it is known to work.

- Testing in isolation of all operations associated with the object.
- The setting and interrogation of all attributes associated with the object.
- The exercise of the object in all possible states.

Traditionally a unit test consists of structural testing which means that we use our knowledge of how the unit is designed internally for the testing and specification testing. We need to perform tests based on the encapsulated state of the object and the interaction of the operations. This is sometimes called state-based testing. This may be done both as specification and structural testing (Jacobson et al. 1992).

10.10 Acceptance Testing

Acceptance testing evaluates the new system to determine if it meets user requirements under operating conditions. When the software and documentation are deemed stable by the test group, it's time to release the software and documentation to a user test group to get user feedback (Schach 1999). A user test group should be composed of all or a sample of people who will work with the system under development. There are two types of acceptance testing (Burch 1992).

10.10.1 Alpha Testing

Alpha testing is conducted in a natural setting with systems professionals in attendance, usually as observers, recording errors and usage problems. Two techniques are applicable to alpha testing.

Usability labs: the design of usability labs differ, but the center theme is constant: get a representative sample of the people who will eventually use the software to do the testing, and place them in a controlled and structured test environment. A usability lab may be a room with one PC, or a large room divided and equipped with one-way mirrors, television cameras and several PCs or workstations.

Usability factors checklist: This checklist can be expanded and tailored. It can also be used along with usability labs. The usability factors checklist gives users the opportunity to evaluate the quality of the new software before it is converted from development to operations. In addition to completing a usability factor checklist, the user test group must also explain to systems professionals why factors were rated low if that is the case. For example, why does a user find the program to be rated low for ease of use? Is it because of poor documentation and lack of instructions? The user should answer such questions and if possible, provide suggestions as to how any or all usability factors can be improved.

Alpha testing is the software prototype stage when the software is first able to run. It will not have all the intended functionality, but it will have core functions and will be able to accept inputs and generate outputs. An alpha test usually takes place in the developer's offices on a separate system.

Any software that will be run on customer equipment must first be reviewed and approved by Corporate Software Quality. The project manager utilizes this prototype to evaluate and provide input to the developer as the design evolves. Although software is usually not distributed to users prior to beta testing, selected end-users may also be involved. Usually, the most complex or most used parts of the code are developed more completely in the alpha, in order to enable early resolution of design questions.

The project manager collaborates with the developer to determine specific goals for alpha testing and to integrate the results into evolving project plans. In-depth software reliability testing, installation testing and documentation testing are not done at alpha test time, as the software is only a prototype. Alpha tester feedback forms are not used, although the developer does request feedback on specific aspects of the software.

10.10.1.1 Setting Customer Expectations

If customers will receive alpha software, they must understand that the product will be only minimally functional and is likely to have problems. The required review by Corporate Software Quality checks for the most serious problems, but customers must still be prepared for unexpected or frustrating experiences. A letter or e-mail accompanying alpha software is strongly recommended. This letter should make customers aware of:

- The software's limited functionality at this early stage
- The likelihood of experiencing problems
- Their mission: Find problems and provide feedback

An example Alpha Transmittal Memo is shown in Fig. 10.1. All software and user documentation in any lifecycle stage must include the Copyright, Ordering information and Disclaimer Notice elements. Although software is usually not distributed to users prior to beta testing, selected end-users may be involved in alpha review. Usually, the most complex or most used parts of the code are developed more completely in the alpha, in order to enable early resolution of design questions.

10.10.1.2 Quality Team Involvement

It is understood that alpha software is not fully functional. However, Corporate Software Quality tests all software that is to be sent to users or run on customer equipment so that possible serious errors can be removed. Examples of such errors are software behavior that compromises a user's system or presence of a virus. This pre-testing of alpha software that is sent to users will protect the reputation of software with customers.

Example Memo to the Recipient of Alpha Software:

The _____ (software name), version _____ is a very early "alpha" release of the software. This means that the software is at the prototype stage when it is first able to run. It does not have all the intended functionality, but it does have core functions and will be able to accept inputs and generate outputs.

Please provide detailed description of identified problems and provide feedback on specific aspects of the software. Kindly provide input while there is still time to make significant changes as the software design evolves.

We ask for your patience with difficulties or problems that you may encounter. Our objective is to hear about these from you during this evaluation, and most of all to obtain your views on the software design approach. In-depth software reliability testing, installation testing, and documentation testing are done at alpha test time, as the software is only a prototype.

Thank you for your participation.

Fig. 10.1 Sample alpha testing transmittal memo

If any end-users or customers will receive software for alpha evaluation, or if software will be run on customer equipment, be sure to send it first to Corporate Software Quality. This prior review and approval is required. Be sure to discuss any exceptions with the Software Quality Manager for your sector.

All software and user documentation in any lifecycle stage must include the Copyright, Ordering Information and Disclaimer Notice elements. In order not to delay project schedules, Corporate Software Quality:

- Uses e-mail notes rather than structured reports on alpha evaluations.
- Works with project managers to complete alpha evaluations within the time needed.

10.10.1.3 Common Problems

- Customer expectations surrounding Alpha software have not been appropriately set and customers are disappointed at the limited functionality and problems encountered.
- Software sent to users or run on customer equipment is not tested by Corporate Software Quality beforehand (EPRI 2006).

10.10.2 Beta Testing

Beta testing is similar to alpha testing, except that no systems professionals are present during user acceptance testing. In addition to employing a usability factors checklist, the user test group records them to the systems people periodically. Modifications are made to make the system ready to be released for full implementation and operations.

A product's beta is an officially released version of a product which includes most of the product's functionality. The beta version is intended for external testing of the product in order to identify configurations that cause problems, as well as collect requirements and suggestions from users.

Before its official release, a beta version always undergoes a full cycle of internal testing, after which the application is sufficiently stable in the majority of computing environments.

A release notes file is supplied with each beta version. Release notes provide the following information:

- the exact version number,
- system and technical requirements for the equipment used for testing,
- the list of changes since the previous version, and,
- Descriptions of known problems (if any) and other relevant information.

Please note that a beta version is not the final version of the product and therefore the developer does not guarantee an absence of errors that may disrupt the computer's operation and/or result in data loss.

Consequently, beta testers use the beta version at their own risk and the company bears no responsibility for any consequences arising out of the use of the beta version.

10.10.2.1 Participating in Beta Testing Enables you to:

- help to improve the quality of the product being tested;
- suggestions on possible ways of improving the product.

10.10.2.2 Reporting Problems:

- To report an error, a detailed description of the steps which lead up to the error and characteristics of the hardware used for testing is necessary.
- Suggestions on improving the product from different testers and users are also included.

10.11 UML Model Testing

Testing is done commonly from program source code and graphical models of software (such as control flow graphs). Briand and Labiche describe the TOTEM

(Testing Object-orienTed systEms with the Unifed Modeling Language) system test methodology (Briand and Labiche 2001). System test requirements are derived from UML analysis artifacts such as use cases, their corresponding sequence and collaboration diagrams, class diagrams and from OCL used across all these artifacts. This approach is not automatic and is meant for system testing, whereas the proposed approach is targeted toward integration testing related to interactions and behaviors of objects. Offutt and Abdurazik developed a technique for generating test cases for code rather than designs from a restricted form of UML state diagrams. The approach performs a limited form of class-level testing, and it does not directly support testing of object interactions. They have also developed a criterion for dynamic testing that involved message sequence paths. They adapt traditional data flow coverage criteria (e.g. all definition—uses) in the context of UML Collaboration Diagrams, but do not address test case generation. We use a different criterion named border testing criteria. Also, our approach generates test data. To our knowledge, no other approaches in UML testing address automatic test data generation (Offutt and Abdurazik 1999). Scheetz et al. developed an approach to generating system (black box) test cases for code from UML class diagrams (Scheetz et al. 1999). Many others have proposed methods for generating test case using UML statechart diagrams.

The scheme for generating Test Cases from collaboration diagram is as shown in Fig. 10.2. There are two major steps in the test data generation algorithm named Distinction and Halving. Each input variable xi of a given input is increased/ decreased by the value UNITxi, while keeping all the other input variables constant. If path P is not traversed for the modified input we say that constraint violation has occurred. If the function F has decreased and constraint violation has not occurred, then the given input variable and the appropriate direction is

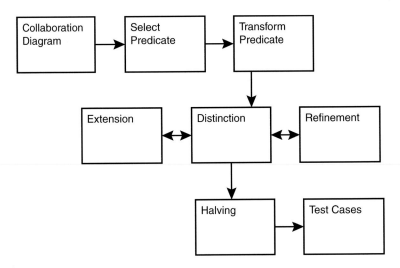

Fig. 10.2 Scheme for test case generation from collaboration diagram

selected. In Distinction step, two inputs Iin (inside) and Iout (outside) are generated such that these two points belong to different sides of border b. The distinction step is carried out in two phases: the extension phase and the refinement phase. In the extension phase the size of the step is doubled after each successful move. Also in the extension phase, when the minimization function becomes negative (or zero), the required program inputs Iin and Iout have been found. Once the extension phase is complete, the refinement phase is carried out. Distinction step is followed by Halving Step. In the Halving Step, the size of the step between Iin and Iout is halved to get the new input Ih. If F(Ih) is negative (or zero), then Ih replaces Iout, otherwise Ih replaces Iin. Here we minimize the distance between the input points obtained in the Distinction Step (Samuel and Mall 2004).

10.12 Testing for Object-Oriented Systems

Testing being the activity of attempting to elicit results that can be monitored and analyzed is not wholly sufficient for the object-oriented paradigm. Object-oriented tests, like object-oriented programming itself, revolves around the concept of reducing effort while maximizing value. Value in this case is the confidence in the thoroughness of the tests. This results in a lengthened test design phase and a shortened test implementation phase.

Elienes outlines three levels of testing when testing object-oriented systems. The first level as he coins, is the strategic level. At this level there should be risk assessment. That is, which components of the system need to be evaluated with the most care, which components do the most other components rely on for functionality and which components are required for fault tolerance. In embedded real time devices some components may be the difference between a system that saves lives and one that takes lives. The second portion of the testing revolves around tactics. However, when and where these modules and objects are going to be tested will be answered. Plans based on the risk assessment should be created. Finally, the tests are implemented and executed at the operational level (Elienes 1995).

10.13 Testing in a Box

Testing for either the inside or the outside of a system solely can be deemed testing from inside a box. This box is merely an analogy for the feeling of either only having internal or external access to a system. The system is in a sense limited to you by your access and knowledge. White-box testing is theoretically capable of finding and correcting all logical errors in the programs structure. However, this is impossible due to the limited nature of human intelligence. Black box testing on the other hand, provides a unique insight into the errors that may arise by the typical use of the system.

10.13.1 Black-Box Testing

Black-box testing demonstrates that software functions are operational, that output is correctly produced from input and that databases are properly accessed and updated. It requires knowledge of the user requirements to conduct such tests. Black-box testing thus does not directly examine the syntax and internal logical structure of the software and is therefore not an alternative to white-box testing. Black-box test cases consist of sets of inputs conditions, either intentionally valid or invalid, that fully exercise all functional requirements of a program (Schach 2007). The goal is to verify the specified behavior in the interface of the unit; we are not interested in how the unit solves this. We send stimuli with different parameters to the unit, and as output we receive responses or perhaps we see a change in some attribute. In traditional testing, the equivalence sets are based upon the parameters, since parameters in object-oriented languages are often references to objects. A common mistake when you test the code is not to check the output data. Just to receive output data is not sufficient; we must also make sure that it is correct. This may involve much work (Jacobson et al. 1992). Both white-box and black-box testing uncover errors that occur during coding, but only black-box testing is focused on uncovering errors that occur in implementing user requirements and systems design specifications. Unlike white-box testing, which is performed early in the testing process, black-box testing tends to be conducted during later stages of testing. Black-box test cases are therefore more appropriate at integration, systems, and acceptance testing levels (Schach 2007).

10.13.2 White-Box Testing

White-box testing is based on the direct examination of the internal logical structure of the software. It uses knowledge of the program structure to develop efficient and defective tests of the program's functionality. One could assume that white-box testing can result in a totally correct program. But, logical paths through a program can become overwhelming even in fairly simple programs. Therefore, exhaustive white-box testing is impracticable (Schach 2007). White-box testing is also called program-based testing, glass-box testing or structural testing. To examine the effectiveness of our test cases we can use measures of test coverage. The least coverage is to exercise each decision-to-decision path at least once. A decision is typically an IF-statement. The minimum requirement should be that all statements have been executed. Normally this is a reasonable goal for test coverage. A more ambitious goal is exercise all pairs of DD paths. It is hardly ever possible to test all the possible paths in the system, regardless of parameters or variable values. Complete path testing can often only be made locally (Jacobson et al. 1992).

10.14 Testing Alternatives

A great number of nuances are being discovered in relation to software testing. These nuances combined with the complexity of software systems provide what is a never ending bug removal cycle. Just as the complexity barrier indicates: chances are testing and fixing problems may not necessarily improve the quality and reliability of the software. Sometimes fixing a problem may introduce much more severe problems into the system, sometimes after bug fixes, such as the telephone outage in California and eastern seaboard in 1991. The disaster happened after changing 3 lines of code in the signaling system (Pan 1999).

Software testing as old as the first program still is a prime target of research and industry specialists. These individuals realize that software bugs may be incomprehensible to us for many reasons. For many, it is the sheer amount of information that is required to analyze all aspects of a system. For others, it is the obtuseness of code or a model. Still, other times there is just not the correct algorithm for solving the problem so it must be completed in a least then optimal method.

However, testing is by no means a waste of resources. It is just beneficial to know the downsides and the tools available to promote better, faster and more efficient testing. Many testing frameworks are in existence to provide testing for anything from embedded systems, to web applications to POSIX implementations in various kernels. The best software engineers know their own limits and where they need to bring in outside assistance, whether in the form of a toolset or more human capital.

10.15 When to Release the Software

After a product has been successfully maintained for many years, it eventually may lose its usefulness and be superseded by a totally different product. A product still may be useful, but the cost of porting it to new hardware or running it under a new operating system may be more than the cost of constructing a new product, and using the old one as a prototype. Testing is potentially endless. We cannot test till all the defects are unearthed and removed.

When will the software ship (hopefully it will). Release time can be seen as a function of resources divided by cost over time. In this scenario the software testing will continue until the resources of money, equipment and human labor are no longer financially viable. This scenario driven by profit provides what someone has deemed as the most cost efficient testing available. The second scenario retains the same function of cost, but is mainly time limited. The software must ship by a certain deadline. This deadline be it arbitrary (someone likes the fifth of October for no valid reason) or purposeful (to mesh with another product's release date) is the sole factor of testing time. This method assumes that resources are bountiful, implementation is complete and you test until you are cut off. It may be obvious to you that these methods are not quality driven and they do not require certain bug quotas to be fixed or any reliability standards. This may seem to be inefficient at worst, but take into consideration that all bugs may never be discovered and fixed, and a system of quotas and quality may be almost impossible to implement while still retaining profitability.

10.16 Chapter Summary and Conclusions

The theme of this chapter is that testing is an activity to verify that a correct system is built. Testing is an expensive activity in the software life cycle because many faults are detected late in the development and long after release. This chapter gives an idea of the different kinds of testing and when to stop testing. To do effective testing, every test should aim to detect fault.

Testing software without running test cases is termed non-execution-based testing. Execution-based testing is also known as program testing and it can be a very effective way to show the presence of faults, but it is hopelessly inadequate for showing their absence.

In execution testing we test different properties of a product like utility, reliability, robustness, performance, and correctness. Execution-based testing should be done by someone else other than the programmer in order to reduce conflict of interest scenarios. Once the components are integrated, system testing ensures that the complete system compiles with functional and non-functional requirements of the system.

Unit testing is performed to test a specific unit. Unit tests are particularly important in the object-oriented paradigm because objects are already designed to be modular and this makes them a prime target of unit tests.

Acceptance testing evaluates the new system to determine if it meets user requirements under the operating conditions specified. It consists of two kinds of testing:

- Alpha testing: this is a closely monitored test normally using advanced users and relying heavily on their input for corrections and bug details before the beta tests.
- Beta testing: a testing approach that provides a copy of the software to the target audience and allows them to utilize it as if it is release ready. In turn, for the normally free use of the software, the software development team is able to track and respond to issues that these users bring to their attention.

Black-box testing thus does not directly examine the syntax and internal logical structure of the software. White-box testing is based on the direct examination of the internal logical structure of the software.

Testing is an endless process. When all the testing has been completed, all the documentation prepared in testing is saved for future use.

10.17 Exercises

1. What are the similarities between product testing and acceptance testing? What are the major differences?
2. What is the role of SQA during the testing phase?
3. Explain why testing can detect the only presence of errors, not their absence.
4. Give three situations where the testing of all independent paths through a program may not detect program errors.
5. Explain why interface testing is necessary even when individual components have been extensively validated through component testing and program inspections.
6. Compare top-down and bottom-up testing by discussing their advantages and disadvantages.
7. What element should an error report contain?
8. Outline a software testing scenario.
9. Explain the purpose of white-box testing and black-box testing.
10. Define alpha and beta tests.
11. What is the difference between testing and debugging?
12. A big issue concerning testing is when to stop testing. In the chapter, what method was proposed? Are there other criteria that might work as well? How do you stop if the goal is to have more or less bugs?
13. What is software quality assurance? What is the difference between quality assurance and software testing?
14. Does every software project need testers?
15. Why does software have bugs?
16. What is a 'walkthrough'? What is an inspection?
17. Which is the best definition of complete testing?
    (a) You have discovered every bug in the program.
    (b) You have tested every statement, branch, and combination of branches in the program.
    (c) You have completed every test in the test plan.
    (d) You have reached the scheduled ship date.

References

Offutt J, Abdurazik A (1999) Generating tests from UML specifications. In: Proceedings of the 2nd international conference on the UML, Fort Collins, TX, 1999. Lecture notes in computer science. Springer

Briand L, Labiche Y (2001) A UML-based approach to system testing. In: Proceedings of the 4th international conference on the UML, Toronto, Canada. Lecture notes in computer science, Spriner

Bruegge B, Dutoit A (2004) Object-oriented software engineering: using UML, patterns, and java, 2nd edn. Pearson Education, Ltd., Upper Saddle River

Burch J G (1992) Systems analysis, design, and implementation. Boyd & Fraser Publishing Company

Elienes A (1995) Principles of object-oriented software development. United Kingdom University Press, Cambridge, United Kingdom

Electric Power Research Institute (2006) Alpha testing. http://www.epri.com/eprisoftware/processguide/alphatest.html. Accessed 6 Oct 2006

Hetzel W C, Hetzel B (1991) The complete guide to software testing. John Wiley & Sons, Inc.

Jacobson I, Christerson M, Jonsson P (1992) Object-oriented software engineering: a use case driven approach. Addison-Wesley

McGregor J D (1994) Planning for testing. http://www.cs.clemson.edu/ ~ johnmc/joop/col2/column2.html. Accessed 6 Oct 2006

Pressman R (2005) Software engineering: a practitioner's approach, 6th edn. McGraw-Hill

Samuel P, Mall R (2004) Test case generation from UML design specifications. Dept. of Computer Science & Engineering IIT, Kharagpur, India

Scheetz M, Von Mayrhauser A, Dahlman F R, Howe A E (1999) Generating test cases from an OO model with an AI planning system. In: Proceedings of the international symposium on software reliability engineering (ISSRE'99), Boca Raton, Florida. IEEE Computer Society Press

Schach S R (1996) Testings: principles and practice. In: ACM computing surveys, vol. 28, no. 1. pp 277–279

Schach S R (1999) Classical and object-oriented software engineering with UML and C++, 4th edn. McGraw-Hill

Schach S R (2007) Object-oriented and classical software engineering, 7th edn. McGraw-Hill

Sommerville I (2004) Software engineering, 7th edn. Pearson Education, Ltd., Boston

Pan J (1999) Software testing. Carnegie Mellon University. http://www.ece.cmu.edu/ ~ koopman/des_s99/sw_testing/. Accessed 25 July 2006

Further Reading

'How to Break Software: A Practical Guide to Testing' This is a practical book on software testing where the author presents a set of experienced based guidelines on designing tests that are likely to be effective in discovering system faults (J.A. Whittaker, 2002, Addison Wesley).

'Software Testing and Verification'. This special issue of IBM systems journal includes a number of papers on testing, good overview, paper on test metrics and test automation. (IBM systems journal, 2002)

'Testing Computer Software' 2nd Edition, is its practical point-by-point guide to everyday software testing, from creating a test plan, to writing effective bug reports, to working with programming staff and management to fix bugs (Cem Kaner, Jack Falk, Hung Q. Nguyen, 1999, Wiley).

Chapter 11
Project Wrap-Up, Delivery, and Maintenance

11.1 Project Management and Success Criteria

"Project management" is a composite of managing many other project elements: people, communication, commitments, resources, requirements, changes, risks, opportunities, expectations, technology, suppliers and conflicts. Nearly every project includes aspects of all previously listed activities and the successful project manager must keep an eye on them all. Activities for a successful project management are (Wiegers 2009):

1. Define Project Success Criteria
2. Define Product Vision and Project Scope
3. Define Product Release Criteria
4. Negotiate Achievable Commitments
5. Study Previous Lessons Learned
6. Conduct Project Retrospectives

11.1.1 Define Project Success Criteria

Wiegers quotes Stephen Covey's words as "Begin with the end in mind" from The 7 Habits of Highly Effective People. Wiegers describes "To begin with the end in mind means to start with a clear understanding of your destination. It means to know where you're going so that you better understand where you are now and so the steps you take are always in the right direction." At the beginning of every software project, the stakeholders need to reach a common understanding of how they will determine whether this project is successful. If you don't know early on how you're going to measure your project's success, you're headed for trouble. Defining explicit success criteria during the project's inception keeps stakeholders focused on shared objectives and aids in establishing targets for evaluating progress. For initiatives that involve multiple subprojects, success criteria will help align all subprojects with the big picture. Ill-defined, unrealistic or poorly communicated success criteria can lead

R. Y. Lee, *Software Engineering: A Hands-On Approach*,
DOI: 10.2991/978-94-6239-006-5_11, © Atlantis Press and the author 2013

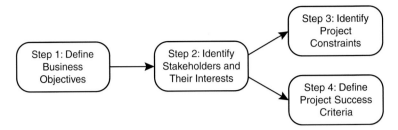

Fig. 11.1 A process for defining success criteria (Wiegers 2009)

to disappointing outcomes. Figure 11.1 describes the four-step process for defining project success criteria. This chapter ideas and methods will promote correct habits and enable project success (Wiegers 2009).

11.1.2 Define Business Objectives

Business objectives are the motivations to take on the project. The enumeration of each goal into an achievable task with success metrics allow for evaluation. For instance it may be necessary to enter a certain market or develop something that is new to a market or perhaps even create a new market. Other times a project may mark the termination of a dying line of products. Whatever the goal may be, it is necessary to make it both clear and transparent. Doing so will allow for the most accurate assessment of completion. These business requirements should not be confused with the structural and technical aspects of the coding process. A product that is developed to specification is essentially wasted if there is no business incentive. Business objectives typically address:

- What a product must be and do, including essential or distinguishing functions it will perform and how well it will perform them.
- Economic constraints, including development costs, cost of materials, and time to market.
- The product's operational and temporal context, such as technologies required for compatibility in the target environment, backward compatibility, and future extensibility.

Business objectives must be SMART: Specific (not vague), Measurable (not qualitative), Attainable (not impossible), Relevant (not unimportant), and Time-based (not open ended).

Table 11.1 illustrates some simple business objective statements. Record your business goals and objectives in a high-level strategic guiding document for the project. Such documents often include a vision and scope document, project charter, project overview, business plan, business case and marketing requirements

Table 11.1 Examples of financial and non-financial business objective

Financial	Nonfinancial
Capture a market share of X % within Y months	Achieve a customer satisfaction measure of at least X within Y months of release
Increase market share in region X by Y % in Z months	Process as least X transactions per day with at least Y % accuracy
Reach a sales volume of X units or revenue of $Y within Z months	Achieve a specified time to market that provides clear business advantages
Achieve X % profit or return on investment within Y months	Develop a robust platform for a family of related products
Achieve positive cash flow on this product within Y months	Develop specific core technology competencies in the organization with competency measured in some way
Save $X per year by replacing a high-maintenance legacy system	Be rated as the top product for reliability in published product reviews by a specific date
Keep unit materials cost below X dollars per unit in the expected Y year lifetime of the product	Maintain staff turnover below X % through the end of the project
Reduce support costs by X % within Y months	Comply with a specific set of Federal and state regulations
Receive no more than X service calls per unit and Y warranty calls per unit within Z months after shipping	Reduce turnaround time to X hours on Y % of customer support calls

document. Some software project management plan templates include a section on management objectives and priorities, which could contain business objectives and stakeholder analysis. Other information might go into other project guiding documents, such as a quality assurance plan that contains product release criteria. As the team gets into design and implementation, they might discover certain business objectives to be unattainable. The cost of materials might be higher than planned or cutting-edge technologies might not work as expected. Business realities also can change, along with evolving marketplace demands or reduced profit forecasts. Under such circumstances, you'll need to modify your business objectives and reassess to see whether the project is still worth pursuing (Wiegers 2009).

A project achieves success by delivering suitable value to various stakeholders. Begin your quest for success by identifying these stakeholders and what is important to them. "Value" could translate to time savings for a corporate department, market dominance for a commercial software vendor, or increased productivity for a user. Look for stakeholders both inside and outside the development organization. Next, perform a stakeholder analysis to reveal the expectations each stakeholder group has for the project.

Identify each stakeholder's interests; Interests include financial benefits, specific time to market, required functionality, performance targets, usability, reliability, or other quality characteristics. Then evaluate how the project will be affected if each interest is or is not satisfied. The project might not be able to fully satisfy everyone's interests. This analysis will help you determine which interests are the most compelling.

Fig. 11.2 Flexibility
diagram for a hypothetical
commercial software product

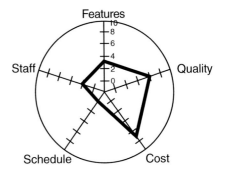

Figure 11.2 illustrates a simple template you can use to document essential stakeholder information. Also assess the relative influence each stakeholder has on the project's decisions. Some stakeholders might wield great political power while others could dictate essential features, impose restricting constraints, or be a potential source of substantial revenue. Key stakeholders are those who can strongly influence the project's decisions—and those whom it's most important to satisfy. Expect to encounter conflicting stakeholder interests. Finance might want the lowest possible unit cost for the product, although the development team wishes to use expensive, cutting-edge technologies to meet stringent performance demands. Different market segments will value different combinations of time to market, feature richness, and reliability. Identifying your key stakeholders will help you to resolve such conflicts as they arise and to negotiate win-win solutions that maximize benefits for the greatest number of stakeholders (Wiegers 2009) (Table 11.2).

- Voting, majority rules. This allows for a democratic style of leadership in which all team members have a perceived equal influence on decision making.
- Reaching unanimous agreement is important for groups that work closely. Maintaining unity and understanding is crucial when working closely with a few individuals. It is not necessary for unanimous agreement in larger more heterogeneous groups.
- Delegating the decision to a single individual is a method that allows for great control and allows for an increased agility, though it may not allow for a large range of creativity unless the person making the decisions is well advised.
- Achieving consensus is vital to maintain continuity. Consensus is not just informing all parties it is an agreement and understanding between all parties on relevant terms and details. Without this it is impossible to maintain a consistent and productive environment.
- Having the person in charge make the decision after collecting input from others aids in promoting consensus. This is derived from the instance immediately above.
- Other scenarios exist, such as boards of directors and oversight committees. It may be found that any number of these methods works best with certain portions of the team, but the goal is to alleviate confusion and create a sense of togetherness among workers and oversight.

Table 11.2 Simple stakeholder analysis example (Wiegers 2009)

Stakeholder	Major Benefits	Attitude	Win Conditions	Constraints
Executives	Increased revenue	See product as an avenue to 25 % increase in market share within 1 year	Richer and more novel feature set than competitors have	Maximum budget = $1.4 M
Manuscript Editors	Fewer errors in their work	Highly receptive, but unwilling to be retained	Automatic error correction capabilities; ease-of-use; high reliability	Must run on existing low-end PC's

It seems paradoxical to say that what form of decision making will be implemented must be decided before decisions are made, but it is necessary. The benefits of speed and conciseness of oversight decisions need to be weighed against the benefit of more thorough and developed plans and ideas that develop from a shared decision making process.

11.1.3 Identify Project Constraints

Wiegers finds that it is possible to build software faster and cheaper. Yet, software development time and creativity are inversely related. You can't accelerate creativity, and software development is a highly creative activity. High-quality deliverables may take a bit longer to initially release, but they save you much time in the long run because you don't have to do extensive testing and rework to fix and maintain them. Software with stringent quality demands, such as safety–critical systems, is expensive because it's imperative to remove defects. The tradeoffs are real, and a project manager must make tradeoffs along five dimensions: features (or scope), quality, staff, cost, and schedule. Some people add an additional dimension, risk. Each dimension fits in one of three broad categories:

- Constraints impose boundaries and restrictions within which the team must operate. For constraints, state the immovable limit.
- Drivers identify key project success goals. Drivers typically afford the project manager a bit of latitude, but they define important targets toward which the team must work.
- Degrees of freedom are factors the project manager can adjust within certain limits. For degrees of freedom, identify the allowable range within which the project manager must operate.

It's important to classify the five project dimensions into these three categories early in your project. One way to represent this information is with a flexibility diagram, illustrated in Fig. 11.2. A flexibility diagram has the five normalized axes extend radially from a center point. A point is plotted for each dimension on a scale that ranges from 0 (a constraint) to 10 (complete flexibility). Figure 11.2 illustrates a flexibility diagram for a hypothetical shrink-wrap software package. The point plotted at zero on the schedule axis indicates that schedule is a constraint. Cost and quality are degrees of freedom that offer more flexibility for the project manager. Connecting the points on all five axes creates an irregularly-shaped pentagon. The flexibility diagram is a qualitative tool intended to help the key stakeholders discuss project constraints and success drivers (Wiegers 2009). It should be noted however that this is merely a tool. Also note that the smaller the pentagon, the more constrained the project is resulting in a lower chance of it being fully successful. Managers often think of schedule as being a constraint when it's really a driver. With proper understanding of a project's drivers and constraints, the project manager can make appropriate tradeoff decisions. Not all project dimensions can be constraints. Project managers must have some latitude to react to schedule slips, scope growth, staff turnover, and other eventualities. A successful manager adjusts the degrees of freedom so as to let the team achieve the project's success criteria—its drivers— within the limits imposed by the constraints.

11.1.4 Derive Project Success Criteria

Each business objective should imply technical success criteria you can monitor prior to release. The development team can't directly meet a business objective of "Capture a 40 percent market share within 12 months". However, they can decompose that objective into specific project actions and product features aligned with achieving the market share target. Disconnects between success criteria and business objectives give stakeholders no way to assess whether the project is likely to meet those objectives. Success criteria shape many aspects of your project, beginning with the functional and nonfunctional requirements specifications. If the stakeholders understand the project's principal business objectives and success criteria, it's easier to make decisions about which proposed product features and characteristics are in scope and which are not. For example, performance goals are often written against either internal benchmarks or external industry reference data. A goal, for example, might compare a new search engine's performance to that of the prior version and also to the performance of a competing product under some set of standard conditions.

Such success criteria allow the project team design tests that measure whether performance, reliability, or throughput goals are being met. Trends in these measures may provide early warning that you might miss a success target, so the team can either take corrective action or redefine the success criteria. Not all of these success criteria can be considered a top priority. You'll have to make thoughtful tradeoff decisions to ensure that you satisfy your most important business priorities. Without clear priorities, team members can work at cross-purposes, which can often lead to rework, frustration and stress. Weigh your success criteria based on how strongly they align with achieving the critical business objectives, so team members will know which ones are essential and which are merely desirable. Consider summarizing your success information similarly to the example form illustrated in Table 11.3. List each business objective, the stakeholder who provided it, corresponding project success criteria, and each criterion's method of measurement along with a well thought out priority weight. Use the stakeholder list to verify that you haven't overlooked any important business objectives. You don't need to associate all stakeholders with every business objective, but every objective should be important to some stakeholder. If you clearly define what success means at the beginning of your project, you greatly increase the chances of achieving it at the end. Understanding your stakeholders' interests, writing clear business objectives, and

Table 11.3 Sample success criteria table (Wiegers 2009)

Business Objective	Stakeholder	Project Success Criteria	Measurement	Weight
Achieve a customer satisfaction measure of at least 4 out of 5 within four months after release	Marketing	Human factors approves user interface design through usability review	All major severity UI design defects are corrected	20
		UI prototype evaluation with focus group results in at least 4.2/5.0 rating and will enable 90 % a high-priority use cases to be performed	Survey of focus group members: count of defined high-priority use cases	30
		Product passes acceptance criteria defined by 80 % of beta site evaluators	Pass/fail rating by beta sites	50

defining corresponding success criteria help to lay the foundation for a happy outcome (Wiegers 2009).

11.2 Project Termination and Release

During this phase, the product is delivered and an overall project history is collected. A handful of key developers, the technical writers, and the team leaders are
involved with wrapping up the system for installation and acceptance. They are
also responsible for collecting the project history for future use (Bruegge and
Dutoit 1999). The goal of a release is to make a work product available to other
project participants, often replacing an older version of the artifact. A release can
be as simple as a two-line electronic message or it can consist of several pieces of
information: the new version of the artifact, a list of changes made since the last
release of the artifact, a list of problems or issues yet to be addressed, and an
author. Releases are used to make a large amount of information available in a
controlled manner by batching, documenting, and reviewing many changes
together. Project and client reviews are typically preceded by a release of one or
more deliverables (Schach 2007).

11.3 Project Wrap-Up and Result Presentation

This is the last phase of SDLC and a presentation will be given to the client by the
development team. First a brief description of the industry, company and specific
facility at which the project will be conducted is given. Then the purpose and goals
achieved will be presented. The project presentation consists of the following steps:

1. Problem description
2. Purpose and goals
3. Approach and methodologies
4. Project deliverables
5. Requirements
6. Software Project Management plan
7. Design
8. Use Cases
9. Standards used
10. Timeline

Presenting the results is the final step in the development cycle. It is an
important step as it is able to convey the projects successes and failures. The
meeting may last up to a couple days and is attended by facilitators, stakeholders
and the architecture team. In advance, the stakeholders are given a workbook
containing a summary of the process, the collection of test cases, and examples of

Table 11.4 Agenda of presentation

Time	Activity
8:30 a.m.	Start
	QARs overview
	Business drivers
	Architecture plans
	Purpose of meeting and expected outcomes
9:30 a.m.	Presentation of analysis of test cases #1 and #2
11:45 a.m.	Review of first two test cases and tailoring of afternoon objectives
Noon	Lunch
1:00 p.m.	Presentation of analysis of two or more additional test cases
4:00 p.m.	Wrap-up
	Review of test cases
	Summary
	Review future activities
5:00 p.m.	End

the test case analysis. A sample agenda is shown below in Table 11.4. During the presentation, the facilitators and stakeholders should probe architectural approaches from the point of view of specific quality attribute requirements. In addition to the specific questions included in the test cases, the participants might generate additional quality-attribute-specific questions for high-priority quality attribute requirements. The conclusions, recommendations and action items resulting from the presentation must be captured in a short report and distributed to the participants (Barbacci et al. 2002).

11.3.1 Postmortem Review

Postmortem reviews focus on extracting lessons from the development team since the software is delivered. Postmortem reviews need to be conducted shortly after the end of the project so that minimal information is lost or distorted by subsequent experience. The end of the project is usually a good time to assess which techniques, methods and tools have worked and have been critical to the success of the system. Even if the results of post mortems are not disseminated through the company via formal channels, they can still be disseminated indirectly to the project participants. Project participants are frequently reassigned to different projects and often disseminate the lessons learned from the old project to other parts of the company.

- Question about problems: What kinds of communication and negotiation problems, that occurred, have emerged in the development of the system?

- Question eliciting: Possible speculation on what kind of information structure is needed for team-solutions; to those problems based on design in conjunction with a model-based object-oriented software engineering methodology.
- Question eliciting's other aspects: What observations and comments do you have about the project that were either concerning or perceived as positive. Think about your expectations at the beginning of the project and how they improved/evolved.
- Open-ended catch-all question: In addition to the above questions, please feel free to discuss any other issues and proposed solutions that you feel are relevant.

It is difficult to anticipate all information needs and plan everything in advance. Issues resulting from a combination of seemingly isolated facts from different areas of the project are difficult to anticipate since no participants have a global view of all the facts and workings. Consequently, a project should be prepared to deal with unexpected situations, often under pressure. We call the communication resulting from such crises unplanned communication events.

11.3.2 Release Management

New versions of a system may be created to fix reported faults or as part of the development process. In general, creating a new system version involves creating new source code and building the system. Creating a release, however, is more complex and expensive. As well as creating new source code and building a system, data and configuration files may have to be prepared and new documentation written. The release must be packaged and distributed to customers (Sommerville 1996).

Over the lifetime of a system, changes are likely to be proposed on a fairly regular basis. Corrective changes are intended to fix faults. Perfective changes are intended to implement new requirements or to improve system maintainability. Adaptive changes are intended to change the system to make it operate in a new environment. The Configuration manager must decide how often the components affected by these changes should be rebuilt into a new version or release of the system.

Sometimes, this decision is forced on management by faults that have been discovered by customers. If these problems cause data corruption or system crashes, the customers must be provided with a fix promptly. Sometimes, these faults are repaired by object-code patching. Object-code patching involves modifying the object code of the current version. The faulty code is replaced by an unconditional branch to the corrected code which then branches back to the end of the code being replaced.

However, this is an error-prone approach to problem repair. A better approach is to create a new system version (or interim release) which incorporates repairs to the critical faults. This interim release may be distributed without new documentation as there is no new functionality to be described.

When a new release of a system is created, the changes which have been made may introduce new faults or bring other existing faults to light. The more changes that are made to a system, the more new faults will be introduced. Therefore, if a release incorporates a large number of changes, it is likely that there will be a correspondingly large number of new faults. These have to be fixed in the next system release.

Lehman's fifth law, the Law of Conservation of Familiarity, suggests that over the lifetime of a system, the incremental system change in each release is approximately constant. This 'law' was derived by analyzing systems over many years and measuring the number of system modules which were modified in each release.

Lehman suggested that if a lot of new functionality was introduced in one release of a system, it would be necessary to issue another release fairly quickly. This would be required to correct errors that have resulted from the system changes and to improve the performance of the delivered release. Over the lifetime of a system, this was seen to be a self-regulating process. There was a limit to the rate at which new functionality could be introduced. This suggests that it is unwise to change too much of a system's functionality at once. Otherwise an excessive number of faults may be introduced. A good change strategy is to interweave fault repair releases and releases which change the system's functionality.

If some system changes are concerned with fault repair and others with changing the system behavior, mixing these changes into a single release could cause problems. The faults reported apply to a given version of the system code and if that code is changed to amend its behavior, it is expensive to check if the faults still apply. All serious faults (faults which cause system corruption) should be repaired before functional or behavioral changes are applied.

Release management is complicated by the fact that customers may not actually want a new release of the system. Some system users may be happy with an existing system version. They may consider that it is not worth the cost of changing to a new release. However, as the system's functionality is enhanced, most customers will eventually decide to change.

This causes CM problems because new releases of the system cannot depend on the existence of previous releases. Consider the following scenario:

1. Release 1 of a system is distributed and put into use.
2. Release 2 follows which requires the installation of new data files but some customers do not need the facilities of release 2 so remain with release 1.
3. Release 3 requires the data files installed in release 2 and has no new data files of its own.

The software distributor cannot assume that the files required for Release 3 have already been installed in all sites. Some sites may go directly from Release 1 to Release 3, skipping Release 2. Some sites may have modified the data files associated with Release 2 to reflect local circumstances. Therefore, the data files must be re-distributed and installed again with Release 3 of the system.

11.4 Development and Maintenance

Once the product has passed its acceptance test, it is handed over to the client. The product is installed and used for the purpose of which it was constructed. However, it will almost certainly need to undergo post-delivery maintenance, either to fix faults or extend the functionality of the product. Because a product consists of more than just the source code, any changes to the documentation, manual or any other component of the product after it has been delivered to the client are examples of post-delivery maintenance (Schach 2007).

11.5 Why Post-Delivery Maintenance is Necessary

There are three main reasons for making changes to a product (Schach 2007):

- A fault needs correcting, whether an analysis fault, design fault, coding fault, documentation fault, or any other type of fault. This is termed corrective maintenance.
- In perfective maintenance, a change is made to the code in order to improve the effectiveness of the product. For instance, the client may wish for additional functionality or request that the product be modified so that it runs faster.
- In adaptive maintenance, a change to the product is made in order to react to a change in the environment in which the product operates.

11.6 What is Required of Post-Delivery Maintenance Programmers?

During the software life cycle, more time is spent on post-delivery maintenance than on any other activity. In fact, on average, at least 67 % of total cost can be attributed to post-delivery maintenance (Schach 2007). Post-Delivery maintenance is the most difficult of all aspects of software production, a major reason is that post-delivery maintenance incorporates aspects of all the other work-flows of the software process. A defect report is filed if, in the opinion of the user, the product is not working as specified in the user manual. One of the first possible causes could be that the user has misunderstood the user manual or is simply using the product incorrectly. Sometimes the user manual might be poorly worded and nothing could be wrong in the code. Another possible cause is that there is actually a fault in the code. Before making any changes, it is vital that the maintenance programmer needs to have above average debugging skills. Suppose that the maintenance programmer has located a fault and must fix it without inadvertently introducing another fault elsewhere in the product, that is, a regression fault. If regression faults are to be minimized, detailed documentation for the product must be available. Having determined the probable fault, the maintenance programmer must test that the modification works correctly and that no regression faults have been introduced in the process. Checking for regression faults is done using a specific set of test data stored precisely for performing such regression testing. Next, the test cases used for modification must be added to the stored test cases. Finally, it is essential that the maintenance programmer document every change made to the system. The other major maintenance tasks are adaptive and perfective maintenance. To perform these, the maintenance programmer must perform the requirements, analysis, design, and implementation workflows, taking the existing product as the starting point. Perfective and adaptive maintenance are adversely affected by a lack of adequate documentation, just like corrective maintenance. Take, for example, a situation where the product has been delivered to the client. But, the client is dissatisfied, because the product does not work correctly, it does not do everything that the client currently wants, or the circumstances for which the product was built have changed in some way. It is important for every software organization to keep its clients happy by providing excellent post-delivery maintenance service. So, for product after product, post-delivery maintenance is the most challenging aspect of software production—and frequently the most thankless. Managers must restrict post-delivery tasks to programmers with all the skills required to properly perform maintenance (Schach 2007).

11.7 Managing Post-Delivery Maintenance

11.7.1 Defect Reports

Changing products is a necessity for all software projects. In order to fully understand the changes that are necessary, defect reports must first be filed. Defect reports are the documents that describe in what manner the product differs from the specification. Defects in the product may range from things that are simple and cosmetic to defects that are capable of causing injury or loss of life. Maintenance programmers work from the defect reports which are normally collected and filed by customer service representatives. Since, it is imperative that defect reports are not necessarily handled in the order obtained, but in the order of importance (the ones that have the greatest adverse consequences first) not all reports will be handled on a first come first served basis. A manager will normally oversee the process to ensure that the changes are occurring in the correct order. Another role of the manager is to decide when an update should be released. As it is substantial work to update documentation and user programs, several changes may be compiled into a single update. Upon a change all customers should be updated and provided with the correct deliverable and documentation.

11.7.2 Authorizing Changes to the Product

A maintenance programmer is assigned the task of determining the fault that caused the failure and repairing it. After the code has been changed, the repair must be tested, as must the product as a whole. Then, the documentation must be reviewed and updated to reflect the changes. In particular, a detailed description of what was changed, why it was changed, by whom, and when must be added to the prologue comments of any changed code artifact. A similar set of steps is followed when performing perfective or adaptive maintenance; the only difference is they are initiated by a change in requirements rather than by a defect report. Before the product is distributed, it must be subjected to software quality assurance testing performed by an independent group; that is the members of the maintenance SQA group must not report to the same manager as the maintenance programmer. Testing during post-delivery maintenance is difficult and time consuming, and the SQA group should not underestimate the implications of the software maintenance with regard to testing. Once the new version has been approved by the SQA group, it can be distributed (Schach 2007).

11.7.3 Ensuring Maintainability

A well-written product goes through a series of different versions over its lifetime. As a result, it is necessary to plan for post-delivery maintenance during the entire software process. During the design workflow, information hiding techniques should be employed; during the implementation variable names should be selected that will be meaningful to future maintenance programmers. Documentation should be complete, correct and reflect the current version of every component code artifact of the product. In other words, just as software development personnel should always be conscious of inevitable post-delivery maintenance, so software maintenance personnel should always be equally conscious of future post-delivery maintenance (Schach 2007).

11.7.4 Problem of Repeated Maintenance

One of the most frustrating difficulties of software development is the moving-target problem. As fast as the developer constructs the product, the client can change the requirements. Not only is this frustrating to the development team, frequent changes can result in a poorly constructed product. These also may result in an increased cost of the product. The more a completed product is changed, the more it deviates from its original design, and the more difficult further changes become. Under repeated maintenance, the documentation is likely to become even less reliable than usual, and the regression testing data may not be up to date (Schach 2007).

11.8 Maintenance of Object-Oriented Software

One reason put forward for using the object-oriented paradigm is that it promotes maintainability. After all, an object is an independent unit of program. A well designed object exhibits conceptual independence, otherwise known as encapsulation. In addition, objects exhibit physical independence; information hiding is employed to ensure that implementation details are not visible outside the object. There are three main obstacles to the proper maintenance of object-oriented software.

1. Hierarchy may not be displayed in the linear fashion but spread over the entire product.
2. Polymorphism and dynamic binding may have a deleterious impact on maintenance
3. The final problem is the fragile base class problem. For instance, a base class does all that is required for the design of new product. A class derived from this base class has features that must be renamed, re-implemented, suppressed, or changed in many other ways if the base class is changed (Schach 2007).

11.9 Post-Delivery Maintenance Skill Versus Development Skills

Skills needed for post-delivery maintenance:

- For corrective maintenance, the ability to determine the cause of a failure of a large product is essential. Though this skill is required throughout product testing and analysis phases, it becomes significantly more important when dealing with maintenance as error reports can be ambiguous or misleading.
- Another skill is the ability to function effectively without adequate documentation. Documentation is derived mainly from development and user experiences. Users are not trained to identify faults and analyze program behavior. Users may report bugs that are actually not bugs or may report that some functionality is not working when it does work, or not know the correct circumstances under which the fault occurs. Maintenance programmers also run the risk of developers intentionally or unintentionally creating incorrect documentation. Developers that take on other's roles during development or that are untrained in the documentation area are a common cause of misinformation. Also, never rule out the possibility that developers attempt to hide flaws by incorrectly documenting code.
- Also skills with regard to analysis, design, implementation and testing are essential for adaptive and preventative maintenance. These activities are also carried out during the development process, and each requires specialized skills

if it is to be performed correctly. A post-delivery maintenance programmer needs skills different from those needed by software professionals specializing in other aspects of software production. Maintenance programmer must be highly skilled in a broad variety of areas (Schach 2007).

11.10   Reverse Engineering

Sometimes the only documentation available for post-delivery maintenance is the source code itself. One way of handling this problem is to start with the source code and attempt to re-create the design documents or even the specifications. This process is called reverse engineering. The process of analyzing a system's code, documentation and behavior in order to identify current components, along with their dependencies is vital to the ability to extract and create system abstractions and design information. The subject system is not altered; however, additional knowledge about the system is produced (SEI 2006).

There are many different reverse-engineering tasks. This section discusses several of the most important: program analysis, plan recognition, concept assignment, re-documentation, and architecture recovery. The first three tasks can be viewed as pattern matching at different levels of abstraction. Program analysis is syntactic pattern matching in the programming-language domain, plan recognition is semantic pattern matching in the programming-language domain, and concept assignment is semantic pattern matching in the application (or end-user) domain.

Assigning each task to an abstraction layer can be difficult. One can argue that re-documentation is a form of reverse engineering, or that it is simply restructuring at the same abstraction level. How one interprets each type of reverse engineering depends on several factors, such as which document you read, what you mean by reverse engineering, and what you mean by re-documentation. Many of these arguments are more in the lines of religion rather than practical differences. Suffice it to say that reverse engineering is not an exact science, and neither is its terminology (Pressman 2005).

Diagrams can be constructed from flowcharts or UML diagrams. These visual aids can help in the process of design recovery. Once the maintenance team has reconstructed the design, there are two possibilities. One is to reconstruct the specifications or modify the reconstructed specifications to reflect the changes. The other is to re-implement the product the usual way. In practice reconstruction of the specifications is an extremely hard task. More frequently, the reconstructed design is modified and the modified design is then is forward engineered.

A related activity often performed during maintenance is restructuring. Reverse engineering takes the product from a lower level of abstraction to a higher level of abstraction, for example from code to design. Forward engineering takes the product from a higher level of abstraction to a lower level. Restructuring which is a process of improving the product without changing functionality also takes place at the same time. In general, restructuring is performed to make the source code easier to maintain. A worse situation occurs if the source code is lost and the executable is available. A possible way to recreate the source code is to use a dissembler to create assembler code and then try to recreate the high level language code. Problems with this kind of approach are (Schach 2007):

1. The names of variables will have been lost
2. Many compilers optimize the code in a way that makes it rather difficult to recreate the source code.
3. A construct in assembler could correspond to a number of different possible constructs in source code.

11.11 Agile Modeling and Extreme Programming

Agile Modeling (AM) is a practice-based methodology for effective modeling of software-based systems. The AM methodology is a collection of practices—guided by principles and values—that are meant to be applied by software professionals on a day-to-day basis. AM is not a prescriptive process, in other words it does not define detailed procedures for how to create a given type of model, instead it provides advice for how to be effective as a modeler. AM is "touchy-feely" in that it is not hard science—think of AM as an art, not a science.

An important concept to understand about AM is that it is not a complete software process. AM's focus is on effective modeling and documentation. That's it. It doesn't include programming activities, although it will tell you to prove your models with code. It doesn't include testing activities, although it will tell you to consider testability as you model. It doesn't cover project management, system deployment, system operations, system support, or a myriad of other issues. This is because AM's focus is on a portion of the overall software process. In fact you need to use it with another, full-fledged process such as eXtreme Programming (XP), DSDM, SCRUM, the Agile Unified Process (AUP), or the Rational Unified Process (RUP). You start with a base process, such as XP or RUP, or perhaps even your own existing process, and then tailor it with AM (hopefully adopting all of AM) as well as other techniques as appropriate to form your own process that reflects your unique needs. Alternatively, you may decide to pick the best features from a collection of existing software processes to form your own process. For XP projects, AM explicitly describes how to improve productivity through the addition of modeling activities, whereas for RUP projects it describes how to streamline modeling and documentation efforts in order to improve productivity.

11.12 Testing During Post-Delivery Maintenance

Through the course of development, the product development team will have broad overview of the product, but, as a result of rapid turnover, members of the postdelivery maintenance team will be involved in the original development. Therefore, the maintainer tends to see the product as a set of loosely related components and is not aware that a change to one code artifact may affect one or more other artifacts. Even though the maintainer wished to understand the product, the pressure to fix it with such little time can make it impossible. Sometimes even the documentation is not be available to assist. One alternative is to use regression testing, that is testing the product against the previous test cases to ensure it still works correctly. This is why it is extremely important to keep test cases. As a result of changes being made the test cases will have to be changed as well. Depending on the maintenance performed, some valid test cases become invalid. There is no extra work involved in maintaining a file of test cases and their expected outcomes. It is sometimes argued that regression testing is a waste of time, however, the dangers of neglecting it are too great to hold the argument. As such regression testing is an essential aspect of maintenance (Schach 2007).

11.13 Metrics and Challenges of Post-Delivery Maintenance

Metrics in software engineering have been discussed for a long time, but not used widely as a means of increasing the quality of the product or process. The real problem is that we cannot measure exactly what we would like to measure; we must assume that there are relationships between that which we can measure and that which we would like to measure. Process related metrics measure things like man-months, schedule time, and number of faults found during testing. Below are the metrics collected when working with OOSE :

- Total development time
- Development time in each process and subprocess
- Time spent modifying models from previous processes
- Time spent in all kinds of subprocesses, such as use case specification, use case design, block design, block testing for each object
- Number of different kinds of fault found during reviews
- Number of change proposals for previous models
- Cost for quality assurance
- Cost for introducing new development process and tools

For instance, if we know the average time to specify a use case, we can predict the time to specify all use cases. These measures vary greatly between different projects, organizations, applications and staffing. Therefore it is dangerous to draw general conclusions on existing data without looking at the specific circumstances. Several product related metrics have been proposed and one is traceability. One example to measure traceability is to measure how many of the original requirements are directly traceable to the use case model. Metrics are more appropriate for object-oriented software (Jacobson et al. 1992):

- Total number of classes
- Number classes reused
- Total number of operations
- Number of operations reused
- Total number of stimuli sent
- Number of classes inheriting
- Number of classes that are dependent
- Number of direct users of a class or operation

The activities of post-delivery maintenance essentially are analysis, design, implementation, testing and documentation. Therefore, the metrics that measure these activities are equally applicable to maintenance. Metrics specific to post-delivery maintenance include measures relating to software defect reports with total number of defect reports and classification of defects.

The challenge of post-delivery maintenance is that changing the maintenance is harder than development, yet maintenance is looked down upon by developers and is also paid less than developers (Schach 2007).

11.14 Chapter Summary and Conclusions

The result of the presentation is the final activity in the project development process. Section 11.1 shows the sample agenda for the presentation. During the project termination and release phase, the product is delivered and the project history is collected. A select few developers, the technical writers and the team leaders are involved with wrapping up the project.

The end of the project is usually a good time to assess which techniques, methods, and tools have worked and to decide which have been critical to the success of the system. The post mortem phase concentrates on this. After post mortem reviews, it is time to release the project. The post-delivery maintenance, is used to either fix faults or extend the functionality of the product.

Once the product has passed its acceptance test, it is handed over to the client. However, it is almost certain to undergo post-delivery maintenance, either to fix faults or extend the functionality of the product.

Post-delivery maintenance is the most difficult of all aspects of software production; a major reason is that post-delivery maintenance incorporates aspects of all the other work-flows of the software process.

The defect report is filed by the user if the product appears to be functioning incorrectly. The maintenance programmer should first consult the defect report file, which contains all reported defects that have not yet been fixed. This, together with suggestions for working around a portion of the product that may be responsible for failure.

Maintenance programmers are assigned the task of determining the fault that caused the failure and repairing it. There are three obstacles to maintenance of object-oriented software. Hierarchy, Polymorphism and Dynamic binding, and fragile base classes can cause issues for maintenance programmers. One way of handling this problem is to start with the source code and attempt to re-create the design documents or even the specifications. This process is called reverse engineering.

Metrics specific to post-delivery maintenance include measures relating to software defects and reports with the total number of defect reports and classification of defects.

11.15 Exercises

1. Why do you think that the mistake is frequently made of considering post-delivery software maintenance to be inferior to software development?
2. Consider a product that determines whether a computer is virus free. Describe why such a product is likely to have multiple variations of many of its code artifacts. What are the implications for post-delivery maintenance? How can the resulting problem be solved?
3. Repeat the problem 11.2 on automated library circulation system of problem.
4. Repeat problem 11.2 for the automated teller machine.
5. If you are a manager in charge of post-delivery maintenance in a large software organization, what are the qualities you look for when hiring new employees?
6. What are the implications of post-delivery maintenance for a one-person software production organization?
7. Why is software maintenance is needed?
8. Why should the role of software architect and project leader be assigned to different people?
9. Give an agenda for a project presentation on library circulation software.
10. Who should decide when software is ready to be released?
11. How can it be determined if a test environment is appropriate?

References

Barbacci M R, Ellison R, Lattanze A J, Stafford J A, Weinstock C B, Wood W G (2002) Quality attribute workshops, 2nd edn. Technical Report CMU/SEI-2002-TR-019 019 ESC-TR-2002-019
Bruegge B, Dutoit A (1999) Object-oriented software engineering: conquering complex and changing systems. Pearson Education, Ltd., Upper Saddle River

Jacobson I, Christerson M, Jonsson P (1992) Object-oriented software engineering: a use case driven approach. Addison-Wesley
Pressman R (2005) Software engineering: a practitioner's approach, 6th edn. McGraw-Hill
Schach S R (2007) Object-oriented and classical software engineering, 7th edn. McGraw-Hill
Sommerville I (1996) Software engineering, 5th edn. Peason Education, Ltd., Boston
SEI (2006) http://www.sei.cmu.edu/str/indexes/glossary/reverse-engineering.html. Accessed 28 July 2006
Wiegers KE (2009) Software requirements. Microsoft press, Redmond, Washington, USA

Further Reading

Papers on software maintenance appear in May 1994 issue of communication of ACM. The July/august 1998 issue of IEEE software contains a number of articles on legacy systems.

'The Art of Project Management's full of practical tools and real experience that will help you succeed with your projects. It is refreshing to see a book on project management that spends as much time on human factors. (Scott Berkun, 2005, O'Reilly)

'Software Project Management: A Unified Framework' The book begins by outlining the "traditional" waterfall approach to software development. The author looks at what changes for management when it comes to today's iterative software processes. Written with an eye toward management, the author takes you through common pitfalls of managing software, (Walker Royce, 1998, Addison-Wesley Professional)

Chapter 12
Software Metrics and Measurements

The previous chapters have provided many details concerning software development and design. They have shown design principles, practices and tools for the development of the best software possible. However, what makes software good or correct and how does one even go about measuring such subjective qualities? Furthermore, why and when do these things need to be measured? This chapter will cover the fundamentals of measuring a project's success as well explain when metrics and measures may not be appropriate.

12.1 Theory and Practice

Metrics are any form of quantitative measure, of any system's expression of chosen traits (Pressman 2005). In simpler terms metrics provide a measure of how much a system or portion of a system is similar to a given construct. It is not only pertinent to have many metrics but the metrics also must be of a good quality. When applied appropriately, software engineers are able to convey to the stakeholders in definite terms, the degree to which a system is compliant with a given set of specifications.

In order to best understand the nuances of metrics and measurements it is necessary to realize the real challenges that exist in the field. Challenges arise from all aspects of the software development lifecycle. Challenges from representational notations to the problem of designing a measurement for some of the more oblique entities of a project are prevalent, but surmountable when the correct concepts and practices are applied. Without good metrics it is impossible to measure software in any capacity and furthermore metrics should be able to measure the benefit of other metrics.

R. Y. Lee, *Software Engineering: A Hands-On Approach*,
DOI: 10.2991/978-94-6239-006-5_12, © Atlantis Press and the author 2013

12.1.1 Challenges Using and Understanding Metrics

Metrics are vital to determining a projects success. However, metrics can be subjective due to the fact that many different aspects of the same entity may be important to different people when looking at achieving some goal. Using the example of software complexity allows for a starting point when examining the challenges of metrics. If you were asked to develop a list of aspects that made software more complex you most likely would begin with attributes such as: degree to which inheritance is used, language which the software is written (a low level language versus a inherently understandable fourth generation language). Also, the number of platforms for which the application must function will undoubtedly create a greater complexity. Using this short list it is possible to begin to see the difficulties in complexity metrics. One possible debate arises from the complexity of inheritance, does inheritance add or remove complexity. Inheritance without doubt makes it harder to understand classes without a greater understanding of the whole, especially when multiple inheritances is present such as with the C++ language. On the other hand, inheritance allows for a uniform relationship between classes where common attributes and methods are defined and hopefully documented.

Thomas McCabe uses control graphs to measure complexity, merely the complexity of the underlying control structure (McCabe 1976). McCabe uses directed call graphs derived from the number of "linearly independent" circuits or simply speaking any sort of branching construct. The idea behind this metric seems simple, provide some sort of maximum number of these circuits and restrict developers to this form, this will allow for a cleaner and more concise coding style and in turn produce less complex code overall. If the only aspect examined is the number of circuits, then a particularly clever programmer would realize that they could reduce the circuit count, by using a goto statement. The usefulness of goto as an understandable program construct is highly debatable. McCabe recognizes the disadvantage of his method and proposes to extend it to encompass the intrinsic complexity gained from operator overloading, data structure malformations and operator misuse (McCabe 1976).

If anything is taken from McCabe's study it should be that a complete analysis of complexity cannot ever be found. As one examines one aspect an issue rises resulting from the scrutiny. Complexity in one analyst's eyes will not be the same in the eyes of the next. The disagreement over what should be correct and proper is precisely what leads to the study of metrics and measurements and more specifically into what constitutes a good metric.

12.1.2 Properties of a Good Measurement or Metric

Software development does not lend itself to the creation of measures and metrics for several reasons. One reason is that in order to obtain the most accurate and pertinent measures there must be a deeply engrossed analysis team in place (Basili and Phillips 1981). An attempt to involve team members so deeply would cause the development team much anguish and most likely skew any sort of metric or measurement being attempted. Knowing this, most companies deploy analyst, but they rely on developers to report their doings using standard forms and accounting procedures.

Even in the most trivial circumstances Basili and Phillips point to a few issues that can arise from trying to measure things like the number of faults or developer hours involved in creating a module. One of the more pertinent issues is time reporting. If an analyst wanted to measure the time spent integrating each of three separate modules into a subsystem, they could merely read the developer's time logs and determine the amount of time integrating each module. There are, however, few methods that the developer could use to log the time spent integrating the modules (Basili and Phillips 1981):

- Take the overall time and divide it by three (the number of modules in this case).
- Denote the time taken per module as the time it took to associate it with any other module.
- Associate the entire time with what the developer deems to be the most significant module being associated.

Saying all of these measurements have their merits and all have their faults is cliché, but pertinent to understand why you cannot mix and match measurements in order to cover for the individual faults of each metric or measurement. Using more than one will cause unnecessary complications. These complications may not be evident when examining the measurement in a vacuum, but the faults are brutally evident when attempting to use these measurements in another metric.

The process for construction of metrics, measurements and their applications should be consistent throughout an organization and should have well established guidelines that are followed closely. In order for the metrics to be used properly, they should be of the least complexity possible.

12.1.3 Etiquette

Measuring and analyzing the software development process is a fundamental part of development. The information that is gained, though pertinent to the understanding of the project as a whole, may come with certain aspects that may provide personal insight regarding the developers. Some metrics may be found to be reflective of a certain individuals' competence, though the metric may not be designed nor actually reflect such a measure. It is necessary to respect the developer and not provide their name or other identifying information to people outside of management. Sommerville cites the ACM/IEEE-CS joint task force in making it clear that the competence and personal character of colleagues should be respected (Sommerville 2004). To do so, it is important to leave out personal information of the developers when communicating information to people that is not their management.

Beside not revealing personal performance information publically there are a few other etiquette matters that should be considered. First, metrics should be considered with sensitivity. Even if personal information is not included some developers may find that they feel targeted and slighted by the presentation of the results. The results of the tests and analysis should not become obsessed with a particular area that seems to be lacking or one portion that seems to be flourishing. In no circumstances should individuals or teams be either, praised or threatened. This is not the point of such measurements. Instead use managerial channels to asses a team or individual's performance (Pressman 2005).

Always keep in mind that less than satisfactory measurements of performance do not necessarily denote less the satisfactory effort or ability. A high number of faults from a certain module during testing may not indicate that the implementation was poor, but maybe the design or theory was not well constructed. Anytime an abnormally good or poor measurement is observed it is prudent to revisit the data collection and analysis of said attribute or even the meta-metric itself.

12.1.4 Private Versus Public Metrics

Metric data will be collected and stored, but not all of this data is fit to be distributed to the public at large. Some of the data collected will be of a nature sensitive to individual teams or developers and should be distributed only to management or quality control teams within the organization. This information can be a strong driver when presented to the team or individual. It will allow them to see the baseline created by their co-workers and where they stand in relation to it. Setting goals and demonstrating progress will drive workers to increase their quality and quantity of work (Pressman 2005).

Some measurements will be worth promoting and publishing. Metrics that indicate performance and reliability of the product seem the obvious choice when such measures are compared to the competition. This will often "prove" some kind of advantage. The measures using collective and assimilated information should be used with caution as they can be misleading and easily misused.

12.1.5 Baseline Measurements

A baseline measurement is one that can be compiled from past projects. Baseline measurements provide a sense of where you are in relation to other projects. Using such measurements analysts should be able to determine if the project is reasonably sound, financially speaking, based on a given schedule. Project data from past projects (the ones being used for the baseline) should be complete and thorough, not rough estimates. The projects should be similar to one another, so that the metrics have some sort of relevance. A final characteristic of a good baseline is that it is composed of as many data sets as possible. Using these techniques it is possible to gauge a projects progress accurately and cost effectively.

12.1.6 Attributes of a Good Metric

Metrics, like the software they evaluate, must be evaluated. Meta-metrics are the description of a metric. Measuring metrics at times is a subjective process; this is because metrics are subjectively analyzed. The quality of metrics can be broken into five categories (Conte et al. 1986):

- Simplicity: Simple metrics provide information in a manner that is easily comprehended by anyone reading it. A simple metric may be the number of faults in a program or the time taken to develop a component. A metric that is not simple for example is a complex derivative based analysis of complexity. In a nutshell simple is easy to understand.
- Validity: For a metric to be valid, they should measure what they claim to measure. For instance if lines of code were to be counted they could be a measure of program size, but if they were to be used as a measure of a programmer's amount of work it would seem incorrect as, lines of code may vary with programming style. Furthermore, the development of a sound and correct algorithm is more difficult then coding a solution.
- Robustness: Being robust means that a measurement should not be easily tampered with. Whether the tampering is merely a side effect of some modifications to the project or if it is done as part of what could be coined creative analysis or the modification of superficial components in order to illicit the desired results.
- Prescriptiveness: Is the test in the right place at the right time? Just like you don't see signs past a sharp curve on the highway informing you that you just passed through the sharp curve successfully, software metrics should be deployed at the correct time. If algorithms are analyzed after they have been coded and integrated it may be difficult to repair them, but if they are tested before integration they will be more easily repaired. Measures must be applied before they become obsolete and their results must be presented to all stakeholders.
- Analyzability: Can statistics be applied to the metric? Normally, a metric that can be properly statistically analyzed will be less prone to subjectivity. Measurements should be just that, depth of nesting, number of global constructs, count of classes, number of memory leaks. All of those previously listed can be

244 12 Software Metrics and Measurements

counted and analyzed, however, things such as the use of Object-Oriented concepts verse not using such concepts is much more capable to subjectivity on the part of the data collection team.

Most developers will experience a slew of metrics and measurements in the course of their career. By paying careful attention to the five core values of a quality metric, it will be possible to determine which measures should be carefully reviewed and which should be reworked or eliminated entirely (Pressman 2005).

12.1.7 Establishing Uniform Measures

Measurements not only rely on consistent data collection and rigorous analysis, but they must also rely on comparative scales of the proper nature (Card and Glass 1990):

- Nominal scales provide discrimination between two objects based on simple and basic characteristics such as color or shape (rounded or square).
- Ordinal scales rely on some sort of ranking, shortest to tallest or heaviest to lightest.
- Interval scales have the characteristic that the distance between two points signifies a degree of distance proportional to the distance.
- Ratio scales are similar to interval scales, but have a fixed absolute zero point.

Human error and bias is one of the main contributors of non-uniform measures. With proper training and experience software engineers can curb their biases and create consistent and uniform measurements. The use of software measurement frameworks, however, facilitate the most accurate and consistent measurements possible.

Software measurement frameworks allow for a consistent and complete software development lifecycle, data collection cycle to occur. By using a software measurement framework, you are assured that data is collected without bias and uniformly amongst all projects implementing it. A software framework collects metrics from the code base itself, as well as from the developers during the development process, in an automated fashion. A good framework is able to collect and format data in a fashion that is consistent with the requirements of both the stakeholders and developers (Zuse 1997).

12.2 Quality Metrics

Software quality is one of the most subjective terms available when determining the goals of an organization. Pressman defines software quality as the following "an effective software process applied in a manner that creates a useful product that provides measureable value for those who produce it and those who use it" (Pressman 2010). Schach would like to point out the fault with most quality definitions. Quality to a software engineer is merely to release a product that meets specification. This attribution to quality standards is lacking. It should contain a pursuit of excellence, excellence in development, delivery and customer satisfaction (Schach 2007). This leads to the definition for this text, software quality is the development, delivery and maintenance of software that meets specifications and customer needs, while not being restricted to simply conforming to specification.

12.2.1 Garvin's Quality Dimensions

Quality dimensions encompass all fields. It is important to look at software from the perspective of an outsider to the development process in order to understand the metrics and measures to use when developing software. David Garvin proposes such a metric. His metric does not apply to software in particular. There are no metrics proposed to subjectively derive any of the points of quality he lists, it is merely a theoretical overview of quality. Garvin lists eight quality dimensions which are listed below, each with a brief description of how it relates to software (Pressman 2010).

- Performance quality, the functionality and feature set that is desirable to the end user.
- Feature set, an appropriate feature set should encompass the user's needs and provide intuitive and useful functionality.
- Reliability, correctly engineered and implemented software will provide the user with the lowest number of faults while functioning to specification.
- Conformance, this is all about the software meeting standards both internally and externally. Software should function within safety parameters when applicable. Software should also conform to design and documentation standards.
- Durability, the length a software system will last is known as its durability. Software needs to be maintainable over time with little to no degradation in fault level.
- Serviceability, relates directly to the ability to modify it and correct faults. The quicker, easier and least intensive that maintenance is the better the serviceability of software will be.
- Aesthetics, the correctness of many aspects of code can be analyzed and systematically scrutinized, but the aesthetic value is much more difficult to compound as a subjective tangible entity. Aesthetics should conform to UI guidelines, but also more importantly it should be pleasing to view and operate.
- Perception, you reputation or the reputation of a genre of software may influence customer's and the general public's opinions of your product rather than the actual product itself. It is necessary to promote the truth about yourself and your product in order to avoid being stereotyped or the victim of prejudice.

12.2.2 McCall's Quality Factors

A more viable set of measures for software was developed by McCall, Richards and Walters. Their measures relate directly to the field of software engineering. Not all the quality factors they list can be directly measured; if indirect measures of these are taken it is possible to assess the software quality. McCall's quality factors are listed below with a brief explanation of each (McCall and Cavano 1978).

- Correctness: The extent to which a program satisfies its specification and fulfills the customer's mission objective.
- Reliability: The extent to which a program can be expected to perform its intended function with required precision.
- Usability: The effort required to learn, operate, prepare input, and interpret output of a program.
- Integrity: The extent to which access to software or data by unauthorized persons can be controlled.
- Efficiency: The amount of computing resources and code required by a program to perform its functions.
- Flexibility: The effort required to modify an operational program.
- Testability: The effort required to test a program to ensure that it performs its intended functions.
- Maintainability: The effort required to locate and fix an error in a program.
- Portability: The effort required to transfer the program from one hardware and/ or software system environment to another.
- Reusability: The extent to which a program or parts of a program can be reused in another application.
- Interoperability: The effort required to couple one system to another (Fig 12.1).

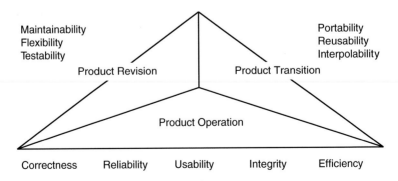

Fig. 12.1 McCall's quality factor illustration (McCall and Cavano 1978)

12.2.3 ISO 9126 Quality Factors

When measuring product quality it is helpful to have general guidelines to follow as you assess a system. The ISO 9126 quality factors define six attributes (each containing sub-attributes) in its model of quality for organizations to use as a general checklist. These qualities include):

- **Functionality** defines how well needs are satisfied by software under the sub-attributes of *suitability, accuracy, interoperability, security,* and *compliance.*
- **Reliability** describes the period of time for which the software will perform its purpose indicated by *maturity, fault tolerance,* and *recoverability.*
- **Usability** indicates the ease-of-use of the software as defined by its *undert-sandability, learnability,* and *operability.*
- **Efficiency** is the extent to which software makes effective use of system resources; included in efficiency is *time behavior,* and *resource behavior.*
- **Maintainability** describes how easily a repair or revision is able to be made to software. This can be described by the sub-attributes of *analyzability, change-ability, testability,* and *stability.*
- **Portability** is defined by a system's *adaptability, conformance, installability,* and *replaceability.*

These guidelines are, of course, very general and leave much room for specification to the individual organizations.

12.2.4 The Quantitative View

The McCall's, Garvin's, and ISO 9126 quality factors, among others, define a very general way to describe the quality of software, however, more exact measures should be preferred when assessing software. The primary problem with using the previously defined quality factors is the level of subjectivity required when directly applying them. Therefore, we will define quantitative measures in subsequent sections that allow us to indirectly measure software quality; this can be done by measuring those attributes of software that allow for such exact metrics which also represent some manifestation of software quality. By doing so we eliminate much of the subjective nature of software quality assessment.

12.3 Design Metrics

The need for design metrics stems from the need for quality design. The design of a program directly impacts the maintainability, efficiency, and adaptability of the software, and a well-written piece of software aims to be easily modified, easy to maintain, and minimally reliant on system resources. Design metrics, which measure can be used to evaluate aspects such as the interface, architecture, individual, and even individual components, aid the developers in achieving such software goals. Constant re-evaluation and revision throughout the design process using design metrics will prevent the need for major revisions down the road.

12.3.1 Interface

While important to the success of a piece of software, the user interface is often times very difficult to measure in terms of usability. Evaluation of the user interface is important, though, and should be included in the assessment of software.

Design metrics can be devised to assess software's usability as it pertains to specific quality factors like those defined by ISO 9126, such as learnability or operability. You may, for example, set a specification for the exact amount of time it should take a user to complete a task or operation in the software. Once these standards are specified, users can be observed and surveyed during and after use of the software to gather numerical data to compare to specified metrics. Sommerville describes some common methods for evaluating the user interface (Sommerville 2004):

- Questionnaires to collect information regarding the users' opinion of the user interface.
- Recording user interaction with the software via video equipment.
- Observing the users as they interact with the software and "think aloud."
- Implementing code to collect data regarding feature use and error commonality.

While metrics exist to measure usability without direct interaction with users, Pressman suggests that user preferences and opinions are most important. He quotes Nielson and Levy as reporting that "one has a reasonably large change of success if one chooses between interface [designs] based solely on users' opinions" (Pressman 2005).

12.3.2 Web Design Evaluation

Still a relatively new topic, design metrics for the Web are much more qualitative. To be useful, metrics for Web design should answer questions such as (Sommerville 2004):

- Is usability promoted by the interface?
- Is the application pleasing to the user?
- Does the design provide the most information with the least effort?

- Is the interface easy to navigate?
- How well does to architectural design accommodate the system's objectives, reduce complexity, and enhance performance?

12.3.3 Object-Oriented Design Metrics

Object-oriented design can be assessed for its complexity, cohesion, and many other attributes. While some may argue that OO design metrics are not formal enough, metrics such as those described in this section can provide valuable, objective insight into the effectiveness of an OO system and its components.

12.3.3.1 Complexity

The complexity of the design of a system most often measures the degree to which components are related. Component dependence on other data and components by looking at a top-down profile of the software design allows complexity to be measured. Complexity in this regard can be measured by counting the number of entry and exit points in components as well as fan-in and fan-out, which is discussed in Sect. 12.3.3.4.

12.3.3.2 Cohesion

The cohesion of a component measures the extent to which properties within the component relates to one another. A components processes and properties should relate to an individual purpose. If cohesion is high, then it is very likely the component is maintainable and adaptable.

12.3.3.3 Coupling

In object-oriented design software, components may share information by passing the item between them. This piece of information is then known as a couple. Coupling measures the amount of these couples being passed between components. Minimizing coupling increases component independence, simplifies design, and enhances re-usability. Components that have a decreased dependence upon each other are referred to as loosely couple components while highly interdependent ones are called tightly coupled.

12.3.3.4 Fan-In and Fan-Out

There are two simple measures of the design of a software's design and components: fan-in and fan-out. Fan-in for a particular component is the number of
components that call the give component. Similarly, fan-out is the number of
components call by said component. It is generally recommended that fan-out be
minimized to less than seven for most components and fan-in be maximized to
promote re-usability.

12.3.4 Architectural Design Evaluation

Evaluating a program's architecture is an important part of the design process,
especially as the complexity of a program grows. Beyond the subjective, qualitative
means for analyzing program architecture, architectural design metrics can provide
a quantitative way to assess the structure and components within a program.

Evaluation of a program's architecture often falls on the measurement of the
complexity of structure and data. Pressman, for example, suggests three complexity measures pertaining to the architecture of a program: structural complexity,
data complexity, and system complexity. These measures are defined as the
following:

- Structural complexity: $S(i) = f_{out}^2(i)$
- Data complexity: $D(i) = v(i)/[f_{out}(i) + 1]$
- System complexity: $C(i) = S(i) + D(i)$

where $f_{out}(i)$ is the fan-out of a module i, and $v(i)$ is the number of input/output
variables passed to and from module i. An increase in these metrics correlates to an
increase in overall architectural complexity (Pressman 2005). These metrics,
though, relate to hierarchical architectures only.

If you want to compare various architectures, though, also suggested are simply
shape metrics such as size, depth, width, and arc-to-node ratio of the architecture
in question. For these metrics:

- size $= n + a$
- $r = a/n$

where n is the number of nodes, a is the number of arcs, and r is the arc-to-node
ration.

12.4 Object-Oriented Metrics

Metrics have been proposed specifically for the object-oriented approach for all
stages of the software development process. Pressman lists the following recommended metrics for object-oriented projects (Pressman 2005):

- Number of scenario scripts—This measures the sequence of steps that detail the interaction between the user and the application. The number of such scripts are in direct relation to the size of the software to be created.
- Number of key classes—Known early on in development, key classes are those components that are independent and reusable. The number of such classes indicate the time required to complete the project and the potential re-usability of code.
- Number of support classes—These classes, such as user-interface classes, database classes, and computational classes, are those required to implement a system but not needed immediately. They are developed for key classes and are developed later in the process. Like key classes, they help determine time requirements for a project.
- Average number of support classes per key class—Previous numbers of support classes per key classes can help teams estimate work load for similar projects.
- Number of subsystems—Knowing the subsystems of a software project can be useful when dividing work and scheduling amongst team members.

12.5 Project Metrics

While measuring the quality of software design is important, so is the measurement of the work that goes into completing a project. Project metrics, used by managers and teams for specific projects, are used to maintain and adapt the work flow of the project by measuring the efficacy of the development processes as they pertain to that project.

Project metrics will be used throughout the development of the software as a way to ensure the project remains both on schedule and that product quality is being maintained. This twofold use for project metrics is described by Pressman:

> The intent of project metrics is twofold. First, these metrics are used to minimize the development schedule by making the adjustments necessary to avoid delays and mitigate potential problems and risks. Second, project metrics are used to assess product quality on an ongoing basis and, when necessary, modify the technical approach to improve quality. (Pressman 2005)

Maintaining the project work schedule, as described above, is a useful aspect which begins by looking at past projects. Collecting data from previous projects will provide a baseline for comparison to the current project. Beginning with project estimation, these baseline metrics will allow teams to estimate the time and effort required to complete the project. This allows the team to create the initial project completion schedule, which could, of course, be modified as the job progresses. Baseline measurements from previous work will also allow teams and managers to monitor the rate at which progress occurs and make any adaptations if necessary. The metrics often used to measure production include the number of models created, errors found, lines of code created, etc. By monitoring the work flow, teams are able to improve efficiency and, hence, reduce the time and cost required to complete the project.

Similarly, maintaining the quality at which the project is completed is a useful result of project metrics. Continuous maintenance of quality can to ensure the absence of major flaws down the road that may require large amounts of time and effort to ameliorate. Much like schedule maintenance, monitoring quality will ultimately save time and cost.

12.5.1 Use-Case Metrics

Metrics for a project pertaining to use-cases provide a non-technical, early-on method for estimating time and effort for a project. Before components are modeled and coding begins, software is often defined using methods such as use-cases. Measuring the number of use cases provides a direct way to help determine the size of a project before major work begins.

12.5.2 Size Metrics

One way to measure projects and compare them is via the use of size-oriented metrics (Pressman 2005). These metrics measure the size of past projects and provide a means for comparing costs, estimating completion time, etc. for current and future projects. Size-oriented metrics may include the following measurements:

- Lines of code
- Number of person-months of effort (for all stages and processes of development)
- Cost of development (for all stages and processes of development)
- Pages of documentation created
- Number of errors reported prior to release
- Number of defects encountered after release
- Number of people on the project

Once compiled, these data points from past projects can be used by organizations to develop metrics for use on current and upcoming projects.

12.6 Process Metrics

Unlike project metrics, which tend to exist for use by a team working on a current project, process metrics tend to be measures across multiple projects and are used by organizations to improve the software process as a whole to improve software quality. Project metrics do, however, contribute to the development of process metrics.

In order to measure processes, we measure the outcomes of said processes to gain insight into their effectiveness. Prior to the start of a new project, the team will often measure the results of previous projects to establish baseline measurements for estimation and goal establishment. These metrics will often include measuring errors, defects, time expended, productivity, etc. These measurements describe how effective the efforts and software development process was for past projects. Once completed, the project's errors, defects, etc. will also be measured and added to the records. These measures allow us to derive process metrics that describe the efficiency of the processes used to complete these attributes.

In his book, Pressman discusses the use of both private and public process metrics. He explains that process data should begin at the individual level to be used privately by the given individual. Private process data of this form is intended to be used for individual improvement. Just above this level of privacy are metrics which are private to a team and public to all members of the team to be used for improving team performance. Metrics at this level may include errors and defects for the entire software project or major parts of it while individual private process data may include such measurements for their specific components and tasks. Public process metrics are those visible to many, if not all, members within the organization. These metrics often include the effort expended, defects found, team size of, and other data for the project in its entirety (Pressman 2005).

12.7 Post Release Metrics

Once completed, existing software can benefit from the use of metrics for the purpose of maintenance. The software maturity index (SMI) proposed by IEEE Std. 982.1-1988 (Pressman 2005) is a metric to designate the stability of the software being maintained. The calculation for SMI includes the following:

- M_T = # of modules in current release
- F_c = # modules in current release that have changed
- F_a = # modules in current release that were added
- F_d = # modules from preceding release that were deleted in current release
- $SMI = [M_T - (F_a + F_c + F_d)]/M_T$

An SMI approaching 1.0 is considered to be near stable.

12.8 Chapter Summary and Conclusions

Software metrics play an important role in every aspect of software engineering as they provide a quantitative, objective view regarding the quality of the various aspects of a system. Before the introduction of specific metrics, this chapter explained the key differences between private and public metrics, between what makes and good and bad metric, and how to establish uniform measures. We have discussed how metrics can play a key role in estimating project scheduling, size, effort required and cost via baseline measurements from past projects. Once began, we have seen how metrics can allow us to measure the quality of the design and architecture of a project, and, more specifically, for the object-oriented approach. And once complete, this chapter explained how project metrics help define process metrics for organizations in order to improve the software engineering process so higher quality software can be produced. Lastly, post release metrics were defined for maintaining software and testing maturity.

12.9   Exercises

1. Briefly describe the properties of a good metric.
2. Not all metrics are available for every member of an organization or even development team to see. Describe the difference between public and private metrics and explain why a metric might be private.
3. Explain and diagram how complexity can be increased/decreased by the fan-in and fan-out of components within a system.
4. Why might a Software Maturity Index approaching 1 be an indication that the software release is becoming more stable?

References

Basili V, Phillips T-Y (1981) Evaluating and comparing software metrics in the software engineering laboratory. ACM. http://portal.acm.org/citation.cfm?id=807913. Accessed 24 July 2009
Card D, Glass R (1990) Measuring software design quality. Prentice Hall
Conte SD, Dunsmore H E, Shen V Y (1986) Software engineering metrics and models. Benjamin-Cummings Publishing Co., Inc.
McCabe T (1976) A complexity measure. IEEE Computer Press Society
McCall J, Cavano J (1978) A framework for the measurement of software quality. ACM Sigmetrics Performance Evaluation Review
Pressman R (2005) Software engineering: a practitioner's approach, 6th edn. McGraw-Hill
Pressman R (2010) Software engineering: a practitioner's approach, 7th edn. McGraw-Hill
Schach SR (2007) Object-oriented and classical software engineering, 7th edn. McGraw-Hill
Sommerville I (2004) Software engineering, 7th edn. Peason Education, Ltd., Boston
Zuse (1997) A framework of software measurement. Hubert and Co.

Chapter 13
Hands-On Software Engineering Project

The difference between the real world and academia can be significant. Some efforts to bridge this gap come from projects that simulate real world problems in a controlled learning environment. The expectations that arise in these settings are not just to deliver a product or service by some arbitrary deadlines, but for the student to engross themselves in the processes and activities, and to learn and hone skills that are highly marketable. To do this, students need to provide honest and constructive feedback for other students, the group, and themselves.

Certain topics require more than a theoretical knowledge. The software development lifecycle and related activities are such things. One of the things that will be inevitable in the course of the project is a narrowing of scope or provided features. This concept should be evident to most upper level students, but there is a great difference between understanding the need and having exercised correctly the option. Another benefit of a hands on development project is the growth of many more skills in relation to being a software engineering professional. These skills result from real client interaction, creation of presentation and documentation materials, peer on peer group interaction, and many other aspects too numerous to list.

13.1 Phase I: Team Composition and Problem Definition

Defining the problem is the first step. Chosen representatives should meet with the customer to discuss and document their needs. The requirements of the project should be clearly understood and the actual product description should be negotiated at this time. Software engineers should make sure that all customer interactions are well monitored, and that they adhere to proper business courtesies when working with customers.

The breakdown of teams will either make or break the project. The project leader should consider all aspects of personality and skill before composing teams.

R. Y. Lee, *Software Engineering: A Hands-On Approach,*
DOI: 10.2991/978-94-6239-006-5_13, © Atlantis Press and the author 2013

13.1.1 Team Composition

The success of a team is based heavily on the members of a team and their ability not only as developers, but as team players. In an academic background, especially one where the students have progressed through the same series of courses, there may be a less than typical diversity of skills. Selecting a project manager that has had some real-world leadership ability is important for the delegation of duties, and for the insurance of a smooth and elegant development process. Selecting the project manager is the first order of business.

The democratic process is particularly useful in determining the project leader. In order to have a fair and unbiased election of a project leader, a closed election, with a round of nominations and runoff of the top two candidates, is quick and effective for electing a popular and capable leader. The first duty of the project manager should be to break the class into teams. It may seem preemptive to divide the class into teams without first accessing their capabilities, but there will be room in the future for tweaking team sizes and members. The point of the project is academic, and introducing students to new roles and challenges is important to maintain their interest (Acharya and Burke 2008). After each team has been designated, a team leader is needed. Each team's leader should be announced to the class.

13.1.1.1 Successful Leadership

Successful leaders are those that are able to effectively communicate goals and motivate their teams to achieve these goals. In software engineering, team leaders should be able to convey the ideas and progress of their developers to the customers in a way that the customer can understand. In turn, they must be able to take the ideas and requirements of the customer and translate them into technical issues for their teams to resolve. Software engineering project leadership requires a few specific tasks of the project leader (Stiller and LeBlanc 2002)

- Establish project files that include items such as work reviews, deadlines, and budgets.
- Conduct peer and self reviews.
- Provides independent product assurance to the customer.
- Management of technical documentation destined to be received by the customer.
- Provide project level technical oversight.
- Announces items of revision to the development teams.

There are, of course, other more subtle tasks for the project manager, and to a slightly lesser extent, the team leader to handle. Managers must create obtainable and definite project goals and deadlines. Not only will deadlines promote the promptness of completion, but they will allow for team members to have a sense of achievement. Leaders need to create opportunities. Good team members will work diligently to complete tasks to the specifications given, and a good team leader will provide adequate tasks and specifications for developers to remain busy and productive (CMPS115).

Sometimes there will be less work than time allotted to working. These times should be used by the team and project leaders to tackle some of the tasks that have not been completed or assigned. By taking on some of the development workload, leaders will provide a positive example and show that they are competent and willing to get their hands dirty, as well as provide management functionality. It should be noted that crucial primary duties should not be sidelined to tackle hands-on development activities.

13.1.1.2 Traits of a Successful Team

Team work is a key component in almost any place of business, including academic institutions. This section will provide some quick pointers on how to get the most out of your team. The success of a team depends on the success of the individuals, not the individual's success at a given problem or task, but their success at being a team player. Team composition is crucial when attempting to create balanced and productive teams. In some instances directed team building exercises may help the team learn to cope with their personality differences and help bonding, but in many instances, this solution is not conducive to deadlines and cost factors. An online guide to time management proposes these solutions for expediting the process of building strong and productive teams (Stiller and LeBlanc 2002):

- Always have clear goals.
- There will always be a contest for authority, so avoid overlapping responsibilities and make clear who is responsible for what.
- Trust is essential between team members, so it is best to create an atmosphere of openness.
- Provide feedback. Feedback, both positive and negative, should be well thought out, honest, and it should be sensitive to the team member's personal reputation.

The above practices should be followed by all team members and not just those in leadership positions. When teams are highly cohesive they present a dynamic entity where the input of each team member is amplified by the effort of the others. Remember that disagreements are natural and beneficial, but they should be resolved in a controlled and professional manner.

13.1.2 Writing for Software Engineering

Clear, concise and properly formatted English documentation is quintessential to the software development process. Yet, this item is too often overlooked. Many times professionals may not be completely proficient in the language in which they are to document their code. This should not prohibit them from writing in a style that is understandable by users and other engineers.

13.1.3 Time and Resource Management

Software development, like any other complex and lengthy undertaking, requires planning, analysis and review. There are a couple of techniques that have been in use for over half a century that apply particularly well to software engineering, the critical path method (CPM), and program evaluation and review technique (PERT). These methods rely on the information acquired during project planning such as estimates of effort, the decomposition of product function and the selection of task sets (Stiller and LeBlanc 2002). Using PERT/CPM the project manager can calculate the following (Stiller and LeBlanc 2002):

- The critical path. The critical path is the sequence of events that determines the maximum time for project completion.
- Create time models for tasks, based upon statistical models.
- Formulate boundary times. Boundary times are the earliest a task can begin and the latest it can end without disrupting the flow of the development process.

The information described above is graphically represented in a PERT/CPM schedule. A PERT/CPM schedule represents a task as a box containing a name and a number. The name is the task name and the number is the time required in man units to complete the task. Tasks are connected by either a line indicating progression or a double line which would indicate the critical path. The following example is a partial PERT/CPM derived from "Project Based Software Engineering" by Stiller and LeBlanc (Stiller and LeBlanc 2002) (Fig. 13.1).

13.1.3.1 Gantt Charts and N^2

Gantt charts are a great way to demonstrate the flow of the project and to show the duration and endowment of tasks to teams or individuals. Gantt charts, however,

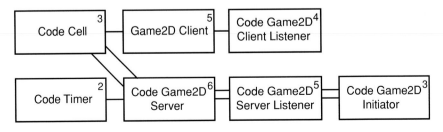

Fig. 13.1 PERT/CPM schedule network for Game2D (Stiller and LeBlanc 2002)

are not sufficient for the representation of task and item dependencies. This is because they do not show relationships between the completion and the startup of connected tasks. Another benefit to the Gantt chart is that it is highly understandable, unlike some of its more verbose counter parts such as the N^2, which though is able to convey inputs and outputs of the task, and it is perpetually more complex. During the project development phase, a Gantt chart spanning the entire development phase should be drafted so that all team members and the customer have an overview and proposed timeline. Internally it may be necessary to create N^2 or other diagrams with more detail to guide the development.

Using the N^2, team members can see what tasks are ready to be under taken. Unlike Gantt charts that progress linearly and rely on a certain sequence of events, N2 provides the activities that must be accomplished before a task can begin. For instance, if Interface task 1 (I_1) can be completed, and then system specification can take place. The following is a Gantt chart of the above procedure, but note how the Gantt chart is ambiguous as to the actual dependencies of the activities.

It should be noted that Fig. 13.2 is not the only format for N^2 diagrams. There are formats such as the line and arrow, and the circle diagram. The diagrams are semantically the same, but there is just a subtle difference in the representations so that non-technical users can understand them without much effort. Consider a few aspects, such as your audience's technical know-how, purpose and time frame when choosing the scheduling diagram (Fig. 13.3).

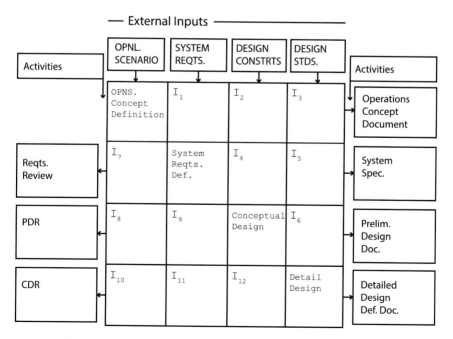

Fig. 13.2 N^2 diagram adapted from Thayer and Dorman (1990) (IEEE)

Fig. 13.3 Gantt Chart of the
same set of tasks in Fig. 13.2
(IEEE)

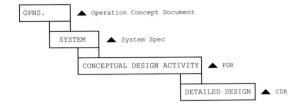

13.1.3.2 Progress Reports

Progress reports are essential in projects where students organize and work at a
pace they set. They are not only important for academic assessment, but for the
student's motivation (Clark et al. 2005). Time management requires plans, and in
order to determine if the plan is being followed, individuals and teams need to
report progress at a regular interval. Work assessment can be broken down cate-
gorically, for better understanding of what each individual spent time working on.
Some potential categories for work are (Fig. 13.4):

- Team Meeting
- Documentation
- Testing
- Code Development
- Customer Client Interaction

    In a real world setting, what gets done on the project at hand is the first and
foremost concern, but in an academic setting, individual effort needs to be coupled
with progress and growth. This is why it is necessary to have peer and self-
assessment, as well as time management analysis. In a personal progress analysis,
students answer questions about themselves and then are given the opportunity to
assess other students that with whom they work closely. Opinions can create
animosity among peers. For the sake of each student's pride and self-respect, the

Name:			*Joe Student*
Date	**Hours Worked**	**Task Type**	**Comments**
01/02/200 9	2	Testing	Wrote test modules for GUI classes.
01/04/20 09	4	Documenta- tion	Documented test modules written on 01/02/2009

Fig. 13.4 Sample student work log

evaluations should be distributed test style, where there should be no conversation and each student may document their own personal assessment of themselves and their classmates with complete honesty. Only after all reports have been collected should students have the opportunity to review the assessment of their peers. Peer surveys describe the attributes of the student on a scale. The scale is fairly common and is as follows:

- A—Always
- U—Usually
- S—Sometimes
- R—Rarely
- N—Never

The type of questions on the survey should revolve around the ethics and activities, such as arriving for meetings on time and willingness to train team members. The questions should not revolve around the individual's ability to create specific code entities or utilize a certain piece of software. The flexibility of these surveys, as well as the amount of data collected (especially from a large class), could warrant the implementation of online automation of survey taking and report generation (Clark et al. 2005) (Fig. 13.5).

13.2 Phase II: Object-Oriented Software Requirements Specification

Object-oriented programming has been discussed in depth in previous chapters of this book and much material can readily be found elsewhere. For these reasons this section will be oriented on practical and implementable documentation that can be created by small teams within a short time frame. This does not mean that the documentation will be lacking in benefit, as it will still be descriptive and relevant to current software engineering fields, it will just be scaled back in scope and complexity to allow for a greater coverage of the essential concepts.

Specification of a system is a daunting task that may seem impossible to cover all the aspects of the system and every single caveat that may arise when applying end users to the functional system. It very well is impossible to cover every aspect of a system, but it is not impossible to create a best effort of understanding. The proper breakdown of the system is essential for understanding and for documenting your understanding. The following is a listing of the most important aspects of a specification document:

1. System Overview: Provide the readers with a quick glance at what will be presented in the project.
2. User Interfaces: How the user will interact with the final product.
3. Functional Description: Describe the functional aspects of the system.

This table shows the rating that the students gave themselves – indicated by a 'Y' and the average rating assigned to them by the rest of their team members indicated by a 'T'.

The ratings are: **A** – Always, **U** – Usually, **S** – Sometimes, **R** – Rarely, **N** -- Never

Meetings	A	U	S	R	N
I arrived on time for meetings	Y	T			
I showed a cooperative attitude during meetings	Y	T			
I was prepared for meetings	T	Y			
I made a meaningful contributions at meetings	Y	T			
I wasted time with irrelevant conversation				Y	T
I identified and raised important issues	Y		T		
I was inattentive at meetings		T	Y		
I brought my individual work at meetings		Y T			
I gave suggestions about others work at meetings					
Work Habits	A	U	S	R	N
I used time effectively		T	Y		
I cooperated with team members	Y	T			
I was willing to share information with team members	Y	T			
I spent time working with other team members on their tasks			T	Y	
I was willing to train team members		Y	T		
I showed initiative by doing library or internet research			Y T		
I undertook tasks that required significant research		Y T			

Fig. 13.5 Sample peer review adapted from (Clark et al. 2005)

I was able to complete individual subtasks with little or no assistance		Y T			
My individual subtasks were completed on time		Y	T		
My individual subtasks were of high quality		Y	T		
I reviewed design documents	Y		T		
I reviewed drafts of the manual		Y T			
I tested software developed by other team members		Y T			
I carried out the duties of my management role	Y	T			
Comments					

Describe one of the highlights of the student's performance.

1.   Keeps meetings on track

2.   Good at keeping control of meetings, and keeping them moving along when they become stuck at some point, or were getting off track of the main agenda.

Suggest one area where the student could improve.

1.   Communicate more, let team members know what is happening.

2.   Improve by asking for help more when there is difficulty.

3.   Did not actually demonstrate much in the way of substantial work effort.

Fig. 13.5   continued

4. Nonfunctional Description: This should focus on aesthetic attributes of the project.
5. Performance Description: This section should take into account the end platform of the operation and what the expected and normal performance benchmarks should be.
6. Exception Handling: Good software relies on quality exception handling as it is impossible to remove all faults from the system. This section should not be substituted with 'better design,' but should be complimented with it.
7. Acceptance criteria: Without this specified it would not be hard to create a successful project, but it is necessary to gauge the true quality of the deliverables.

For the most part this section should be in simple written English, but it is unavoidable that some jargon and diagrams will be required to convey concepts. These sections should be explained thoroughly in the literature as these documents are the primary insight by stakeholders into the development process.

13.2.1 Specification Documentation

Specification documentation comes in many forms; different documentation is required for each of the seven sections listed above. Some sections will require object diagrams or use case diagrams, while other sections will require carefully written documentation.

The systems overview section should be a brief overview of functionality, compatibility and project timeline. Basically, this should be an overview of anything that you may want to know about the project. For this reason it should not be dense or convoluted with many diagrams and flow charts, but be brief and concise. The most important points it should cover are:

- Development cycle description: who will do what, where and when.
- What actual project deliverables should encompass.
- Development paradigms that will be employed. Some paradigms that should be noted in this portion are peer programming, object oriented, model driven architecture and service oriented architecture. The list is almost infinite.
- Platform requirements, which includes whether the project will require multi-platform development tools or will only be targeted at one system.

The most important aspect of a user may be how they will interact with the final product. The user interface section should cover this in detail. For this section it is very appropriate to use mock ups of the interface as well as written descriptions. Mock ups of user interfaces should do more than show an image, but should have callouts and highlights of the most important features.

The functional description is needed to develop use cases and process flow diagrams. Functional descriptions can easily become highly technical. They are undoubtedly one of the most technically intense portions of the design document. To combat this, the use of diagrams showing flow control can be used as well as simple walkthroughs of scenarios.

The non-functional description should cover the important aspects of the project that are unique and special. Many times the form of comments, efficiency, overhead and other similar aspects should be covered in this section. This section, however, should not be brought down in quality with a huge increase in length with overly ambiguous statements about "ample comments" or "optimal efficiency". Instead, it should set specific guidelines for many of the non-functional aspects. Guidelines should be testable and when appropriate, the test used to measure them should be described as well.

The performance description in some cases will overlap with the non-functional requirements. This is okay as the sections are somewhat similar. The performance description should cover a more distant view of the system, where the non-functional requirements should cover specific performance issues. This section should cover hardware requirements, as well as architecture and the specialized processing units required. Both minimum and recommended system setups should be listed if appropriate.

This, in many cases, will become a very lengthy section. Each possible exception should be documented here. Exceptions should be grouped in a standard way to make their reference easier as this section may encompass a large number of pages. Each error should be listed, as well what action will take place. Some common groupings are:

- By error type (file, interface, user invoked).
- Catastrophic (complete system failure).
- By modules (what module did the error occur in).

Acceptance criteria are the items by which the deliverables will be accepted or rejected. This section can pose technical dilemmas for software engineers and may contain legal jargon as pertinent to faults and accident liability, but an attempt should be made to make some important points clear and concise. The main points of this section are:

- Important deliverable deadlines.
- Required uptime of implemented system.
- Throughput or load of the system.
- Fault tolerance.
- Content of deliverables.

13.2.2 Change Management

Any good development team will find issues with the specification document at some point during the development process. This is perfectly acceptable and desired as it promotes review and scrutiny of the concepts and design. This process of discovery and revision needs careful and well documented control in order to assure that only desirable changes are implemented, and that changes are not being made to make up for a lack of experience or effort by the development teams. A good change request form should cover the following:

- Who it was requested by.
- When it was requested.
- Why it was requested.
- What the change entails.
- Whether the change was accepted or rejected.
- Who approved or rejected the change.

Since most changes increase cost and project length, senior developers should evaluate them closely before approving them. Before any changes are approved, the impact on deliverables needs to be documented, e.g. documentation, cost, deadlines and current work assignments (Thayer and Dorman 1990) (Fig. 13.6).

13.3 Phase III: Object Oriented System Design

System design is the critical step between specification and implementation. It is here that a project is either made or broken. Specification is the development process of designing classes, objects, data stores, user interfaces and many other important project aspects. The first step to designing a good working system is a Stakeholders and Interests List. This list is extremely important and should not be pushed aside for what may seem like more pressing issues.

The following is a brief outline of what is required in a specification document. The main parts of the document are an understanding of the stakeholder's needs, the system interface and the system composition. There are many more kinds of documents and diagrams that can be used to supplement and complement the following, but the following sections are absolutely necessary. Each section will provide a brief explanation and an example of what is expected to be contained in each portion of the specification.

13.3.1 Stake Holders and Interests List

The first step to this list will be to determine the stakeholders. A simple example would be a point of sale system or POS. In this scenario we can document at least two stakeholders quickly, the first being the cashier physically moving the product in exchange for currency. The second stakeholder is the salesperson. The salesperson will have sold a good or service and directed a customer to a cashier to handle the actual transaction. From this rudimentary knowledge, a stakeholders and interests list can be started such as the one in Fig. 13.7.

13.3.2 Use Case

All good software has a particular use in mind when it is being developed. This use is described in a use case. A use case expands on the stakeholders and interests list and presents, typical and atypical interactions of the stakeholders with the system in questions. Use cases are broken into three separate scales. The first is a brief overview. In this scenario the system and actors are roughly discussed and an outline format is used to document the flow of interaction. Most often, alternate

Change Request Form

Form # 1b

Requestor: _____ Jon Stewart _____

Signature: _____ Jon   Stewart _____   Date:

_____ 01/02/2009 _____

Description of Change:

Increase processing specification from recommended 1G ram to 1.5 G ram to accommodate expanded undo capabilities.

Review team lead: ___ Sheila Wilson _____

Approved x Rejected ___

Reasons:

It was not accounted for with change 1A, initial testing has deemed it necessary to make this change.

Impact on Current Proceedings:

Changes are required to specification document section 7.

Comments:

None.

Review Team Lead Signature: _____ Bill Stevens _____

Date: _____ 03/08/2009 _____

Project Manager Signature: _____ Susan Strong _____

Date: _____ 03/09/2009 _____

Fig. 13.6 A change request form

Stakeholders and Interests:
■ Cashier: wants fast and accurate payment, does not want errors in processing of transactions as it costs them personally.
■ Salesperson: desires commissions processing.

Fig. 13.7 Stakeholders and interests list adapted from Larman (2005)

scenarios are explored, but some of the more remote cases are normally omitted. In a casual scenario the outline form is translated to well-structured English paragraphs. This setup requires slightly more detail to be added to create a comprehensive flow of a written scenario. The final version is what is called fully dressed. After several brief and casual use cases are identified, this version is constructed. Trying to increase the verbosity of the system explanation, preconditions and success guarantees should be added (Larman 2005). The following is an extract of a use case from "Applying UML and Patterns", by Craig Larman (Fig. 13.8).

13.3.3 Use Case Diagrams

The use case diagram is a powerful diagram in automated code generation tools. For practical purposes use case diagrams extract the pertinent and necessary information from use case scenarios and present it in a fashion that is not only extremely simple to understand, but is also very easily converted to code through the use of UML code tools. As use case models are described heavily elsewhere in this text, the following example will briefly enumerate the cashier actor from Fig. 13.9 in a use case diagram in order to demonstrate how a written scenario, as shown in Fig. 13.8, can be turned into a graphical representation.

13.3.4 Class and Object Diagrams

No specification would be complete without a modeling of the objects and classes that are going to be used to compose the software. A comprehensive set of class and object diagrams are the last specification tasks before coding begins. Class and object diagrams are more valuable than maybe first expected. Besides from the fact that they are invaluable when you begin coding, if you are developing a system in one of the many object oriented languages supported, there are multiple tools that are capable of rendering your diagrams as source code. This eliminates many of the trivial tasks of typing what is deemed to be shell code (the classes, method and attributes), allowing for directly proceeding to inner workings of the methods and classes. Class diagram notation has been covered in great detail later, but to keep

Scope: NextGen POS application

Level: user goal

Primary Actor: cashier

Stakeholders and Interests:

- Cashier: Wants accurate and fast entry with no payment errors.
- Customer: Wants purchase with minimal effort.
- Manager: Wants ability to quickly override operations.
- Company: Wants accurate records.

Preconditions: cashier is authenticated.

Success guarantee (or post-conditions): Sale is saved. Tax is correctly recorded. Accounting and inventory are updated. Commissions are recorded. Receipt is generated. Payment authorization approvals are recorded.

Main Success Scenario:

1. Customer arrives at POS with goods.
2. Cashier starts new sale.
3. Cashier enters identifier.
4. System records line item and presents description, price and running total.
5. System presents total with taxes.
6. Customer pays and system handles transactions.
7. Receipt presented.
8. System logs sale to inventory and accounting systems.
9. Customer leaves with receipt and goods (if tangible).

Extensions:

1. Manager override is possible at all times.
2. Cash transactions are calculated from received payment, payment is collected and stored securely, and change is calculated and presented automatically.

Special requirements:

1. Touch screen UI.
2. Credit response within 30 seconds, 90% of the time.

Open Issues:

1. Tax law variations?
2. How are cashier transaction drawer disputes handled/resolved/avoided?
3. What customization is needed for different kinds of businesses?

Fig. 13.8 An abbreviated fully dressed use case adapted from Larman (2005)

Fig. 13.9 Use case diagram representing the cashier actor

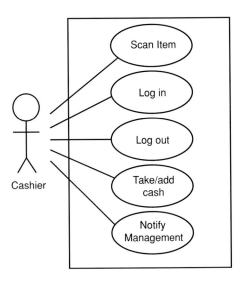

Fig. 13.10 Partial domain model of a POS system adapted from Larman (2005)

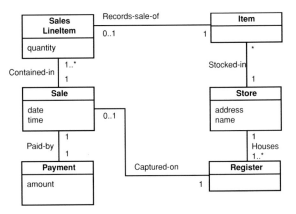

with the theme of a cross section of specification, the following is a brief adaption of a partial domain model in class diagram notation (Fig. 13.10).

13.3.4.1 Software Engineering Ethics

Ethics are important in all fields and software is not the exception. Software engineers should adhere to a high level of professionalism and integrity in their work. One of the most highly regarded codes of ethics is set down by the Association for Computing Machinery. Their ethics in short provide a set of guidelines for professional and proper conduct. The following are the eight key principles according to the ACM (2009):

1. **Public**—Software engineers shall act consistently with the public interest.
2. **Client and Employer**—Software engineers shall act in a manner that is in the best interests of their client and employer, and be consistent with the public interest.
3. **Product**—Software engineers shall ensure that their products and related modifications meet the highest professional standards possible.
4. **Judgement**—Software Engineers shall maintain integrity and independence in their professional judgment.
5. **Management**—Software engineering managers and leaders shall subscribe to and promote an ethical approach to the management of software development and maintenance.
6. **Profession**—Software engineers shall advance the integrity and reputation of the profession that is consistent with the public interest.
7. **Colleagues**—Software engineers shall be fair to, and supportive of their colleagues.
8. **Self**—Software engineers shall participate in lifelong learning regarding the practice of their profession and shall promote an ethical approach to the practice of the profession.

13.4 Phase IV: Implementation

Implementation can by far be one of the most enjoyable phases of the development process. Coding is a very simple activity when the specification is correctly completed and there are no or very few ambiguities left to overcome. Implementation hazards such as complex languages, ambiguous error messages and large API's can be overcome easily with modern practices and tools. Use the following guide as a reference to correct implementation practices.

- There is much coding that can be completed autonomously. Autonomous systems are able to translate UML or other high level documentation to code. These tools should be used as often and completely as possible as they are capable of creating concise implementations of specifications.
- Create consistent style. All team members working on implementation should follow the same coding style which should contain rules and structure as explained in the implementation chapter. Whatever style is chosen, it should be enforced to retain consistency and it should be clear and verbose.
- Changes should be logged, not only in work logs and external documentation, but within the source code for auditors to review.

13.4.1 Commenting Code

Commenting code is extremely important to understanding it. Another item that can be automatically generated is documentation. This leads to strict and specific comment styles. Comments should be verbose enough to convey understanding, but not lengthy and complex creating more confusion than mere source code. Schach defines the minimal coding requirements for a code artifact as follows (Schach 2007):

1. The name of the artifact.
2. A brief description of what the code artifact does.
3. The programmer's name.
4. The date the artifact was coded.
5. The date the artifact was approved.
6. The name of the person who approved the artifact.
7. The arguments of the artifact.
8. A list of each variable in the artifact and a brief description of each variable.
9. The names of any files accessed by this code artifact.
10. Input–Output, if any.
11. Error handling capabilities.
12. The name of the file containing test data (used for regression testing).
13. A listing of each modification made to the artifact, the date the modification was made, who performed the modification and who approved the modification.
14. Any known faults.

13.4.1.1 End User Documentation

Documentation for the end user is an important part of the development process. Though it may not necessarily take shape during the implementation phase of development, it is important to be mindful of the aspects that it should cover when completed. For any system to be complete, documentation must be provided at multiple levels to suit users of different skills and purposes. Sommerville provides the following breakdown of documentation, as well as a description of each different variety. All items listed should be included with the project deliverables (Sommerville 2004) (Fig. 13.11).

The following is a brief description of the five documents listed above (Sommerville 2004):

1. A functional description should provide users with the knowledge of what services the product provides. This document should be comprehensive enough for the user to determine if this will solve the task at hand.
2. An introductory manual is an invaluable piece of documentation. This document should have a liberal amount of pictures and samples. It has to also be deemed appropriate to cover common error avoidance and recovery in this work.

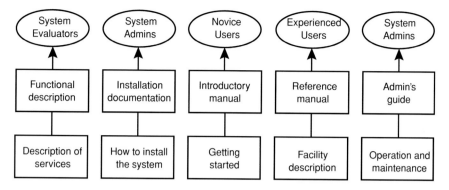

Fig. 13.11 Type of document to support each user task (Sommerville 2004)

3. A system reference manual is necessary to provide reference to all system functions, errors and how to recover there from.
4. A system installation manual should contain pertinent information concerning installation. This information at the minimum should include recommended and minimal hardware specifications, installation media inventory, preparatory procedures for systems receiving the install and an installation walkthrough.
5. A system administrator's manual should be included in some systems documentation. This manual should document the system's faults and configurations for advanced implementations.

13.5 Phase V: System Integration and Testing

In the integration and testing phase, all the planning and programming will come to its first major test. Integration into a release system requires that the project is tested and complete. Though it is still possible to provide finishing touches, the product should be nearly complete. This sub chapter will provide examples of proper tests and testing procedures so that it is easier to implement them during this phase of the project.

13.5.1 Testing

Testing is basically composed of two different varieties; quality testing and performance testing. Quality testing is increasing the confidence with which the software will perform to specification under appropriate conditions. Performance testing creates a benchmark of the ability of the software; this may be measured in execution time, throughput, bandwidth consumption, etc. Testing theory mostly revolves around the idea that software is inherently flawed and it only requires the correct test case to provide insights into the flaws.

Test cases should focus on common fault areas, particularly tricky code segments, and areas with a low fault tolerance. This can be a challenging feat as test
plans should be drawn up before implementation begins. This assures that there are
appropriate resources (including time) to execute the necessary tests. Proactive test
planning normally fits very well with black-box testing where specifications are
used to design testing scenarios which are applied to the developed program's
segments and the results are compared to the expected results.

13.5.2 Quality Testing

Quality testing should be done methodically and comprehensively. Quality testing
is one of the few in roads to product quality assurance. Product testing normally
advances in three phases. The first phase in quality assurance is a quality
inspection. Before a quality inspection occurs, the inspection team needs to collaborate with the developers of the particular piece of code if possible, and derive a
checklist for the quality inspection. The development checklist that follows is
adapted from Ian Sommerville (Sommerville 1996).

- Data Faults:

    - Are all variables initialized before use?
    - Have all constants been named?
    - Lower array bounds checked?
    - Are string delimiters required and verified?

- Control Faults:

    - For each conditional statement is the condition correct?
    - Are there any infinite loops?
    - In case statements are all cases counted for?

- I/O Faults:

    - Are all input variables used?
    - Are unassigned variables output?

- Interface faults:

    - Do all function and procedure calls have the correct amount of parameters?
    - Do formal and actual parameter types match?
    - Are the parameters in the correct order?
    - Do components that access shared memory have the same shared memory
      structure?

- Storage management faults:

    - Has dynamic storage been allocated correctly?
    - Has dynamic storage been deallocated correctly?

- Exception management faults:
  - Have all possible error conditions been taken into consideration?
  - Are useful errors generated per fault for both end users and developers?

After completing the code walk through and having answered the previous questions, there are numerous other methods for testing and verifying code as described in prerequisite chapters. Some of these methods are clean room testing, black-box testing, mathematical verification, static analysis, object orient testing, etc.

13.5.3 Performance Testing

Performance testing is where developers get to demonstrate the power and performance characteristics of their system. It is important to note, however, that performance is relative. Performance is relative to the specifications and special characteristics of a system, should a performance test be chosen. Marketing a system relies heavily on these benchmarks.

There are two main forms for performance benchmarks. The first sort of benchmark is called processor bound. There are several variations of this benchmark and MIPS, Sieve and Dhrystone are three of them. Processor bound benchmarks measure the number of instructions executed in a given time. These benchmarks are essential when determining how much work can be accomplished with processor heavy applications.

The second benchmark is deemed the Input/Output bound benchmark, which measures all other aspects of performance. Some common items are bridges, gateways, database servers, physical storage, volatile storage, operating systems and networks. These tests can be harder to perform than processor bound benchmarks due to the fact that they encompass a huge range of software and hardware combinations and intricacies.

13.5.4 Reporting Test Results

Nothing is better than a graph when it comes to documenting a systems performance. Graphs provide stakeholders an insight into the benchmark without making the results over complex or technical. Graphs however should be well documented and should not be convoluted. Figure 13.12 is a processor bound benchmark adapted from Burch (Burch 1992). Graphs and accompanying written documentation should be simple and accommodate the audience. If you are writing to technical publishers for an end user, the language should reflect this difference. Technical publishers and technical review committees will expect technical

Fig. 13.12 Example
processor bound benchmark
(Burch 1992)

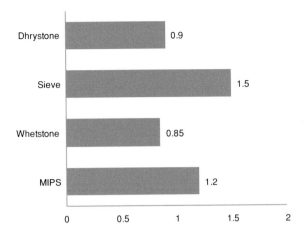

documentation. End users that are looking to purchase a product in your market
will expect illustrations, comparisons and easy to understand language with
minimal jargon.

13.5.5 When and How to Comprise Time and Functionality

Sometimes even the best design plans and schedules are either not realistic or for
some reason fall behind and are not fully executable by the deadlines at hand. In
this case, it is advisable and necessary to cut functionality. In a software engineering class project completed by software engineering students at Robert Morris
University, the project was estimated at 40-20-20 (design, code and testing).
However, in the end being an academic setting the requirements gathering and
research took approximately 70 % of the time allotted to the project. Coding and
testing were given 20 and 10 % respectively (Acharya and Burke 2008).

In this scenario the learning of Monopoly and various tools, platforms and
techniques took precedence over features such as trading properties, which was
dropped in the favor of implementing the project in platform independent C#
(Acharya and Burke 2008). In any project it is easier to create loftier goals than
practically accomplishable. Even with goals that are reasonable for the scope of
the project, there will need to be considerations made with respect to deadlines and
features. A short guide is provided for when, what and how to properly work when
running behind schedule.

1. Determine the goal of the project.

   (a) What fits best with the mission? Check the mission statement and project
       goals.
   (b) What is essential and what is not essential?

2. Determine how much time needs making up.

   (a) Is it a big setback or only minor?

   (b) Minor setbacks can be fixed with more time input or slight tweaks to future schedules.

   (c) Major setbacks will require feature omissions or major reworking of project goals.

3. Determine what needs tweaking.

   (a) If a setback is caused by one certain feature, this features specification may need to be revisited, or if it is beyond the ability of the team to implement it, special training or specialists will need to be brought into resolve to issue.

   (b) If the setback is due to not enough time and not from the complexity, adding more work time or removing functionality will be required.

4. Make the changes required to bring the project back on schedule.

5. Receive permission to implement changes and document these changes accordingly.

13.6 Phase VI: System Demonstration

The hard work is now done. The project has reached release and it is time to bring to the stakeholders a working demonstration along with promotional materials. The point of a product demonstration is to show the stakeholders what has been done and what has not been done. The presentation should take place in a comfortable atmosphere where an honest exchange is possible. If the development has been undertaken with skill and professionalism then the product demonstration should be easy and enjoyable for both the presenters and the presentees.

There is no better way to get the good points of a software developer's work across to their audience then a well planned, developed and executed demonstration. In the same respect software demonstrations can leave a foul taste in the stakeholder's mouth at its completion. This section will focus on the do's and do not's of software project demonstrations.

13.6.1 What to Bring

The demonstrators should wear professional dress and maintain proper business procedure with addressing and interacting among themselves and with stakeholders. If the audience has a good impression of the presenters then they will have a good impression of the products. The presenters of any product should attempt to bring a sample of the product. This can be difficult if the product is large (server software, large embedded devices, etc.) when this is not possible there should be representations even if the device is as mundane as a vehicle electrical control unit. Also, there should be a well thought out and designed visual demonstration of code, interfaces and the system in action.

There are many other tips, suggestions and techniques for creating engaging and professional presentations that can be found in books outside of the scope of this text. The most important thing to keep in mind as a software engineer is to retain your professional appearance. If you believe that you, your team and your product are of a professional grade then your stakeholders are much more likely to share the same attitude.

13.6.2 The Demonstration

The demonstration will consist of a visual demonstration assisted with explanation. The presentation teams should create a presentation that is well thought out and covers all aspects of the deliverables. Aspects that should be covered are:

- User Interfaces
- Deployment walkthrough
- Strengths of the system
- Weaknesses of the system
- Performance test results

The above items should be covered thoroughly with ample diagrams, pictures and illustrations. Some important things to note about visual aids are the write ups for demonstrations. Pictures should be of a high quality. Taking screen shots of a piece of software is a great way of show casing it. However, in many instances the screenshot encompasses irrelevant things such as background tasks or large pieces of the software that are irrelevant to point being made. These aspects should be trimmed, which allows for more focus as well as a decreased file size and greater clarity.

Written notes and key points are essential to drive the pictures, videos and other media's points home. Poorly written comments and factoids will make these items shrink in grandeur. Making sure all items are proof read and accurate is a necessity. A good visual presentation only contains the writing that is necessary to complete the thoughts started with the other sensory media.

13.6.3 Presenting

Not everyone is a naturally born public speaker, but anyone can give a good presentation if they follow some very simple tips. First, practice, practicing will not only help make the presentation more fluid and natural, but will instill conviction and showcase professionalism. The next important aspect is to prepare. Preparation the day before of any materials is liable to throw a curve ball. Team members should be familiar with the material that all presenters are bringing. This will cut down on any gut reactions that may be witnessed by the audience. This brings me to the last point respect the team. Do not interject unnecessarily or make subtle suggestions that you may not have been in favor of a certain aspect of the project.

13.7   Phase VII: Product Delivery With Documentation

The project is almost over, success or failure is something that needs to be delivered to those that paid for it. Deliverables for projects come in many forms depending on the type of project. In the least, the software developed and the user documentation should be provided for the product to be delivered. In some instances however, there will need to be setup of the system or end user training. In any circumstances the deliverables should be delivered in a professional nature, reflective of the atmosphere of the entire project.

13.7.1 Peer Reviews

Peer reviews are a powerful tool when assessing the end value of an individual's input to the project. Peer reviews should provide insight into the growth of the student developer, as well as to the areas that may require improvement or polishing. They should be administered similar to tests so that students can write their own honest evaluations of their peers without influence of others. Peer reviews after the project is complete should contain the same questions as the progress reports had, plus more feedback on growth. Some characteristics that should be added to the peer review after the completion of the project are:

- Technical ability adaptation (the growth of coding, debugging and design skills).
- Communication, or how well the student developer communicated during the project outside of designated work time (did the student developer attempt to motivate the project to a greater amount of success)?
- It may be appropriate to ask for more lengthy written evaluations from each individual on their own performance. Not only is self-assessment a valuable skill, but it also helps provide insight into some of the comments received regarding the individual's reviews.

13.8 Chapter Summary and Conclusions

There is more to software development than coding; proper design and testing along with an emphasis on strong deliverables is essential to a successful project. The Software Development Life Cycle (SDLC):

- Planning
- Analysis
- Design
- Implementation
- Maintenance

Different stakeholders and end users have different needs. It is the job of the software engineer to accommodate each user type with appropriate documentation and systems capability. Software specification comes in both written and illustrative types. Both types have merits.

- Written documentation: verbose, complex and detailed.
- Illustrative: more understandable at a glance and less verbose.

A learning exercise has to have an objective and a way to measure the level of success that was achieved when attempting to reach this objective. One way to measure success is by an honest evaluation by peers. Peer evaluations should have the following traits:

- Peers should be in an environment where they can honestly assess themselves and their peers without being biased.
- Peer evaluations should provide relevant questions to the phase of development.
- An overall evaluation should be performed to determine the amount of personal growth.

13.9 Exercises

1. How many times should peer reviews be completed?
2. Name and explain two differences between Gantt and N^2.
3. Explain the importance of benchmarks.
4. Name and differentiate between the two main types of benchmarks.
5. Complete a mock demonstration of any existing software product as if you had developed it.
6. What are the main tenants of the Software Engineering ethics listed in this chapter?
7. What should be delivered at the project's completion?
8. What are the traits of a successful team? Name a trait that you think is important that is not listed in this chapter.

9. List and explain five items that are learned from the project, that you are more knowledgeable about than with only theoretical exercises.
10. Write problem statements for a software engineering problem, and have a peer review it and provide feedback.

References

Acharya S, Burke D (2008) Incorporating gaming in software engineering projects: case of RMU monopoly. IISCI. http://www.iiisci.org/journal/CV$/sci/pdfs/. Accessed 29 Sept 2009
Association for Computing Machinery (2009) Software engineering code of ethics and professional practice. ACM. http://www.acm.org/about/se-code. Accessed 15 Aug 2009
Burch J G (1992) Systems analysis, design, and implementation. Boyd and Fraser Publishing Company
Clark N, Davies P, Skeers R (2005) Self and peer assessment in software engineering projects. In: International conference proceeding series, vol. 106. ACM.
Larman C (2005) Applying UML and patterns: an introduction to object-oriented analysis and design and iterative development. Prentice Hall
Schach S R (2007) Object-oriented and classical software engineering, 7th edn. McGraw-Hill
Sommerville I (1996) Software engineering, 5th edn. Peason Education, Ltd., Boston
Sommerville I (2004) Software engineering, 7th edn. Peason Education, Ltd., Boston
Stiller E, LeBlanc C (2002) Project-based software engineering: an object-oriented approach. Addison-Wesley
Thayer R, Dorman M (1990) System and software requirements engineering. IEEE Society Press

About the Author

Dr. Roger Lee is a professor at Central Michigan University in the Department of Computer Science, where he specializes in topics in software engineering. He received his Ph.Ds from Shizuoka University and University of Southern Mississippi. At Central Michigan University, he teaches courses in object-oriented programming and software engineering using the principles taught in this book. Similarly, his research and publications cover areas such as component-based software engineering, requirements engineering, software architecture, and object-oriented analysis and design. He is the director of the Software Engineering and Information Technology Institute (SEITI) where he oversees research activities. He serves as Editor-in-Chief of the International Journal of Software Innovation and managing editor for the International Journal of Networked & Distributed Computing as well as the International Journal of Computing & Information Science (ICIS). He is also the founder and CEO of the Association for Computer and Information Science (ACIS); this organization sponsors numerous conferences such as the annual International Conference on Computer & Information Science (ICIS) and the Software Engineering, Artificial Intelligence, Networking, and Parallel/Distributed Computing Conference (SNPD); these conferences are also cosponsored by the IEEE Computer Society.

R. Y. Lee, *Software Engineering: A Hands-On Approach*,
DOI: 10.2991/978-94-6239-006-5, © Atlantis Press and the author 2013

Index

A

Access control, 171
Activity diagram, 51, 57, 58
Actors, actors-primary and sec, 41, 42
Aggregation, 44, 115
Agile development, 179
Alpha testing, 206–208, 214
Analysis modeling, 109, 110, 119
Analysis object model, 110, 150, 154
Application domain, identifying, 89, 152
Application domain, modeling, 40, 152
Architecture, 47, 82, 110, 130, 137, 141, 250
Architecture, design evaluation, 250
Architecture, models, 110
Architecture, object-oriented, 137, 141
Architecture, system design, 141
Associations, 44, 46, 115, 158, 188

B

Baselines, 86, 242–243, 251, 254
Beta testing, 203, 207–209, 214
Black-box testing, 202, 212, 214, 274, 275
Boundary value, 193
Bugs, 9, 110, 174, 192, 213, 214, 232
Business objectives, 218, 219, 223

C

Change management, 265
Class diagrams, 47, 48, 56, 110, 113, 119, 152, 158, 160
Classes, concepts, 20, 21, 42
Classes, definition, 20, 42
Classes, metrics for, 235, 240, 244, 247
Class modeling, 113

Classifier, 157
Coding principles, 30, 180
Cohesion, 141, 143, 249
Communication, 8, 71
Communiction, project, 71
Complexity, metrics, 240
Complexity, of metrics, 240
Complexity, of software, 4
complexity, organizational, 77, 93
Component-based design, 131
Component-based development, 179
Component models, 115, 191, 131, 132
Components, definition, 35, 54, 110, 131, 132, 179
Contextual instance, 157, 158, 160
Contextual type, 157
Control specification, 98
Correctness, 119, 155, 196, 200, 201, 214, 246
Correctness, class implementor, 156
Correctness proving, 196, 201, 202
Cost estimation, 7, 62–64, 66
Coupling, definition, 141
Critical path, 258
Critical path method, 258
Customer, communication, 68, 92, 98
Customer, involvement, 84, 92, 109, 207

D

Data design, 142, 143
Data flow, diagrams, 104, 114, 128
Database, 105, 111, 119, 121, 187, 188, 251, 275
Data modeling, 119
Debugging, in post-delivery, 229
Defect reports, 230, 236, 237

R. Y. Lee, *Software Engineering: A Hands-On Approach*,
DOI: 10.2991/978-94-6239-006-5, © Atlantis Press and the author 2013

Dependencies, 22, 23, 52, 67, 110, 162, 233, 259
Deployment diagram, 41, 54, 55, 57
Design, architectural, 89, 137, 139, 141, 249, 250
Design, definition, 125
Design, metrics, 247–249
Design, object-oriented, 136
Design, too much, 144
Design constraints, 91, 104, 105, 127, 136, 139, 151
Design model, 71, 110, 120, 130, 141, 150, 151, 187, 188
Design patterns, 137, 149, 150, 152, 154
Design process, 125, 126, 134, 137, 248, 250
Domain analysis, 76, 89, 99
Domain requirements, 81, 83, 98, 99
Dynamic model, 110, 142, 193

E

Efficiency, 12, 22, 65, 77, 82, 147, 155, 179, 246, 247, 253, 264
Efficiency, class implementor, 156
Elicitation. *See* Requirements elicitation
Errors, definition, 13, 14, 93, 104, 108, 122, 140, 170, 187, 206, 207, 212, 228, 253, 273
Estimation, 62–64, 78, 251
Ethics, software engineering, 270
Events, 40, 43, 104, 117, 118, 135, 258
Events, in use cases, 43, 46, 81, 87, 94, 112, 192, 252
Events, state diagram, 50, 51, 56, 210
Exception handling, 121, 187, 263
Execution based testing, 196, 198, 200, 202, 203, 214
Extends, 30, 45, 95, 138, 141
Extreme programming, 179, 234

F

Failure, 7, 9, 13, 64, 88, 94, 104, 122, 140, 144, 192, 194, 199, 205, 225, 232, 237, 279
Fault, definition, 18, 162, 182, 184, 186, 192–197, 202, 211, 227–230, 236, 241, 242, 245, 265, 274
Forward engineering, 164
Frameworks, non-functional requirements, 81, 82, 87, 89, 98, 99, 106, 108, 214, 265
Functional description, 261, 263, 264, 272
Function-oriented design, 127, 128

G

Generalization, 26, 32, 35, 45, 65, 95, 114
Glass-box testing, 203, 212
Granularity, 139

I

Implementation workflow, 185–189, 230
Information hiding, 22–24, 32, 37, 129, 130, 178, 231, 232
Information hiding, language choice, 178, 179
Inheritance, 19, 25, 26, 30, 32, 36, 45, 115, 117, 149, 153, 165, 178, 240
Inheritance, metrics, 98, 186, 218, 235–237, 239–245, 247, 254
Integration testing, 185, 210
Interface, 18, 19, 22, 24, 25, 31, 36, 74, 83, 91, 105, 111, 116, 122, 130, 133, 137, 138, 140, 144, 154, 155, 163, 165, 186, 204, 212, 248, 251, 264, 266, 278
Interface, requirement, 74, 105, 151
ISO 9126 quality factors, 247

L

Lines of code, 18, 186, 213, 243, 251, 252

M

Maintenance, concepts, 24, 76, 85, 133, 178, 180, 229–232, 235, 236, 252, 273
Measurement. *See* metrics
Metrics, challenges, 161, 186, 189, 235, 239, 240, 256
Metrics, definition, 235, 236
Metrics, implementation workflow, 187
Metrics, maintenance, 235
Metrics, object-oriented, 249, 250
Metrics, of design, 247, 248
Metrics, of process, 163, 252
Metrics, of quality, 244–247
Metrics, post release, 253, 254
Metrics, project, 251, 252
Metrics, size, 252
Modeling, 8, 39, 40, 56, 109, 110, 112, 113, 119, 128, 147, 156, 187, 234, 268
Modularity, 21, 22, 24, 37, 130, 134, 137, 138
Multiplicity, 46, 47, 120, 159, 187

N

Non-execution based testing, 191, 196, 214
Notes, 56, 209, 278

O

Object-oriented, analysis, 104, 113, 114, 119, 121, 143, 147
Object-oriented, concepts, 17−37
Object-oriented, design, 129, 130, 134−139, 142, 147, 151, 164, 178, 249
Object-oriented, integration, 185
Object-oriented, maintenance, 232
Object-oriented, metrics, 249, 250
Object-oriented, modeling, 39, 156
Object-oriented, programming, 17, 19−21, 27, 131, 169, 211, 261
Object-oriented, system design, 134, 266
Object-Oriented Software Requirements Specification, 104, 261
Object-oriented, testing, 211

P

Packages, 55, 162
Peer reviews, 279
Performance description, 263, 265
Planning, 6, 7, 61−67, 72, 77, 78, 140, 179, 191, 192, 194, 258, 273, 274
Planning, extreme programming, 179, 234
Planning, time management, 65, 167, 257, 260
Polymorphism, 30, 31, 178, 232
Postcondition, 152, 157, 159, 187
Precondition, 152, 157, 187
Problem definition, 255
Process, metrics, 252
Project management, 3, 4, 10, 65, 76, 217, 234
Project planning, 62, 63, 65, 67, 72, 78, 258
Prototyping, 14, 94, 107

Q

Quality, issues, 88
Quality, metrics, 244
Quality assurance teams, 91, 92
Quality function deployment (QFD), 93, 94

R

Refinement, 103, 108, 122, 138, 143, 144, 169, 191, 211
Regression testing, 112, 172, 203, 230, 231, 235, 272
Reliability, 4, 63, 72, 87, 108, 151, 155, 171, 199, 202, 207, 213, 214, 219, 220, 223, 242, 245−247

Reporting, 209, 241, 248, 275
Requirement, definition, 14, 73, 81, 83
Requirement, elicitation, 81, 83, 85, 90
Requirements analysis, 104, 105, 107, 147, 162, 165, 174, 186, 230
Requirements scrubbing, 73
Requirements specification, 96, 103−108, 261
Resources, 5, 8, 9, 22, 45, 54, 61, 63, 65, 66, 68, 69, 73, 74, 77−79, 119, 155, 172, 178, 200
203, 213, 247, 248, 274
Responsibilities, 5, 47, 77, 109, 113, 117, 120, 121, 170, 174, 188, 193, 195
Reuse, 22, 23, 152, 179, 181, 186, 236
Reverse engineering, 164, 187, 233
Reviews, postmortem, 126
Reviews, requirement, 94, 103, 122, 144
Risks, 16, 30, 204, 217, 251
Roles, 6, 20, 47, 53, 57, 70, 93, 95, 113, 133, 162, 174, 188, 232, 256

S

Scenario, 7, 48, 49, 76, 94, 96, 97, 112, 118, 140, 268
Scenario-based modeling, 112
Scope, 4, 62, 63, 73, 78, 81, 85, 90, 94, 176, 222
Sequence diagram, 49, 53, 56, 57, 95, 110, 117, 118
Software crisis, 3, 4
Software engineering, 3, 5, 6, 10, 61, 255, 257, 270
Software maintenance. *See* Maintenance
Software metrics. See Metrics
Software project management plan, 76, 77, 219, 225
Software quality, 12, 82, 180, 194, 196, 207, 208, 231, 244−247, 252
Specification documentation, 264−265
Spiral model, 14−15, 163
Stakeholders, 5, 6, 12, 15, 84, 85, 91, 112, 166, 217, 219, 220, 222, 225, 226, 239, 243, 244, 264, 266, 268, 269, 275, 277, 278, 280
State diagrams, 50−51, 210
Stress testing, 204
Structured programming, 17, 21
Stubs, 182, 185
Subclass, 25, 26, 30, 32, 33, 34, 57, 142, 153
Superclass, 26, 30−32, 34, 45, 57, 153

Swimlane, 52, 53, 58
System testing, 204, 210, 214

T
Tasks, 4, 6, 19, 61, 66, 67, 70, 71, 76, 81, 82,
    85, 86, 98, 116, 118, 120, 121, 135,
    163, 172–175, 194, 203, 230, 233, 253,
    256–260, 262, 263, 268, 278
Testability, 234, 246, 247
Test cases, 49, 172, 182, 191–193, 196,
    202–204, 210, 212, 214, 225, 226,
    230, 235, 274
Testing, 4, 14, 22, 23, 49, 61, 83, 105, 108,
    112, 118, 143, 155, 166, 169, 170, 172,
    180, 181, 183
Testing, correctness, 155, 196, 200–202, 214
Testing, inspection, 196–198, 274
Testing, objectives, 192
Testing, performance, 204, 273–275
Testing, reliability, 199
Testing, robustness, 199–200
Testing, utility, 199
Test planning, 191, 194, 274

U
UML, 8, 39–58, 95, 109, 110, 112, 119, 123,
    151, 152, 156–158, 163, 164, 166,
    209–211, 233, 268, 271
UML, model testing, 209–211
UML, models, 8, 39–58, 109, 156, 163, 164,
    209, 268
Unit testing, 22, 172, 185, 205–206, 214

Use case diagram, 48–49, 99, 268, 270
Use cases, 43, 46, 48, 81, 87, 94–97, 99, 104,
    112, 115–118, 150, 154, 192, 205, 210,
    225, 235, 252, 266–268
User interface, 19, 75, 83, 87, 116, 151, 152,
    165, 248, 251, 264
Users, types of, 112, 126, 155
Uses, 45–46

V
Validation, 85, 93, 98, 111, 179
Validation criteria, 98
Validation logic, 111
Validation testing, 00
Verification, 108, 174, 201, 275
Verification, mathematical, 275
Verification, of requirements, 108
Version control, 171

W
Walkthrough, 120, 196–198, 205, 264
Waterfall model, 12–14
Web application, testing, 200, 204
Web design, 204, 248
White-box testing, 211, 212, 214
Workflow, 163, 185, 186, 189, 191, 194, 195,
    230, 231

X
XP. See Extreme programming

Exact Statistical Inference
for Categorical Data

Exact Statistical Inference
for Categorical Data

Guogen Shan
University of Nevada, Las Vegas, NV, USA

AMSTERDAM • BOSTON • HEIDELBERG • LONDON
NEW YORK • OXFORD • PARIS • SAN DIEGO
SAN FRANCISCO • SINGAPORE • SYDNEY • TOKYO
Academic Press is an imprint of Elsevier

Academic Press is an imprint of Elsevier
125 London Wall, London, EC2Y 5AS, UK
525 B Street, Suite 1800, San Diego, CA 92101-4495, USA
225 Wyman Street, Waltham, MA 02451, USA
The Boulevard, Langford Lane, Kidlington, Oxford OX5 1GB, UK

Notices
Knowledge and best practice in this field are constantly changing. As new research and experience
broaden our understanding, changes in research methods, professional practices, or medical treatment
may become necessary.

Practitioners and researchers must always rely on their own experience and knowledge in evaluating
and using any information, methods, compounds, or experiments described herein. In using such
information or methods they should be mindful of their own safety and the safety of others, including
parties for whom they have a professional responsibility.

To the fullest extent of the law, neither the Publisher nor the authors, contributors, or editors, assume
any liability for any injury and/or damage to persons or property as a matter of products liability,
negligence or otherwise, or from any use or operation of any methods, products, instructions, or ideas
contained in the material herein.

ISBN: 978-0-08-100681-8

British Library Cataloguing in Publication Data
A catalogue record for this book is available from the British Library

Library of Congress Cataloging-in-Publication Data
A catalog record for this book is available from the Library of Congress

For information on all Academic Press publications
visit our website at http://store.elsevier.com/

ELSEVIER Book Aid International

Working together
to grow libraries in
developing countries

www.elsevier.com • www.bookaid.org

CONTENTS

List of Figures vii

List of Tables.. ix

Preface.. xi

Chapter 1 Exact Statistical Inference for a 2 × 2 Table **1**

1.1 Exact Testing Procedures 5

1.2 Comparison of Exact Approaches 17

Chapter 2 Exact Statistical Inference for a 2 × *K* Table **29**

2.1 Testing Trend for Binary Data from a 2 × *K* Table 29

2.2 Testing for Hardy-Weinberg Equilibrium 37

Chapter 3 Sample Size Determination Using Exact
Approaches **43**

3.1 Exact Sample Size Computation for a Clinical Trial with
Historical Controls 44

Conclusions 47

Bibliography 49

LIST OF FIGURES

1.1   Tail probability plots for a binomial comparative study based on three test statistics. 12

1.2   Tail probability plots for a binomial comparative study based on partial maximization by using the Z-pooled test statistic. The two green lines are the exact 0.999 confidence interval for the nuisance parameter, and the purple dot is the value for the BB p-value. 14

1.3   Two-sided and one-sided type I error rate comparisons among the five exact approaches with a balanced sample size of 100 per group at the significance level of $\alpha = 0.05$, based on the test statistics T_{PD}, T_{ZuP}, and T_{ZP} from the first row to the third row. 18

1.4   Two-sided and one-sided type I error rate comparisons among the five exact approaches with unbalanced sample size, $n_t = 100$ and $n_c = 50$ at the significance level of $\alpha = 0.05$, based on the test statistics T_{PD}, T_{ZuP}, and T_{ZP} from the first row to the third row. 21

1.5   Power comparisons for two-sided and one-sided problems among the five exact approaches with balanced sample size, $n_t = 100$ and $n_c = 100$ at the significance level of $\alpha = 0.05$, under the alternative $p_c = 0.3$ and $p_t = p_c + \theta$, based on the test statistics T_{PD}, T_{ZuP}, and T_{ZP} from the first row to the third row. 23

1.6   Power comparisons for two-sided and one-sided problems among the five exact approaches with unbalanced sample size, $n_t = 100$ and $n_c = 50$ at the significance level of $\alpha = 0.05$, under the alternative $p_c = 0.3$ and $p_t = p_c + \theta$, based on the test statistics T_{PD}, T_{ZuP}, and T_{ZP} from the first row to the third row. 25

2.1   Plots of the tail probability as a function of the nuisance parameter for the animal carcinogenicity study with $K = 4$ and a sample size of 10 per group. 33

2.2   Type I error rate for the five exact approaches when $K = 3$ and a sample size of 30 per group at the significance level of $\alpha = 0.05$, the left plot with the score value $d = (0, 1, 2)$, and the right plot with the score value $d = (0, 1, 4)$. 34

2.3   Power comparison among the five exact approaches when $K = 4$, a sample size of 30 per group, and the score value $d = (0, 1, 2, 3)$. 36

2.4   Power comparisons among the C approach, the M approach, and the C+M approach, using the χ^2 test with total sample sizes of 25, 50, 100, and 300 from the first row to the fourth row. 40

LIST OF TABLES

1.1   A 2×2 Contingency Table 2

1.2   A Randomized Placebo-Control Two-Arm Study for Patients with Chronic Noncancer-Related Pain 2

1.3   Association Between Smoking and UADT Cancer 4

1.4   Airway Hyper-Responsiveness (AHR) Status Before and After Stem Cell Transplantation (SCT) 5

2.1   A $2 \times K$ Contingency Table 30

2.2   Data From the Animal Carcinogenicity Study with $K = 4$ 33

PREFACE

With the development of computational techniques (e.g., super-computers, parallel computing) and statistical software packages (e.g., SAS, R, Stata, StatXact, SPSS, Matlab, PASS), exact statistical inference for categorical data analysis is increasingly available for use in practice. In the cases that traditional asymptotic approaches do not have satisfactory performance with regards to type I error control and accurate sample size determination, exact approaches should be utilized. This book provides an overview of exact approaches, including Fisher's exact approach, which is also known as the exact conditional approach, and several efficient exact unconditional approaches. Real examples are provided to illustrate the application of these exact approaches, and these approaches are also comprehensively compared in many important statistical problems.

The first chapter reviews the three sampling methods to generate data, then presents the five exact approaches. Data that can be organized in a 2×2 contingency table is considered in this chapter. Among the five approaches, one is the exact conditional approach, and the remaining four are unconditional. This book is the first to comprehensively compare the performance of the five exact approaches for data from a binomial comparative study. Chapter 2 deals with data from a $2 \times K$ table by applying the exact approaches. Such data is commonly obtained from a dose-response study, and a genetic study. The last chapter is given to sample size determination based on exact approaches. Power analysis is an essential part of a research proposal, and accurate sample size determination would increase the chance of the proposal being funded and finished in a timely manner.

I thank those who provided valuable comments and helpful suggestions about the book, including anonymous reviewers for this book. I am grateful to Prof. Chris Lloyd from Melbourne Business School for developing the most recent exact approach for categorical data analysis. I also thank Profs. Daniel Young, Weizhen Wang, Changxing Ma, Gregory Wilding, and Alan Hutson for their valuable comments. Finally, I would like to thank my wife, Yanjuan, for her continued support of my academic career, and our parents for taking care of us and our children.

Exact Statistical Inference for a 2 × 2 Table

A 2×2 contingency table commonly arises in a comparative study (e.g., a study to compare the response rate between two treatments) or a cross-sectional study (e.g., a study to test the association between two dichotomous variables). Barnard [1] was the first to describe three distinct sampling methods to generate a 2×2 contingency table; see Table 1.1. They are often termed as a 2×2 independent study, a 2×2 comparative study, and a double dichotomy study with both marginal totals fixed, one marginal fixed, and no marginal fixed, respectively. In a double dichotomy study with no marginal fixed, the total sample size of a study, N, is considered fixed.

Independent Study
In the first sampling method for a 2×2 independent study, both marginal totals of a 2×2 table are considered as fixed, that is, sample sizes (n_1, n_2) for the factor A and (m_1, m_2) for the factor B, are known before the study. One classical example is the experiment described by Fisher [2]: a lady claimed that she could tell whether milk was poured before or after tea in a cup. In this interesting experiment, eight cups were prepared with four of each kind. The lady was informed that among these eight cups, four were prepared with tea first and the remaining four with milk first. After the lady tasted all eight cups, she reported which four cups she thought had milk added first. It is obvious in this experiment that both marginal totals are fixed, with four for each kind on both marginal totals from the truth and the lady's answer. Such studies are relatively rare in practice due to the fact that subjects in the study were informed about the number of each kind, and for this reason, a 2×2 independent study will not be further discussed in detail here.

Comparative Study
A 2×2 comparative study involves two independent groups with sample sizes n_1 and n_2. At the end of the study, the associated number of events (e.g., response, survival) x_1 and x_2 are observed from the first group and the second group, respectively. It is often interesting to compare the response

Exact Statistical Inference for Categorical Data. http://dx.doi.org/10.1016/B978-0-08-100681-8.00001-4

Table 1.1 A 2 × 2 Contingency Table

		Factor A		
		Yes	No	Total
Factor B	Yes	n_{11}	n_{12}	m_1
	No	n_{21}	n_{22}	m_2
	Total	n_1	n_2	N

rate between the two groups. The following Phase III study is used to illustrate the setting of a 2 × 2 comparative study.

Example 1.1. A randomized, placebo-controlled two-arm Phase III clinical trial was conducted to evaluate oral lubiprostone for constipation associated with non-methadone opioids in patients with chronic noncancer-related pain [3]. Patients were randomized into either the treatment group treated with lubiprostone or the placebo group, and they were followed for 12 weeks in the study. The data is displayed in Table 1.2. At the end of the study, $x_1 = 58$ responders out of $n_1 = 214$ were recorded from the treatment group, while $x_2 = 41$ out of $n_2 = 217$ patients were observed from the placebo group.

The response rates, the primary endpoint, are estimated to be 27.1% and 18.9% for the treatment group and the placebo group, respectively. To compare the response difference between two groups, Pearson's χ^2 test statistic

$$T_{\chi^2} = \frac{(n_{11}n_{22} - n_{12}n_{21})^2 N}{n_1 n_2 m_1 m_2}$$

is used for testing the null hypothesis

$$H_0 : p_1 = p_2$$

against the alternative hypothesis

Table 1.2 A Randomized Placebo-Control Two-Arm Study for Patients with Chronic Noncancer-Related Pain

		Treatment Group	Placebo Group
Response	Yes	58	41
	No	156	176
Total		214	217
Source: From Jamal et al. [3], with permission.			

$$H_a : p_1 \neq p_2.$$

This test can be found in the function *prop.test* from statistical software *R*, and the *freq* procedure from SAS to compare two independent proportions. It should be noted that the χ^2 test statistic is equivalent to the Z test statistic with a pooled variance estimate, which is given as

$$\frac{\hat{p}_1 - \hat{p}_2}{\sqrt{\hat{p}(1 - \hat{p})(1/n_1 + 1/n_2)}},$$

where $\hat{p}_1 = x_1/n_1$, $\hat{p}_2 = x_2/n_2$, and $\hat{p} = (x_1 + x_2)/(n_1 + n_2)$. It is obvious that the Z test statistic can be applied to a one-sided problem, but the χ^2 test statistic T_{χ^2} is only used for a two-sided problem.

The asymptotic limiting distributions of the χ^2 test and the Z test are often used for statistical inference, and they are appropriate for use in practice only when cell frequencies are large enough. The χ^2 test is not recommended for use when the lowest expected frequencies from the four cells is less than 5 [4, 5]. However, Cochran [6] argued that the cut point value 5 is chosen arbitrarily, and this cut point may be modified when new evidence from data becomes available. For data with small cell frequencies, exact approaches (e.g., Fisher's exact conditional approach) are generally recommended [2, 7, 8]. Several exact approaches [2, 8–15] will be discussed later in Section 1.1.

Double Dichotomy Study
In a double dichotomy study, only the total sum is fixed, which is common in a cross-sectional study for testing an association between two dichotomous variables. A sample of size N is drawn from a population, and each member of the sample is classified according to the two dichotomous variables, A and B. For such studies, the row and column totals are not fixed in advance; only the total sum is fixed. One typical example is a cross-sectional study to test the association between smoking and cancer.

Example 1.2. Krishnatreya et al. [16] reported a retrospective study of upper aero digestive tract (UADT) cancer patients from 2010 to 2011 from the hospital cancer registry. For the $N = 56$ patients documented with the occurrence or presence of synchronous primaries, each patient was asked about his/her smoking status, and was tested whether or not UADT appears at both index and synchronous. Data from this study is presented in Table 1.3. One of the main research questions from this study was to test the association between the smoking history and the presence of UADT synchronous cancers.

Table 1.3 Association Between Smoking and UADT Cancer			
		UADT tumors	
		Yes	No
Smoking history	Yes	45	1
	No	5	5
Source: From Krishnatreya et al. [16], with permission.			

The Pearson χ^2 test was used for testing the association, and the p-value was found to be much less than 0.05. Then, the authors concluded that smoking was significantly associated with the occurrence of synchronous primaries in UADT. They also mentioned that the Yates' correction was used in the χ^2 test statistic as small expected frequencies were observed from the table.

In addition to the commonly used Pearson χ^2 test statistic, the likelihood ratio χ^2 test, often referred to as the G test, is an alternative to test the hypothesis of independence. Based on the standard maximum likelihood method, the likelihood ratio χ^2 test will be close in results to the Pearson's χ^2 test for large samples. The likelihood ratio χ^2 test statistic has the form as

$$T_{\mathrm{LR}} = 2 \sum_{i=1}^{2} \sum_{j=1}^{2} n_{ij} \log \left(\frac{n_{ij} N}{m_i n_j} \right),$$

where $0 \log 0 = 0$. Although these asymptotic tests perform well in the presence of large sample sizes, they could perform poorly in a small sample setting [17].

In addition to the cross-sectional study, a matched-pairs design is another important application of a double dichotomy study. With the total N subjects enrolled in a study, each subject is measured twice, before and after an intervention.

Example 1.3. Bentur et al. [18, p. 847] conducted a study on airway hyper-responsiveness (AHR) status before and after stem cell transplantation (SCT) on 21 patients; see Table 1.4 for the data. The AHR status for each patient is assessed using a methacholine challenge test (MCT) twice, before and after SCT. A positive MCT (AHR yes) is defined by $PC_{20} < 8$ mg/ml.

Table 1.4 Airway Hyper-Responsiveness (AHR) Status Before and After Stem Cell Transplantation (SCT)			
		Before SCT	
		AHR yes	AHR no
After SCT	AHR yes	1	7
	AHR no	1	12
Source: From Bentur et al. [18], with permission.			

In addition to a matched-pairs study where each subject is measured twice, it could be a study in which each subject is matched with an equivalent from another study. In practice, data from another experiment is already exist or easy to obtain. Such designs can be used to reduce the influence of possible confounding factors. Traditionally, the χ^2 test and the likelihood ratio test are used for testing the association between two dichotomous variables.

Let $p_{ij} = n_{ij}/N$ be probability for the i-th level of the factor A and j-th level of the factor B. Suppose $p_1 = p_{11} + p_{21}$ and $p_2 = p_{11} + p_{12}$ are the marginal probabilities. The difference between these two proportions is often the parameter of interest, $p_1 - p_2$, or equivalently $p_{21} - p_{12}$. To make a statistical inference for this parameter, the most commonly used test statistic is the McNemar test [19]:

$$T_{\mathrm{MC}} = \frac{(n_{21} - n_{12})^2}{n_{21} + n_{12}}.$$

It should be noted that only the off-diagonal numbers, n_{12} and n_{21}, from a 2 × 2 table are used in the test statistic, and the diagonal values, n_{11} and n_{22}, have no influence on computing the test statistic and the p-value calculation. There has been a long-term debate over whether all values should be used in the test statistic.

1.1 EXACT TESTING PROCEDURES

When sample size in a study is increased from small to large, asymptotic approaches are traditionally used for data analysis. However, the significance value they provide is only an approximation, because the sampling distribution of the test statistic is only approximately equal to the theoretical limiting distribution, for example, a χ^2 distribution, a standard normal distribution. The approximation is inadequate in cases where the total sample size is small, or the expected values for cells in the table are low.

In discrete data analysis, unsatisfied type I error control from traditionally used asymptotic approaches has been observed in many statistical problems. In a comparative binomial study, Pearson's χ^2 test is often associated with an inflated type I error rate, while the χ^2 test based on Yates' correction [20] is always conservative, with actual type I error rate being less than the nominal level, and often less than half of the nominal level [7, 11, 21–23]. Uncontrolled type I error rate in a study could lead to either under- or overestimated sample size calculation. Several modified χ^2 test statistics were proposed to increase the performance of the Pearson's χ^2 test, for example, the uncorrected χ^2 test [24] and re-corrected χ^2 test [25]. Uncontrolled type I error occurs not only in a 2×2 table, but also in other types of data. For example, a dose-response study to test a trend for data in a $2 \times K$ table, the traditionally used test statistic, the Cochran-Armitage test [4, 26] always has an inflated type I error rate as the total sample size goes to infinity [27].

In light of the problems of type I error control, procedures based on exact probability calculations may be considered in order to preserve the nominal level of a test. Two basic exact approaches, the conditional approach and the unconditional approach, will be introduced first, followed by another three exact unconditional approaches. To avoid too many mathematical notations and symbols, we use a comparative binomial study to explain the computation of these five exact approaches.

1.1.1 Conditional Approach

For the cases where asymptotic approaches are not adequate (e.g., the total sample size is small, the expected sample size for some cells is too small), exact approaches should be considered to make proper statistical inference. Fisher [2] was among the first to propose an exact approach by fixing both marginal totals to control for any nuisance parameter in the tail probability. This is an exact conditional approach and is referred to be as the C approach. This approach was originally developed for analyzing a 2×2 table, but it can be applied to a general $R \times C$ contingency table. Mehta and Patel [28] developed a network-based algorithm to implement Fisher's exact approach for different types of categorical data. But, the main application of Fisher's approach lies in a simple 2×2 table.

Generally speaking, a test statistic should be used in conjunction with the conditional approach to determine the tail area. A test statistic is used to order all possible tables in the sample space where they all have with the same marginal totals as the observed table. As we all know, the limiting distribution of a test statistic and its property are very important in asymptotic approaches for p-value calculation and efficiency comparison, but not in exact approaches. It is only used for the purpose of ordering all tables from the sample space. The probability of each table can be calculated exactly from a hyper-geometric distribution whose probability density function is only based on the values from a table.

Under the conditional framework with both marginal totals fixed, the value at the $(1, 1)$ cell, n_{11}, determines the other three values in a 2×2 contingency table. Therefore, we use n_{11} to represent the complete data $(n_{11}, n_{12}, n_{21}, n_{22})$ for simplicity. The probability of a 2×2 table as in Table 1.1 under the conditional approach is computed as

$$P_C(n_{11}) = \frac{m_1!m_2!n_1!n_2!}{N!n_{11}!n_{12}!n_{21}!n_{22}!}. \tag{1.1}$$

Then, the p-value is computed by adding the probabilities of the given table and other more extreme tables. For example, in a one-sided hypothesis problem that rejects the null hypothesis with a large test statistic, all the tables with the test statistic values being larger than or equal to that of the given table's are in the rejection region and their probabilities are added together to compute the p-value. Although the assumption for the limiting distribution of a test statistic is not needed in exact approaches, some assumptions related to a study itself must be satisfied, for example, the independence assumption of participants. These assumptions can be checked from the study.

Fisher's exact approach has been applied to many statistical problems, such as an association test between two categorical variables, a trend test with binary endpoints [14], and proportion comparison for binary clustered data [29]. While some theorists argued that Fisher's exact test can only be applied to a study that was originally designed with both marginal totals fixed, actually, Fisher's idea is a general approach, and it has been applied to many studies whose marginal totals are not fixed. As aforementioned, a study with both marginal totals fixed is rarely found in practice. One frequently used area of Fisher's exact approach is where the traditionally used χ^2 test can not be applied due to a relatively small expected frequency. When this assumption of the χ^2 test is not satisfied, the exact conditional approach is the alternative that should be used to guarantee the type I error rate. The exact conditional approach is widely available in the majority of statistical software (SAS, R, StatXact, Stata, SPSS, etc.). For a simple 2×2 table, the p-value calculation should not take a long time even for a large sample size.

The data from Example 1.1 is used to illustrate the application of the conditional approach. This is a randomized placebo-control two-arm study for patients with chronic non-cancer-related pain [3]. If this study assumes that the treatment response rate should be higher than that from the placebo group in advance, then a one-sided hypothesis would be appropriate with the alternative hypothesis as $H_a : p_t > p_c$, where p_t and p_c are the response rate for the treatment group and the placebo group, respectively. In this study, the response rates for the treatment group and the placebo group are estimated as $p_t = 27.1\%$ and $p_c = 18.9\%$, respectively, from the observed data in Table 1.2. When both marginal totals are fixed as in the conditional approach, the value, n_{11}, determines the other three values, and the sample space can be simplified as a collection of all possible n_{11} values. Given the marginal totals, n_1 and n_2 for column totals, m_1 and m_2 for row totals as in Table 1.1, the range of the possible values for n_{11} is from $\max(0, n_1 + m_1 - N)$ to $\min(n_1, m_1)$. For this particular example, this range is from 0 to 99, therefore the size of the sample space for the conditional approach is 100. For each data point in the sample space, its probability can be computed from Equation (1.1). The null hypothesis will be rejected when $n_{11} \geq 58$, therefore, the p-value is calculated as $\sum_{n_{11}=58}^{99} P_C(n_{11}) = 0.028$.

When a hypothesis testing problem is two-sided, multiple approaches have been proposed to compute its p-value. Among these approaches, the most commonly used one is from Irwin [30] who proposed computing the two-sided p-value by adding all data whose probability is smaller than or equal to that of the observed data. In other words, the table probability in Equation (1.1) is used as a test statistic and the tail area includes all tables with smaller probabilities. The second approach uses the test statistic: $|n_{11} - n_1 m_1 / N|$ to determine the tail area that is defined as a collection of tables whose test statistics are at least as large as that of the given data. Another widely used approach doubles the one-sided p-value, which may be larger than 1 in some cases [5, 31]. It is obvious that different approaches for a two-sided problem generally do not have the same p-value, thus they may lead to different conclusions. It should be noted that the two-sided exact conditional p-value would be strictly defined when the test statistic for ordering the sample space is only used to compute a two-sided asymptotic p-value, such as the χ^2 test statistic.

1.1.2 Unconditional Approach Based on Maximization

The exact conditional approach is the alternative of traditional asymptotic approaches when asymptotic approaches do not control for the type I error rate. However, the conditional approach is often criticized for being conservative from an unconditional framework, which is often based on results from studies with small sample sizes. The conservativeness of the exact conditional approach has been discussed in many research articles. Andrés and Tejedor [32] compared the conditional approach and the unconditional approach for binomial comparative studies under one-sided and two-sided alternatives with various sample size ratios between two groups. They found that the loss of power from the C approach as compared with the exact unconditional approach, is often slight. Later, Crans and Shuster [33] continued the debate on which exact approach is the most powerful and the most appropriate for use in binomial comparative studies. The results indicated that the C approach is indeed conservative as the actual significance level is less than 0.035 for a sample size up to 50 at the nominal level of 0.05.

To address the conservativeness of the exact conditional approach due to the small size of the sample space, Barnard [34] was the first to propose an unconditional approach where only the column totals (n_1 and n_2 as in Table 1.1) are fixed, for testing the hypotheses as $H_0 : p_1 = p_2$ against $H_a : p_1 \neq p_2$. This study belongs to the comparative study mentioned before. Under the null hypothesis, it states that both groups have the same response rate, for example, $p_1 = p_2 = p$, which is a nuisance parameter in the table probability, specifically,

$$P(n_{11}, n_{12}|p) = b(n_{11}, n_1, p) \times b(n_{12}, n_2, p),$$

where $b(x, y, z) = \binom{y}{x} z^x (1 - z)^{y-x}$ is the probability density function of a binomial distribution.

Before computing the exact unconditional p-value, the tail area needs to be determined, and a test statistic is often used in this procedure for ordering the sample space. For a given test statistic T, such as, the χ^2 test, the likelihood ratio test, or the score test, the tail area is calculated as $\Omega_T(\mathbf{x}^*) = \{\mathbf{x} : T(\mathbf{x}) \geq T(\mathbf{x}^*)\}$, where $\mathbf{x} = (n_{11}, n_{12}, n_{21}, n_{22})$ is a data point, and $\mathbf{x}^*$ is the observed data. In a binomial comparative study, $\mathbf{x}$ is equivalent to (n_{11}, n_{12}) as the column totals n_1 and n_2 are given. The unconditional p-value is then computed as

$$PM = \max_{p \in [0,1]} \sum_{\mathbf{x} \in \Omega_T(\mathbf{x}^*)} P(\mathbf{x}|p).$$

The nuisance parameter, p, in the tail probability is eliminated by the maximization step. For this reason, this approach is referred to as the M approach. The choice of the test statistic would affect the tail area, and further affect the p-value calculation.

By fixing the number of subjects from each group, the size of the sample space in the exact unconditional approach is $(n_1+1)(n_2+1)$, which is much larger than that from the conditional approach. For data in Example 1.1, the size of the unconditional space is $215 \times 218 = 46870$ while the size of sample space for the conditional approach is only 100. The null distribution of the unconditional approach could be much less discrete than that of the conditional approach, which may lead to a powerful testing procedure. However, the performance comparison between these two exact approaches is still unclear in general. The preference for the approach often depends on the specific problem. The M approach was developed for comparing two binomial comparative trials, and this approach was extended to a double dichotomy study with only the total sum fixed [15, 35]. In such studies, an additional nuisance parameter is added to the tail probability function. In other words, the p-value is computed by maximizing the tail area over two nuisance parameters instead of one from a binomial comparative study. It will be computationally intensive, but it is still feasible with the usage of current computational resources and software packages.

The unconditional approach for a two-sided problem is relatively computationally easy as compared to the approach for a one-sided problem. The null hypothesis space for a two-sided problem is a one-dimensional line, $p_1 = p_2 = p$, while it becomes a two-dimensional space: a triangle $p_1 \leq p_2$, in a one-sided problem. Then, the p-value has to be computed by maximizing the tail probability over the triangle space for testing a one-sided hypothesis. It is computationally intensive to find the global maximum of the tail probability over a triangle space by using the traditional grid-search method, even with the help of numerical search algorithms. The monotonicity property is an important property of a test statistic to reduce the computational intensity in finding the maximum of the tail probability. In general, the monotonicity property states that if one data point is in the tail area, then certain data points in the neighbor should also be included in the tail area. In a binomial comparative study, if (n_{11}, n_{12}) is in the rejection region for testing the null hypothesis $H_0 : p_1 \leq p_2$, then

$(n_{11} + 1, n_{12})$ and $(n_{11}, n_{12} - 1)$ should also be in there, since these two data points have even stronger support for the alternative hypothesis H_a : $p_1 > p_2$. Röhmel [36] proved that the Farrington and Manning test statistic satisfies the monotonicity property for testing non-inferiority/superiority for two binomials [37]. Commonly used test statistics for comparing two binomial proportions belong to the Farrington and Manning test statistic. The monotonicity property has to be checked for a one-sided problem when the exact unconditional approach is used.

The exact unconditional approach and the exact conditional approach could be substantially different from each other even for a study with moderate sample sizes [38, 39]. With the decreased discreteness of the null distribution from the unconditional approach, it would be expected that the unconditional approach is less conservative with a larger size of the null space. However, it was found that the unconditional approach has low power in two binomial comparative studies by using some test statistics, for example, the proportion difference [40]. The trend could be reversed when another test statistic is utilized. The performance of the exact unconditional approach and the exact conditional approach highly depend the choice of the test statistic in two binomial comparative comparisons. In a trend test with binary endpoints, Mehta et al. [41] found that the actual type I error rate is generally more conservative using the conditional strategy as compared with the unconditional approach, although the difference between the tests diminishes with increasing sample sizes. Both approaches have nearly identical power when the sample sizes are large, but for small sample sizes, the unconditional approach is generally more powerful due to the less discrete null distribution. In some scenarios, the conditional approach was shown to be more powerful than the unconditional approach.

The binomial comparative trial in Example 1.1 is used to illustrate the application of the M approach based on three commonly used test statistics for testing the null hypothesis: $H_0 : p_t \le p_c$ against the alternative $H_a : p_t > p_c$, where p_t and p_c are the response rates for the treatment group and the control group, respectively. Three test statistics considered are: the proportion difference (PD), the Z test with an unpooled variance estimate (ZuP), and the Z test with a pooled variance estimate (ZP):

$$T_{PD} = \hat{p}_t - \hat{p}_c,$$

$$T_{ZuP} = \frac{\hat{p}_t - \hat{p}_c}{\sqrt{(\hat{p}_t(1 - \hat{p}_t)/n_1 + \hat{p}_c(1 - \hat{p}_c)/n_2)}},$$

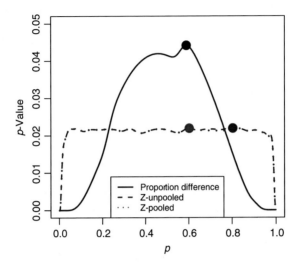

Figure 1.1 Tail probability plots for a binomial comparative study based on three test statistics.

and

$$T_{ZP} = \frac{\hat{p}_t - \hat{p}_c}{\sqrt{(\hat{p}(1 - \hat{p}))(1/n_1 + 1/n_2)}},$$

where $\hat{p}_t = n_{11}/n_1$, $\hat{p}_c = n_{12}/n_2$, and $\hat{p} = (n_{11} + n_{12})/(n_1 + n_2)$. The monotonicity property is satisfied for all three test statistics [36]. Therefore, the unconditional p-value based on the M approach is obtained from the boundary of the null space, which is the common probability of the two groups, p.

In the M approach, the first step is to determine the tail area for the given data based on a test statistic. Different test statistics may lead to a different tail area. The tail probability curve is drawn as a function of the nuisance parameter, p. Figure 1.1 presents the three tail probability plots as a function of p based on the three test statistics. It can be seen that the plot based on the T_{PD} is very different from those based on the two Z test statistics. The final p-value is computed as the maximum of each curve: 0.044, 0.022, and 0.022 based on the test statistic T_{PD}, T_{ZuP}, and T_{ZP}, respectively. These maximum values are found when $p = 0.588, 0.803$, and 0.602, respectively, and they are marked in the figure with big dots. The R package, *Exact*, can be used to compute these M p-values. It is noticeable that the tail probability curve is not smooth, with multiple local spikes as seen in the plots. The traditional grid search algorithm is commonly used to search for the maximum of a tail probability plot with multiple spikes.

1.1.3 Unconditional Approach Based on Partial Maximization

In the unconditional M approach, the p-value is computed as the maximum of the tail probability over the whole parameter space of the nuisance parameter. When the parameter space is not bounded, it is a challenge to compute the p-value based on the M approach without some essential properties of the tail probability being satisfied. It has been observed that the tail probability as a function of the nuisance parameter is often erratic, and it is difficult to search for a global maximum over an unbounded space. In addition to this computational consideration, Berger and Boos [42] argued that some of the possible nuisance parameter values should not be included in the p-value computation if they are not completely supported by the data, such as the values outside of the confidence interval of the parameter. For these reasons, they proposed an unconditional approach based on partial maximization, referred to as the BB approach, and the associated p-value is defined as

$$P_{\mathrm{BB}} = \max_{p \in C_{1-\eta}} \sum_{\mathbf{x} \in \Omega_T(\mathbf{x}^*)} P(\mathbf{x}|p) + \eta,$$

where $C_{1-\eta}$ is a $1 - \eta$ confidence interval for the nuisance parameter under the null hypothesis, and η has to be determined before data analysis and it is often chosen to be 0.001 or 0.01. The confidence interval $C_{1-\eta}$ is generally two-sided, but it can be one-sided for a one-sided hypothesis testing problem. It has been shown that the unconditional p-value based on partial maximization is valid [42]. A p-value, PX, is valid [43] if

$$P(PX \le \alpha) \le \alpha$$

is satisfied for any nuisance parameters. One obvious application of the BB approach is to compare two independent Poisson rates [44, 45] where the incidence rate is not bounded in such studies.

Berger [46] compared the BB approach and the M approach for data from a binomial comparative study. The Z-pooled test statistic T_{ZP} was used, and the confidence interval $C_{1-\eta}$ was calculated from the Clopper-Pearson exact method for a binomial proportion [47]. The results indicated that the confidence interval based approach can improve the power of a binomial comparative study. The power gain often occurs when the p-value of the M approach is obtained from the outside of the confidence interval $C_{1-\eta}$.

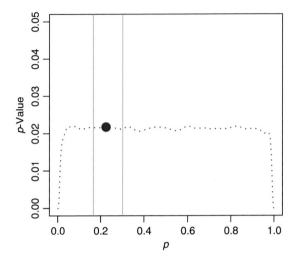

Figure 1.2 Tail probability plots for a binomial comparative study based on partial maximization by using the Z-pooled test statistic. The two green lines are the exact 0.999 confidence interval for the nuisance parameter, and the purple dot is the value for the BB p-value.

We use the binomial comparative study in Example 1.1 based on the Z-pooled test statistic T_{ZP} to illustrate the computation of the BB p-value with $\eta = 0.001$. The exact confidence interval for the data is computed as $C_{1-\eta} = (0.167, 0.302)$, which is represented with two vertical lines in Figure 1.2. The first part of the BB p-value is $\max_{p \in C_{1-\eta}} \sum_{\mathbf{x} \in \Omega_T} P(\mathbf{x}|p) = 0.022$, then the final BB p-value is 0.023 after adding $\eta = 0.001$. This example shows the case that the BB approach could be slightly conservative as compared to the M approach when the first part of the BB p-value is very close to or the same as the M p-value.

1.1.4 Unconditional Approach Based on Conditional p-value and Maximization

The exact conditional approach is often conservative, with the actual unconditional level of a test being much less than the nominal level. To address the conservativeness of the C approach, Boschloo [9] proposed using the p-value of the C approach as the test statistic. Basically, Boschloo's approach is to identify the largest λ such that $P(P_C \leq \lambda) \leq \alpha$ is satisfied for all possible nuisance parameter values: $\max_p P(P_C \leq \lambda|p) \leq \alpha$. This approach can be viewed as a combination of the C approach and the M approach (referred to as the C+M approach). The C+M p-value is computed as

$$P_{C+M} = \max_{p \in [0,1]} \sum_{\mathbf{x} \in \Omega_C(\mathbf{x}^*)} P(\mathbf{x}|p),$$

where $\Omega_C(\mathbf{x}^*) = \{\mathbf{x} : P_C(\mathbf{x}) \leq P_C(\mathbf{x}^*)\}$ is the tail area, and P_C is the C p-value.

When $\lambda = \alpha$, $P(P_C \leq \lambda) \leq \alpha$ is always true as from the C approach. It follows that $\lambda \geq \alpha$. Therefore, the C+M approach is at least as powerful as the C approach.

The C+M approach has not been widely used in practice, possibly because of the confusion that comes from using the C p-value as the test statistic. The C p-value is often used as the p-value for statistical inference. The C+M approach was shown to be uniformly more powerful than the C approach in a binomial comparative study [40], and it was recommended for use. For the binomial comparative Example 1.1, the p-value based on the C+M approach is 0.023, which leads to the same conclusion as others. The C+M p-value may be computed from the R package, *Exact*.

1.1.5 Unconditional Approach Based on Estimation and Maximization

The exact unconditional M approach could be computationally intensive when multiple nuisance parameters are presented. For this reason, Liddell [48] was the first to propose an approach by computing the exact distribution of the proportional difference of two independent binomial distributions at a single point, the maximum likelihood estimate (MLE) for the common proportion under the null hypothesis. In Liddell's approach, one only needs to find the exact distribution at one point instead of the whole parameter space as in the M approach. It is computationally easy to obtain the p-value. Later, Storer and Kim [49] extended Liddell's approach to other commonly used test statistics. This approach is often called the approximate unconditional approach. Since the nuisance parameter in the table probability is replaced by an estimate of the parameter, this approach is referred to as the E approach.

If the null hypothesis is rejected for a large test statistic, then the tail area based on the test statistic, T, is computed as $\Omega_T(\mathbf{x}^*) = \{\mathbf{x} : T(\mathbf{x}) \geq T(\mathbf{x}^*)\}$. It is often the case that a test statistic has a closed formula, therefore it is computationally easy. For each data point in the tail area, its probability is a function of the nuisance parameter. In a binomial comparative study, the E p-value is computed as

$$P_{\mathrm{E}} = \sum_{\mathbf{x} \in \Omega_T(\mathbf{x}^*)} P(\mathbf{x}|\hat{p}),$$

where $\hat{p} = (n_{11}+n_{12})/(n_1+n_2)$ is the MLE of the common proportion under the null hypothesis. The tail area does not depend on the MLE value. The E approach is a general approach, and it has been applied to other studies [50, 51].

The E p-value only needs to evaluate the tail probability at a single point. For this reason, this approach was attractive in the days when computational resources were a problem for most practitioners. The E approach guarantees the test size at a single estimated value, but not for all the possible values of the nuisance parameter. For this reason, the E approach is not exact.

Lloyd [13, 31, 50, 52–55] proposed a new approach for the p-value calculation based on estimation and maximization. The estimation step is used to obtain a flatter p-value plot, and the maximization step is used to guarantee the nominal level. The p-value plot based on a test statistic in the M approach is generally erratic, and it is computationally difficult to search for the global maximum, especially for the case with multiple spikes. It was shown in Lloyd [52] that the p-value plot by using the E p-value as the test statistic tends to have a much flatter plot. This important step may allow one to avoid the situation where the maximum of the tail probability is obtained from unlikely values of the nuisance parameter, such as the values outside of a confidence interval. Although the E p-value is only approximately valid, the following maximization step makes the approach exact with the type I error rate guaranteed. The approach is referred to as the E + M approach. The E + M approach has been applied to many important statistical problems [15, 45, 50, 56–61].

The estimation step could be computationally difficult with a large size sample space, since the E p-value for each data point needs to be computed. Parallel computing is a useful tool to reduce the computational time significantly by computing the E p-values at the same time for all tables. Some of the packages have been developed in R to conduct the parallel computing, for example, *multicore, parallel*. For a study with a small to moderate sample size, a personal computer may be sufficient to serve this purpose.

The E p-value is used as a test statistic in the E + M approach to find the tail area including the tables whose E p-values are less than or equal to that of the given table: $\Omega_E(\mathbf{x}^*)\{\mathbf{x} : P_E(\mathbf{x}) \leq P_E(\mathbf{x}^*)\}$. The E approach is not exact, and is slightly liberal in general. The maximization step would make it exact, and the E + M p-value is computed as

$$P_{E+M} = \max_{p\in[0,1]} \sum_{\mathbf{x}\in\Omega_E(\mathbf{x}^*)} P(\mathbf{x}|p).$$

In the E + M approach, the estimation step can be applied multiple times before the final maximization step, such as E^2+M with two E steps. Lloyd [52] found that a single application of the E step has already produced a flatter p-value plot, and the improvement from multiple E steps is slight. For this reason, a single E step is recommended for use in practice.

The E + M p-value based on the test statistic T_{ZP} with pooled variance estimate for the binomial comparative Example 1.1, is 0.024, thus the null hypothesis is rejected. The E + M p-values based on the other two test statistics, 0.022 for T_{PD} and 0.024 for T_{ZuP}, are very close to that based on the test statistic T_{ZP}.

1.2 COMPARISON OF EXACT APPROACHES

We compare the performance of the five exact approaches numerically by enumerating all possible tables in the sample space. This is a numerical study and no simulation is involved. The significance level is set as 0.05, which is commonly used in practice. Both one-sided and two-sided problems are studied. When the hypothesis is two-sided, the test statistic is computed as the square of a test statistic for a one-sided hypothesis.

Comparative Study
We first investigate the type I error rate control in a binomial comparative study, with various sample size combinations $(n_t, n_c) = (50, 50), (100,100), (300, 300), (100,50), (50, 300)$, and $(300,100)$. Figure 1.3 shows the type I error curve for the five exact approaches based on the three test statistics $(T_{PD}, T_{ZuP},$ and $T_{ZP})$, with a balanced sample size of 100 per group. The plots on the left side are for a two-sided problem, and these on the right side are for a one-sided hypothesis problem. It can be seen that the performance of the M approach depends on the choice of the test statistic. This approach has a good type I error rate control when the Z-type test statistics are used. The C approach is generally conservative when compared with other approaches. The BB approach often performs better than the M approach, but the full maximization of the BB type I error curve could be larger than

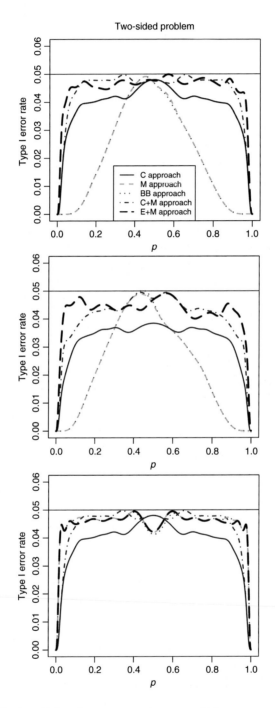

Figure 1.3 Two-sided and one-sided type I error rate comparisons among the five exact approaches with a balanced sample size of 100 per group at the significance level of $\alpha = 0.05$, based on the test statistics T_{PD}, T_{ZuP}, and T_{ZP} from the first row to the third row.

(Continued)

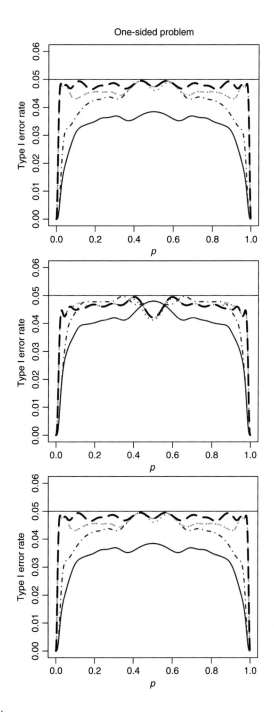

Figure 1.3, Continued

the nominal level as seen in Figure 1.4 for type I error comparison with unbalanced sample size $(n_t, n_c) = (100, 50)$. Overall, the E+M approach and the C+M approach have good performance with regards to the type I error control, with the actual type I error rate curve being closer to the nominal level.

Having studied the type I error rate among the five exact approaches, we compare their power under the alternative, $p_t = p_c + \theta$, for θ from 0 to $1 - p_c$. Figure 1.5 presents the power study for a balanced study with a sample size of 100 per group. Multiple p_c values are considered, and the typical plots with $p_c = 0.3$ are presented. The C approach is the least powerful approach among these five exact approaches in the balanced case. All the other four approaches have similar power in the one-sided problem. In the two-sided problem the C+M approach is generally less powerful than the other three exact approaches (the M approach, the BB approach, and the E+M approach), and the power difference is substantial when the test statistics T_{ZP} and T_{ZuP} are used. For the unbalanced study with sample size $(n_t, n_c) = (100, 50)$, see Figure 1.6, the C approach is more powerful than the M approach and the BB approach based on the test statistic T_{ZuP}, and this trend is reversed when the other two test statistics are used. The C+M approach and the E+M approach are often the most powerful approaches, and the C+M approach is slightly more powerful than the E+M approach is some cases.

The C+M approach and the E+M approach generally have good performance with regards to power. The performance of the C+M approach is consistent with the choice of a test statistic, while the E+M approach is not. For the E+M approach, the test statistic T_{PD} is preferable for a one-sided problem, and T_{ZuP} and T_{ZP} for a two-sided problem, although the power difference is often small.

Matched-Pairs Study
Matched-pairs studies are utilized in many study designs to account for population heterogeneity. When the outcome is binary, McNemar's test [19] is commonly used for testing the equality of two marginal probabilities for data from a 2×2 contingency table. In addition, the likelihood ratio test can also be used for this problem.

Lloyd [31] compared the performance of three exact approaches based on three test statistics for matched-pairs studies. The three exact approaches considered are the M approach, the BB approach, and the E+M approach.

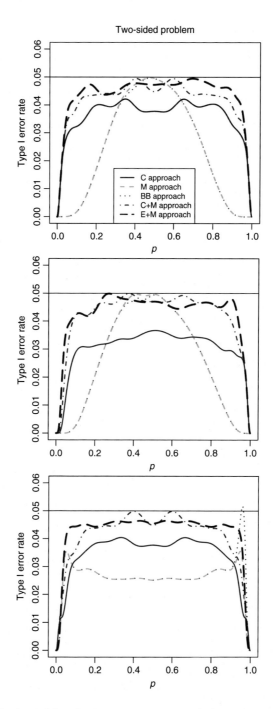

Figure 1.4 *Two-sided and one-sided type I error rate comparisons among the five exact approaches with unbalanced sample size, $n_t = 100$ and $n_c = 50$ at the significance level of $\alpha = 0.05$, based on the test statistics T_{PD}, T_{ZuP}, and T_{ZP} from the first row to the third row.*

(Continued)

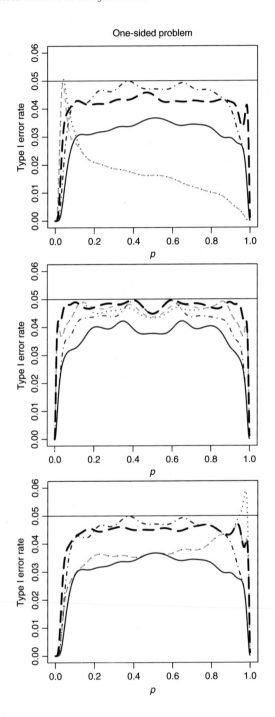

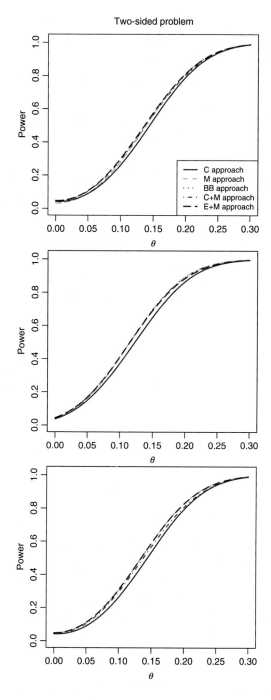

Figure 1.5 Power comparisons for two-sided and one-sided problems among the five exact approaches with balanced sample size, $n_t = 100$ and $n_c = 100$ at the significance level of $\alpha = 0.05$, under the alternative $p_c = 0.3$ and $p_t = p_c + \theta$, based on the test statistics T_{PD}, T_{ZuP}, and T_{ZP} from the first row to the third row.

(Continued)

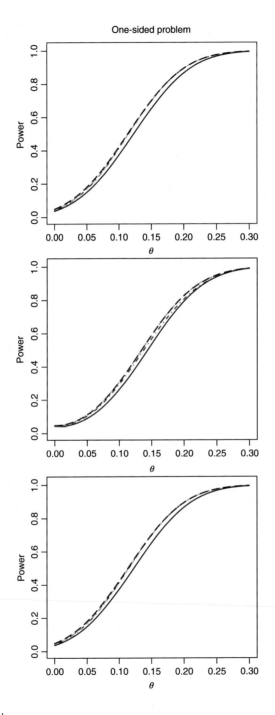

Figure 1.5, Continued

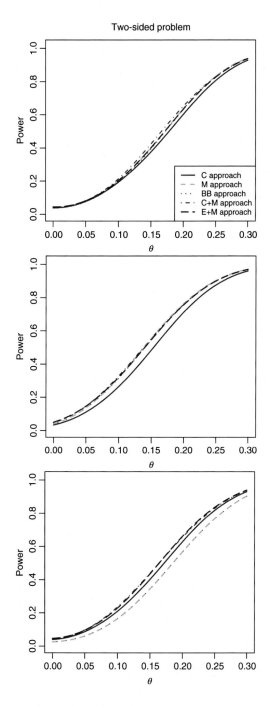

Figure 1.6 Power comparisons for two-sided and one-sided problems among the five exact approaches with unbalanced sample size, $n_t = 100$ and $n_c = 50$ at the significance level of $\alpha = 0.05$, under the alternative $p_c = 0.3$ and $p_t = p_c + \theta$, based on the test statistics T_{PD}, T_{ZuP}, and T_{ZP} from the first row to the third row.

(Continued)

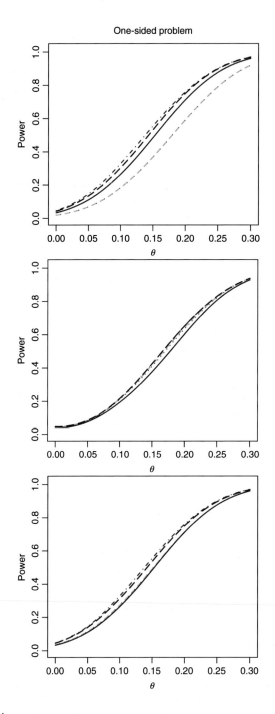

Figure 1.6, Continued

The other two exact approaches, the C approach, and the C + M approach are not included in his article for comparison [31]. In addition to the McNemar test statistic and the LR test statistic, the third test statistic is the conditional sign test with the nuisance parameter estimated as the value from the null hypothesis. Various configurations were considered, and the three exact approaches were compared by calculating the proportion of the parameter space in which one approach is more powerful than another. It was shown that the E + M approach dominates the other two exact approaches.

Later, Lloyd and Moldovan [50] investigated the performance of the same three exact approaches [31] for testing non-inferiority in matched-pairs studies. They developed the likelihood ratio test as an alternative to the score test statistic derived by Nam [62]. They illustrated the application the three exact approaches based on the two test statistics with a very interesting example reported by Kao et al. [63] for comparing two diagnostic procedures. The E + M approach was shown to be more powerful than the M approach and the BB approach under various conditions, and the test statistic does not make much difference in power when the E + M approach is used.

CHAPTER 2

Exact Statistical Inference for a 2 × K Table

We have studied the exact approaches for data that can be organized in a 2 × 2 table in the last chapter. These exact approaches are now applied to a general case for data that can be organized in a 2 × K table. For such studies, one factor is binary, and the other is ordinal or nominal with K levels ($K \geq 3$). One example is a dose-response study to test the equality of K binomial populations, under either an ordered alternative or a general alternative [14, 64]. Another important application is to test the Hardy-Weinberg Equilibrium in population genetics. The exact approaches have been successfully applied to these important statistical, medical, and genetic applications [51, 65].

2.1 TESTING TREND FOR BINARY DATA FROM A 2 × K TABLE

The problem of testing a dose-response relationship among K binomial populations exists in a wide range of applications. Suppose that $d_1, d_2, \ldots, d_K$ are the K ordered dose levels as $d_1 < d_2 < \cdots < d_K$ in a study. The number of subjects for i-th group is n_i, ($i = 1, 2, \ldots, K$), which is considered as fixed for the study. When the outcome is binary, the response rate is the primary endpoint of interest to test the dose-response relationship. Let x_i be the number of responses observed out of n_i subjects from the i-th group. Data from such studies can be organized in a 2 × K table; see Table 2.1.

Let p_i be the response rate at the dose level of d_i; it is often of interest to test the null hypothesis

$$H_0 : p_1 = p_2 = \cdots = p_K = p,$$

against an ordered alternative of the form

$$H_a : p_1 \leq p_2 \leq \cdots \leq p_K,$$

with at least one strict inequality.

The Cochran-Armitage (CA) test (Cochran [4], and Armitage [26]) is by far the most frequently used test for detecting a trend with binary endpoints.

Exact Statistical Inference for Categorical Data. http://dx.doi.org/10.1016/B978-0-08-100681-8.00002-6

Table 2.1 A 2 × K Contingency Table				
	Dose Level			
	1	**2**	**...**	**K**
Response	x_1	x_2	$\cdots$	x_K
No response	$n_1 - x_1$	$n_2 - x_2$	$\cdots$	$n_K - x_K$
Total	n_1	n_2	$\cdots$	n_K
Source: From Corcoran et al. [69], with permission.				

When the suspected ordering is correct, the CA test is always more powerful than the χ^2 test that is used for testing a general alternative. The CA test statistic is given as

$$T_{CA} = \frac{\sum_{i=1}^{K} x_i d_i - \hat{p} \sum_{i=1}^{K} n_i d_i}{\sqrt{\hat{p}(1 - \hat{p}) \sum_{i=1}^{K} n_i (d_i - \bar{d})/N^2}},$$

where $\hat{p} = \sum_{i=1}^{K} x_i/N$, $N = \sum_{i=1}^{K} n_i$, $\bar{d} = \sum_{n=1}^{K} n_i d_i/N$. The T_{CA} asymptotically follows a normal distribution. The null hypothesis is rejected at the significance level of α when the value of the test statistic is greater than $Z_{1-\alpha}$ which is the $1 - \alpha$ upper quantile of a standard normal distribution. The properties of the asymptotic limiting distribution of the CA test was studied in a small sample setting by Agresti and Yang [66], and in a large sample setting by Kang and Lee [27]. Both results pointed out that the type I error rate is not well controlled even with sufficiently large sample sizes. In addition, Kang and Lee [27] theoretically proved the inflated type I error rate of the CA test: the actual type I error is always greater than the nominal level, as the total sample size goes to infinity when the ratios of sample size among the K groups keep constant. As a result of an inflated type I error rate, the power of the study is always overestimated. But, the quantity of the overestimated part is generally unknown, thus we would recommend using the CA asymptotic approach with caution, due to the unsatisfactory type I error control.

To control for the type I error rate, exact approaches should be utilized to preserve the nominal level of a study. The column totals, the number of subjects for each group, are fixed from such studies. If the row total, the total number of responses $\sum_{i=1}^{K} x_i = g$, is also considered fixed, then the probability of each table can be calculated from a hyper-geometric distribution. This approach is the C approach where both marginal totals are fixed. The C approach was suggested by Mehta et al. [41] to compute exact power for the CA test. Let $\mathbf{x} = (x_1, x_2, \ldots, x_K)$ be a vector for the number of responses, and $\mathbf{x}^*$ be the observed data. The conditional p-value is calculated as

$$P_C = \sum_{\mathbf{x} \in \Omega_C(\mathbf{x}^*)} \frac{\prod_{i=1}^K \binom{n_i}{x_i}}{\binom{N}{g}}, \tag{2.1}$$

where $\Omega_C(\mathbf{x}^*)$ is the tail area for the observed data $\mathbf{x}^*$, and defined as $\Omega_C(\mathbf{x}^*) = \{\mathbf{x} : T_{CA}(\mathbf{x}) \geq T_{CA}(\mathbf{x}^*) \text{ and } \sum_{i=1}^K x_i = \sum_{i=1}^K x_i^* = g\}$. Mehta et al. [41] found that the C approach is generally conservative when compared to the unconditional approach.

The calculation of the M p-value can be followed from the last chapter under a binomial comparative setting. The only difference lies in the tail probability, with K binomial density functions in this setting for testing a trend. The tail probability under the null hypothesis with the common response rate p is

$$P(\mathbf{x}|p) = \prod_{i=1}^K b(x_i, n_i, p),$$

and the M p-value is calculated as

$$P_M = \max_{p \in [0,1]} \sum_{\mathbf{x} \in \Omega_T(\mathbf{x}^*)} P(\mathbf{x}|p),$$

where $\Omega_T(\mathbf{x}^*) = \{\mathbf{x} : T_{CA}(\mathbf{x}) \geq T_{CA}(\mathbf{x}^*)\}$ is the tail area. The M approach was extensively compared with the C approach by Tang et al. [10, 67], and they concluded that the M approach is often associated with a considerable power gain when compared to the C approach.

Instead of maximizing the tail area over the complete domain of the nuisance parameter, the partial maximization approach finds the p-value from a portion of the nuisance parameter space, which is the confidence interval of the nuisance parameter. The BB p-value is computed as

$$P_{BB} = \max_{p \in C_{1-\eta}} \sum_{\mathbf{x} \in \Omega_T(\mathbf{x}^*)} P(\mathbf{x}|p) + \eta,$$

where $C_{1-\eta}$ is the $100(1 - \eta)\%$ interval for p based on the Clopper-Pearson exact approach [47], and $\eta = 0.001$ is the penalty value [42] as recommended. Freidlin and Gastwirth [68] extended the BB approach for testing a trend in a $2 \times K$ table, and revealed that the BB approach is more powerful than the C approach in many cases.

In addition to these three exact approaches, the C approach, the M approach, and the BB approach, we also consider another two exact unconditional approaches that are constructed from a combination of existing approaches. They can be viewed as a two-step procedure, with the second step as the maximization in both approaches to guarantee the nominal level. The C+M exact approach uses the p-values from the C approach to obtain the tail area, and the C+M p-value is calculated as

$$P_{C+M} = \max_{p\in[0,1]} \sum_{\mathbf{x}\in\Omega_C(\mathbf{x}^*)} P(\mathbf{x}|p),$$

where $\Omega_C(\mathbf{x}^*) = \{\mathbf{x} : P_C(\mathbf{x}) \leq P_C(\mathbf{x}^*)\}$ is the tail area, and P_C is the p-value based on the C approach as in Equation (2.1).

The other two-step testing procedure is the E+M approach where the E p-value obtained from the first step is used as a test statistic in the second maximization step. The E p-value is used to order the sample space, not as the final p-value. The E approach does not guarantee the type I error rate, but the following maximization step makes the test exact. The E+M p-value is computed as

$$P_{E+M} = \max_{p\in[0,1]} \sum_{\mathbf{x}\in\Omega_E(\mathbf{x}^*)} P(\mathbf{x}|p),$$

where $\Omega_E(\mathbf{x}^*) = \{\mathbf{x} : P_E(\mathbf{x}) \leq P_E(\mathbf{x}^*)\}$ is the tail area, $P_E(\mathbf{x}^*) = \sum_{\mathbf{x}\in\Omega_T(\mathbf{x}^*)} P(\mathbf{x}|\hat{p})$, is the E p-value, and $\hat{p}$ is the MLE of the nuisance parameter, p, for the given data $\mathbf{x}^*$. Shan et al. [14] extended the E+M approach which was originally proposed by Lloyd [52] for a 2×2 table, to the problem of testing the equality of response rates in K binomial populations against an ordered alternative. The E+M approach was compared with the C approach, the M approach, and the BB approach, and was shown to be associated with considerable power gain.

Data from an animal carcinogenicity study with $K=4$ and a balanced sample size of 10 per group [69] is used to illustrate the application of the five exact approaches. Data is presented in Table 2.2. The score value $d=(0,1,5,50)$ is chosen to represent the dose level in the study for p-value calculation. The tail probability plots for each approach are displayed in Figure 2.1. At the significance level of $\alpha=0.05$, the null hypothesis is rejected by using the M approach, the BB approach, and the E+M approach with p-values 0.037, 0.038, and 0.044, respectively. The confidence interval for the nuisance parameter for the BB approach is from 0.017 to 0.372, which is indicated by the two vertical lines in the figure. The maximum of

Table 2.2 Data From the Animal Carcinogenicity Study with $K=4$				
	Dose Level			
	1	2	3	4
Response	1	0	1	3
No response	9	10	9	7
Total	10	10	10	10

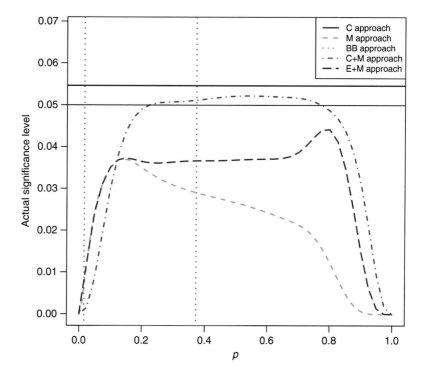

Figure 2.1 Plots of the tail probability as a function of the nuisance parameter for the animal carcinogenicity study with $K=4$ and a sample size of 10 per group.

the tail probability is obtained within the confidence interval, therefore, the BB p-value would be $\eta = 0.001$ larger than the M p-value. For the other two conditional approaches, their p-values (0.055 for the C approach and 0.052 for the C+M approach) are greater than 0.05. It can be seen that the p-value based on the C+M approach is only slightly above the nominal level.

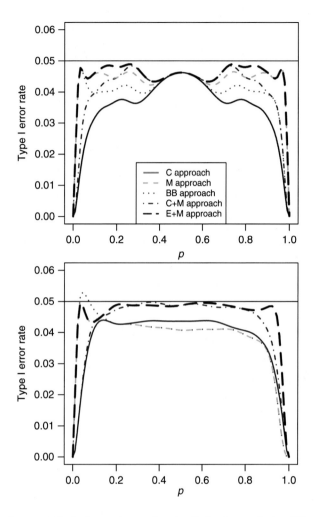

Figure 2.2 Type I error rate for the five exact approaches when $K=3$ and a sample size of 30 per group at the significance level of $\alpha = 0.05$, the left plot with the score value $d = (0, 1, 2)$, and the right plot with the score value $d = (0, 1, 4)$.

To assess the performance of the five exact approaches, we start with the type I error rate comparison. Figure 2.2 shows the actual type I error rate plots for the exact approaches when $K=3$ and a sample size of 30 per group for the dose values $d = (0, 1, 2)$ and $d = (0, 1, 4)$ at the significance level of $\alpha = 0.05$. The value of 0 in the dose score represents the control group. The first dose value is for a linear relationship, and the second is for a quadratic relationship. For the BB approach, when the maximum over the full space is outside of the confidence interval, the unconditional p-value over the complete domain may be larger than the nominal level. All other unconditional approaches guarantee the type I error rate as the last step in these approaches is the full maximization step, and the exact conditional approach respects the type I error rate that has been theoretically proved. The C+M approach is generally less conservative as compared to the C approach. The M approach performs liberally, depending the choice of sample size and dose value. The C+M approach and the E + M approach generally perform better with regards to type I error control. More type I error comparisons among exact approaches may be found in Shan et al. [14].

We further compare the exact approaches with regards to power under various conditions. The tail area from the type I error control study for each approach is used to compute power. Suppose the tail area for the S approach is Ω_S, where $S = \{C, M, BB, C + M, E + M\}$. For a given alternative $p_i, i = 1, 2, \ldots, K$, the power for the A approach is calculated exactly from binomial distributions as

$$\text{Power} = \sum_{\mathbf{x} \in \Omega_S} \prod_{i=1}^{K} b(x_i, n_i, p_i).$$

The alternative p_i values are obtained from a curve which is plotted as a function of a parameter γ from a logistic regression model [10]:

$$p_i = \frac{e^{\log(p_1/(1-p_1)) + \gamma d_i}}{1 + e^{\log(p_1/(1-p_1)) + \gamma d_i}}, \quad i = 2, 3, \ldots, K.$$

Figure 2.3 presents the power comparison when $K = 4$, a balanced sample size of 30 per group, $d = (0, 1, 2, 3)$ and $p_1 = 0.05$. For a given γ, each p_i value $(i = 2, \ldots, K)$ can be computed from the aforementioned formula as a function of p_1 and the associated dose value, d_i. Power plots are then drawn as a function of γ. As the value of γ increases, the distance between p_i values also increases. Therefore, power for each approach is an increasing function of γ. Power plots for the C approach and the C+M approach are displayed on the top of the figure. The C+M approach is at least as powerful as the C approach. This plot illustrates this property. The M approach and the BB approach have similar performance with regards to power, as seen from the middle plot in the figure. The bottom plot is for the power comparison between the BB approach, the C+M approach, and the E + M approach. The E + M approach and the BB approach are more powerful than the C+M approach in this configuration. This trend is not always true, as seen from the numerical studies by Shan et al. [14]. Nevertheless, it has been found

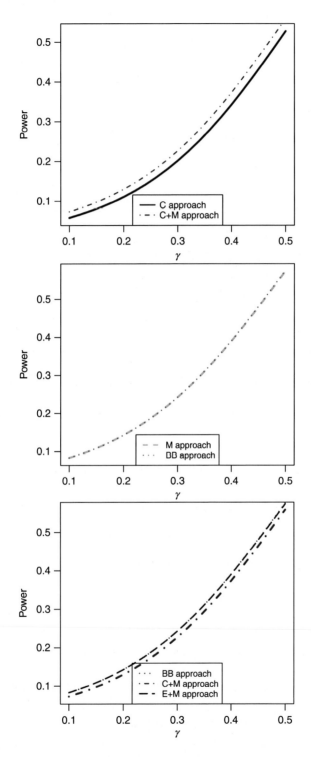

Figure 2.3 Power comparison among the five exact approaches when K = 4, a sample size of 30 per group, and the score value d = (0, 1, 2, 3).

that the M approach and the BB approach are generally not as powerful as the E + M approach [14].

In addition to the commonly used CA test for detecting a trend in a dose-response study with binary endpoints, several other test statistics have been developed. The recent one is based on a new test by Baumgartern, Weiß, and Schindler (BWS) [70], who developed a rank based test for comparing two populations. This test was shown to be at least as powerful as the well known nonparametric tests. Later, Neuhäuser [71] applied the modified BWS test for detecting trends among binomial proportions. Recently, Shan et al. [72] improved the test developed by Neuhäuser [71], by using the exact expected value and variance of the quantities in the test statistics. These two test statistics were used in conjunction with exact approaches, and the results indicated that the E + M approach based on these two test statistics could be slightly more powerful than that based on the CA test in some cases. Shan et al. [72] provided a detailed comparison among these testing procedures.

The commonly used CA test depends on the choice of the dose values $(d_1, d_2, \ldots, d_K)$. To reduce the influence of the dose value assignment, Bartholomew [73] developed a new test statistic for qualitatively ordered samples based on the isotonic regression method. Consiglio et al. [61] considered the exact approaches for testing trend with binary endpoints based on the Bartholomew's test statistic, instead of the traditional CA test statistic. The M approach, the BB approach, the E + M approach, and the C approach were compared, and the first three exact unconditional approaches were shown to be more powerful than the C approach.

2.2 TESTING FOR HARDY-WEINBERG EQUILIBRIUM

The assessment of the Hardy-Weinberg equilibrium (HWE) is one of the first important questions in population genetics to check whether the genotype frequencies have changed from one generation to another [74–76]. When the seven conditions (mutation is not occurring, all mating is totally random, et al. [74]) are met, both the allele frequencies and the genotype frequencies remain constant in a population. This is known as the Hardy-Weinberg Equilibrium. For simplicity, we will focus on the approaches to test the HWE for a diallelic locus with alleles A and B. When the HWE is satisfied, the probabilities of the genotypes AA, AB, and BB are p^2, $2p(1 - p)$, and $(1 - p)^2$, respectively, where p is the marginal probability for the gene A in the population. Let n_{AA}, n_{AB}, and n_{BB} be the sample sizes for the genotypes AA, AB, and BB, respectively.

Traditionally, the χ^2 test is used to test for the HWE, with the test statistic

$$T_{CS} = \frac{4N(n_{AA}n_{BB} - n_{AB}^2/4)^2}{n_A^2 n_B^2},$$

where N is the total number of subjects as $N = n_{AA} + n_{AB} + n_{BB}$, and n_A and n_B are the total number of A and B genes as $n_A = 2n_{AA} + n_{AB}$ and $n_B = 2n_{BB} + n_{AB}$, respectively. It follows that $n_A + n_B = 2N$. This test statistic asymptotically follows a χ^2 distribution with df$= 1$. The second test statistic that may be considered is the likelihood ratio test statistic [77]:

$$T_{LR} = \frac{N^N}{(2N)^{2N}} \frac{2^{n_{AB}} n_A^{n_A} n_B^{n_B}}{n_{AA}^{n_{AA}} n_{AB}^{n_{AB}} n_{BB}^{n_{BB}}}.$$

It is well known that $-2T_{LR}$ follows a χ^2 distribution with df$= 1$ asymptotically. The third test statistic considered is the probability for a data point $\mathbf{x} = (n_{AA}, n_{AB}, n_{BB})$, and it is calculated as

$$T_{PB} = \frac{N! n_A! n_B! 2^{n_{AB}}}{(2N)! n_{AA}! n_{AB}! n_{BB}!}.$$

It has been pointed out by many researchers [65, 78–80] that asymptotic approaches may not be appropriate when the total sample size is small or the expected values for some cells are too small. One solution to the unsatisfied performance from asymptotic approaches is the exact conditional approach. In addition to the fixed number of genotypes n_{AA}, n_{AB}, and n_{BB}, the total number of A genes, n_A, is also considered fixed. Under the exact conditional framework, the probability for data $\mathbf{x} = (n_{AA}, n_{AB}, n_{BB})$ is calculated as $P_{PB}(\mathbf{x})$. This probability is free of any nuisance parameter under the conditional approach with both marginal totals fixed. The tail area can be determined by using one of the three test statistics aforementioned. Then, the C p-value is computed by adding the probabilities of data in the tail area. The C approach for testing independence in a 2×2 table has been studied for decades [2, 5]. Guo and Thompson [79] were among the first to develop an efficient algorithm for the conditional approach in application to loci with multiple alleles. Recently, Engels [65] proposed a substantially improved algorithm based on a lattice-like network [28] to implement the exact conditional approach efficiently for large sample sizes. This new algorithm is about two orders of magnitude faster than the existing ones.

In addition to the exact conditional approach to guarantee the type I error rate, exact unconditional approaches may also be considered to raise the significance level of studies with small sample sizes where the C approach is often conservative as seen in many statistical problems. Haber [81] was one of the first researchers to introduce the unconditional test based on maximization for testing HWE to loci with two alleles. Under the null hypothesis with HWE satisfied, the probability for data $\mathbf{x}$ is a function of the nuisance parameter p,

$$P(\mathbf{x}|p) = \frac{N!}{n_{AA} n_{AB} n_{BB}} 2^{n_{AB}} p^{2n_{AA}+n_{AB}} (1-p)^{2n_{BB}+n_{AB}},$$

where p is the probability of the gene A. The M p-value [81] is given as

$$P_M = \max_{p\in[0,1]} \sum_{\mathbf{x}\in\Omega_T(\mathbf{x}^*)} P(\mathbf{x}|p),$$

where $\Omega_T(\mathbf{x}^*) = \{\mathbf{x} : T(\mathbf{x}) \geq T(\mathbf{x}^*)\}$ is the tail area, and $\mathbf{x}^*$ is the observed data. Haber [81] showed that the M approach generally has more power than the conditional approach in small sample sizes.

Another exact approach is the C + M approach which is a combination of the C approach and the M approach. The p-value from the C approach is used as a test statistic in the following maximization step. This approach was first proposed by Boschloo [9] with the aim to reduce the conservativeness of the C approach. Specifically, the C + M p-value is defined as

$$P_{C+M} = \max_{p\in[0,1]} \sum_{\mathbf{x}\in\Omega_C(\mathbf{x}^*)} P(\mathbf{x}|p),$$

where $\Omega_C(\mathbf{x}^*) = \{\mathbf{x} : P_C(\mathbf{x}) \leq P_C(\mathbf{x}^*)\}$ is the tail area, and P_C is the conditional p-value. All these exact approaches respect the type I error rate.

When the HWE does not hold, a second parameter is needed to fully define the probabilities of the three diallelic genotypes AA, AB, and BB. One example [81] is

$$p_{AA} = p^2 + \theta p(1-p),$$

$$p_{AB} = 2p(1-p)(1-\theta),$$

$$p_{BB} = (1-p)^2 + \theta p(1-p),$$

where θ is the inbreeding coefficient [78], and $\theta \in [\max(-p/(1-p), -(1-p)/p), 1]$. When $\theta = 0$, the probabilities satisfy the HWE. We compare these three exact approaches based on one of the three test statistics, the χ^2 test statistic, at the nominal level of $\alpha = 0.05$. For a given p value, the power of each exact approach can be drawn as a function of θ. Figure 2.4 presents

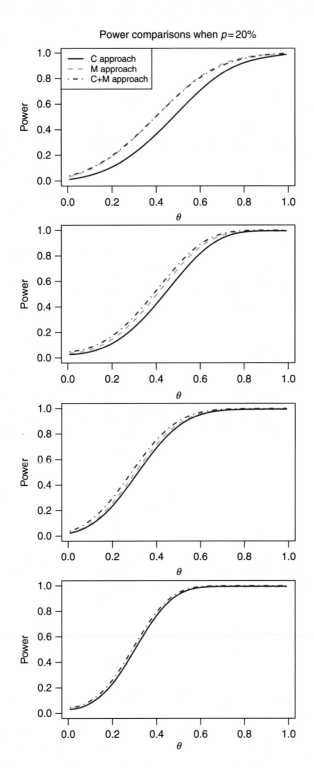

Figure 2.4 Power comparisons among the C approach, the M approach, and the C+M approach, using the χ^2 test with total sample sizes of 25, 50, 100, and 300 from the first row to the fourth row.

(Continued)

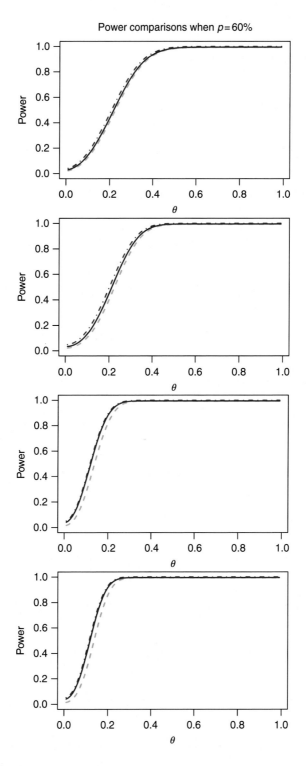

Figure 2.4, Continued

the power plots for sample size $N = 25, 50, 100$, and 300 when $p = 20\%$ and 60%. When the sample size is small, the M approach is more powerful than the C approach, and the power gain is considerable, as already shown from the results by Haber [81]. However, this trend could be reversed as the sample size increases. The C+M approach is at least as powerful as the C approach by nature of the C+M approach. When the sample size is small, the C+M approach is competitive to the M approach. Shan [51] compared the performance of the C+M approach based on all the three different test statistics as aforementioned. The C+M approach, based on the χ^2 test and the data probability, generally outperform the approach based on the likelihood ratio test, although the difference is often negligible.

The other two exact approaches, the BB approach and the E+M approach, may also be included in the future for a comprehensive comparison. We will leave this to interested readers. One interesting topic is to apply the efficient algorithm developed by Engels [65] to other important statistical problems, such as the agreement test for data from a $K \times K$ table as discussed in the next chapter. Engels demonstrated the efficiency of the algorithm to obtain the p-value for testing the HWE when compared to the existing algorithms. It would make a significant contribution to the exact approaches if his algorithm can be generalized to other problems.

CHAPTER 3

Sample Size Determination Using Exact Approaches

Sample size determination plays an extremely important role in a study to address research questions. The study time is significantly affected by the number of subjects enrolled; so is the budget of a research proposal. Underestimating the number of subjects could lead to an unsuccessful project, and overestimated sample size would cause unnecessary waste of resources, or even treat more patients at risk with a possibly harmful therapy, such as a cancer clinical trial. The traditionally used sample size determination is often based on asymptotic approaches, that could lead to over- or underestimated sample sizes.

To overcome the unreliable sample size calculation from asymptotic approaches, exact approaches may be utilized as an alternative to improve the efficiency of a study. Sample size calculation based on the exact conditional approach has been increasingly available for use in practice since the development of the network algorithm for the C approach [82], and the StatXact software [83] and other statistical software packages based on exact approaches for exact statistical inference and exact sample size determination.

The exact conditional approach for sample size calculation has been used in many statistical problems. Mehta et al. [41] presented the exact sample size computation based on the C approach for detecting a trend in a dose-response study by using the Cochran-Armitage test statistics. They demonstrated that the power from asymptotic approaches can be rather misleading and the exact sample size computation based on the C approach is recommended. Later on, the C approach was used for exact sample size computation for ordered categorical data based on the Wilcoxon rank-sum test statistic [64, 84]. Other test statistics, such as the one based on the proportional odds model [64], may also be considered for sample size calculation. With the increased sample size for a study, it becomes computational and a Monte Carlo simulation may be utilized for power calculation [84].

Exact Statistical Inference for Categorical Data. http://dx.doi.org/10.1016/B978-0-08-100681-8.00003-8

An alternative to the exact conditional approach is the exact unconditional approach. The most frequently used unconditional approach is the one based on maximization [34, 85]. Both approaches are exact with the significance level being less than or equal to the nominal level. Suissa and Shuster [86] were the first to consider the exact unconditional approach based on maximization for sample size calculation of a binomial comparative study where the data can be organized in a 2×2 contingency table. One marginal total, the number of subjects for each group, is fixed. The hypothesis was one-sided, and the Z-statistic with the unpooled variance estimate was considered. For a balanced study, the sample size based on the M approach is always less than that based on the C approach for the cases considered as the sample size from 10 to 150, at the significance level of $\alpha = 0.01, 0.025$, and 0.05. Sample size calculations based on asymptotic approaches were added as a reference, and they were shown to be liberal.

Later, Suissa and Shuster [87] compared the exact sample size calculation based on the M approach and the C approach in a matched-pairs study with binary endpoints. For data from such studies, the C approach uses the discordant pairs only in data analysis, but the M approach takes into account the total number of pairs. The McNemar test is commonly used for a matched-pairs design. The square root of that test statistic was used in Suissa and Shuster's work for the one-sided hypothesis problem. They found that the M approach requires a smaller sample size than the C approach for $\alpha = 0.01, 0.025$, and 0.05, and pre-specified power values of 80% and 90%. Later, Hoover [88] extended the exact approaches for matched-pairs designs with three possible outcomes instead of two for one factor, and derived the exact sample size calculation based on the general sign test, which can be considered as a modification of the McNemar test.

As more powerful exact approaches are being developed for use in practice, it is also important to develop exact sample size determination based on these exact approaches. Recently, Shan et al. [89] considered the E + M approach to calculate sample size for a clinical trial with historical controls. The sample size savings from this efficient exact approach is substantial when compared with the sample size calculation based on other exact approaches.

3.1 EXACT SAMPLE SIZE COMPUTATION FOR A CLINICAL TRIAL WITH HISTORICAL CONTROLS

Makuch and Simon [90] developed the commonly used method to calculate sample size for a clinical trial with historical controls. Suppose n_c and n_e

are the total number of subjects in the control group and the experimental group, respectively. Let x_c and x_e be the associated number of responders. The subjects in the control group are obtained from a historical database. It is often of interest to test the hypotheses

$$H_0 : p_e \leq p_c$$

against the alternative

$$H_a : p_e > p_c,$$

where p_e and p_c are response rates for the experimental group and the control group, respectively. The Z-statistic with the pooled variance estimate was used for sample size computation:

$$T(x_c, x_e) = \frac{\hat{p}_e - \hat{p}_c}{\sqrt{\frac{x_c + x_e}{n}(1 - \frac{x_c + x_e}{n})(\frac{1}{n_c} + \frac{1}{n_e})}},$$

where $\hat{p}_e = x_e/n_e$ and $\hat{p}_c = x_c/n_c$ are the estimated response rates. The test statistic asymptotically follows a normal distribution, and the null hypothesis is rejected when the test statistic is above $Z_{1-\alpha}$ at the significance level of α when the asymptotic approach is used for statistical inference.

Makuch and Simon [90] used the angular transformation of estimated response rates to improve the variance-stabilizing properties. There is no closed formula for the sample calculation, and it has to be solved from an equation iteratively [90]. They also tabulated the sample sizes for commonly used cases in clinical trials.

Sample size computation based on the approach by Makuch and Simon [90] performs well when the sample size is large. In the case with small to moderate sample sizes, exact approaches would be preferable to guarantee the type I error rate. Chang et al. [91] presented the exact sample size calculation based on the BB approach [92]. Suppose $\mathbf{x} = (x_c, x_e)$ is a data point, and $\mathbf{x}^*$ is the observed data. The tail area is $\Omega_T(\mathbf{x}^*) = \{\mathbf{x} : T(\mathbf{x}) \geq T(\mathbf{x}^*)\}$, and the associated BB p-value is

$$P_{BB} = \max_{p \in C_{1-\eta}} \sum_{\mathbf{x} \in \Omega_T(\mathbf{x}^*)} P(\mathbf{x}|p) + \eta,$$

where $P(\mathbf{x}|p) = b(x_c, n_c, p)b(x_e, n_e, p)$ is the probability for data $\mathbf{x}$, $C_{1-\eta}$ is the one-sided $100(1 - \eta)\%$ interval for p, $(0, p_{1-\eta})$ [43], and $\eta = 0.001$ is the penalty value [42]. At the significance level of α, the tail area can be determined. Power of a study is then calculated under the alternative with the expected response rate for the experimental group, p_e. The final sample size n_e, is the smallest sample size such that the power of the study is above the pre-specified value. Chang et al. [91] observed some important differences between the exact sample size and the sample size from Makuch and Simon [90], although they often have very similar results.

The exact unconditional approach based on estimation and maximization [52] has been shown to gain some power when compared with other exact approaches in several statistical problems [14, 45, 50, 54]. The estimation step in the E + M approach may be able to generate a flatter tail probability curve, and this may increase the significance level of a test and finally lead to a possible power gain. Shan et al. [89] were the first to extend the E + M approach for the sample size computation in a clinical trial with historical controls. The E + M p-value is computed as

$$P_{E+M} = \max_{p \in [0,1]} \sum_{\mathbf{x} \in \Omega_E(\mathbf{x}^*)} P(\mathbf{x}|p),$$

where $\Omega_E(\mathbf{x}) = \{\mathbf{x} : P_E(\mathbf{x}) \leq P_E(\mathbf{x}^*)\}$ is the tail area from the estimation step, and $P_E(\mathbf{x}^*) = \sum_{\mathbf{x} \in \Omega_T(\mathbf{x}^*)} P(\mathbf{x}|\hat{p})$, and $\hat{p}$ is the MLE of the nuisance parameter p under the null hypothesis.

Since the problem is one-sided, the monotonicity property needs to be checked in order to guarantee that the actual type I error rate occurs at the boundary of the null space. The test statistic used here belongs to the commonly used test statistics for comparing two independent binomial distributions [36, 37], and the monotonicity property was shown to be satisfied for these test statistics for testing non-inferiority or superiority [36, 37].

The sample size search algorithm is similar to that for the BB approach, as the smallest n_e such that the power of the study based on the E + M approach is above the pre-specified value. More detailed search steps can be found in Shan et al. [89]. Multiple design configurations were considered by Shan et al. [89]. The sample size from the two exact approaches are close to each other when the required sample size is small. The E + M approach generally requires a smaller sample size than the BB approach and the asymptotic approach due to Makuch and Simon [90]. In the example by Shan et al. [89] to detect a 20% increase in the response rate from the new treatment as compared to the existing study with the response rate estimated as 10%, 49 subjects are required from the BB approach, while the E + M approach needs only 41 subjects to attain 90% power at the significance level of $\alpha = 0.05$. The sample size saving by using the E + M approach in this example is substantial.

CONCLUSIONS

This book introduced the frequently used and newly developed exact approaches for categorical data analysis. The exact conditional approach is widely available from existing statistical software, such as StatXact, SAS, and R. The exact unconditional approach based on the maximization and the one based on partial maximization have been added to statistical software recently. The other two efficient exact approaches, the C+M approach and the E+M approach, are only available for certain data (e.g., a binomial comparative study). The development of a software package for statisticians, biostatisticians, and other practitioners to use in practice, is extremely important.

Application of efficient exact approaches for data from a $K \times K$ table, a $R \times C$ table, a $2 \times 2 \times 2$ table, or a $2 \times K \times K$ table are practically important. We realize that it is too computationally intensive without an efficient algorithm to determine the rejection region. The existing network-based algorithm is a general approach, and it may not be the best algorithm for a particular problem. The improved algorithm developed by Engels [65] can potentially be used to motivate the research in this area for the problems, such as reliability testing, and homogeneity testing among strata [93].

In addition to the exact p-value calculation, the computation for an exact confidence interval is another important research topic. Exact confidence intervals may be obtained by inverting an exact test [94–100]. One example is the exact confidence interval for a binomial proportion based on Clopper and Pearson's approach [101], or Blaker's approach [102]. It has been noticed that these exact intervals may result in a wider interval. For this reason, Wang [103] proposed an optimal interval based on an inductive order of the sample space, that can be calculated from the R package, *ExactCIdiff* [104]. Later, Wang extended this exact confidence interval construction approach for other important statistical problems [105–108]. The optimal exact confidence interval proposed by Wang [103] could be computationally intensive for data beyond a 2×2 table, then the approach proposed by Buehler [109] can be used to compute exact confidence intervals by using existing asymptotic intervals to order the sample space. This approach has been successfully applied to many important statistical problems [8, 13, 29, 110].

Sample size determination based on exact approaches has been studied for many years [83, 86, 87, 89, 111, 112]. The exact conditional approach and the unconditional approach based on full maximization or partial maximization were traditionally used in sample size calculation. The other two exact approaches, the C+M approach and the E + M approach, are rarely used to compute sample size. These two approaches have been shown to gain power when compared with others, and it is important to develop software packages for sample size determination based on these efficient approaches.

BIBLIOGRAPHY

[1] Barnard GA. Significance tests for 2×2 tables. Biometrika 1947; 34(1-2):123-38, URL: http://view.ncbi.nlm.nih.gov/pubmed/20287826.

[2] Fisher RA. The design of experiments. 9th ed. Edinburgh, UK: Macmillan Pub Co; 1935. URL: http://www.worldcat.org/isbn/0028446909.

[3] Jamal MM, Adams AB, Jansen JP, Webster LR. A randomized, placebo-controlled trial of lubiprostone for opioid-induced constipation in chronic noncancer pain. Amer J Gastroenterol 2015; 110(5):725-32, doi:10.1038/ajg.2015.106.

[4] Cochran WG. Some methods for strengthening the common χ^2 tests. Biometrics 1954;10:417-51.

[5] Agresti A. Categorical data analysis. 3rd ed. Hoboken, NJ: Wiley; 2012. URL: http://www.worldcat.org/isbn/0470463635.

[6] Cochran WG. The χ^2 test of goodness of fit. Ann Math Stat 1952;23(3):315-45, doi:10.1214/aoms/1177729380.

[7] Campbell I. Chi-squared and Fisher-Irwin tests of two-by-two tables with small sample recommendations. Stat Med 2007;26(19):3661-75, doi:10.1002/sim.2832.

[8] Lloyd CJ, Moldovan MV. Exact one-sided confidence bounds for the risk ratio in 2×2 tables with structural zero. Biomet J 2007;49(6):952-63, doi:10.1002/bimj.200710357.

[9] Boschloo RD. Raised conditional level of significance for the 2×2-table when testing the equality of two probabilities. Stat Neerland 1970;24(1):1-9, doi:10.1111/j.1467-9574.1970.tb00104.x.

[10] Tang ML, Ng HK, Guo J, Chan W, Chan BP. Exact Cochran-Armitage trend tests: comparisons under different models. J Stat Comput Simulat 2006;76(10):847-59, doi:10.1080/10629360600569519.

[11] Hirji KF, Tan SJ, Elashoff RM. A quasi-exact test for comparing two binomial proportions. Stat Med 1991;10(7):1137-53, URL: http://view.ncbi.nlm.nih.gov/pubmed/1876801.

[12] Tang ML, Poon WY, Ling L, Liao Y, Chui HW. Approximate unconditional test procedure for comparing two ordered multinomials. Comput Stat Data Anal 2011;55:955-63, doi:10.1016/j.csda.2010.08.009.

[13] Lloyd CJ, Moldovan MV. Constructing more powerful exact tests of equivalence from binary matched pairs. Aust NZ J Stat 2011;53(1):27-42, doi:10.1111/j.1467-842x.2011.00597.x.

[14] Shan G, Ma C, Hutson AD, Wilding GE. An efficient and exact approach for detecting trends with binary endpoints. Stat Med 2012;31(2):155-64, doi:10.1002/sim.4411.

[15] Shan G, Wilding G. Unconditional tests for association in 2×2 contingency tables in the total sum fixed design. Stat Neerland 2015;69(1):67-83, doi:10.1111/stan.12047.

[16] Krishnatreya M, Rahman T, Kataki AC, Das A, Das AK, Lahkar K. Synchronous primary cancers of the head and neck region and upper aero digestive tract: defining high-risk patients. Ind J Cancer 2013;50(4):322-6, URL: http://view.ncbi.nlm.nih.gov/pubmed/24369209.

[17] Lydersen S, Fagerland MW, Laake P. Recommended tests for association in 2×2 tables. Stat Med 2009;28(7):1159-75, doi:10.1002/sim.3531.

[18] Bentur L, Lapidot M, Livnat G, Hakim F, Lidroneta-Katz C, Porat I, Vilozni D, Elhasid R. Airway reactivity in children before and after stem cell transplantation. Pediat Pulmonol 2009;44(9):845-50, URL: http://view.ncbi.nlm.nih.gov/pubmed/19670401.

[19] McNemar Q. Note on the sampling error of the difference between correlated proportions or percentages. Psychometrika 1947;12(2):153-7, URL: http://view.ncbi.nlm.nih.gov/pubmed/20254758.

[20] Yates F. Tests of significance for 2 × 2 contingency tables. J R Stat Soc A (Gen) 1984;147:426-3.

[21] Upton GJG. A comparison of alternative tests for the 2 × 2 comparative trial. J R Stat Soc A (Gen) 1982; 145(1):86-105.

[22] Hirji K. Exact analysis of discrete data. Boca Raton, FL: Chapman and Hall/CRC; 2005. doi: 10.1201/9781420036190.

[23] Pearson ES. The choice of statistical tests illustrated on the interpretation of data classed in a 2 × 2 table. Biometrika 1947;34(1-2):139-69, URL: http://view.ncbi.nlm.nih.gov/pubmed/20287827.

[24] Fleiss JL, Cohen J. The equivalence of weighted kappa and the intraclass correlation coefficient as measures of reliability. Educat Psychol Measur 1973;33(3):613-19, doi:10.1177/001316447303300309.

[25] Fleiss JL, Levin B, Paik MC. Statistical methods for rates and proportions. Technometrics 2004;46(2):263-64, doi:10.1198/tech.2004.s812.

[26] Armitage P. Tests for linear trends in proportions and frequencies. Biometrics 1955;11(3):375-86, doi:10.2307/3001775.

[27] Kang S, Lee J. The size of the Cochran-Armitage trend test in 2 × c contingency tables. J Stat Plan Infer 2007;137(6):1851-61, doi:10.1016/j.jspi.2006.03.009.

[28] Mehta CR, Patel NR. A network algorithm for performing fisher's exact test in r by c contingency tables. J Amer Stat Assoc 1983;78(382):427-34, doi:10.2307/2288652.

[29] Shan G, Wang W. Exact one-sided confidence limits for Cohen's kappa as a measurement of agreement. Stat Meth Med Res 2014;In press, doi:10.1177/0962280214552881.

[30] Irwin JO. Tests of significance for differences between percentages based on small numbers. Metron 1935;12(2):84-94.

[31] Lloyd CJ. A new exact and more powerful unconditional test of no treatment effect from binary matched pairs. Biometrics 2008;64(3):716-23, doi:10.1111/j.1541-0420.2007.00936.x.

[32] Andrés, Tejedor. Is Fisher's exact test very conservative? Comput Stat Data Anal 1995;19(5):579-91, doi:10.1016/0167-9473(94)00013-9.

[33] Crans GG, Shuster JJ. How conservative is Fisher's exact test? A quantitative evaluation of the two-sample comparative binomial trial. Stat Med 2008;27(18):3598-611, doi:10.1002/sim.3221.

[34] Barnard GA. A new test for 2 × 2 tables. Nature 1945;156:177.

[35] Shuster JJ. Exact unconditional tables for significance testing in the 2 × 2 multinomial trial. Stat Med 1992;11(7):913-22, URL: http://view.ncbi.nlm.nih.gov/pubmed/1604070.

[36] Röhmel J. Problems with existing procedures to calculate exact unconditional P-values for non-inferiority/superiority and confidence intervals for two binomials and how to resolve them. Biomet J 2005;47(1):37-47, URL: http://view.ncbi.nlm.nih.gov/pubmed/16395995.

[37] Röhmel J, Mansmann U. Unconditional non-asymptotic one-sided tests for independent binomial proportions when the interest lies in showing non-inferiority and/or superiority. Biomet J 1999;41(2):149-70, doi:10.1002/(sici)1521-4036(199905)41:2\%3C149::aid-bimj149\%3E3.0.co;2-e.

[38] Routledge RD. Resolving the conflict over Fisher's exact test. Can J Stat 1992;20(2):201-9, doi: 10.2307/3315468.

[39] Seneta E, Phipps MC. On the comparison of two observed frequencies. Biomet J 2001;43(1): 23-43, doi:10.1002/1521-4036(200102)43:1\%3C23::aid-bimj23\%3E3.0.co;2-8.

[40] Mehrotra DV, Chan IS, Berger RL. A cautionary note on exact unconditional inference for a difference between two independent binomial proportions. Biometrics 2003;59(2):441-50, URL: http://view.ncbi.nlm.nih.gov/pubmed/12926729.

[41] Mehta CR, Patel NR, Senchaudhuri P. Exact power and sample-size computations for the Cochran-Armitage trend test. Biometrics 1998;54(4):1615-21, doi:10.2307/2533685.

[42] Berger RL, Boos DD. P-values maximized over a confidence set for the nuisance parameter. J Amer Stat Assoc 1994;89(427):1012-16, doi:10.2307/2290928.

[43] Casella G, Berger RL. Statistical inference. 2nd ed. Belmont, CA: Cengage Learning; 2001. URL: http://www.worldcat.org/isbn/0534243126.

[44] Han C. Comparing two independent incidence rates using conditional and unconditional exact tests. Pharmaceut Stat 2008;7(3):195-201, doi:10.1002/pst.289.

[45] Shan G. Exact unconditional testing procedures for comparing two independent Poisson rates. J Stat Comput Simul 2015;85(5):947-55, doi:10.1080/00949655.2013.855776.

[46] Berger RL. More powerful tests from confidence interval p values. Amer Stat 1996;50(4):314-18, doi:10.1080/00031305.1996.10473559.

[47] Clopper CJ, Pearson ES. The use of confidence or fiducial limits illustrated in the case of the binomial. Biometrika 1934;26(4):404-13, doi:10.2307/2331986.

[48] Liddell D. Practical tests of 2×2 contingency tables. Statistician 1976;25(4):295-304, doi:10. 2307/2988087.

[49] Storer BE, Kim C. Exact properties of some exact test statistics for comparing two binomial proportions. J Amer Stat Assoc 1990;85(409):146-55, doi:10.2307/2289537.

[50] Lloyd CJ, Moldovan MV. A more powerful exact test of noninferiority from binary matched-pairs data. Stat Med 2008;27(18):3540-49, doi:10.1002/sim.3229.

[51] Shan G. A note on exact conditional and unconditional tests for Hardy-Weinberg equilibrium. Human Hered 2013;76(1):10-17, doi:10.1159/000353205.

[52] Lloyd CJ. Exact p-values for discrete models obtained by estimation and maximization. Aust NZ J Stat 2008;50(4):329-45, doi:10.1111/j.1467-842x.2008.00520.x.

[53] Lloyd CJ. Exact tests based on pre-estimation and second order pivotals: non-inferiority trials. J Stat Comput Simul 2009;80(8):841-51, doi:10.1080/00949650902806476.

[54] Lloyd CJ. On the exact size of tests of treatment effects in multi-arm clinical trials. Aust NZ J Stat 2014;56(4):359-69, doi:10.1111/anzs.12089.

[55] Lloyd CJ. P-values based on approximate conditioning and. J Stat Plan Infer 2010;140(4):1073-81, doi:10.1016/j.jspi.2009.10.007.

[56] Shan G. More efficient unconditional tests for exchangeable binary data with equal cluster sizes. Stat Probabil Lett 2013;83(2):644-49, doi:10.1016/j.spl.2012.11.014.

[57] Wilding GE, Consiglio JD, Shan G. Exact approaches for testing hypotheses based on the intra-class kappa coefficient. Stat Med 2014;33(17):2998-3012, doi:10.1002/sim.6135.

[58] Shan G, Ma C. Exact methods for testing the equality of proportions for binary clustered data from otolaryngologic studies. Stat Biopharmaceut Res 2014;6(1):115-22, doi:10.1080/19466315. 2013.861767.

[59] Shan G. Exact approaches for testing non-inferiority or superiority of two incidence rates. Stat Probabil Lett 2014;85:129-34, doi:10.1016/j.spl.2013.11.010.

[60] Shan G, Ma C. Efficient tests for one sample correlated binary data with applications. Stat Meth Appl 2014;23(2):175-88, doi:10.1007/s10260-013-0251-6.

[61] Consiglio JD, Shan G, Wilding GE. A comparison of exact tests for trend with binary endpoints using Bartholomew's statistic. Int J Biostat 2014;10(2):221-30, URL: http://view.ncbi.nlm.nih.gov/pubmed/25324456.

[62] Nam JM. Establishing equivalence of two treatments and sample size requirements in matched-pairs design. Biometrics 1997;53(4):1422-30, URL: http://view.ncbi.nlm.nih.gov/pubmed/9423257.

[63] Kao CHH, Shiau YCC, Shen YYY, Yen RFF. Detection of recurrent or persistent nasopharyngeal carcinomas after radiotherapy with technetium-99m methoxyisobutylisonitrile single photon emission computed tomography and computed tomography: comparison with 18-fluoro-2-deoxyglucose positron emission tomography. Cancer 2002;94(7):1981-86, URL: http://view.ncbi.nlm.nih.gov/pubmed/11932900.

[64] Shan G, Ma C. Unconditional tests for comparing two ordered multinomials. Stat Meth Med Res 2012;In press, doi:10.1177/0962280212450957.

[65] Engels WR. Exact tests for Hardy-Weinberg proportions. Genetics 2009;183(4):1431-41, doi:10.1534/genetics.109.108977.

[66] Agresti A, Yang M. An empirical investigation of some effects of sparseness in contingency tables. Comput Stat Data Anal 1987;5(1):9-21, doi:10.1016/0167-9473(87)90003-x.

[67] Tang ML, Chan PS, Chan W. On exact unconditional test for linear trend in dose-response studies. Biomet J 2000;42(7):795-806, doi:10.1002/1521-4036(200011)42:7\%3C795::aid-bimj795\%3E3.0.co;2-g.

[68] Freidlin B, Gastwirth JL. Unconditional versions of several tests commonly used in the analysis of contingency tables. Biometrics 1999;55(1):264-7, doi:10.2307/2533920.

[69] Corcoran CD, Mehta CR. Exact level and power of permutation, bootstrap, and asymptotic tests of trend. J Mod Appl Stat Meth 2002;1:42-51.

[70] Baumgartner W, Weiß P, Schindler H. A nonparametric test for the general two-sample problem. Biometrics 1998;54(3):1129-35, doi:10.2307/2533862.

[71] Neuhäuser M. An exact test for trend among binomial proportions based on a modified Baumgartner-Weiß-Schindler statistic. J Appl Stat 2006;33(1):79-88, doi:10.1080/02664760500389756.

[72] Shan G, Ma C, Hutson AD, Wilding GE. Some tests for detecting trends based on the modified Baumgartner-Weiß-Schindler statistics. Comput Stat Data Anal 2013;57(1):246-61, doi:10.1016/j.csda.2012.04.021.

[73] Bartholomew DJ. A test of homogeneity for ordered alternatives. Biometrika 1959;46:36-48, URL: http://elibrary.ru/item.asp?id=10030424.

[74] Hardy GH. Mendelian proportions in a mixed population. Science 1908;28(706):49-50, doi:10.1126/science.28.706.49.

[75] Crow JF. Eighty years ago: the beginnings of population genetics. Genetics 1988;119(3):473-6, URL: http://www.ncbi.nlm.nih.gov/pmc/articles/PMC1203431/.

[76] Edwards AW. G. H. Hardy (1908) and Hardy-Weinberg equilibrium. Genetics 2008;179(3):1143-50, doi:10.1534/genetics.104.92940.

[77] Weir BS. Genetic data analysis II: methods for discrete population genetic data. 2nd ed. Sunderland, MA: Sinauer Associates Inc; 1996. URL: http://www.worldcat.org/isbn/0878939024.

[78] Emigh TH. A comparison of tests for Hardy-Weinberg equilibrium. Biometrics 1980;36:627-42.

[79] Guo SW, Thompson EA. Performing the exact test of Hardy-Weinberg proportion for multiple alleles. Biometrics 1992;48(2):361-72, URL: http://view.ncbi.nlm.nih.gov/pubmed/1637966.

[80] Rohlfs RV, Weir BS. Distributions of Hardy-Weinberg equilibrium test statistics. Genetics 2008;180(3):1609-16, doi:10.1534/genetics.108.088005.

[81] Haber M. An exact unconditional test for the Hardy-Weinberg equilibrium. Biomet J 1994;36(6):741-9, doi:10.1002/bimj.4710360614.

[82] Mehta CR, Patel N, Senchaudhuri P. Exact stratified linear rank tests for ordered categorical and binary data. J Comput Graph Stat 1992;1(1):21-40, doi:10.1080/10618600.1992.10474574.

[83] Mehta CR, Patel NR, Senchaudhuri P, Corcoran CD. StatXact 2014; doi:10.1002/9781118445112. stat04892.

[84] Hilton JF, Mehta CR. Power and sample size calculations for exact conditional tests with ordered categorical data. Biometrics 1993;49(2):609-16, URL: http://view.ncbi.nlm.nih.gov/pubmed/8369392.

[85] Basu D. On the elimination of nuisance parameters. J Amer Stat Assoc 1977;72(358):355-66, doi:10.2307/2286800.

[86] Suissa S, Shuster JJ. Exact unconditional sample sizes for the 2 × 2 binomial trial. J R Stat Soc A (Gen) 1985;148(4), doi:10.2307/2981892.

[87] Suissa S, Shuster JJ. The 2 × 2 matched-pairs trial: exact unconditional design and analysis. Biometrics 1991;47(2):361-72, URL: http://view.ncbi.nlm.nih.gov/pubmed/1912252.

[88] Hoover DR. Extending power and sample size approaches developed for McNemar's procedure to general sign tests. Int Stat Rev 2005;73(1):103-10, doi:10.1111/j.1751-5823.2005.tb00253.x.

[89] Shan G, Moonie S, Shen J. Sample size calculation based on efficient unconditional tests for clinical trials with historical controls. J Biopharmaceut Stat 2014;In press, doi:10.1080/10543406.2014.1000545.

[90] Makuch RW, Simon RM. Sample size considerations for non-randomized comparative studies. J Chron Diseas 1980;33(3):175-81, doi:10.1016/0021-9681(80)90017-x.

[91] Chang MN, Shuster JJ, Kepner JL. Sample sizes based on exact unconditional tests for phase II clinical trials with historical controls. J Biopharmaceut Stat 2004;14(1):189-200, doi:10.1081/bip-120028514.

[92] Berger RL. Power comparison of exact unconditional tests for comparing two binomial proportions. tech. rep.. Department of Statistics, North Carolina State University, Department of Statistics, North Carolina State University; 1994.

[93] de Leon A, Chough K. Analysis of mixed data: methods & applications. Boca Raton, FL: Chapman and Hall/CRC; 2013. doi:10.1201/b14571.

[94] Wilson EB. Probable inference, the law of succession, and statistical inference. J Amer Stat Assoc 1927;22(158):209-12, doi:10.1080/01621459.1927.10502953.

[95] Tony Cai T. One-sided confidence intervals in discrete distributions. J Stat Plan Infer 2005;131(1):63-88, doi:10.1016/j.jspi.2004.01.005.

[96] Shao J. Mathematical statistics. Springer Texts in Statistics, New York: Springer-Verlag; 1999. doi:10.1007/b98900. URL: http://dx.doi.org/10.1007/b98900.

[97] Yang J, Zhang R, Liu M. Construction of fractional factorial split-plot designs with weak minimum aberration. Stat Probabil Lett 2007;77(15):1567-73, doi:10.1016/j.spl.2007.03.043.

[98] Wu SS, Wang W, Yang MCK. Interval estimation for drop-the-losers designs. Biometrika 2010;97(2):405-18, doi:10.1093/biomet/asq003.

[99] Gart JJ, Krewski D, Lee PN, Tarone RE, Wahrendorf J. Statistical methods in cancer research. Volume III—The design and analysis of long-term animal experiments. IARC Scientific Publications 1986;(79):1-219, URL: http://view.ncbi.nlm.nih.gov/pubmed/3301661.

[100] Wallis S. Binomial confidence intervals and contingency tests: mathematical fundamentals and the evaluation of alternative methods. J Quantit Linguist 2013;20(3):178-208, doi:10.1080/09296174.2013.799918.

[101] Clopper CJ, Pearson ES. The use of confidence or fiducial limits illustrated in the case of the binomial. Biometrika 1934;26(4):404-13, doi:10.1093/biomet/26.4.404.

[102] Blaker H. Confidence curves and improved exact confidence intervals for discrete distributions. Can J Stat 2000;28(4):783-98, doi:10.2307/3315916.

[103] Wang W. On construction of the smallest one-sided confidence interval for the difference of two proportions. Ann Stat 2010;38(2):1227-43, doi:10.1214/09-aos744.

[104] Shan G, Wang W. ExactCIdiff: an R package for computing exact confidence intervals for the difference of two proportions. Roy J 2013;5(2):62-71.

[105] Wang W, Zhang Z. Asymptotic infimum coverage probability for interval estimation of proportions. Metrika 2014;77(5):635-46, doi:10.1007/s00184-013-0457-5.

[106] Wang W. An inductive order construction for the difference of two dependent proportions. Stat Probabil Lett 2012;82(8):1623-28, doi:10.1016/j.spl.2012.03.035.

[107] Wang W. Exact optimal confidence intervals for hypergeometric parameters. Journal of the American Statistical Association 2014;In press, doi:10.1080/01621459.2014.966191.

[108] Wang W, Shan G. Exact confidence intervals for the relative risk and the odds ratio. Biometrics 2015;In press, doi:10.1111/biom.12360.

[109] Buehler RJ. Confidence intervals for the product of two binomial parameters. J Amer Stat Assoc 1957;52(280):482-93, URL: http://www.jstor.org/stable/2281697.

[110] Lloyd CJ. Efficient and exact tests of the risk ratio in a correlated 2×2 table with structural zero. Comput Stat Data Anal 2007;51:3765-75, URL: http://portal.acm.org/citation.cfm?id=1234418.1234637.

[111] Wilding GE, Shan G, Hutson AD. Exact two-stage designs for phase II activity trials with rank-based endpoints. Contemp Clin Trials 2012;33(2):332-41, doi:10.1016/j.cct.2011.10.008.

[112] Shan G, Ma C, Hutson AD, Wilding GE. Randomized two-stage phase II clinical trial designs based on Barnard's exact test. J Biopharmaceut Stat 2013;23(5):1081-90, doi:10.1080/10543406.2013.813525.

Printed in the United States
By Bookmasters